LAW, LIBERTY, AND THE PURSUIT OF TERRORISM

It is commonly believed that a state facing a terrorist threat responds with severe legislation that compromises civil liberties in favor of national security. Roger Douglas compares responses to terrorism by five liberal democracies—the United States, the United Kingdom, Canada, Australia, and New Zealand—over the past 15 years. He examines each nation's development and implementation of counterterrorism law, specifically in the areas of information gathering, the definition of terrorist offenses, due process for the accused, detention, and torture and other forms of coercive questioning.

Douglas finds that terrorist attacks elicit pressures for quick responses, which often allow national governments to accrue additional powers. But emergencies are neither a necessary nor a sufficient condition for such laws, which may persist even after fears have eased. He argues that responses are influenced by institutional interests and prior beliefs and are complicated when the exigencies of office and beliefs point in different directions. He also argues that citizens are wary of government's impingement on civil liberties and that courts exercise their capacity to restrain the legislative and executive branches. Douglas concludes that the worst antiterror excesses have taken place outside of, rather than within, the law and that the legacy of 9/11 includes both laws that expand government powers and judicial decisions that limit those very powers.

Roger Douglas is Professor of Law at La Trobe University.

Law, Liberty, and the Pursuit of Terrorism

Roger Douglas

The University of Michigan Press
ANN ARBOR

Published in the United States of America by
The University of Michigan Press
Manufactured in the United States of America
♾ Printed on acid-free paper

2017 2016 2015 2014 4 3 2 1

A CIP catalog record for this book is available from the British Library.

Library of Congress Cataloging-in-Publication Data

Douglas, Roger (Roger Neil), author.
Law, liberty, and the pursuit of terrorism / Roger Douglas.
pages cm
Includes bibliographical references and index.
ISBN 978-0-472-11909-7 (hardcover : alk. paper) — ISBN 978-0-472-02966-2 (e-book)
1. Terrorism. 2. Terrorism—Prevention—Law and legislation. 3. National security—Law and legislation. 4. Civil rights. 5. Government information—Access control. 6. Detention of persons. 7. Torture. I. Title.

K5256.D68 2014
363.325'156—dc23

2014010710

In memory of Alan Douglas (1920–2009)

Contents

Preface and Acknowledgments

Some years ago, Joo-Cheong Tham, a colleague at La Trobe University Law School, suggested that we propose a subject on Australian counterterrorism law. We duly drafted the relevant documentation, but the head of the school suggested that our ambitions were far too modest and that our subject should compare the counterterrorism laws of a number of countries. For a variety of reasons, we never got around to doing so.

In 2006, I was planning to take some well-earned study leave, a condition for which was that I propose a project. At the time, I had largely completed a study of the uneasy relationship between Australian law and the Australian Communist Party, one of the underlying themes of which was the symbiotic relationship between the party and its adversaries, each of which somehow convinced themselves that the party constituted a threat to bourgeois Australia. Laws were enacted to deal with the threat, but they proved largely unworkable, because they were conditioned on there being evidence, and there was pitifully little. This could be and was interpreted as evidence of the party's devilish cunning, and this, in turn, prompted years of extralegal anticommunist measures. A common argument against banning the party was that doing so would drive it underground. Ironically, one of the effects of law's constraint on anticommunism was to drive some anticommunist activities underground. With these memories in mind, I proposed a comparative study of the counterterrorism laws of Australia, Canada, New Zealand, the United Kingdom, and the United States, with a view to examining some of the ways in which law both facilitated and restrained counterterror activities.

Like most projects, this one has proved much more demanding than I had expected. Counterterror law is wide ranging and extends to areas such as asset freezing, money laundering, emergency preparedness, and infrastructure security. It overlaps with other bodies of law. Especially in the United Kingdom and the United States, it continues to be in a state of flux. Moreover, the threat of terrorism is elusive, as is information about what governments do with their powers, despite legal constraints. Furthermore, testing one of the most plausible explanations for preferences in relation to counterterror measures—namely, that they reflect underlying political dispositions rather than the "objective" threat—is difficult, given the paucity of information available in the public domain. This difficulty is a pity, because I find the explanation persuasive.

This book does not attempt to be a comprehensive summary of counterterrorism law in the five countries. Rather, it examines a number of areas of counterterror law with a view to setting out salient features of the laws in the five countries. These areas have been chosen partly because they represent some of the areas that most concern legal scholars. They have also been chosen because they illustrate different relationships between laws, institutions, public opinion, and beliefs.

My argument (adapted from earlier research) is that counterterror law has been a response to pressures from the enforcement arms of the executive for greater powers to fight terrorism but that, in a sense, it continues to be a force for liberty. One reason is that executive ambitions meet resistance, from opposition parties, from organised civil libertarians, from the public (up to a point), and sometimes from the courts. But, because the executive does not always get its way, executive deviance may become tempting and facilitated by various forms of delinquency neutralisation. One of these draws on the ambiguity of law and involves reliance on interpretations that would seem strained to almost anyone but those who passionately want to be convinced of the rightness of their interpretation. (Executive deviants are not alone in this respect; one also encounters some impressive examples in the law reviews.) Executive deviance varies, major reasons being variations in temptation, opportunity, and capacity. This is reflected in the contrast between the law-bound criminal justice system and the far less law-bound regimes operating in places where prisoners in the War on Terror are kept. It also helps explain cross-national differences: using war rather than law as a tool in the fight against terrorism is more likely to seem to make sense to the United States than to New Zealand. My overall suspicion is that the recent response to terrorism has been disproportionate, even allowing for the enormity of the 9/11 attacks. However, part of my argument is that the uncertainty surrounding law and terror means that beliefs about what is appropriate must necessarily reflect basic political orientations. It follows that my suspicions must partly be a product of my own political orientations. Terrorism and the law relating to it continue to be in a state of flux. To the best of my knowledge, this book's statements about fact and law were correct as of 30 June 2012.

The law has not stood still since that date, and neither have terrorists and counterterrorists. I have made reference in the text to some of the more recent legal developments, none of which have been particularly surprising. There have been several terrorist attacks, one particularly serious when measured by injuries (but not by deaths), others less serious. Most plots continue to be frustrated, the proposal to place a bomb on a Canadian train being thwarted partly on the basis of information supplied from Canada's Muslim community. Recent (June 2013) revelations about the extent to which the US government has used its surveillance powers have provoked predictable outrage, and predictable claims that it has saved lives. Mistreatment of prisoners transferred to Afghanistan forces has continued to be a problem, and recently resulted in decisions by the United Kingdom and Australian governments to cease handing prisoners over to some Afghan authorities. None of these developments (which are not discussed elsewhere in this book) is inconsistent with the analysis I have developed on the basis of pre 30 June 2012 material, but recent US polls on support for surveillance suggest that its partisan correlates are dictated more by the president's party than by party-related dispositions and underlying civil libertarianism.

Books, even when written by a congenital introvert, are a team effort. Above all, I would like to thank my wife, Robin Burns, not only for her direct contribution to the book—she read and commented on a draft—but also for doing far more than her share of gardening and housework and for tolerating the absentmindedness inherent in thinking about the book when politeness would have dictated thinking about more important things. As always, I am grateful for her support and encouragement. Thanks are also due to Melody Herr, commissioning editor at the University of Michigan Press. She played a role not unlike that of a first-rate dissertation supervisor, encouraging me to develop my early proposal, pointing out when draft chapters needed tightening, and suggesting ways to overcome some of the more serious weaknesses in successive drafts.

I also owe much to my colleagues at La Trobe University Law School, who provide a congenial and collegial work environment. Professors Jianfu Chen and Paula Baron arranged my teaching load so as to give me time to work on the book. I have talked with numerous colleagues about my arguments: I would particularly like to thank Jeffery Barnes, Magda Karagiannakis, Keith Kendall, Oliver Mendelsohn, Marilyn McMahon, Jill Murray, Balu Rao, Savitri Taylor, John Willis, Ann Wardrop, and David Wishart. Thanks are also due to La Trobe's law librarian, Dennis Warren, whose skills at tracking down elusive sources have proved invaluable.

Abbreviations

AGC	assistant general counsel
ASIO	Australian Security Intelligence Organisation
ASIO Act	Australian Security Intelligence Organisation Act 1979 (Cth)
CAA	Crimes Act 1914 (Cth)
CAE	Canada Evidence Act RSC 1985, c C-5
CAU	Communications Analysis Unit (FBI)
CBRN	chemical, biological, radiological, and nuclear
CCC	Criminal Code of Canada RSC 1985, c C-41
CIPA	Classified Information Procedures Act of 1980, PL 96-456, 94 Stat 2015, codified at 18 USC App
CPR	Civil Procedure Rules 1998 (UK), SI 1998/3132
CSIS	Canadian Security Intelligence Service
CSRT	Combatant Status Review Tribunal
Cth	Commonwealth of Australia
ECHR	European Convention for the Protection of Human Rights and Fundamental Freedoms
ECtHR	European Court of Human Rights
FISA	Foreign Intelligence Surveillance Act of 1978, PL 95-511, 92 Stat 1783, codified at 50 USC Ch 36
FISC	Foreign Intelligence Surveillance Court
IEEPA	International Emergency Economic Powers Act of 1977, PL 95-223, 91 Stat 1628, codified at 50 USC Ch 35
IRPA	Immigration and Refugee Protection Act, SC 2001, c 27
NSIA	National Security Information (Criminal and Civil Proceedings Act 2004 (Cth)
NSL	national security letter
NSLB	National Security Law Branch
NZSIS	New Zealand Security Intelligence Service
OPR	Office of Professional Responsibility (Department of Justice)
PIRA	USA Patriot Improvement and Reauthorization Act of 2005, PL 109-177, 120 Stat 192

POAC	Proscribed Organisations Appeals Commission (Procedure) Rules 2001 (UK), SI 2001/1286
RIPA	Regulation of Investigatory Powers Act 2000 (UK), c 23
SIAC	Special Immigration Appeals Commission Act 1997 (UK), c 68
TA	Terrorism Act 2000 (UK), c 11
T(IA)A	Telecommunications (Interception and Access) Act 1979 (Cth)
Torture Convention	Convention against Torture and Other Cruel, Inhuman or Degrading Treatment or Punishment 1465 UNTS 85
TSA	Terrorism Suppression Act 2002 (New Zealand)
USAPA	USA Patriot Act of 2001, PL 107-56, 115 Stat 272

Introduction

Outrages tend to provoke demands for government responses, and responses tend to include legal innovations. It is therefore unsurprising that terrorist acts have stimulated the development of laws aimed at punishing, denouncing, and discouraging terrorism. However, countries react differently, partly because they experience terrorism differently and partly because responses to terrorism depend on far more than the nature of terrorist attacks and the threat they imply. This book examines the legislative and judicial responses of five liberal democracies to terrorism, both prior to and after the 9/11 attacks.

One of this book's objectives is to identify the nature of those responses. The most obvious examples include laws whose operation is conditioned on some kind of nexus with "terrorism" or "terror," but there are also more-general laws whose timing, context, and justification suggest that they can be understood as responses to terrorist attacks and fears of terrorism. Moreover, since long-standing general laws may sometimes obviate the need for specific counterterror legislation, this book will include references to such laws when they have obvious bearing on the legality of counterterror measures and where the corresponding areas of law in at least some of the jurisdictions make some provision for terrorism-related legal consequences. My aim is to provide an overview and to identify both cross-national differences and areas where legal responses have been or are substantively similar.

My second objective is to contribute to an understanding of the development of counterterror laws in the five countries. In doing so, I address four questions. To what extent can counterterror measures be understood as a hasty response to terrorist attacks? To what extent do responses vary institutionally? What is the role of underlying political beliefs in determining how political actors respond to actual and possible terrorism? And insofar as cross-national differences emerge, how are these to be explained?

The answer to the first question might seem obvious. Civil libertarians assert that the executive's strategy is opportunistic, prompted either by a desire to be seen to be doing something or by a perception that attacks and the subsequent public response provide a brief window of opportunity for the enactment of measures that would normally be politically unacceptable. Moreover, measures passed in haste will be ill-considered and may therefore be defective from both an instrumental and an expressive perspective. Authoritarians tend partly to agree, while arguing that speedy responses are needed in order to respond to new and terrifying threats, they also seem to agree with civil libertarians' charge that pressures for a speedy response are opportunistic in the sense that they represent unique windows of opportunities for the passage of the kind of measures needed to combat terrorism. This is implicit in their general opposition to sunset clauses. If they were confident that the measures would demonstrate their value, such opposition would seem pointless. If, however, they were concerned that the measures would not survive the closer scrutiny they would receive prior to the expiry of the sunset period, resistance would make considerable sense. Moreover, as we shall see in chapters 1 and 2 of this book, there are good evidentiary and theoretical reasons for expecting that terrorist attacks will result in heightened estimates of the terrorist threat posed by terrorism and in heightened receptivity to reactive measures.

Examination of the history of the development of counterterror laws throws light on some of these issues. First, it provides evidence of the degree to which counterterror measures are indeed introduced and passed in haste. Second, if legislation passed after lengthy deliberation tended to be no more "repressive" than legislation passed in haste in other jurisdictions, this would cast some doubt on the "haste" hypothesis insofar as it implies opportunism on the part of the proponents of the new laws. Third, if measures introduced in haste were particularly likely to be subsequently repealed, this would tend to bear out the "brief window of opportunity" perspective.

For reasons given in chapter 2, the "institutional" hypothesis is plausible. It is also readily tested. If enthusiasm for stronger executive powers is greatest within the executive (or, to be more precise, its muscular arms) and least within the judiciary, executive proposals would tend to be "watered down" in the legislature, and it would be exceptional for the legislature to seek to amend legislation so as to confer powers on the executive additional to those it had sought. Courts, however, would sometimes construe powers narrowly and would sometimes find that legislation fell foul of constitutionally protected rights.

The "political predispositions" hypothesis is almost irresistible. We are accustomed to thinking in terms of goodies and baddies: left versus right; authoritarians versus liberals; Democrats versus Republicans; believers versus the damned. Debates on counterterror legislation sometimes suggest that the forces of security are in battle with the forces of liberty. In chapter 2, I advert to a considerable body of academic literature suggesting that our political dispositions can indeed be parsimoniously modeled on a few dimensions, usually one or two, but possibly and less parsimoniously up to six. Further, albeit with some dissent, the literature suggests that ranks on the dimensions are relatively stable and partly determined by such considerations as child rearing and even DNA. On their face, they appear to have implications for preferences among possible reactions to terrorism.

One complication is provided by the fact that in parliamentary democracies and, to a lesser extent, the United States, party discipline means that individual legislators must subordinate their views to those of the party to which they belong, the views of which may, in turn, be strongly influenced by whether the relevant party is the party of the president or prime minister. Nonetheless, given the hypothesised differences between liberals and conservatives, one might expect that "conservative" legislative majorities would be more likely than "liberal" majorities to favour wide-ranging counterterror laws and that popular support for additional counterterror measures would be greater among the supporters of conservative parties. One would also expect that changes in the political complexion of governments and legislatures would be reflected in amendments to laws relating to terrorism.

Finally, insofar as laws are reactive, one might reasonably expect that they would reflect national experiences of terrorism (or its absence). But given the expected importance of institutions and political predispositions, one might also expect that they would reflect variations in national institutional structures and the predispositions of the elected government.

The Five Countries

In this book, I examine the terrorism laws of the national governments of five common-law countries: the United States, the United Kingdom, Canada, Australia, and New Zealand. While additional insights might be gained from an examination of subnational legal systems, Northern Ireland in particular,[1] the cost would be a vastly more complicated book.

While the five countries are all well-established liberal democracies, they differ in a number of respects. The United States maintains a high level of separation between the executive and legislative arms; in the other four countries, the prime minister (the de facto head of government), the members of the cabinet, and other ministers normally must be members of parliament and normally hold office only for as long as they have the confidence of a majority in the lower house. Voting on bills in the parliamentary democracies is normally done strictly along party lines, especially in Australia and New Zealand. Even the current US Republicans are less monolithic than the parliamentary parties. Despite party discipline, governments do not always get their way. Close elections sometimes mean that the government depends for its continuity on nongovernment members of parliament who support the government on confidence motions but reserve the right to vote against it on bills they do not like. This has proved salient in Canada but not in Australia, where the recent minority Labor government showed little interest in expanding counterterror powers and where its minor liberalising amendments have received cross-party support. More important, control of the lower house does not guarantee control of the upper house, and parliamentary committees are often far less partisan than the parliament itself.

In the United Kingdom, Australia, and New Zealand, differences between the major parties have become increasingly blurred, but if one looks closely, one can still find echoes of once-deep partisan cleavages and corresponding social ones, and smaller parties provide refuges for the less nonideological. Names may sometimes be misleading. Australia's Liberal Party is closer to a conservative party, and its coalition party, the National Party, draws its support mainly from Australia's small nonurban minority. The "conservative" parties tend to be somewhat to the left of the US Republicans. (They tend to accept the desirability of universal health insurance, for instance.) The Labour (UK and NZ) and Labor (Australia) parties were once well to the left of the US Democrats, but differences have decreased over the past 50 years. Barack Obama would be an acceptable Labor leader in all three countries, but their leaders would probably struggle to win a Democratic presidential primary (even if they had been born American).

The Canadian party system has been more fluid and fragmented, but parties can be ranked along a right-left continuum, with varyingly labeled Conservatives tending towards the right, Liberals to the middle, and the Bloc Québécois and the New Democratic Party towards the left. The United States, the traditional home of blurred partisan differences, now gives many of its voters a rather starker ideological choice than that provided by the Labor/Labour parties and their conservative opponents. In all five countries, there have been changes in the governing party between 2001 and 2011, which provides a basis for teasing out the impacts of partisan-related beliefs and the exigencies of being in government rather than opposition.

All five countries maintain a sharp distinction between the political and judicial arms, but they vary in the powers they confer on their courts. Almost since its founding, the United States has given courts the power to strike down legislation on the grounds of its inconsistency with a variety of specified rights. That precedent did not commend itself to British institutional reformers or to the drafters of the New Zealand, Canadian, and Australian constitutions. However, the Canadian and Australian constitutions impose limits on the legislature's powers. Constitutional entrenchment of separation of powers sets (indeterminate) limits on the degree to which legislatures can allocate functions to bodies other than courts and on the degree to which they can require courts to perform nonjudicial functions and act in uncourtly ways. Federal division of powers sets some limits on the powers of national (and provincial or state) legislatures.

The Charter of Rights and Freedoms is now entrenched in Canada. By virtue of its obligations under the European Convention for the Protection of Human Rights and Fundamental Freedoms (ECHR), the United Kingdom is effectively bound by the convention. The convention does not invalidate legislation contrary to its provisions, but it does expose governments to damages awards by the European Court of Human Rights (ECtHR) for failure to comply with the convention, except in circumstances where signatories are permitted to "derogate" from the convention. Political considerations have generally precluded derogating legislation and would constitute a major obstacle to withdrawal from the convention. Indeed, the convention has been given domestic legal force by the Human Rights Act 1998 (UK), passed under the Blair government. New Zealand's Bill of Rights Act 1990 gives legal force to the rights set out in the International Covenant on Civil and Political Rights (ICCPR) but is subject to legislation to the contrary. Australian politicians have generally resisted calls to limit their powers, and two attempts to amend Australia's constitution to provide greater protections for rights each failed to achieve majority support in national referenda. Proposals for statutory bills of rights have fallen through at the commonwealth level, but since 2011, drafters of commonwealth legislation have been required by statute to certify that proposed legislation is compatible with the specified human rights conventions.[2] The countries also differ in two other respects. First, as we shall see in chapter 1, they vary in their experiences of terrorism. Second, they obviously vary in their capacity to throw their weight around internationally.

Outline

Chapters 1 and 2 examine the "terrorist threat" and the variety of possible responses to the threat. In chapter 1, I examine national experiences of terrorism and perceptions of the threat posed by terrorism, arguing that terrorism generally does not seem to constitute a major threat to any of the five nations. There is some evidence to suggest that terrorist attacks produce a temporary increase in the perceived threat, but the evidence also suggests that fears of attacks remain high even after long attack-free periods.

Chapter 2 examines whether heightened fears of terrorism are likely to provoke or facilitate "tougher" counterterror laws. It argues that while laws represent only one of a variety of possible responses to threatened terror, "tougher" laws are a likely response. However, it also argues that receptivity to tougher laws will vary within governments and within populations. It discusses why institutional roles and interests are likely to be reflected in varying degrees of enthusiasm for greater government powers and why preferred responses to terrorism might be expected to reflect ideology and its analogues.

Chapters 3 through 9 examine the nature and evolution of seven areas of terrorism-related law. In many ways, the five countries' laws are functionally similar, but there are striking cross-national differences in the use of legal powers and in governments' willingness to bypass legal constraints in the name of fighting terror. There are also some substantive cross-national differences, and within countries, laws have changed over time. These differences throw light on the power of particular explanations for responses to terrorism.

Chapter 3 examines the emergence of statutory definitions of the term *terrorism* and their implications. While the chapter highlights the diversity of ways in which *terrorism* and cognate terms have been defined, it argues that the definitions reflect a broad consensus as to what the term entails. It also identifies contested aspects of the standard definitions and their implications. There is little evidence to suggest that the definitions were enacted in haste. There is some evidence that resolution of the definitional issue turns partly on institutional interests, but there is virtually none to suggest that courts disagreed with the statutory definitions. Parliamentary debates evidenced a nexus between underlying beliefs and preferred definitions, but these have not been reflected in changes to the definitions upon changes of government.

Chapter 4 relates to counterterrorism surveillance. Aspects of the history of the relevant US law seem to bear out the haste hypothesis. The circumstances surrounding the passage of the USA Patriot Act seem to provide powerful evidence of executive opportunism and legislative fearfulness, and its subsequent history goes a long way towards bearing out this analysis. But an attempt to strengthen surveillance powers following the earlier Oklahoma bombing came to naught, which indicates that responses to terror may depend on who is responsible for the attack. Moreover, in some ways, the 2001 amendments simply gave the US government powers that were already enjoyed by other governments, and laws subsequently conferring surveillance powers in other countries have passed with little reference to terrorism. Indeed, in relation to domestic terrorism, the US law is in some ways less government-friendly than the laws of the other countries. Moreover, while surveillance laws have tended to meet legislative resistance, they have generally survived judicial scrutiny.

The obverse of interest in other people's secrets is the desire to conserve one's own, which is the subject of chapter 5. Laws provide considerable formal protection for classified information, although they have not proved capable of preventing errors (such as mislaying laptops and electronically stored data in public places) or theft of poorly protected information (most notably in the United States). These laws have been left largely (but not completely) untouched by counterterror concerns. More problematic is the situation where governments want to keep their secrets yet use them as grounds for judicial decisions with implications for liberty and other interests. By 2001, courts and legislators had already addressed aspects of this problem, and post-9/11 measures have generally built on pre-2001 precedents. On the whole, the legislation in this area cannot be understood in terms of heightened fears, but it nonetheless represents one area of law where the priorities of the political arms have sometimes proved hard to reconcile with courts' concerns with protecting due process rights, especially in Canada and the United Kingdom, though far less so in the United States. There is some evidence of partisan conflict over the issue, but there is little evidence to suggest that changes of government are reflected in corresponding changes to law and practice.

An element common to the legislation of all five jurisdictions is provision for the proscription of terrorist organisations, as discussed in chapter 6. Proscription legislation is not readily understood in terms of heightened fears or distinctive executive interests. Prior to the 9/11 attacks, the United States and the United Kingdom had already established proscription regimes, and the regimes elsewhere owed much to the UK precedent, except that the Australian and New Zealand regimes were less intrusive. Proscription appealed more to governments than to opposition, though not by much. While proscription legislation aroused criticism, it passed through legislatures largely unaltered, except in Australia and New Zealand, where narrowly circumscribed powers were later expanded by successive pieces of legislation. Courts have left proscription legislation largely unscathed, partly because of the obstacles facing organisations that might want to contest their status and partly because courts have been unimpressed by constitutional arguments based on the implications of proscription for those who want to make nonfungible contributions to assist organisations' nonterrorist activities. Partisan differences bear a limited but predicted relation to stance on proscription, though not—except in one minor respect—to the point where changes of government have produced relevant changes to legislation.

Terrorist acts normally fall within one or more of the standard categories of criminal offences, and sentencing laws enable appropriately heavy sentences for any terrorist charged and convicted of a "nonpolitical" criminal offence. All five jurisdictions have, however, created special terrorism offences, which are detailed in chapter 7. These include offences relating to terrorist organisations. They also include precursor offences, designed to catch people who have begun making plans for some form of terrorist attack.

The legislative history of these offences provides limited support for the haste hypothesis, and there is evidence to suggest that institutional perspectives play some role in relation to its enactment and fate. Relevant government bills have sometimes met legislative resistance. But courts have generally upheld the legislation, and interpretative decisions have rarely been subject to subsequent legislative change. There is evidence of the relevance of partisan differences, but these are sometimes weak and not easily separated from government/opposition differences and, to date, have rarely been reflected in amendments to post-2001 legislation following changes of government. However, one context in which post-9/11 innovations have proved highly controversial relates to investigatory detention, an issue that produced sharp divisions between governments and parliaments.

While the criminal justice system serves as a basis for preventive detention, governments doubt that it is sufficient, and all jurisdictions have devised alternative forms of preventive detention, to deal with cases where the criminal justice system appears to be inadequate. These are discussed in chapter 8. They have proved to be highly controversial. The most notorious form of preventive detention has involved the detention of prisoners taken in the War on Terror. Most jurisdictions make or have made special provision for would-be immigrants who are believed to constitute security risks and who cannot be deported. Some make provision for detention for the purposes of avoiding a terrorist attack and to facilitate postattack investigations. In two jurisdictions, laws provide for a form of house arrest for potential terrorists.

Some of the relevant legislation predates the 9/11 attacks, but some seems explicable in terms of heightened fears. In one sense, there is a relationship between institutions and acceptance of preventive detention. Courts have typically found aspects of preventive detention regimes to be contrary to constitutional and quasi-constitutional protections. Executive and legislative differences are more complex. In the United States, beliefs have trumped institutional interests, with President Obama's attempt to close Guantánamo Bay being frustrated by congressional refusal to allow government funds to be used for that purpose. In the United Kingdom, it is difficult to disentangle the impact of institutional interests and beliefs. In Australia, institutional interests seem to trump beliefs.

Detention, whether for investigative or preventive purposes, carries with it the risk of abuse, especially in the absence of external supervision. This is the subject of chapter 9. Public denunciation of torture and the mistreatment of prisoners coexists with the temptation to torture or at least to use its fruits. The treatment of prisoners at Guantánamo Bay and in Afghanistan and Iraq will become a staple of future civil libertarian cautionary tales, and executive abuse coexists with attempts to keep it secret and to deny its unlawfulness.

The circumstances prompting ill-treatment of prisoners have not prompted attempts to rewrite anti-torture laws so as to permit torture in certain circumstances, but US law has been amended both to make it clearer that torture is not permitted and to exculpate prior torture in certain circumstances. Voting on these measures has been strongly related to party. US courts have affirmed the duty of governments to comply with exacting standards, but litigants in torture cases have tended to fall foul of procedural obstacles.

The other four countries' records are better but not perfect. Their laws are more exacting than US law, and their courts and governments are more receptive to torture victims' civil claims. Poll data help explain why terrorism-related concerns have not prompted changes in the relevant laws. In all five countries, there is widespread opposition to the official use of torture, with opposition varying cross-nationally. However, poll data suggest the importance of belief as a determinant of preferred responses to torture. Acceptance of torture (in specified circumstances) varies by party, with voting respondents on the right considerably more willing to accept that torture can be justified than are voters in the centre and, a fortiori, on the left.

Conclusions

The analysis in this book warrants several conclusions. First, while there is evidence to support aspects of the haste hypothesis, terrorism-related laws have sometimes been passed in conditions of relative calm. Moreover, there is also evidence to suggest that legislation passed in haste is sometimes no more draconian than similar legislation passed after greater deliberation in other jurisdictions and that "hasty" legislation survives almost as well as legislation passed after careful deliberation.

Second, the analysis highlights the importance of institutional considerations. It is almost unheard of for legislatures to amend government proposals by increasing government powers and expanding the scope of antiterror measures. (There are, however, cases where legislatures have nonetheless given the executive most of what it sought.) One also rarely finds courts ruling that the political arms have underestimated their legislative and executive powers. But—especially in the United States—the courts have tended to be sympathetic to the conferral and use of the powers conferred by contemporary counterterror legislation. If law is what the courts say it is, civil libertarians' confident assertions as to the unconstitutionality of recent counterterror legislation have generally not been borne out.

Third, the role of preexisting beliefs is equivocal. On the whole, roll call votes and poll data suggest that votes and support for counterterror measures vary depending on whether a person's party loyalties lie with a party on the right or on the left. But partisan divisions often coexist with considerable bipartisanship. Observed relationships are occasionally in the "wrong" direction, and critics of counterterror measures typically do little to change them upon their subsequently coming to power. The effects of civil libertarianism can be blurred and even trumped by the exigencies of office and by attitudes towards the possible targets of counterterror laws.

Fourth, national differences are sometimes reflected in countries' responses to terrorism in general and in differences in the content of their national counterterrorism laws. But the relationship between national differences and national responses to terrorism is far from simple. National responses cannot be ranked along a simple "repressiveness" dimension. National institutions are loosely coupled, so that "tough" executive action does not necessarily coexist with relatively "tough" legislation. Tough legislation may coexist with liberal courts. Responses to attacks may be influenced by preexisting laws and may involve imitation rather the innovation. Bills of rights may matter, but the mildest response to terrorism has been that of New Zealand, a country whose constitution imposes almost no restrictions on what its unicameral parliament may do.

The analysis in this book also highlights the ambiguous role played by law in the context of counterterrorism. Law both empowers and constrains governments. In the conclusion, I address the implications of these findings, arguing that while law has been a response to fears of terrorism, it has also been a constraint. It is a constraint partly because of politics: while governments tend to want greater powers, quests for power attract widespread opposition, even against the backdrop of terrorist attacks. It is also a constraint because when powers are granted, their exercise is often heavily circumscribed. Moreover, legislation is also constrained by international law and politics and by constitutional and quasi-constitutional limits on legislatures' powers.

But law's role and fate in the post-9/11 decade highlights what any lawyer knows: first, laws are malleable; second, they are not self-executing. Law's malleability is demonstrated by the fact that virtually all of the major counterterrorism cases have involved dissenting judgments and different outcomes at different levels. This may overstate malleability a little: cases tend to be fought and fought to higher levels because each side has some chance of success, and if this condition is satisfied, it is likely that there will be disagreement between judges. More interesting is the way in which judges have responded to ambiguity. In the United States, the Supreme Court's habeas corpus decisions coexist with other highly deferential decisions, some of which seem flawed by highly questionable logic. In the United Kingdom and Canada, courts have tended to be much less deferential. Decisions by Australian courts reflect the Australian Constitution's limited protection of fundamental rights, tempered by the common-law presumption that legislation should be interpreted to minimise inconsistency with international law and common-law rights.

Malleability is one reason laws have not always been sufficient to control executive illegality. Potential lawbreakers may believe that they are complying with the law or, alternatively, that their interpretation of the law is sufficiently plausible to ensure that even if it does not prevail, they will not be punished. But potential lawbreakers may also take comfort from the improbability of being caught or of being punished if they are caught. Where law seems to get in the way of achieving valued outcomes, institutional culture is likely to encourage deviance. It certainly seems to have done so in the United States and may have done so even in New Zealand.

Executive deviance seems to have been far more widespread in the United States than elsewhere. This is not surprising: in terms of lives lost, the 9/11 attacks were the most serious attacks on the US homeland in its history. This, coupled with the humiliation entailed, could be expected to make for receptivity to punitive responses. Moreover, detention and mistreatment of prisoners flow directly from the decision to use massive military force against symbols, supporters, and agents of terrorism. The United States could do so. Smaller powers could do no more than help, and small powers are more accustomed to accommodating the demands and expectations of other countries. Their responses reflected a corresponding assessment that international law was a tool to be used in combating terrorism, rather than an obstacle towards doing so.

ONE

The Specter of Terrorism

> Reports that say that something hasn't happened are always interesting to me, because as we know, there are known knowns; there are things we know we know. But there are also unknown unknowns—the ones we don't know we don't know. And if one looks throughout the history of our country and other free countries, it is the latter category that tends to be the difficult ones.
>
> *Donald H. Rumsfeld*

> Many of you may have seen recent press reporting about a . . . survey that found people are now much less concerned about terrorism than they were after the London bombings. The decrease in public concern about terrorism, at one level, is not surprising. Public attention spans are often short and Australians tend to have an optimistic perception of the security environment. Over the last five years, the issue of terrorism has rarely been far from centre-stage in the media, but Australia has not experienced a recent attack on its soil. So it is almost inevitable that a type of "terrorism fatigue," if you will, would set in. Unfortunately, such complacency . . . makes us vulnerable.
>
> *Paul O'Sullivan, director-general of the Australian Security Intelligence Organization, 2006*

Civil libertarian critiques of responses to terrorism frequently assume that counterterror polices are distorted by exaggerated assessments of the seriousness of the terrorist threat, especially in the aftermath of spectacular terrorist attacks. This conclusion is defended partly on the basis of theory and partly on the basis of evidence suggesting that estimates of the threat are unwarranted by what is known about its "true" magnitude and that this is particularly likely immediately following terrorist attacks. This chapter develops and examines these arguments. It concludes that they are cogent but not conclusive. They depend on the optimistic assumption that the objective terrorist threat will continue to be slight, and while that assumption may be warranted, one cannot be certain of it. While poll data yields evidence of cognitive error, it also yields evidence to suggest that the political salience of the threat is small, notwithstanding that the perceived risk remains high.

Sources of Misperception

When people form opinions about the risk of terrorist attacks, they necessarily do so in a state of considerable ignorance as to terrorists' intentions. They are thrown back on a variety of cognitive shortcuts. One is known as "availability" ("the ease with which instances or associations can be brought to mind").[1] Typically, frequent events are more available than infrequent ones, but what terrorism lacks in frequency is made up by its visibility, reinforced by television footage of the aftermath of terrorist attacks in foreign countries and by periodical replays of the collapsing towers in New York, the red London bus with its top sheared off, or the smoke billowing from the Taj Mahal hotel in Mumbai. Given the generally accepted trope that terrorists aim for drama, their success will be reflected in an overassessment of the risk they pose. Availability will be highest immediately following terrorist attacks on symbols with which one can identify, but memories are likely to persist long after the attack.

Perception of low-risk high-intensity threats is also likely to be distorted by worst-case fears (which become serious when compounded with failure to discount for improbability). Worst-case reasoning shares something in common with availability. Actual "very bad" cases stand out more than not-so-bad ones, and warnings of "worst cases" are likely to receive more publicity than warnings of minor attacks. Worst-case reasoning is aggravated by the difficulties most people have with probabilities. As probabilities decrease, people find it increasingly difficult to distinguish between the implications of small and very small probabilities, and they make their assessment of the danger on the basis of the nature of the threatened outcome rather than on its likelihood. Sunstein reports studies finding that perceptions of riskiness do not vary when the risk is 1/100,000 rather than 1/1,000,000 and that perceptions even vary little between risks of 1/650, 1/6,300, and 1/68,000.[2] Assume that an honest and infallible oracle has helpfully provided the information that within a given country and a given period, there is a 1/1,000,000 chance of a terrorist attack, which, if it takes place, will kill 100,000 people and cost $500 billion in property damage. A coldhearted insurer would require a premium based on the value of a tenth of a life and aggregate premiums of a little more than $500,000 to insure against the risk. But the risk assessor in the street would assess the risk at a considerably higher level. This suggests that perceptions of the threat of terrorism may be heavily influenced by remote possibilities of really serious attacks.

Moreover, even after controlling for the "objective" seriousness of the threat, people appear to be willing to pay far more to reduce the likelihood of a threat from 1 percent to zero than they are to reduce it from 2 to 1 percent. Where the threat also arouses a high level of emotion, the price people are willing to pay for its elimination is even higher, and it is also even less dependent on perceived probabilities.[3] Given that terrorism involves low probabilities and that the threat is likely to arouse strong emotions, one would expect that even small threats would be accompanied by willingness to make considerable sacrifices in order to minimise or eliminate the likelihood of their eventuating.

One interpretation of these findings is that they indicate that people are likely to overreact to low-probability high-cost threats. However, there are several problems with this analysis. First, the existence of overreaction is ultimately dependent on what the objective threat actually is. Availability considerations may affect the likelihood of a threat being overestimated rather than underestimated, but the extent to which it does so is ultimately dependent on whether the threat actually is large or small. To state the obvious, if someone who saw the first of the 9/11 attacks had fallen victim to availability reasoning and concluded that the risk of further attacks was much higher than they had previously thought, they would, in fact, have been correct, at least in relation to the next few hours. Second, the analysis assumes that if we know the likelihood of an event and its effects (measured in dollars and lives), we can determine its "expected value." While we might have a good start at making such determinations, the analysis makes some arbitrary assumptions. It discounts emotions and their implications, a particularly egregious omission in an age where keeping a stiff upper lip is no longer de rigueur. That people are willing to pay a certain amount to halve a risk and three times that amount to eliminate it might seem irrational, but it might simply reflect awareness that the cost of halving a risk can be far more than double the cost of eliminating the risk altogether, coupled with a subjective preference for certainty.

There is no reason to assume that civil libertarians are immune to such biases. While infringements of civil liberties are often relatively invisible,[4] availability and worst-case reasoning can be mobilised to support civil libertarian as well as authoritarian arguments. The left's success in conflating anticommunism with McCarthyism highlights the use that can be made of highly visible threats to liberty (availability). Roach and Trotter have argued, "Claims of wrongful conviction are a potent political force; miscarriages of justice are public problems that can go to the top of the political agenda and command attention across the political spectrum."[5] Civil libertarian responses to repressive measures typically include what generally turn out to be exaggerated claims for what governments might do with added powers (worst-case reasoning). In short, we have some evidence of what Vermeule calls "libertarian panics."[6] However, the examples of the costs of repression tend to achieve visibility gradually and too late to make an impact on the passage of the legislation (if any) that prompts them.

An alternative argument contends that overestimation in risk perceptions is exaggerated because those with the capacity to influence perceptions have an interest in exaggerating the risk. Mueller provides considerable evidence of patently untenable claims in relation to the post-2001 terrorist threat and argues that at least some of these claims were knowingly dishonest and that others reflected the makers' economic and personal interests. He contends that the success of some claimants in securing currency for their untenable claims accounts for why threat perceptions are exaggerated.[7] Exaggerated claims do indeed seem to have been made. Whether they were made sincerely or insincerely is probably unknowable and is largely irrelevant to the question of whether they were misleading. What matters is whether exaggerated views are particularly likely to receive currency, and they may well have been. Mueller reports evidence to the effect that media were far more likely to report news suggesting that the threat was serious than news suggesting that it was not, thereby enhancing the availability of material consistent with terrorism as a serious threat. But threat entrepreneurs are not the only people in the business of threat perception. A comprehensive study of the social creation of the perception of the terrorist threat would also require an analysis of the role of civil libertarians in contributing to countervailing fears that freedoms were under threat.

How Serious Is the Threat?

National Experiences of Terrorism

Terrorist Attacks

To judge from the past, the threats posed by terrorism are manageable. Terrorist attacks occur, but they are rare; and when they occur, they rarely involve more than one death. However, far more devastating attacks do take place, and most of the deaths attributable to terrorism are attributable to a handful of attacks. If past patterns were to continue, terrorism would constitute a relatively trivial threat, even allowing for the rare devastating attacks.

While the United States has had a history of political violence and continues to have a relatively high homicide rate, terrorist attacks on American soil are exceptional. Paul Wilkinson estimated that there were only 20 terrorism-related deaths in the United States between 1985 and 1994.[8] The 1995 Oklahoma bombing, in which 165 people were killed, represented an attack of a completely different order, but it was an exception. The Global Terrorism Database lists only 11 other fatal terrorist attacks during the years 1995–2000, resulting in a total of 12 deaths.

The 9/11 attacks were unparalleled in terms of both loss of life and economic loss, but despite apocalyptic fears, the post-9/11 period has been remarkably free of fatal terrorist attacks. One candidate for a terrorist attack was the posting of letters laced with anthrax spores to various targets, including politicians and journalists,[9] but the motive for this attack was unclear. Almost all attacks appear to have been the work of lone offenders or small groups. Two involved attacks on Jewish targets, apparently intended to express opposition to Israel and to US support for Israel.[10] Others involved attacks on abortionists, Unitarians, the IRS, the media, and a military recruiting station, and involved only one or two deaths.[11] The 2009 massacre of 12 fellow soldiers and a civilian by a Muslim army psychiatrist was far more serious.

In a typical year, Americans are somewhat more at risk of being killed in terrorist attacks when outside the United States. Some of these deaths have been incidental to foreign terrorist attacks; others have targeted Americans. Some guidance as to the level of "foreign" attacks on US citizens is provided by the US State Department's annual reports on global terrorism and the subsequent Country Reports on Terrorism and data from the National Counterterrorism Center but fatalities there attributed to "international terrorism" include attacks by international terrorists on targets located in the United States. Figures for 2001 reflect the 9/11 attacks. Since 2001, the number of such deaths from foreign attacks—27 (2002), 35 (2003), 56 (2005), 28 (2006), 19 (2007), 33 (2008), 9 (2009), and 15 (2010)—has far exceeded the number of terrorism-related deaths within the United States.[12]

Canada has experienced few lethal attacks since Laporte's assassination in 1971. There were three fatal attacks on Turkish diplomats by Armenian terrorists in 1984–85, and the Global Terrorism Database lists two more attacks whose motivation is unclear.[13] There is one dramatic exception to this record: in 1985, Sikh extremists placed bombs on Air India flights from Toronto and Vancouver. The flight from Toronto exploded over the Irish Sea, killing all 329 passengers and crew. That from Vancouver exploded after being unloaded, killing two baggage attendants.[14] Since then, Canada has remained free of major terrorist attacks,[15] and minor incidents noted by the Canadian Security Intelligence Service (CSIS) have involved property damage but no loss of life or physical injury.[16] Canadians have, however, been killed in foreign attacks. Twenty-four Canadians died in the 9/11 attacks, two in the 2002 Bali bombings, and another two in the 2005 London bombings. A Canadian diplomat died in a 2006 suicide bombing in Afghanistan.[17]

Australia has not experienced a lethal domestic terrorist attack since 1980, when the Turkish consul general was assassinated in Sydney.[18] However, Australians have suffered heavy casualties in foreign attacks. Of the 202 killed in the 2002 Bali bombings, 88 were Australians, as were four of the 20 killed in the 2005 Bali bombings. Fifteen Australians died in the 9/11 attacks. Three Australians were killed in the July 2009 attack on the Marriott Hotel in Jakarta.

Australians were also among those killed in the 2003 Riyadh attack (one), the 7 July 2005 London bombings (one), and two Iraq bombings.

New Zealand has experienced only two fatal terrorist attacks. In 1984, a caretaker was killed by a bomb left in the foyer of the Wellington Trades Hall, and the following year, a French agent planted two bombs intended to destroy the *Rainbow Warrior*, a ship that the organisation had been using to protest against French nuclear testing in the Pacific. After the first bomb, a photographer who had been on the dockside went on board to recover his photographic equipment before the *Rainbow Warrior* sank. He was killed when the second bomb exploded.[19] The Global Terrorism Database lists only one fatal terrorist incident in New Zealand (involving an unknown assailant). There have been no post-9/11 attacks there. However, at least seven New Zealanders have been killed in foreign attacks: two in the World Trade Center, three in the 2002 Bali attacks, one in the 2005 London bombing, and one in the 2009 Jakarta attack.

The United Kingdom's experience has been different. In Northern Ireland, terrorism has been a real threat for much of its history, culminating in a 30-year war that began in 1969 and peaked in 1972, when 467 died in Northern Ireland as a result of violence associated with the conflict over whether Northern Ireland was to remain part of the United Kingdom. Of those that died, 321 were civilians, with the remainder being soldiers (103), members of the Ulster Defence Regiment (26), and police (17). Between 1969 and 1994 (after which the annual death rate fell sharply), there were 3,159 terrorism-related deaths in Northern Ireland. Most of the casualties (2,216) were civilians; the others were soldiers in the British Army (445), members of the Ulster Defence Regiment or its successor (197), or members of the Royal Ulster Constabulary (194) or the Royal Ulster Constabulary Reserve (101).[20] Civilian casualties included both Catholics and Protestants, in proportions roughly similar to their proportion of the population.[21] Between 1995 and 2000, there were another 131 terrorism-related deaths, and 121 of the dead were civilians (including 38 members of Republican or loyalist paramilitaries).[22] The post-9/11 period coincided with a continuing decline in Irish violence. According to one source, there were 16 conflict-related deaths in Northern Ireland in 2001, 11 in 2002, 10 in 2003, 4 in 2004, 8 in 2005, 3 in 2006, 2 in 2007, and none in 2008.[23] There were at least three conflict-related deaths in 2009.

Northern Ireland bore the brunt of the conflict, but there were frequent attacks on targets in England (most of which were not lethal). Among the casualties were English politicians, including the secretary of state for Northern Ireland who was killed by a car bomb in 1979.[24] Less-discriminating bombings caused considerable civilian casualties and included the 1974 bombings of two pubs in Birmingham, which took at least 21 lives; bombings earlier that year that killed 17; and a 1994 bombing at Warrington, which killed two.[25] According to the Global Terrorism Database, Irish Republican groups were responsible for 51 fatal terrorist attacks on the British mainland (173 deaths) between 1971 and 1980, 32 (135 deaths) between 1971 and 1980, 12 (39 deaths) between 1981 and 1990, and 7 (10 deaths) between 1991 and 2000.

By comparison, the United Kingdom's experience of other forms of political violence has been mild. There have, however, been several lethal terrorist attacks. In addition to attacks by Irish groups, the Global Terrorism Database lists 29 other fatal terrorist attacks between 1971 and 2001, each typically involving a single death. Twelve took place between 1971 and 1980, causing a total of 16 deaths.[26] In the following decade, there were 13 attacks, causing a total of 14 deaths (excluding those caused by the destruction of a plane over Lockerbie, Scotland, which killed 270 people). Between 1991 and 2001, there were four attacks, with five deaths. More than half the attacks were by unknown groups or people.[27] Of the rest, all but a handful were associated with a variety of Arabic and Islamic groups. In addition, a siege at the Iranian embassy in London ended with the death of five of the six hostage takers and one of the hostages.[28]

The post-9/11 period has seen one major terrorist attack and a number of attacks causing one or more deaths. The gravest attack occurred on 7 July 2005 and involved the coordinated bombing of three London trains and a bus, in which 56 people (including the four bombers) were killed. Those responsible were British nationals who were sympathetic towards but acting independently of al-Qaeda.

United Kingdom nationals have also been the victims of overseas attacks. Sixty-seven British citizens were among those killed in the 9/11 attack.[29] Twenty-four British citizens were among those killed in the October 2002 Bali bombings, and Britons were among those killed in the 12 May 2003 attack on three Saudi Arabian residential compounds.[30] In November 2003, there was a suicide attack on the British consulate and the Istanbul branch of the HSBC, with 33 killed, including the British consul and two other British citizens. Al-Qaeda gunmen killed a British cameraman in an attack on a BBC news crew in June 2004 and killed a British national living in Riyadh in September 2004. British citizens were also the victims of an attack in Iraq (October 2004) and the explosion of a car bomb in Qatar (2005).[31]

Thwarted Plans

Thwarted plans provide an ambiguous guide to the threat posed by terrorism. On one hand, they indicate that the threat is reduced by the diligence of security services, the police, and the public. On the other, they suggest that even in countries that have been largely free from terrorist attacks, this is not through want of would-be terrorists. It seems unrealistic to treat thwarted attacks as irrelevant to the dimensions of the terrorist threat.

In each of the five countries, police and security agencies claim to have frustrated terrorist attacks. Federal Bureau of Investigation statistics relating to terrorist incidents within the United States between 12 September 2001 and 31 December 2005 suggest that the FBI prevented almost as many terrorist attacks as actually took place (21 compared with 27) but that the attacks would not have involved many casualties had they taken place. The prevented attacks were typically acts of domestic terrorists, a majority of which involved right-wing extremists.[32] A study of the period 2001–2011 concluded that there had been at least 30 foiled attacks involving "international terrorism," some of which would have involved considerable loss of life if executed.[33] Several of these involved threats to aircraft and were detected only when the offender was in the process of trying to cause an on-flight explosion. Richard Reid managed to board a Paris-Miami flight with explosives packed into the soles of his shoes and was overpowered while attempting to detonate the explosives.[34] More recently, Umar Farouk Abdulmutallab attempted to destroy an aircraft carrying 290 passengers and crew. According to an FBI agent's affidavit, Abdulmutallab succeeded in setting off an explosion sufficient to set his pants and the wall of the aircraft on fire. The fire was extinguished, and Abdulmutallab was subdued.[35] In 2010, two bombs placed on cargo flights bound for the United States were intercepted en route, after the Saudi government had received and communicated details of the bombers' plans.

Most of the other thwarted conspiracies involved plans for bomb attacks on buildings and in public places. In 2010, a would-be car bomber was arrested after the vehicle he abandoned had attracted the attention of a suspicious bystander.[36] Most of the other foiled attacks were identified at a much earlier stage, sometimes well before the offender had taken any steps to acquire the bomb, other than those done with the knowledge of the police.[37]

A former director-general of the United Kingdom Security Service reported that between 2001 and 2007, the United Kingdom

> faced 15 serious plots and many smaller ones. The plots were of varying complexity and sophistication, and most involved a network of people overseas as well as people based in the UK. We detected and thwarted, with police, a dozen of them.[38]

Plots that were not thwarted by the police included the 7/7 attacks, the attempted 21 July attack (which failed as a result of a manufacturing error by the bomb makers), and Richard Reid's attempt to destroy an aircraft. The most impressive police success was the frustration of a 2006 conspiracy to blow up a number of flights from London Heathrow Airport to North American destinations, a legacy of which is limits on the right of passengers to bring fluid containers aboard aircraft.[39] Two planned bomb attacks failed only because the bombs failed to explode.[40] Several planned bomb attacks were frustrated after having been discovered by British and Pakistani intelligence.[41]

By 2005, the Royal Canadian Mounted Police had reportedly "'disrupted' at least half a dozen 'national-level' terrorist groups," but details are lacking.[42] The only foiled attack on Canada that gave rise to a criminal prosecution involved plans to bomb a number of targets in the Toronto area. The plans came to the notice of the authorities well before any serious steps had been taken to implement them.[43]

In December 2001, Singapore authorities uncovered plans by Jemaah Islamiyah to attack a number of targets, including the Australian High Commission.[44] Australian authorities have also successfully prosecuted a number of people on the basis of planned acts of terrorism. As in Canada, the police and security services were aware of the plans from an early stage.[45] New Zealand police claimed to have foiled a terrorist conspiracy in 2007, but the solicitor-general concluded that New Zealand law could not support terrorism charges, given the facts alleged against the arrestees. After years of wrangling about the admissibility of surveillance evidence, firearms charges against 13 remaining defendants were dropped as unsustainable. One defendant died. In 2012, four were charged with firearms offences and involvement in an organised criminal group. The jury convicted on the firearms offences but could not agree on the criminal organisation charges.[46]

Drawing conclusions from thwarted attacks is difficult. In relation to some international plots, few details have emerged. Far more material has emerged from criminal trials, but the implications of the material are unclear. In several cases, the circumstances indicate that it was only good luck, incompetence, or both that frustrated the plan. This was clearly the case in relation to two attempts to destroy aircraft, and there can be little doubt that those responsible for leaving car bombs in London and New York intended that they explode. In other trials, the implications of the facts are more ambiguous. Typically, the trials indicate that the defendants were people who probably would have been pleased if their plans had come to fruition; but they also highlight massive gaps between intentions and capacities and indicate that the relevant terrorists were sometimes more attracted to the thought of violence than to its actual execution.[47] One of the 7/7 conspirators decided against being a suicide bomber and abandoned his bomb in some wayside bushes. Some of the Toronto conspirators and Abdul Kadir, one of the conspirators plotting to blow up John F. Kennedy International Airport in New York, seem to have been anxious to minimise civilian casualties. Parties to conspiracies sometimes drifted away without coconspirators being particularly concerned. The trials suggest the possibility that if left to their own devices, the terrorists might simply have decided to abandon their plans. The police, understandably, decided not to find out.

Assessing the Risk

If reasoning by induction was sound logic, we could conclude that the risk of a terrorist attack causing one or more deaths in a particular year and in a particular large city in one of the five countries is very small and that the risk of a major attack is tiny. We also have grounds for believing that the size of the risk may be partly due to the vigilance of counterterrorist forces, coupled with fortuitous mistakes on the part of would-be terrorists. But rejoicing in good news is something we regard with natural suspicion, borne of ancestral fears of the price of hubris.

Out of deference to the gods, some qualifications are in order. First, if terrorism is treated from an internationalist perspective, the picture is far less rosy. In Iraq and Afghanistan in particular, terrorist activity has been and continues to be a problem, partly attributable to policies pursued by liberal democratic governments in response to the perceived threat of terrorism. (It is also attributable to decisions made by terrorists.)

Second, one cannot necessarily extrapolate from the past to the future. A theme of many surveys of the recent history of terrorism is its fluidity. A popular paradigm emphasises waves of terrorism, perhaps as many as four since the 1970s.[48] A methodologically sophisticated time-series study has identified "breaks" in patterns of terrorism, with 9/11 representing one such break.[49] Other studies highlight the degree to which the demographic and social attributes of terrorists[50] and the nature of terrorism can vary even within relatively short periods.[51] This is not surprising, since terrorist groups are likely to react to counterterrorism moves and other changes to their environment by adopting different strategies.[52] Sometimes, changes are for the good, but in countries where the terrorist threat borders on nonexistent, substantial change can only be for the worse.

Third, even if the dynamics of terrorism were stable over time, experience cannot provide a reliable guide to the likelihood of extremely rare events, except in the sense that it will suggest that they will continue to be extremely rare. The effect of this is that it may be impossible to know whether the risk of, say, a terrorist nuclear attack on a given large city in a given year is 1/100 or 1/10,000. Yet a difference of this magnitude has important implications for determining whether and what precautions should be taken against this possibility.

These problems are not altogether insuperable. Intelligence agencies, media organisations, journalists, and other researchers may be able to detect changes that foreshadow possible changes to the risk of terrorist attacks, and laypeople may be able to make some informed guesses based on accessible information. For instance, the 9/11 attacks did not entirely come as a bolt from the blue. But for reasons discussed here, estimates of the parameters of terrorist threats are likely to be vague. This can be demonstrated by insurers' apparent inability to estimate the likelihood and magnitude of catastrophic attacks and by the vagueness of government specifications of the dimensions of the threat.

Insurers

If anyone can dispassionately assess the risk posed by terrorism, it ought to be the insurance industry. Moreover, if risks can be calculated with some precision, it should be possible to charge premiums that would-be insureds are prepared to pay, especially if it is true that laypeople tend to overestimate the risk of terrorism. Up to a point, these assumptions have been borne out. However, especially in the aftermath of 9/11, insurers have tended to require special terrorism insurance for at least some lines of cover. For other lines, risk aversion on the part of insurers has meant that premiums have been set at a level that has limited the take-up of such insurance. Uncertainty associated with the danger of some forms of terrorist attack has prompted insurers to refuse cover for damage occasioned by such attacks. Problems associated with the underprovision of affordable terrorism insurance have prompted government intervention in numerous countries, including the United Kingdom, the United States, and Australia, but not Canada and New Zealand.

The events of 9/11 demonstrated the resilience of the insurance industry. Despite the unprecedented losses, the insurance industry met its legal obligations,[53] and perhaps even more surprisingly, the price of insurance company stock recovered to close to where it had been prior to the attack. However, the immediate lesson that insurance companies derived from the attack was that it was no longer wise to treat losses due to terror as simply another type of loss. Post-9/11 commercial property insurance policies excluded coverage for terror-related losses.[54] The supply of terrorism insurance almost dried up, and while it began to recover, take-up was slow.[55] Insurers were less concerned by the threat of noncommercial losses. In at least some OECD countries, the terms of personal lines of insurance have not been changed to exclude terrorism risks.[56]

The history of terrorism insurance points to a number of conclusions. First, even now, insurance companies regard some insured risks as insignificantly affected by threatened terrorism.[57] Second, there is evidence that, in some respects, commercial terrorism risks are sufficiently predictable for a competitive terrorism insurance market to have emerged in the United States. Premiums have declined: they accounted for 10 percent of all premiums paid for commercial property insurance in early 2003, but by late 2004, they had fallen to 4 percent, where they have remained. For some insureds, premiums may be as little as 0.02 percent of the value of their insured property.[58] Take-up rates rose substantially between early 2003 and late 2004, from about a quarter of all insured businesses to around half, and they were close to 60 percent by 2006.[59] However, terrorism insurance was less available, more expensive, and often capped, where the relevant premises were located in high-risk areas.[60]

Third, governments in many countries have been persuaded that the problems of risk determination require special legislation aimed at placing some of the risk of exceptional attacks on governments. The United Kingdom passed such legislation following massive property damage caused by attacks on property by the IRA, and the United States and Australia did so following the 9/11 attacks. In the latter two countries, the legislation was and is subject to sunset clauses, but it has not been allowed to expire.[61]

Fourth, the ongoing problems surrounding the determination of premiums point to a perception on the part of risk assessors that the terrorism risk is serious but, to a considerable extent, incapable of precise calculation. While suggesting that insurers' strategies for risk assessment and risk management have become more sophisticated, an OEDC report on insurance against terrorism risk points out that calculating the likely costs of attacks on particular targets requires access to a vast amount of information if it is to be of value and that such calculations are of little assistance in the absence of information about the likelihood of a particular target being attacked.[62]

Fifth, the difficulties surrounding decisions in relation to the provision of terrorism insurance not only reflect the difficulty of determining the likelihood and likely severity of terrorist attacks; they also reflect features of the risk, which means that insurers may find it harder to manage a series of terrorist attacks than a series of natural disasters whose aggregate effects may be as disastrous. In particular, the different kinds of risks associated with major terrorist attacks may be highly correlated, involving claims against different lines of insurance. Liabilities for terrorism-related losses may accrue at the very time that the attack has led to a loss of financial confidence, thereby reducing the value of insurers' assets. Also, given the proclivities of some terrorist groups, there may have been a series of simultaneous attacks.[63] This means that the determination of what to offer and at what price is harder than the determination of the likelihood and likely severity of possible terrorist attacks, but this suggests, in turn, that insofar as insurers in a free[64] market do offer terrorism insurance, they consider that it is nonetheless possible to make plausible estimates of the likelihood and likely severity of the risk of terrorism, along with the hazards introduced by correlated risks.

Sixth, insurers are reluctant to provide coverage against the risk of chemical, biological, radiological, and nuclear (CBRN) weapons. Private insurers regard these risks as uninsurable and exclude them from coverage. Some government schemes exclude some or all CBRN risks from their statutory compensation schemes. Germany excludes all CBRN risks. Australia excludes damage attributable to radiation or nuclear attack. Belgium permits coverage for loss due to nuclear bombs to be excluded from coverage.[65] US terrorism legislation does not preclude compensation for CBRN risks, but it does not require insurers to offer insurance against such hazards for states that approve CBRN exclusion clauses.[66] Many states also allow exclusion of losses indirectly flowing from such attacks, such as losses caused by fire.[67] The United States provides for partial coverage. The United Kingdom, France, Spain, and the Netherlands provide general coverage, even for CBRN risks.[68] CBRN incidents may also be covered indirectly. Several jurisdictions provide set ceilings on the government's exposure.[69]

Finally, premium setting and its analogues highlight the degree to which the risk of terrorism is geographically contingent. In the United States, location is a major determinant of premiums.[70] In Australia, the premiums payable by insurers to the Australian Reinsurance Pool Corporation vary sharply according to whether the business is located in the central business district (CBD) of a city of more than 1 million people, elsewhere in a large city or anywhere in a city of more than 100,000 people, or elsewhere in Australia. Since 2003, premiums payable as a percentage of underlying premiums have been 12 percent for CBD premises, 4 percent for premises in other urban areas, and 2 percent for premises elsewhere.[71] The stability of those contributions also suggests an assessment that the risk of attack has remained relatively constant.[72]

Terrorism insurers are the only group to have attempted to attach numbers to the threat of terrorism. Implicit in their numbers is the conclusion that terrorism poses little threat to commercial property, other than property located in the CBDs of large and medium-sized cities, and that there is a nontrivial but incalculable threat posed by CBRN attacks—which is more or less the conclusion to be drawn from past experience.

Government Fears

When it comes to assessing the risks of terrorism, governments enjoy several advantages over laypeople. They have access to far more data, some of which they may be able to keep secret from the public. They also have access to skilled analysts. However, governments may have political reasons for deliberately exaggerating the threat, and a mixture of availability, the seduction of worst-case scenarios, and institutional cultures may also lead governments astray.

Space does not permit a detailed analysis here of government perceptions or of what underlay them, and in any case, disentangling the influences of political calculation and self-deception would be extremely difficult. Goldsmith's account of the "threat matrix" presented each day to the president highlights the degree to which those responsible for the country's security were (and may still be) daily confronted with pages of threats distilled from billions of intercepted phone calls and e-mail messages, including numerous plans for CBRN attacks. Self-evidently, none of these eventuated, but those exposed to the daily reports admit to being terrified by what they encountered, notwithstanding that none of the threats has yet been put into practice.[73] Low-probability threats were to be treated as certainties, and Goldsmith sympathised, but not to the point of accepting the logic of this analysis.[74] Dame Elizabeth Manningham-Buller has highlighted similar problems of information overload during her term as director of the United Kingdom's MI5 and was also concerned about the possibility that al-Qaeda might have and use CBRN weapons.[75] Mueller is less forgiving, and his examples of the use of funds ostensibly intended for security suggest either that members of Congress were not particularly concerned about the dangers posed by terrorism or—if they were—that their concern was not sufficient to persuade them to resist pork-barrel temptations.[76]

Publicly, governments are concerned about the threat. But the most striking feature of their descriptions of the threat is not that they are clearly misleading; it is that they have tended to be so vague as to be almost unfalsifiable. Here, I shall examine three sets of sources: speeches in support of counterterror legislation; colour-coded terrorism alerts; and reports from security services. Speeches justifying counterterror legislation naturally referred to the evils of terrorism and the need to combat it, but there is little to suggest that they could not have been written by intelligent laypeople with no access to such restricted information as the government might have had in its possession.

When the British home secretary moved the second reading of the Terrorism Bill in 1999, his speech addressed the evils of terrorism, the deaths and injuries it had caused in the United Kingdom, and recent examples of terrorism in the United Kingdom and abroad. His justification for the legislation was not that there was a known threat of a known magnitude but that one could not say there was no threat.[77] Post-9/11 speeches treat the 9/11 attacks as heralding a new paradigm, such that the threat must be treated as far more serious than it had previously been. In the House Judiciary Committee's deliberations on what became the USA Patriot Act, Chairman Sensenbrenner argued that "our lives were changed forever," but he was not sure how. His analysis of the problem posed by terrorism emphasised uncertainty: "We are uncertain who the enemy is. We are more uncertain than ever before about the next move of the enemy. Because of this uncertainty, we have had to change the way we think about the safety and security of our country and its people."[78] Introducing Bill C-36 on 10 October 2001, the Canadian minister of justice and attorney general justified the legislative package on the grounds that "[t]he world changed on September 11 in a way that changed our collective sense of safety and security."[79]

The New Zealand minister for foreign affairs and trade considered that "[t]errorism has become the greatest contemporary threat to the world's peace, prosperity, and security."[80] Less apocalyptically, the Australian attorney-general admitted that there was "no known specific threat of terrorism in Australia at present," but he justified his government's much more wide-ranging package of bills on the grounds that

> since September 11 there has been a profound shift in the international security environment. This has meant that Australia's profile has risen and our interests abroad face a higher level of terrorist threat. . . . Terrorism has the potential to destroy lives, devastate communities and threaten the national and global economy.[81]

These speeches were given within months of 9/11, at a time when one would expect governments still to be coming to grips with the devastating attacks. But there is little to suggest that governments subsequently developed a significantly more accurate assessment of the threat. A crude measure of government threat assessments is provided by the much-mocked color-coded alert systems. The United States defined "threat conditions" by reference to a five-color hierarchy: green for low, blue for guarded, yellow for elevated, orange for high, and red for severe. The codes were determined by the attorney general in consultation with officials of the Department of Homeland Security and could be assigned generally or for particular areas or sectors. They reflected both the likelihood and gravity of threats. Assignment of a threat level had implications for measures that must be taken to meet the threat. However, the presidential directive establishing the advisory system did not specify criteria for determining whether a given threat should be placed in a given category.[82]

The United States changed its assessed threat level on numerous occasions in the early years of its operation. More recently, the level became more stable and more particularised.[83] It began at yellow on 12 March 2002, increased to orange on 10 September, and was lowered to yellow on 24 September. It was raised to orange on 7 February 2003 and lowered to yellow on 27 February, increased to orange on 19 March and lowered to yellow on 16 April, raised to orange on 20 May and lowered to yellow on 30 May, and increased to orange on 21 December. On 9 January 2004, it was lowered to yellow, where it has generally stayed. However, between 1 August and 10 November 2004, it was orange for the financial services sectors in New York City, northern New Jersey, and Washington, DC; and between 7 July and 12 August 2005, it was orange for mass transit. On 10 August 2006, following discovery of the Heathrow plot, it was raised to red for flights from the United Kingdom to the United States and to orange for other US or US-bound flights. Three days later, the red threat was lowered to orange, where it stayed until 2010, when colour-coded threat warnings were abandoned.

Since 2006, the United Kingdom Home Office has used a five-tier ranking: critical (an attack is expected imminently), severe (an attack is highly likely), substantial (an attack is a strong possibility), moderate (an attack is possible but not likely), and low (an attack is unlikely). All probabilities are probabilities of attacks in the near future.[84] These assessments lend themselves to falsification. If the risk is "critical" for a long period but no attacks occur, the risk has been overestimated, although the significance of this will depend on whether the overestimation is a result of the success of the police and others in frustrating what would otherwise have been a terrorist attack.

British threat levels have fluctuated. Since 1 August 2006, when the level was severe, it has changed to critical (10 August), severe (13 August), critical (30 June 2007), severe (4 July), substantial (20 July 2009), severe (22 January 2010), and substantial (24 September 2010).[85] In one case, threat assessments under an earlier system involved a kind of "false negative": shortly before the 7/7 attacks in 2005, the threat level was lowered (under an earlier model) to "medium."[86] At times, these forecasts have constituted "true positives": the United Kingdom has experienced several attempted attacks during periods when the risk has been assessed as high or critical. But there have also been false positives: there have been periods lasting for months during which attacks have been forecast as imminent and have never come to pass. There have been no cases of true negatives: forecasts of peace that were coupled with peace.

The Australian National Counter-Terrorism Alert System uses four measures to communicate the threat level (low, medium, high, and extreme) and provides for the possibility of alert levels tailored to risks posed to particular locations. A "medium" alert means no more than an assessment that an attack could occur.[87] Since 2001, the threat of a domestic terrorist attack has been classed as medium.[88] Threats of attacks on Australian targets overseas and on UK, US, and Israeli targets in Australia have been ranked as high.[89]

Colour coding is crude, given that risks are typically to particular targets rather than to particular countries. Given that the US system was, at most, an ordinal measure of the seriousness of the risk, it is difficult to know whether "yellow" alert is an overestimate of the "true" risk. That the measure has fluctuated while actual attacks have not tells little about the reliability of the government measure, since the absence of forecast attacks may reflect that awareness of the danger enabled governments to head off attacks. (It may also reflect that fears turned out to be misplaced.)

Governments also publish more-precise information. The United Kingdom Security Service appears to have concluded that al-Qaeda and its associates constitute the only serious international terrorist threat to the United Kingdom. It has reported a steady increase in the number of people tracked by the service, from 250 in 2001 to 2,000 in 2007, by which time the service was also tracking 200 networks. The service explained that while this increase is partly due to increased capacities, it is also attributable to a growth in the numbers involved in Islamist extremism.[90]

Concerns about terrorism are the "top" or "major" priority of the Canadian Security Intelligence Service. Its public report for 2002 indicated concerns about the possibility that CBRN weapons could be acquired or used by terrorist groups, reporting that "as a result of the Afghan war, new information has come to light indicating that Osama Bin Laden's search for CBRN weapons was even more assiduous, and in some respects had progressed further, than previously believed."[91] The CSIS's concern was primarily with the danger posed by al-Qaeda and people associated with it. The problems posed by terrorism were exacerbated by technological advances—which facilitated travel, communication, money transfers, and encryption—and by the evolving nature of terrorism. The report noted that much terrorist-related activity within Canada seemed to be related to attempts to mobilise economic and political support for groups engaged in foreign conflicts and that coercive fundraising within immigrant communities was a problem. Similar themes were expressed in subsequent reports, although the 2003 report concluded that the threat had increased and that "emerging terrorist threats and tactics have become more lethal."[92]

The Australian Security Intelligence Organisation (ASIO) also regards counterterrorism as its dominant concern. Al-Qaeda had regarded Australia as a target even before 9/11 and continued to do so, but ASIO was also particularly concerned by the activities of Jemaah Islamiyah, which had been linked with plans to attack Western targets in Singapore, including the Australian High Commission, and which had been responsible for the 2002 Bali bombings. However, in its 2002–3 report to parliament, it also reported that raids on Australians associated with Jemaah Islamiyah yielded no evidence of cells or of planned attacks or the wherewithal to conduct them. Like Canada, its reports express concerns about the possibility of terrorists gaining access to CBRN weapons. Following the Madrid and London bombings, reports noted the emergence of homegrown groups, observing that while "autonomy imposes certain operational constraints on groups, it also makes detection by security agencies more difficult."[93]

The annual reports of the New Zealand Security Intelligence Service (NZSIS) suggest that the service was generally optimistic, while naturally reluctant to conclude that there was no terrorist threat to New Zealand. In the aftermath of 9/11, the NZSIS concluded that "there is no evidence of a serious terrorist threat against New Zealand," but it added that "there is no room for complacency."[94] By 2004, it was concerned that al-Qaeda's mutation from a centralised organisation into an "inspirational force" meant that it was harder to assess the nature of the al-Qaeda threat and that there was a potential threat from New Zealand supporters of "Islamic extremist causes."[95] These concerns were reiterated in the NZSIS's 2005 report, with the 7 July London bombings confirming the danger of attacks from local groups. However, the NZSIS was not aware of any specific terrorist threat.[96] Its 2006 report concluded that the risk of an attack on New Zealand or on New Zealand interests remained low ("possible, but it is not expected"), but it once more warned of the dangers of radicalisation and the speed at which it could take place.[97] The NZSIS's 2008 report does not attempt to specify the threat with any degree of precision.

We might like the parameters of the threat specified with a greater degree of precision, but in an address to the Risk Management Institution of Australia, Australia's director-general of security, Paul O'Sullivan, argued that if so, we are doomed to frustration.

> [I]n addition to understanding, and dealing with, present risks—of which, only some are known—we need to anticipate future risks. History holds valuable insights, but ultimately provides unreliable testimony concerning

> the possibilities of the future. And the gravity of the present—our immediate horizon—creates powerful biases that will always prove difficult to overcome. Risk managers will look to statistics. But . . . "terrorism does not follow simple statistical patterns." And a threshold event like September 11 somewhat defies the statistical framework informing risk analysis, because it embodies such a radical asymmetry between probability and consequence.[98]

Vagueness is inescapable. So is error. Indeed, if governments accurately assess an increase in the threat level, they may well have the information to enable them to thwart the plot, in which case its threat is diminished. If there is a plot and governments do not know of it, they will underestimate the threat and may well be shown to have done so.

Public Perceptions of the Risk of Attacks

There is a vast body of survey data bearing on public perceptions of the threat of terrorism. In numerous polls since the 9/11 attacks, Americans have been asked how likely it is that there will be further acts of terrorism in the United States over the next several weeks. Another series of polls asked about the likelihood of another terrorist attack within the next few months. Table 1 reports the distributions of answers to these polls. Variants include references to "major" or "deadly" attacks, to the likelihood of such attacks within longer periods, and to the likelihood of attacks within particular communities. Outside the United States, polls tapping fears of terrorism are far rarer but are sufficient to enable limited cross-national comparison. Response categories are typically "very likely," "somewhat likely," "not very likely," "not at all likely," and "don't know" or "not sure."

The series of polls tapping fears of attacks within the next few weeks and the next few months show similar trends. In the immediate aftermath of the 9/11 attacks, most Americans considered that further attacks were either very or somewhat likely. By December 2001, fears were evaporating, and between 2002 and 2009, they declined yet further, only to rise back to 2002 levels in the aftermath of the attempted 2009 Christmas Day bombing. However, fears may also rise in response to attacks on terrorist targets: the killing of Osama bin Laden was reflected in a sharp increase in the percentage of respondents who feared a terrorist attack within the next few weeks.

The polls suggest that respondents correctly assess the likelihood of attacks as smaller when the relevant period is relatively short. This is consistent with other poll data that suggest that the perceived likelihood of terrorist attacks when people are asked about the likelihood of attacks within the next year, few years, or, a fortiori, the next five years. US data also suggest that people correctly rank the likelihood of a terrorist attack in their community over the next few weeks as far lower than the likelihood of an attack within the United States. In November 2001, 23 percent ranked the likelihood of local attacks as very or somewhat likely, but the figures were lower in subsequent polls, with the relevant percentages ranging between 10 percent (August 2009) and 17 percent (July 2002, May 2010).

These figures suggest that aggregate responses are "rational" in the sense that perceived likelihoods vary according to the time within which the attack might take place and the breadth of the area in which the attack might take place. But the data also suggest that these variations make far less impact than they ought to. The likelihood of an attack within weeks should be about one-third of the likelihood of an attack within months, which should, in turn, be about one-fourth of the likelihood of an attack within a year. The likelihood of an attack in a random American's community will be only a tiny fraction of the likelihood of an attack somewhere in the United States.

TABLE 1. Summary of Polls Relating to the Perceived Likelihood of Terrorist Acts within the United States

Date	#	V	Sw	NT	N	Dk	Date	#	V	Sw	NT	N	Dk
Oct 01	(1)	40	45	10	13	2	8 Oct 01	(1)	46	39	8	3	4
Nov 01	(1)	24	50	16	6	4	25–28 Oct	(1)	53	35	8	2	2
Dec 01	(1)	17	55	27	8	3							
2002	(5)	14	44	29	10	3	2002	(9)	27	45	19	5	3
2003	(5)	13	45	30	10	2	2003	(4)	17	48	19	5	3
2004	(3)	10	39	36	13	2	2004	(4)	19	47	23	7	4
2005	(4)	9	37	39	13	2	2005	(1)	9	43	35	7	6
2006	(4)†	12	38	37	10	2	2006	(3)	14	44	30	9	4
2007	(5)†	10	31	9	17	2	2007	(4)	15	37	33	12	4
2008	(3)*	8	26	40	21	7	2008	(2)	8	33	40	16	3
2009	(2)†	10	27	39	22	2	2009	(3)	8	30	41	18	4
2010	(2)*	14	38	36	14	2	2010	(4)	20	40	28	10	4
May 11	(1)*	26	42	23	6	2	2011	(2)	15	41	31	11	2
							Apr 12	(1)	10	27	37	20	6
							2013	(2)	20	39	28	9	5

Source: www.pollingreport.com/terror.htm; http://www.pollingreport.com/terror2.htm, http://www.pollingreport.com/terror6.htm.

Note: Polls conducted in the United States questioning the perceived likelihood of an attack within (a) the next several weeks, and (b) the next few months. Reported probabilities are: very likely; somewhat likely; not too likely; not at all likely, and don't know or unsure. Cells report row percentages. Individual polls are cited for 2001. For other years, poll results are averaged. The number of polls for each year is listed in parentheses in the column headed "#."

Left-hand side: How likely is it that there will be further acts of terrorism in the United States over the next several weeks? Very likely, somewhat likely, not too likely, or not at all likely? (USA *Today*/Gallup; and CNN/Opinion Research (*)).

Right-hand side: How likely do you think it is that there will be another terrorist attack in the United States within the next few months? Very likely, somewhat likely, not too likely, or not at all likely? (CBS).

The distributions of responses suggest that Americans have overestimated the risks they face from terrorism, which is what one would expect, given availability and well-documented responses to low-probability high-cost events. Moreover, poll data suggest a particular tendency to overestimate the likelihood of CBRN attacks. Immediately after 9/11, 68 percent of respondents thought that an attack within the next 10 years by terrorists possessing nuclear or biological weapons was very likely or somewhat likely.[99] Two-thirds of respondents thought that terrorist groups currently had access to nuclear weapons, and 47 percent thought that terrorists would detonate a nuclear bomb in the United States within 10 years.[100] Respondents to a 2007 poll were asked, "How would you rate the likelihood of each of the following happening as a terrorist attack in the United States?" (the number of respondents ranking each scenario as very or somewhat likely is given in parentheses):

A suicide bomber in a shopping mall (82 percent)
A chemical attack using a poison gas (70 percent)
A biochemical attack using diseases such as anthrax or small pox (69 percent)
An attack on a nuclear power station (62 percent)
Another attack using airplanes like 9/11 (48 percent)
A nuclear bomb exploding in a city (42 percent)[101]

Cross-national comparisons suggest that UK respondents rate the likelihood of domestic terrorist attacks as high. In March 2004, most respondents thought that it was almost certain (28 percent) or very likely (29 percent) that there would be a major terrorist attack within the next two or three years. Their pessimism was borne out by the London bombings the following year. In the aftermath of the 7/7 bombings, 9 out of 10 respondents thought that a further terrorist attack was almost certain (45 percent) or very likely (47 percent). In a poll conducted 18 months later, 54 percent considered that there would probably be another attack on the scale of the 7/7 attacks, and another 20 percent considered that an attack would be thwarted by the activities of the police and security service. Only 7 percent thought that there would not be an attack. In response to a 2010 poll in which American, British, and Canadian respondents were asked about the likelihood of a terrorist attack in the next year, British respondents were far more likely than Americans to consider an attack to be very likely (30 percent compared to 14 percent).

In two 2003 polls, only 12 percent of Canadians thought that a terrorist attack within the coming year was very likely. But in 2005 and 2006 polls, sizeable majorities thought that the likelihood of an act of terrorism within the next few years was either very likely (24 percent in 2005, 32 percent in 2006) or likely (38 and 39 percent).[102] By 2010, only 5 percent of Canadians thought that it was very likely that there would be a terrorist attack within the next year, and 54 percent thought that an attack was either not too likely or not likely at all.[103]

A series of surveys of Canadian business executives indicated that, on average, they saw the likelihood of a major terrorist attack within the next 12 months as between 0.12 (September 2002) and 0.24 (July 2005). By comparison, probabilities for the United States were 0.27 and 0.50, and the July 2005 probability for the United Kingdom was 0.42.[104] Given the limitation to serious acts of terrorism within a year, the Canadian executives seem to have been more apprehensive than randomly selected Canadians but, like randomly selected Canadians, less pessimistic than UK respondents.

In January 2003, Australians ranked the likelihood of a domestic attack within the following 12 months as high (18 percent as very likely, 35 percent as likely), but these figures had fallen sharply by 2007 (4 percent as very likely, 30 percent as likely).[105] However, in a 2009 poll, 12 percent strongly agreed and 43 percent agreed that acts of terrorism in Australia will be part of life in the future.[106]

The United Kingdom figures stand out. They suggest that UK respondents may be more pessimistic about the likelihood of terrorist attacks on their country than are Americans, notwithstanding the United Kingdom's much smaller population. The Canadian and Australian figures are consistent with what one would expect on the basis of the two countries' prior experiences of domestic terrorism, but insofar as a country's vulnerability to terrorist attacks is a function of population, they may actually overstate the relative risk of attacks in the two countries. If so, this would not be surprising. Images of terrorist attacks in the United States and the United Kingdom will probably have influenced Canadians' and Australians' perceptions of the risks of domestic terrorism. After all, they have no domestic images to draw on (although Australian fears may have been influenced by the Bali bombings).

TWO

Responding to the Threat

> My blood was boiling. We were going to find out who did this and kick their ass.
> *George W. Bush*[1]

> Today I want to reassure Canadians that their government has listened to them and acknowledged their desires for action.
> *Anne McLellan, minister for justice and attorney general, introducing Canada's 2001 counterterrorism legislation*[2]

Threats tend to elicit responses, but the relationship between threats and responses is likely to be complex. People may respond by taking steps which they believe will reduce their vulnerability. Or, unable to conceptualise such steps, they may descend into mental illness. In the absence of further manifestations of the threat, they usually revert to traditional practices. People also have expectations of governments. In the short term, they are likely to expect and welcome symbolic reassurance. They also expect that governments will take measures to minimise future threats, although they may leave it to the government to decide what these measures might be. Governments may respond in a variety of ways. These include responding to the emotions unleashed by terrorist attacks, but they are also likely to include measures designed to reduce the likelihood of future attacks.

Responses may include war, incapacitation, deterrence, symbolic reassurance, protection, harm minimisation, and concessions, and they will usually involve a mixture whose content changes over time. Facilitating these responses may involve removing limits on powers, but it may also involve providing added resources. These responses seem to lie along a continuum from coercion to accommodation, but while it is possible to conceptualise responses in these terms, it is also important to recognise that some responses are not so easily conceptualised. Governments may respond to threats with both coercion and concessions. A government might rationally conclude both that its coercive arms should be legally constrained and that they should be given added resources so that they can perform their functions effectively notwithstanding the legal constraints on their behaviour. This chapter nonetheless assumes that bundles of responses can be ranked along a coerciveness-accommodation continuum parsimoniously, if approximately, and that the same can be said for legislative and judicial responses.

Choices are likely to turn on a variety of considerations. Governments normally insist that their measures are rational and more or less proportionate, and while there is considerable evidence to the contrary, responses can be partly understood in terms of their probable effectiveness and their probable cost. They are likely to be influenced by timing: initial responses are likely to be complicated by ignorance and are more likely to reflect expressive considerations, possibly at the expense of instrumental ones. Institutional interests and cultures are likely to influence preferences. Preexisting belief systems are likely to affect the choice of response, and government choices are likely to be influenced by (and to influence) public opinion. These generalisations apply to both legal and nonlegal responses, but—I shall argue—there are some grounds for believing that instrumental considerations may play a greater role in influencing decisions about the content of law than in relation to the use of more extreme responses.

Rationality

Governments and their critics both agree that counterterrorism measures should be calculated to reduce the terrorist threat, and the ubiquity of public statements to this effect suggests that counterterror policies should therefore tend to be both effective and cost-effective. Governments may pursue such policies simply because they are staffed by reasonably public-spirited decision makers who are dispassionate and devoted to the public interest. To some extent, this is the case. Alternatively, governments have good reasons for pursuing such policies. Since people expect governments to provide security, future terrorist attacks may come at some cost to those who might have been able to avoid them. (But this is not necessarily so: 9/11 generated political capital for the Bush administration.) Moreover, given scarce resources, governments have some incentive to use their resources as effectively as possible.

But even if public officials act rationally, this does not necessarily mean that they act effectively and proportionally. There are several reasons why counterterror measures may fall short of cost-effectiveness—or its human rights analogue, proportionality. First, from some perspectives, ineffective and expensive strategies are rational. The pork-barreling associated with the use of counterterror funds[3] made no sense from the standpoint of threat minimisation, but given that parochialism can trump patriotism (just as patriotism tends to trump internationalism), members of Congress who used counterterror funds as a source of bribes to their electorates may have been acting rationally. Critics of counterterror measures point to other conflicting objectives, such as catering to or reflecting the emotions generated by a terrorist outrage. But while such measures may be ineffective and may even backfire, catering to emotions may not be irrational. Law, after all, treats retribution as a legitimate purpose of punishment.

A second and related reason why counterterror measures may fall short of cost-effectiveness is that cost-benefit and proportionality analyses involve subjective assessments of values and relative values. Whether measures do or do not satisfy the effectiveness/proportionality standards will depend on such considerations as the relative weight to be attached to the interests of neighbours, fellow nationals, and foreigners; whether revenge can count as a benefit, even if it serves no instrumental purpose; and the value one is prepared to assign to a hypothetical reduction of risk. International standards on human rights law may provide what looks like a relatively objective yardstick, but to understand responses to terrorism, it seems necessary to recognise that those standards may be contested.

Third, choice of response is necessarily based on imperfect information. One obstacle to assessing the rationality of responses to terrorism is that their effects are often extremely difficult to determine. Methodologically sophisticated assessments of the impact of counterterrorism measures are rare. A 2006 paper reported the results of a literature survey that started with the identification of more than 20,000 works on terrorism. The researchers found that of these, only 290 articles and 64 books made any reference to an evaluation of counterterror measures. Closer inspection of the abstracts, notes, and titles of the 290 articles yielded 94 promising articles, of which 79 could be tracked down. Of these, only 21 actually attempted an analysis of the impact of a program, and only 7 were methodologically sophisticated enough to warrant confidence in the findings.[4] These 7 articles generally provided evidence that some measures (notably military intervention) made things worse. Other measures (criminal sanctions) seem to have made no difference. Even when measures did influence behaviour, there seem to have been displacement effects.

Responses are likely to be further complicated by the difficulty of knowing whether what worked in one context will work in another. Terror groups are notoriously diverse. Their aims, structures, and strategies are likely to change in response to changes to their environment. In addition, political, religious, and ideological objectives are likely to coexist with organisational and personal objectives. Like governments, terrorist groups are far from being monolithic wholes. Complicating matters still further are the blurred boundaries between terrorists and their immediate milieu, with moves in both directions as terrorists tire of being terrorists and as disaffected potential terrorists join or find themselves involved in terrorist groups. Information about terror groups and about their reaction or likely reaction to particular measures is in danger of being out of date, inaccurate, and limited.

Yet there is some evidence that governments act as if they were semirational. First, faced with growing evidence of the futility of military involvement in Iraq (which was justified partly as a counterterror measure) and Afghanistan, governments have withdrawn or have started withdrawing, rather than continue to pay and inflict the costs of continued involvement. Second, their policies tend to be roughly consistent with their capacities. The United States can sometimes afford to use military force in attempts to achieve its aims. Canada, Australia, and New Zealand recognise that their success in countering international terrorism is dependent on the cooperation of other countries. This means being nice to the United States and providing symbolic or practical support for some of its wars. But it also means cooperating with other countries and treating international law as a resource rather than a cost. So, for example, Australia's response to the Bali bombings was not to send commandos into Sumatra but to offer assistance to the Indonesian police.

Third, counterterror measures tend to involve experimentation and a willingness to abandon policies that seem not to be working. Canada resolved the limited problem posed by secessionist terrorism by attending to Québécois grievances. Even in the early 1970s, the UK government was exploring the possibility of concessions in exchange for peace in Northern Ireland. Having tried internment and found that it exacerbated the problem, it abandoned that solution. Having introduced repressive legislation in response to particularly serious attacks, it arranged inquiries into their operation and frequently, if gradually, alleviated their repressiveness. Spain seems to have achieved a settlement with the ETA. Finally, if one accepts that the current terrorist threat is negligible, it follows that government strategies have, at worst, not been particularly counterproductive.

There are, of course, the exceptions. Exhibit 1 is the Iraq War fiasco, which highlights the fact that a devastating war may be the result not of inadequate information but of a determination by decision makers not to allow inconvenient facts to get in the way of their folly. It also highlights the possibility of responses that are devastating, whether assessed from the standpoint of the nation, the government, those responsible for the decision, or those the war was supposed to help. Exhibit 2 is the torture and mistreatment of suspected terrorists and known nonterrorists in Guantánamo Bay and elsewhere.

There are also likely to be cases where it is not clear whether or to what extent counterterror policies are working or have worked, which complicates the enterprise of assessing the degree to which government policies are dictated by their probable effectiveness. War seems unreliable. Conciliation seems promising. However, complicating attempts to relate this to the relative rationality of coercive and accommodative responses is the question of the role of government threats in convincing terrorists that they might have to settle for less than they would have liked. After all, if terrorist threats can extract concessions, it is not clear why government threats cannot.

Timing

A common criticism of post-9/11 measures is that they were taken in haste. Haste, of itself, is not necessarily a bad thing. If responses actually had the potential to ward off further attacks, it would be highly desirable that they be taken quickly. Moreover, it is possible that those responsible for the measures have been thinking about them for some time, believe with some justification that they could work, and see the aftermath of an attack as a propitious time for their introduction. But if the measures are taken in response to an unexpected attack, there is a considerable danger that should those responsible for them have little basis for knowing whether they will make any difference to the danger posed by the threat, they may be responsive to the temptations of expressive politics.[5] Policymakers themselves feel the mixture of emotions that follow exposure to an outrage. There are also opportunistic politicians who believe that there is political capital to be won by measures that demonstrate confidence and resolve and a determination to punish those responsible for the outrage.

Poll data throws some light on whether there is indeed political capital to be made out of postattack toughness. As noted in chapter 1, they suggest that fears of terrorism increase after attacks and tend to subside within months. They also suggest that attacks may increase support for illiberal measures but that this support erodes over time. Immediately after the Oklahoma bombing in 1995, half of Americans surveyed thought that it would be necessary for them to give up some civil liberties to curb terrorism, but this figure had fallen to 29 percent two years later.[6] Following 9/11, far more people thought that such a measure would be necessary.[7] (There is also evidence for the unsurprising finding that people were even more willing to give up other people's liberties.)[8]

Until 2006, sizeable majorities considered that curbing terrorism would require the average person to give up some civil liberties. But by 2006–7, majorities no longer saw the need to surrender any more of their liberties. (Logically, this might simply reflect the fact that some liberties had already been given up and that people did not want to give up the liberties that remained.) Then, in 2010, following the attempted Christmas Day bombing in 2009, a majority once more considered that it was necessary to give up some liberties.[9]

Even in the immediate aftermath of terrorist attacks, belief in the necessity of giving up some liberties coexisted with a belief that the danger that the government would fail to enact "strong new laws" was only slightly greater than the danger that it would enact laws "which excessively restrict the average person's civil liberties": 39 percent shared the former concern, and 34 percent feared the latter danger. By November 2002, concerns about lost liberties outweighed concerns about weak laws. By 2008 (by which time new laws had been enacted), 31 percent were concerned about reticence, and 54 percent were concerned about threats to liberties.[10] Other polls suggest similar levels of anxiety about threats to liberty.[11]

Outside the United States, pollsters have not generated such a rich body of time-series data. The limited evidence suggests that fear of terrorism increases receptivity to illiberal measures. In two 2005 UK polls, majorities agreed that it was sometimes necessary to restrict civil liberties without a court's approval, the majority increasing from 58 percent to 70 percent in the aftermath of the 7/7 attacks.[12] A 2008 poll indicated that 41 percent favoured giving equal weight to concern over civil liberties and to defeating the threat from terrorism, but 38 percent favoured giving more weight to defeating the threat from terrorism.[13] Canadian polls conducted in 2001 suggest some (but not much) support for limiting liberties, and a 2004 poll found that only a bare majority disagreed that Canadian police and security services were going too far in their use of antiterrorism powers.

These figures must be handled with care. They reflect sentiment rather than the considered response of people who are familiar with the content of existing and emerging laws. Sentiments might strengthen the resolve of those who favour tougher laws, but they hold out little promise of long-term electoral gains for those who favour illiberal legislation.

The chapters that follow will tend to bear out the importance of timing in relation to postattack legislation. But in those chapters, I shall argue that the relationship between attacks and legislation is more complex than the critique of hastiness suggests.

Institutional Interests, Preferences, and Practices

A common civil libertarian complaint is that terrorist attacks are seized on as opportunities for governments to expand their powers.[14] This complaint, which overlaps with but also refines the "timing" argument, assumes that the impetus for coercive responses tends to come from the executive arm rather than the legislative and, a fortiori, the judicial arms. There is an authoritarian variant on this: namely, that security is protected by the executive, sometimes assisted by legislatures, and only too often imperiled by the judiciary.

The "institutional" argument assumes that the executive arm tends to favour coercion, that legislatures are less supportive, and that courts seek to constrain legislatures. This assumption seems self-evident in the light of both history and recent experiences. But in extreme forms, it sits uneasily with governments' willingness to initiate measures whose effect has been to impose some constraints on their coercive capacities.

That said, there are several reasons why the executive arm may be particularly likely to want to include repressive measures within its armory of responses to the threat of terrorism. The most obvious is that coercion is largely an executive function and is performed by specialised agencies. Members of agencies specialising in coercion and intelligence gathering believe that their activities are socially valuable, and they are likely to be wary of those who seek to impose limits on the circumstances in which they may use their powers. Restraints may be experienced both practically and morally. Practically, they may be treated as obstacles to the agencies' proper performance of their functions. Morally, they may be treated as downgrading the value of those functions or as reflecting adversely on the agencies' competence and integrity. Agencies' views are not necessarily accepted by the political executive, but the more salient a threat is, the more attentive the elected executive is likely to be to the security forces.

At the other extreme are the courts. Their role and likely response is more complex. Courts are relevant in two related respects. First, government and legislative decisions are likely to be made in the shadow of the law. This does not necessarily mean that the political arms will comply with "law." They may quite excusably get it wrong: after all, if law is what courts say it is, those who get it wrong sometimes turn out to be in the company of almost half (and sometimes more than half) of the judges who handle the subsequent litigation. The political branches may also know that law rarely moves fast, so they can enjoy the fruits of their illegality pending a final decision. Governments may calculate that they can get away with infringements: not all irregularities will come to the notice of those affected, and not all of those who have been affected will have access to the courts.

Moreover, legislators may support unconstitutional legislation for opportunistic reasons. They may calculate that legislation will be able to do some good before it is eventually struck down. Muscular conservatives may support repressive legislation, hoping that if it is struck down, that will discredit the courts. Liberals may support electorally popular repression in the expectation that it will be struck down, thereby both propitiating the voters and appeasing their consciences.[15] But officials are aware that failure to comply with law can be hazardous. Besides, while legislators may sometimes knowingly pass unconstitutional legislation, political expediency may dictate attentiveness to its likely fate in the courts. If legislation is indeed a response to a brief window of opportunity, legislators are likely to be mindful of the need to ensure that it has a reasonable chance of survival.

Courts also matter because they may quash unlawful decisions, and governments almost invariably comply with their decisions. But the degree to which courts matter depends on the degree to which their responses to threats differ from those of the political arms. There are several grounds for believing that they will. Indeed, the obverse of civil libertarian concerns about overweening executives is authoritarian concern about the pernicious role of courts and lawyers.

First, judges' professional reputation is bound up with a perception that they are committed to applying the law and acting on evidence. Moreover, their decisions, much of the material on which they are based, and the reasoning in terms of which they are justified are public. Courts are expected to afford a particularly high level of procedural fairness to those who appear before them. The heroic judge applies the law to the evidence, come what may. The heroic spy is prepared to disregard legalities for a greater cause. Law and facts may well be ambiguous, and judges sometimes have little alternative but to make both in their own image. But unlike other political actors, judges can take pride in choosing law over political preferences when they see conflict between the two.

Second, judges' decisions may be subject to a rather different kind of "availability bias" than that which arguably influences the behaviour of the executive and legislative branches. Trials have the potential to focus on the implications of laws for particular individuals, and one would expect attention to the individual to mean that the highly visible effects of denial of civil liberties will be more apparent than any contribution to the collective good that such denial may produce. Moreover, organisations sponsoring attacks on repressive laws are likely to select cases that emphasise the unjust results that can follow from contested laws.

Further, if executive and legislative decisions are responses to a sudden crisis, the delay that typically characterises judicial proceedings will mean that the court will be considering the issue in calmer circumstances and with the advantage of being able to see whether and how the measure has been working. Judges also enjoy a degree of security denied to members of the political branches. If they allow someone who turns out to be a threat to the state to go free, they have someone to blame: the government, for not presenting them with strong enough evidence to warrant their doing what it wanted (and what they themselves might have wanted). Moreover, judges are almost immune from dismissal and demotion, which means that they are largely immunised against some of the pressures and temptations that can lead members of the political branches away from the path of civil libertarian virtue.

The effect of these considerations is blurred somewhat by judicial reluctance to become involved in security-related issues. Judges are not immune from the fears generated by terrorist attacks and are sometimes concerned about how to deal with factual issues that cannot be resolved with any degree of precision on the basis of normal curial procedures. They are sometimes sensitive to issues concerning the separation of powers, and while courts have retreated from the position that security decisions lie outside the purview of judicial review, they are sometimes willing to grant governments a very broad discretion in relation to security matters. Governments that want to wage wars on terror still have considerable freedom in relation to how they do so, but—as we shall see—one of the legacies of the War on Terror has been a series of decisions that have made it clear that while wars on terror are permitted, they must be conducted subject to law.

To varying degrees, legislators and the elected executive are accountable to the electorate. Politicians who disregard public opinion do so at their peril, and attempts to explain past and current illiberalism have argued that illiberal measures have sometimes been pursued in order to appease the general public rather than in response to their perceived merits.[16] An analysis of West Germany's reaction to the violence of the 1970s argues that the Social Democrats favoured a restrained response but considered it electorally unsustainable.[17] More recently, Roach has argued that the unelected Canadian Senate may be more protective of the rights of unpopular minorities than is the elected House of Commons,[18] and there is evidence that US Democrats' votes on counterterror issues have been prompted by a fear of looking "soft."[19] But the poll data previously described suggest that the political costs of being "soft" can be exaggerated, especially when "softness" involves protecting the liberties of nationals.

Beliefs and Dispositions

When asked, most people are able to locate themselves on unidimensional scales tapping the degree to which they are "liberal" or "conservative," "left" or "right." People appear to have some understanding of what these terms mean, and position on the scales tends to be related to stances in relation to a variety of issues, including that involving civil liberties. In any case, there is some evidence to suggest that attitudes towards civil liberties issues tend to be related and that they bear some relation to attitudes towards equality and hierarchy. They are often assumed to be relatively stable. This stability was implicit in the idea that they reflected personality and its antecedents. Alternatively, it could be explained in terms of both the role of social position as a determinant of beliefs and the role of beliefs in determining how people constructed their social environment. If so, it would be reasonable to assume that preferred responses to terrorism would reflect preexisting dispositions, and the stock responses to be found in the relevant legislative debates seem to confirm this expectation.

As a description of the belief systems of nonactivists, this analysis is hard to reconcile with Converse's classic 1964 study, which found that mass attitudes on economic and foreign policy issues bore little relation to their self-placement on a liberal-conservative scale and that attitudes measured in 1958 correlated very weakly with responses to the same items in a poll two years later.[20] His findings bear only tangentially on whether popular attitudes to liberty-related issues are more coherent and more stable, but they do demonstrate that one should not lightly assume that they are. Converse did find, however, that attitudes appear to be much more coherent among activists.

Subsequent research has tended to support the proposition that people can be meaningfully ranked on a liberalism-conservatism scale.[21] Moreover, twin studies suggest that scale scores reflect both childhood environment and genetic influences, and there is some evidence linking beliefs with the interaction between particular genes and environmental factors.[22] Other studies have suggested that liberalism-conservatism may be better understood as involving several related (but stable) dimensions. Eysenck developed a two-dimensional model—one dimension of which tapped civil libertarianism, while the other tapped egalitarianism—and found some evidence to bear out his analysis.[23] Gastil and colleagues tested Wildasky's hypothesis that people constructed their responses to political issues according to their "ways of life" and that these could be classified two-dimensionally: according to the degree to which the person values autonomy over conformity to the group and according to the degree to which the person attaches moral significance to social differentiation. They found that rank along these dimensions predicted responses on particular issues reasonably well, even among people who knew relatively little about politics. Even among the politically active, they predicted policy preferences somewhat better than did party allegiance and ideological self-identification.[24]

The dimensional analysis has implications for understanding reactions to coercive measures. In particular, it suggests what seems plausible in any case—namely, that responses to threats will be influenced by their attractiveness, given the person's prior dispositions. First, we are likely to draw on ideology, or "way of life," as a heuristic device to assist us in determining responses to situations about which we know very little. Second, ideology is likely to determine how people process information. We tend to welcome information that reinforces our prejudices and to filter out information that does not. Third, in some cases, ideology can be the basis for a sense of identity. Where moralities or "ways of life" are at stake, issues become personal. Policies symbolise the degree to which the views of "people like us" prevail. So the emotional stakes may be higher than the practical ones. But much depends on what aspects of an issue are prompting the reaction. Converse's research reminds us that very few people react to the finer details of a political measure, and his research suggests that what matters to members of the political elite may be of little significance to the less informed. So while it may be possible to predict who will react most favourably to a president who promises tough action, it may be harder to use a person's dispositions to predict whether and how that person will react to a proposal to change the law with respect to applications for warrants to access stored communications.

Moreover, relative civil libertarianism is not everything. Among egalitarian libertarians, its implications will be blurred in relation to racist terrorists and gun-toting militiamen, and when it is militias rather than Muslims who most symbolise a terrorist threat, Republican authoritarianism is blunted. Ideology may also conflict with role. Groupthink may triumph over personal views. Members of parliament must become accustomed to voting for laws that garner their disapproval, and members of Congress may be subject to pressures to conform to the views of the party majority.

Law as a Response to Terrorism

On the whole, one would expect the preceding generalisations to apply to counterterrorism legislation. However, law differs from some other counterterror responses in ways that are potentially relevant to this book's discussion. First, laws tend to be general. A law that can be used in a particular way in relation to Islamist terrorism is also available for use against terrorists in general. This will not particularly concern pacifists, but it is likely to concern people who might simultaneously favour the torture of Muslims and envisage a positive role for terrorists who want to overthrow any government that wants to take away their guns. Second, laws are formally public, and governments and people tend to behave themselves better when their activities are public, which is one reason why privacy is popular. Governments may want to engage in unpalatable practices while pretending that they do not, and those who vote for them may agree. Third, law usually evolves slowly. Even when laws are enacted with what looks like unseemly haste, they often receive considerable attention. More important, laws usually require judicial interpretation, which normally involves delay and close scrutiny. It also means that the payoff for trying to use loose language to allow unpalatable exercises of power is likely to be minimal.

Conclusions

This chapter examined several possible reasons responses to fears of terrorism have taken the form they have, noting the potential importance of effectiveness, timing, institutional concerns, and preexisting beliefs. It has argued that legal responses to terrorism may be constrained by considerations that do not necessarily apply to the same extent in relation to nonlegal responses. The following chapters examine various legal responses and the degree to which they can be explained in these terms.

THREE

What Is Terrorism?

> I know that African tribes yield only to violence. To exercise this violence with crass terrorism and even with gruesomeness was and is my policy.
>
> *Lieutenant General Luther von Trotha, commander of German forces in South West Africa, 1904–5*[1]

The previous chapters assume that there is a degree of agreement as to the meaning of the word *terrorism*. Otherwise, it would have been necessary to justify my implicit assumption that some activities could be classed as terrorism while others (such as a war characterised by "shock and awe") could not. In the absence of agreement about what terrorism entails, little could be gained by reference to the results of polls in which people are asked about the likelihood of terrorist attacks. Moreover, in referring to the "threat" of terrorism, I have assumed that terrorism is reprehensible: otherwise, it would have been better to refer to the "likelihood" or even the "promise" of terrorism.

This chapter addresses these assumptions by analysing the extent to which and the ways in which the national legislatures of the five countries have defined *terrorism* and cognate terms. Legislative definitions are not conclusive, but they and the debates surrounding them are suggestive. Importantly, they suggest that both across and within legislatures, there is a substantial consensus as to what terrorism entails. But there is also a degree of dissensus, stemming partly from ambivalence in relation to the legitimacy of lesser forms of political violence and partly from reluctance to protect "good terrorists" from the moral and legal implications of their falling within the statutory definitions.

An Elusive Term?

Despite the famously tortuous history of attempts to reach international agreement on a definition of terrorism, a degree of consensus has been achieved, helped perhaps by the transformation of successful freedom fighters from potential terrorists into their potential targets.[2] Resolutions of the

United Nations Security Council indicate a consensus that terrorism is evil, but the consensus is partly achieved by fudging the question of what terrorism actually entails. However, something akin to a definition emerges from the International Convention for the Suppression of the Financing of Terrorism (the Terrorist Financing Convention).[3] This convention does not define the term *terrorism*, but it makes it an offence to provide funds for any act "intended to cause death or serious bodily injury to a civilian, or to any other person not taking an active part in the hostilities in a situation of armed conflict, when the purpose of such act, by its nature or context, is to intimidate a population, or to compel a government or an international organization to do or to abstain from doing any act" (Art 2(1)(b)). It also applies to acts contrary to a number of specified conventions, thereby implying that such acts constitute forms of terrorism.[4] The specified conventions extend to behaviour regardless of whether it satisfies the "purpose" requirement of the Terrorist Financing Convention, but they also cover virtually all the kinds of activities by which a terrorist might conceivably seek to achieve his or her purposes.

The most recent "terrorism convention" follows the Terrorist Financing Convention in including both harm and purpose elements. The International Convention for the Suppression of Acts of Nuclear Terrorism, adopted at New York on 14 September 2005, applies to the possession and use of nuclear material or devices with intent to cause death or serious injury or substantial damage to property or to the environment, and to their use with the intent of coercing persons, international organisations, or states, as well as to credible threats of such use (Art 2, pars 1–2).

Significantly, the conventions are neutral in relation to the motivation of those who breach their conditions. It is not an excuse that the target of the act is a vicious government or the supporters of a vicious government. This is probably not surprising: conventions owe their existence in part to the willingness of vicious governments to accede to them.

Some scholars have argued that there is now sufficient consensus to warrant the proposition that it is possible to identify forms of terrorism in addition to those proscribed by the "terrorism conventions," which are also unlawful under international law.[5] However, it is difficult to formulate a simple definition of what constitutes terrorism under customary international law. Nonetheless, international law now seems to recognise something in the nature of a definition of terrorism.[6]

National Definitions

Terrorism existed long before legislative attempts to address it as a distinctive phenomenon, and until the turn of the century, the term *terrorism* was usually either undefined or defined on an ad hoc basis for the purposes of particular pieces of legislation. In the United States, counterterror legislation continues to be based on numerous ad hoc definitions that vary from context to context. Elsewhere, post-2000 legislation has included a comprehensive definition that governs almost all contexts in which legal relevance is attached to terrorism and terrorism-related activity.

Defining Terrorism, 1973–2002: An Overview

The earliest references to terrorism in national legislation are found in legislation giving legal effect to the Geneva Conventions and, incidentally, to the conventions' prohibitions on "terrorism."[7] The conventions did not, however, include a definition of the term *terrorism*, and the earliest statutory definition appears to be the United Kingdom's definition in section 28(1) of the Northern Ireland (Emergency Provisions) Act 1973 (UK, c 53),[8] enacted in response to the upsurge of violence in Northern Ireland. This definition survived in successive emergency acts, until the last of these, the Northern Ireland (Emergency Provisions) Act 1996 (UK, c 22, as amended), was repealed by the Terrorism Act 2000 (UK).[9] This act included a definition of terrorism that applies to virtually every situation in which legal consequences attach to the fact that behaviour constitutes "terrorism."[10]

The earliest reference to terrorism in US federal legislation occurs in the Foreign Intelligence Surveillance Act of 1978 (FISA), permitting surveillance for the purposes of investigations into "international terrorism," for which it offers a definition that has proved resilient.[11] Variants appear in numerous other pieces of US legislation, either reproduced, by reference, or by reference to legislation that defines the terrorism in almost identical terms.[12] Section 1801(c) of the Foreign Relations Authorization Act, Fiscal Years 1988 and 1989 (FRAA),[13] included a different definition of terrorism for the limited purpose of determining the content of annual country reports on terrorism. Under the USA Patriot Act of 2001, the definition has acquired considerably greater significance: it is now relevant to whether a body can be listed as a "foreign terrorist organization." Section 212(a)(3)(B)(iii) was added to the Immigration and Nationality Act of 1952 (INA) in 1990 and amended in 2001.[14] The INA definition of "terrorist activity" uses a quite different formula to that found in FISA and the FRAA. It is relevant to whether a person is eligible for entry to the United States and to whether a body may be listed as a "foreign terrorist organization." Other definitions include those of "international terrorism" in the Federal Courts Administration Act of 1992,[15] the "federal crime of terrorism" in section 702(a) of the Antiterrorism and Effective Death Penalty Act of 1996 (AEDPA),[16] "domestic terrorism" in section 802 of the USA Patriot Act of 2001,[17] and "act of terrorism" in section 102(1) of the Terrorism Risk Insurance Act of 2002 (TRIA).[18]

Legislation clarifying the powers of the Australian Security Intelligence Organization (ASIO) defined "security" to include protection from "terrorism" and included a definition of terrorism;[19] and an overhaul of censorship legislation replaced relatively open-ended political censorship powers with more-limited powers, which included the power to exclude materials that advocated terrorism (which was not defined).[20] After a brief life, these two references to terrorism were removed from the legislation. In the ASIO legislation, the concept of "terrorism" was largely subsumed by a related concept, "politically motivated violence" (which included terrorism offences but not terrorism).[21] In the customs regulations, it was subsumed by a prohibition on material that promoted, incited, or instructed in matters of crime and violence.[22] When references to terrorism were reintroduced to the ASIO legislation, the term was defined by reference to a general definition adopted in the aftermath of 9/11.

In 2002, Australia enacted a series of counterterror measures. These were dependent on the existence of a "terrorist act," which was defined in an amendment to the Criminal Code 1995 (Commonwealth),[23] in terms similar to those used in UK legislation. The definition is the only extant definition of terrorism under Australian commonwealth law.

New Zealand's International Terrorism (Emergency Powers) Act 1987 attached consequences to and included a very broad definition of an "international terrorist emergency."[24] The Immigration Act 1987 (NZ) operated in relation to "acts of terrorism," which were defined somewhat differently. (The term is not defined in the Immigration Act 2009 (NZ).) The two 1987 definitions were left intact by the post-9/11 Suppression of Terrorism Act 2002 (NZ), which included yet another definition, based on the UK and Canadian definitions.

Except for its Geneva Convention legislation, Canadian legislation appears to have made no reference to *terrorism* or cognate terms until 1992, when the term appeared, undefined, in migration legislation.[25] The 2001 amendments to the criminal code attached a variety of consequences to "terrorist activity" and included a definition, based on the UK definition but including a number of innovations, of which many found their way into New Zealand law and some into Australian law.[26]

Comparing Definitions

Broadly, there are three types of definition regime. In the United States, definitions appear to have been devised to deal with particular problems, and while FISA-type definitions predominate, other definitions govern important areas of counterterror laws. In the United Kingdom and Australia, there is a general definition of terrorism, which governs virtually all contexts in which it is relevant that "terrorism" is involved. The post-9/11 Canadian and New Zealand definitions have similarly general application. However, there is one important difference. Like the UK and Australian definitions, they include a general definition of terrorism, which resembles those definitions in both structure and content. However, following the precedent set by the Terrorist Financing Convention, Canada also defines terrorist activity to include activities falling within a number of specified offences that implement Canada's obligations under terrorism conventions.[27] New Zealand's definition is similar to Canada's, except that it defines terrorism to include offences against the conventions, rather than by reference to preexisting or concurrently created offences designed to implement New Zealand's obligations under the conventions. There is overlap between the categories, but there will be acts that are terrorist only because they either constitute a convention offence or fall within the general definition. The inclusion of offences against the conventions within the definition is also a feature of several US definitions, including that of the INA (which is predicated on offences against some of the conventions) and the definition of a "federal crime of terrorism" (whose elements include commission of one or more specified federal offences, which include those against laws giving effect to conventions).

Despite these differences, definitions typically include a number of elements. All include a "harm" element, which defines the physical or economic harm that terrorism entails (or, possibly, threatens). Most include an "intended purpose" element (which limits "terrorism" to acts done with the intention that they will produce particular results); and many include a "motivation" element (not generally found in US legislation, but an aspect of the general definitions in the other four jurisdictions).

The Harm Requirement

Broadly, the harm requirement is satisfied if the relevant act involves either serious violence to the person or behaviour that endangers human life. In relation to the level of violence required, several of the US definitions seem relatively relaxed. While "domestic terrorism" (18 USC § 2331) requires violence that is dangerous to human life, the harm elements of "international terrorism" (FISA) and "terrorism" (§ 140 of the FRAA) are satisfied by "violence," and under the Terrorism Risk Insurance Act of 2002 and its successors, a "violent act" suffices.

However, several US definitions include behaviour that does not involve violence to the person. For example, the category "federal crime of terrorism" (AEDPA) includes attacks on infrastructure, federal government property, and computer systems. The category "act of terrorism" (TRIA) covers acts that endanger property and infrastructure.

The general Canadian, New Zealand, and Australian definitions are based to a considerable extent on the 2000 UK definition.[28] In general, the UK and Australian definitions set a lower harm threshold than do the definitions used in Canada and, a fortiori, New Zealand, especially in relation to behaviour that causes property damage. In relation to behaviour that involves violence to the person, there is a rough consensus. Violence is not enough: all four definitions require that the violence be "serious" or at least involve physical harm or danger to life.[29] All four general definitions accept that creating a serious risk to the health or safety of a population also satisfies the harm element.[30] The inclusion of convention offences means that in Canada and New Zealand, there may be exceptional circumstances where nonserious violence can constitute terrorism.[31]

There is far less agreement in relation to property damage. In the United Kingdom and Australia, the harm requirement is satisfied by "serious damage to property" and by serious interference with or destruction of electronic systems.[32] In Canada and New Zealand,[33] more is needed. Property damage can satisfy the requirement only if it is likely to produce harm that would fall within one of the "violence" categories.[34] In Canada, serious interference with or disruption to an essential service, facility, or system satisfies the harm requirement (subject to a "legitimate protest" qualification). The relevant New Zealand provision requires serious interference with "infrastructure" and applies only if that interference endangers life. Yet New Zealand recognises one form of harm that might not fall within the other definitions: the release of a disease-bearing organism that could devastate the national economy.[35]

Acts that are contrary to the terrorism conventions and that involve harm to property generally fall within the harm criteria prescribed by the general definitions. Typically such acts involve conduct that is also likely to endanger life or at least bring harm to infrastructure. This is not the case in New Zealand, however. Attacks on property that threaten infrastructure but not life do not fall within New Zealand's general definition, although they do fall within the Terrorist Bombings Convention, if the incident involves at least one non-New Zealander as perpetrator or victim.[36]

"Terrorism" (UK) and "terrorist acts" (Australia) include threats of such acts.[37] In New Zealand, a threat to produce a relevant outcome would not constitute a "terrorist act." In Canada, "terrorist activity" includes conspiracies, threats, attempts, being an accessory after the fact, and counseling in relation to terrorist activities.[38]

Intended Effect: Impact on Government and Civilians

Virtually all definitions require that the harm be done or threatened with the intention to coerce governments or intimidate populations. The widely used FISA definition requires that the act or acts (1) be such that they would be an offence under American law if committed in the United States and

> (2) appear to be intended—
> (A) to intimidate or coerce a civilian population;
> (B) to influence the policy of a government by intimidation or coercion;
> (C) to affect the conduct of a government by assassination or kidnapping.[39]

There are, however, variants. FISA-like definitions made more recently include affecting the conduct of government through the use of weapons of mass destruction. The FRAA definition of "terrorism" requires that it be "politically motivated," rather than that it be intended to coerce or intimidate. While there are some circumstances in which this difference would be material to whether conduct constituted terrorism,[40] politically motivated violence will normally imply an intention to coerce or intimidate. Like the terrorism conventions on which it is based, the INA definition treats intended impact as largely irrelevant. Intimidation of civilians does not satisfy the "intended effect" requirement for "federal crimes of terrorism," but retaliation against government does.[41]

The UK legislation requires that the action or threatened action be "designed to influence the government or to intimidate the public or a section of the public." "Government" was initially defined to include not only the government of the United Kingdom but also governments of parts of the United Kingdom and of other countries. It was subsequently amended to extend to international organisations.[42] Unlike the Australian, Canadian, and New Zealand definitions, the UK definition provides that if the action satisfying the harm requirement involves the use of firearms or explosives, it is terrorism, regardless of whether the "influence or intimidate" requirement is satisfied (s 1(1B)). This exception has the potential to produce rather odd results. If a religiously motivated person unleashes anthrax bacteria, this is not terrorism unless there is an intent to coerce or intimidate. If the person uses a shotgun, it is terrorism regardless of whether the offender intends to coerce or intimidate (although a political, religious, or ideological requirement is needed).

The Australian "intimidation" requirement is similar to the United Kingdom's but requires an intention to coerce governments and not simply to influence them.[43] In practice, little is likely to turn on this distinction, but it would mean that a violent attack on the government (which was not intended to intimidate the public) would not constitute terrorism if the actor intended that the attack would persuade the government to have second thoughts about the moral justification for a particular policy. The Canadian and New Zealand definitions do not require an intention to intimidate or coerce, as long as the activity falls within a listed terrorism convention. In relation to acts defined other than by reference to the conventions, they resemble the Australian definition in requiring coercion rather than influence, regardless of whether the offence involves the use of firearms or explosives. The Canadian definition is, however, slightly broader than the Australian and original UK definitions, in that it includes coercion of domestic and international organizations.[44] It also extends to an attempt to intimidate any person, rather than "a section of the public."[45] New Zealand law includes attempts to coerce international organisations,[46] but it also includes a slightly stricter intention requirement: it is not enough that there be an intention to coerce government; there must be an intention to do so "unduly" (s 5(2)(b)). One day, if New Zealand is unlucky, a court will have to decide when coercion is "undue."

On the whole, these definitions resemble the FISA definition. But whereas FISA requires merely that the act appears to be intended to coerce or intimidate, the UK legislation and legislation based on it requires that it be done with the intention that it achieve the particular outcome. This requires the existence, not merely the apparent existence, of the relevant intention.

Purpose/Intention to Advance a Cause

Whether or not relevant actors are intending to advance a cause is largely irrelevant to US definitions, although the FRAA requires acting for a political motive. Motivation is, however, an additional element in the UK, Canadian, New Zealand, and Australian definitions. Not only must the act be done with the intention of causing particular impacts on government and the public, but it must be done to advance particular causes. The UK requirement, which was initially that an act be "for the purpose of advancing a political, religious or ideological cause" (s 1(c)), has been subsequently amended so that "racial" causes are also included.[47] The Canadian, New Zealand. and Australian requirements are similar to the original UK requirement.[48] However, as with the intention requirement, there is no purpose requirement in Canada and New Zealand when the relevant act falls within a listed terrorism convention. The requirement means that the relevant laws do not extend to a hypothetical serial killer who gains satisfaction from causing fear among women but is not ideologically or religiously committed to doing so. Nor would they cover the case of a person motivated solely by greed who attempted to extort money from a large retail chain by leaving poisoned products on the shelves of its supermarkets, notwithstanding that the offender believed that the threat would cause widespread fear.

Qualifications: Advocacy, Protest, Dissent, and Industrial Action

The Canadian, New Zealand, and Australian definitions include a further limitation: each definition provides that in certain circumstances, behaviour that would otherwise constitute terrorism will not do so if the act constitutes advocacy, protest, dissent, or industrial action. In Canada, an act that falls within one or more of these categories and involves disruption to an essential service does not constitute terrorism unless it is intended to cause serious harm, endanger a life, or endanger the health or safety of the population.[49] It is not terrorism even if it causes substantial property damage that is likely to produce such harm. Australian legislation is similar.[50] In New Zealand, disruption of essential services cannot of itself constitute terrorism, whether engaged in by protesters or otherwise. New Zealand law nonetheless includes limited protection for protesters, by providing that the fact that a person is participating in a protected activity is not, by itself, sufficient evidence that the person is acting for a prohibited purpose or intends to cause a prohibited outcome.[51] Even in the absence of this proviso, it is hard to see how that participation could be considered as such evidence. US and UK law include no such provisions.

Qualifications: Armed Conflict

Read literally, many of the definitions include war within the rubric of terrorism. War, after all, involves the use and threat of violence in order to coerce governments. War is, in a sense, the most extreme form of terrorism, and the costs and casualties of war so vastly exceed those of other forms of violent politics that one could be forgiven for wondering why there should be so much concern about those other forms of violence. If terrorism per se is bad, how can war per se not be much worse? But all five countries maintain military forces and sometimes use them.

National definitions have dealt with this problem in at least three ways. One is to limit terrorism to attacks on civilian populations and to exempt from the definitions attacks that do not fall foul of the law of international armed conflict.[52] This is the approach taken by Canada and New Zealand. Under Canadian law, acts that would otherwise fall within the general definition of terrorism do not do so if they take place in the course of armed conflict and are consistent with the body of international law applicable to the conflict. This exception also applies to offences under the legislation governing the terrorist bombings convention.[53] New Zealand law includes an international law defence but expressly defines terrorism to include acts that take place in the course of armed conflict and are intended to cause death or serious bodily injury to noncombatants.[54]

These provisions effectively mean that acts in the course of armed conflict do not constitute terrorism as long as they comply with the Geneva Conventions. Acts by national armed forces are protected, but so are acts by enemy armed forces. Acts by guerilla armies may also be protected either under the protocols to the conventions or under Common Article 3. If the Prince Edward Island Liberation Army pursued its objectives by attacks limited to the Canadian armed forces, it could not be proscribed under Canadian counterterrorism legislation. If, contrary to the Geneva Conventions, it murdered civilians, it would lose this protection.

On the whole, this is a conceptually elegant solution to awkward questions otherwise implicit in counterterrorism legislation, but it requires a deep commitment to international law. The US definitions tend to achieve a similar result, albeit less elegantly. Some definitions (including the FISA definition) confine terrorism to attacks on civilian targets. They do not extend to attacks on armed forces and therefore to attacks by armed forces on other armed forces. However, on their face, they appear to include military attacks on civilians, whether the attack would be permitted under the Geneva Conventions or not.

The FRAA definition limits terrorism to attacks on civilians by subnational groups. It therefore excludes any activities by national armies. The INA definition of "terrorist activity" applies only to acts that are also prohibited under several of the earlier "terrorism conventions." In addition, many definitions (including the FISA and related definitions) require that the act be one that is, in any case, an offence against US law or would be if committed in the United States. The elements of US terrorism offences are such that there are almost no circumstances in which a person can be guilty of a terrorism offence without also being guilty of a nonterrorism offence or of knowing assistance to terrorist organisations (whose listing is constrained by the FRAA and INA definitions). This protects members of the United States and other armed forces, except insofar as their behaviour would be unlawful under nonterrorism legislation.

The UK and Australian definitions do not expressly exclude acts in the course of armed conflict and, on their face, would include acts of war, whether they are engaged in by government forces, allied forces, foreign forces, or enemy forces. In the United Kingdom, that acts by government forces seemed to fall within the definition of terrorism provoked some concern in the Parliament, where the government argued, first, that the UK armed forces were protected because the legislation was not expressed to apply to the Crown;[55] second, that, in any case, the definition did not cover any action in armed conflict;[56] and, finally, that even if it did, the director of public prosecutions would not prosecute.[57] The first consideration meant that the activities of members of the UK armed forces were not covered by the legislation but would not protect a member of a foreign force. Immunity protections for the Australian crown are weaker, but it is likely that Australian courts would interpret the legislation in the light of the practicalities of national defence. The second consideration was not developed, but the conclusion appears to be correct. Prosecuting a participant in international armed conflict for behaviour not constituting a breach of international law would constitute a breach of the Geneva Conventions. Given the presumption against a legislative intention to legislate contrary to international law and given the absence of any extrinsic materials to suggest such an intention, it is likely that the court would read the legislation down.

The question arose in the trial of a defendant on charges of disseminating terrorist publications, where his defence was that force against the military was justified. Among questions asked by the jury was whether the use of force by coalition forces in Afghanistan was terrorism. The judge's answer was that

> the use of force by Coalition forces is not terrorism. They do enjoy combatant immunity, they are ordered there by our government and the American government, unless they commit crimes such as torture or war crimes.[58]

The defendant was convicted and appealed, but it was not necessary for the appeal court to decide whether the trial judge's answer was correct.

Even read down, the UK and Australian definitions cover some acts in the course of armed conflict that would not fall within the Canadian and New Zealand definitions. The former definitions catch terrorist acts that are not contrary to international law and that take place in the course of armed conflict not amounting to international armed conflict, or activity falling within Protocol II. Since these acts are not contrary to international law, they do not fall within the Canadian definition, and they fall within the New Zealand definition only insofar as they involve attacks on civilians. It would not be terrorism for a guerilla group to attack a Canadian army base or the New Zealand navy. However, while international law does not forbid such attacks, it does not preclude countries from punishing people who participate in them.[59] There is therefore no international law-based presumption in favour of such guerillas under UK and Australian law, and if their behaviour falls within the natural meaning of the relevant definition, it would constitute terrorism.

Implications

Definitions matter because they have implications for the scope of counterterror laws, but their significance depends on those laws. For this reason, their history provides limited guidance to the extent to which counterterror laws can be understood in terms of the opportunities and pressures generated by terrorist attacks. It suggests several conclusions. First, the timing of legislative definitions indicates that they can scarcely be treated as ill-considered. Second, their history provides some evidence of the conflicting priorities of the executive and legislative arms but little evidence of conflict between the political and judicial arms. Third, there is no evidence to suggest that definitions can be understood as a response to an illiberal public. But there is some evidence to suggest that choice of definitions can be understood in terms of tolerance of unconventional politics.

A Response to Heightened Fears?

While several of the general definitions were enacted as part of a package of post-9/11 measures, they can scarcely be treated as ill thought through. First, all the definitions can trace their ancestry to prior to the 9/11 attacks, and none of them was adopted in circumstances that suggest it could only have been adopted in the immediate aftermath of the attacks. The widely used FISA definition was a response not to a terrorist attack but to government abuse of surveillance powers. The UK definition of 2000 was included in legislation that had had a four-year gestation period and that had been designed for an era in which it was hoped that Northern Irish terrorism would have largely ceased to be a problem. Moreover, while the Canadian, Australian, and New Zealand definitions were adopted following the 9/11 attacks, they were heavily based on the UK definition, except insofar as they were narrower. The relevant Australian and New Zealand bills were not finally passed until July and November 2002.

Institutional Responses

There is some evidence that governments favoured slightly wider definitions than the legislatures. In the United Kingdom and Australia, governments defended proposed definitions on the grounds that flexibility was desirable and that governments could be trusted with the powers in question. However, despite having a large parliamentary majority, the UK government agreed to an amendment adding a limited "intimidate or influence" element (which subsequently found its way into the other three countries' definitions). The Canadian government (which also had a large parliamentary majority) agreed to expand its "protest" exception to include unlawful as well as lawful protests. The Australian bill had originally proposed a definition based on an early version of the proposed UK legislation. A Senate committee recommended the addition of a "coerce or intimidate" requirement to deal with what would otherwise be a danger of overbreadth,[60] and the Liberal-National government later agreed to amend the legislation accordingly, by replacing a "lawful protest" exception with one that extended to unlawful but nonviolent protests. It probably had no choice. It needed Labor Party support to secure the passage of the legislation through the Senate.

Definitions have rarely given rise to litigation, and insofar as courts have considered the meaning and validity of definitions, they have generally agreed with the government. The only exception is *R v Khawaja*, a Canadian case where a defendant charged with terrorism offences argued that the motivation requirement represented an unconstitutional interference with freedom of political and religious expression. Justice Rutherford agreed:

> It seems to me that the inevitable impact to flow from the inclusion of [the requirement] will be to focus investigative and prosecutorial scrutiny on the political, religious and ideological beliefs, opinions and expressions of persons and groups, both in Canada and abroad. Equally inevitable will be [a] chilling effect. There will also be an indirect or re-bound effect . . . , as individuals' and authorities' attitudes and conduct reflect the shadow of suspicion and anger falling over all who appear to have any connection with the religious, political or ideological grouping identified with specific terrorist acts.[61]

This heartfelt expression of dissent from post-9/11 politics demonstrates admirable judicial independence and praiseworthy unchillability. But it is also puzzling. It seems to imply that but for the motivational element, police and security agencies would focus considerably less on those with particular beliefs. But their pre-2001 practices suggest otherwise.

While the judgment may have provided symbolic satisfaction to Canadians for whom the motivational element issue has acquired considerable symbolic importance, it did nothing for Khawaja. Rutherford held that the offending clause could be severed from the definition, thereby saving the government from having to prove the motivation element of Mr. Khawaja's alleged offence. Khawaja's application for leave to appeal to the Supreme Court against the interlocutory decision was dismissed.[62] The issue subsequently arose in

United States v Nadarajah (an extradition case)[63] and in R *v Ahmad*,[64] where the court decided not to follow *Khawaja*. Khawaja was subsequently convicted, and he appealed unsuccessfully to the Ontario Court of Appeal, which dismissed the appeal in a judgment that was also highly critical of Rutherford's handling of the "chilling" issue.[65] The parties to the extradition case were also unsuccessful on appeal.[66] The Supreme Court granted leave to appeal on grounds including the motivation requirement ground but subsequently and unanimously concluded that the motivation requirement did not fall foul of the Charter.[67] Otherwise, in relation to definitions, courts seem to have been content to let legislative decisions prevail.

Political Beliefs

The nature of opposition to the legislation suggests that stances on definitional issues were prompted in part by preexisting attitudes. In the United Kingdom, the "protest" issue aroused a degree of cross-partisan concern, but concerns were particularly likely to be expressed by backbench Labour members of parliament and by Liberal Democrats. Similar concerns were expressed by New Democrats and members of the Bloc Québécois in Canada; by the Labor Party, the Australian Democrats, and the Greens in Australia; and by the Greens in New Zealand. The same groups also expressed concerns about the danger that the legislation could catch "good terrorists."

However, these partisan differences should be kept in perspective. In the United Kingdom, the Labour government made no attempt to accommodate backbench concerns about possible overreach or the impact of the legislation on good terrorists, beyond assurances that the legislation would be used responsibly. In Canada, a proposed amendment to remove the "ideological purpose" element was supported by the Progressive Conservatives and the Canadian Alliance, although their primary concern seems to have been to expand the coverage of the act and ease the task of prosecutors.[68] Once the Australian government agreed to extend the scope of the "protest" exception, the Labor Party voted with the government on definitional issues; and in New Zealand, there was broad support for the definition from the major parties. Moreover, definitions have proved remarkably stable, notwithstanding changes in government. The United Kingdom expanded the "motivation" requirement to include racially motivated terrorism and extended the scope of the definition to cover terrorism against international organisations, but elsewhere there have been no changes, even where incoming governments had opposed the original definitions. On becoming the government, the Canadian Conservative Party did not attempt to eliminate the "ideological motive" requirement.

The Role of the Public

The parliamentary history of the post-9/11 legislation suggests that definitions cannot be readily understood as a response to authoritarian pressures from the public. Insofar as there was public input into the legislation, it came overwhelmingly from civil libertarians and the political left.[69] Moreover, parliamentary opposition to the legislation was overwhelmingly based on the civil libertarian objections, rather than on arguments that the definitions were underinclusive. There were no attempts to amend the definition to relax the "harm" or "intimidate and coerce" requirements. There were also, however, moves to eliminate the "ideological motive" element. Parliamentary critics of this element argued that it should be deleted because attention to motive discriminated against people pursuing collective goals and could encourage discrimination on religious, political, and ideological grounds. Had they got their way, their amendment would have broadened the ambit of counterterror law and eased the task of prosecutors, but on the whole, that does not seem to have been their intention. Rather, the element seems to have acquired symbolic significance, especially in Canada. The paucity of calls to broaden the scope of counterterror laws suggests that opposition parliamentarians did not envisage that there was political capital to be gained from advocating broad definitions or that, if they did, they were not interested in trying to attract it. If, as seems likely, responses to terrorism are influenced by images of massive terrorist attacks, popular ideas of what constitutes terrorism might well be considerably narrower than those embodied in the definitions.

Conclusions

There is considerable agreement as to what constitutes terrorism, but the term *terrorism* is necessarily vague. Acts of terrorism rank along a continuum. At one extreme is the typical attack that causes physical and social harm but poses no serious threat to the social and political order. If the threat of terrorism were limited to such attacks, there would be little need for special terrorism laws. However, even minor attacks may have corrosive effects if they become frequent. Nor is it self-evident that terrorism should be confined to acts against the person. Acts against property can harm people. The destruction of a factory may strip hundreds of their employment. Bombing a metro system may mean that thousands have to spend far more time getting to work. International law recognises the emotional significance of national monuments, artistic treasures, and places of worship. Another consideration is that the low harm threshold makes proof of guilt easier, especially in relation to preparations and conspiracies. Proving an intention to cause at least some serious physical injury will be easier than proving an intention to cause serious physical injury to more than a specified number of people. If the harm caused or threatened barely crosses the harm threshold, proving the additional intent will be correspondingly harder. Defenders of broader definitions also argued that political good sense would reduce the danger of abuse, thereby highlighting one of the issues that pervades counterterrorism law and practice: whom does one trust to do the right thing, and by what process can they be made accountable? The legislatures' answer has been politicians and politics, but only up to a point.

FOUR

Gathering Information

Sunlight is said to be the best of disinfectants; electric light the most efficient policeman.

Louis Brandeis (but not with surveillance in mind)[1]

The greatest problem with the Patriot Act may not be that it is unconstitutional, as some argue, but that, in too many respects it is not.

Susan N. Herman[2]

The best friend of prevention is information. If you have the right information you can prevent. Without that information, you can't.

John D. Ashcroft[3]

If terrorist conspiracies are to be thwarted, it is almost essential that governments engage in surveillance and almost inevitable that this will involve the surveillance of numerous nonconspirators. This effect is bad enough (although arguably a price to be paid for security), but there is a worse one. National histories disclose long traditions of surveillance targeting "loyal" radicals who want social change but who are basically content to work within the system to achieve it. If those who conducted oversurveillance diligently exonerated nonthreats and turned their attention elsewhere, surveillance might be nonproblematic. But the historical record is discouraging.

First, there are cases where surveillance has thrown up information that is irrelevant to whether the target engages in unlawful behaviour but that nonetheless discredits its target. Governments and their agents have sometimes been unable to resist the temptation to use such information to weaken their political adversaries. Second, while information acquired through surveillance ought to have the potential to exonerate as well as incriminate, there seems to be a bias in favour of looking for evidence that confirms suspicions. This may help explain why agents and governments may believe they are acting properly when they use "irrelevant" information to discredit people whose politics may be objectionable but who are working within the constitution to achieve their ends.

These abuses are well documented, and the political heirs to their victims have long memories. Defenders of surveillance are worried about the errors attending undersurveillance; critics are worried by traditions of oversurveillance. Post-9/11 hindsight lends some support to the advocates of wide surveillance powers, and post-9/11 legal developments provide some support for arguments that the 9/11 attacks spawned unnecessarily broad surveillance laws.

This chapter recognises the obvious: the 9/11 attacks enabled the US government to acquire powers it would otherwise have been hard-pressed to secure. But, I shall argue, the legislation was less ill-considered than the rapidity of its passage suggests. On the whole, the measures were ones that had already been introduced in other countries or were subsequently introduced in calmer times. They fell short of what the administration wanted, as was demonstrated by subsequent administration programs, and they have generally survived constitutional scrutiny. There is little evidence that the 9/11 attacks or others were directly reflected in expanded surveillance powers in the other jurisdictions.

There is ample evidence of the degree to which fondness for surveillance is an executive, rather than a legislative, taste, but this has been manifested not so much in the abuse of powers as in behaviour that appears to have exceeded legal powers. Contrary to what one might expect on the basis of timing and institutional proclivities, courts have generally upheld both surveillance legislation and surveillance practices. Legislative innovations cannot be treated as an opportunistic appeal to popular prejudices. Poll data provide little evidence of widespread popular support for broad surveillance powers either in the immediate aftermath of terrorist attacks or later.

Stances on surveillance reflect political dispositions as well as institutional interests and cultures. Legislative votes on surveillance measures suggest that voting is related to general political dispositions and sometimes more to dispositions than to whether one's preferred party is in government. Poll data suggest a similar tendency among the general public.

Information-Gathering Regimes

Surveillance powers tend to vary depending on whether the information is to be used as evidence in legal proceedings or for security purposes, and there is a grey area reflecting the overlap between law enforcement and intelligence gathering. In the United States, intelligence-gathering powers vary depending on whether the target is a local or foreign adversary. Elsewhere this distinction is less important.

Law Enforcement

Law enforcement agents may collect information in a variety of ways: searches and seizures, interception of communications, analysis of patterns of communication, use of eavesdropping devices, commandeering or asking for records, trawling through rubbish bins, talking to potential witnesses, infiltrating criminal groups, and interviewing suspects. Most (but not all) of these methods require formal authority, especially where they are intrusive or involve interference with privacy. In general, searches, interception, and bugging require warrants from a judicial or quasi-judicial officer, who must be persuaded that there is probable cause warranting their issue. There may also be a requirement that the information is such that less-intrusive information-gathering procedures are impractical. The target of the warrant must normally be notified, either before or after execution of the warrant (depending on its nature). Most jurisdictions now require monitoring of warrants. For some less-intrusive procedures of information collection, administrative subpoenas may suffice, and undercover and public surveillance generally requires no more than administrative authorisation. On the whole, requirements are independent of whether the relevant crime involves terrorism.

These requirements receive considerable constitutional protection. In the United States, the primary basis for such protection is the Fourth Amendment; and section 7 of the Canadian Charter of Rights and Freedoms provides a right "to be secure from unreasonable search or seizure." Under Article 8 of the ECHR, "[e]veryone has the right to respect for his private and family life, his home and his correspondence." Some protection from surveillance and questioning is also provided by constitutional protections of freedom of expression and due process. However, even in the absence of constitutional protections, intrusive surveillance by law enforcement is strictly regulated. This does not mean that it is always in accordance with the relevant law.

There are, of course, variations—over time and place and according to the type of search or surveillance. Warrants of search and seizure normally require probable cause, but in Australia, it is enough that "there are reasonable grounds for suspecting that there is, or that there will be within the next 72 hours, any evidentiary material at the premises."[4] In the United Kingdom, special rules govern search and seizure for the purposes of terrorism investigations. Warrants are needed, but the test relates to whether the material likely to be found will be of substantial value to a terrorist investigation, rather than to whether it is likely to be evidence of an offence.[5]

The requirements for warrants to intercept communications differ from those governing search and seizure. Historically these did not require judicial approval, except where they would otherwise involve trespass.[6] However, judicial and legislative concerns with protecting privacy interests have resulted in a complex body of law concerned with both restraining and permitting interference with privacy interests. Different jurisdictions have adopted different formulas for doing so. US federal law criminalises the unauthorised interception of any "wire, oral or electronic communication," the use of devices to bug communications, and the use or transmission of details of intercepted communications. However, these activities may be authorised if a judge finds that strict conditions are met, including a nexus between the target, the offence, and the facilities being intercepted or the place of interception, and authorisations must require compliance with procedures designed to protect the communications of third parties.[7] After interception has been completed, the target must normally be given expeditious notification of details of the surveillance.[8] These requirements may be waived in limited circumstances.[9] This does not cover the situation where law enforcement agents seek access to information held by one person and relating to another. These include stored electronic communications (the most important form of which is copies of e-mails held by an Internet service provider). Access normally requires compliance with the search warrant procedures, but after 180 days, the government may give notice to the subscriber or customer. If so, a court may issue an order on being satisfied that the information is "relevant and material to an ongoing criminal investigation."[10]

In the United Kingdom, interception and bugging require warrants, which are issued not by judges but by the home secretary, who must believe that the warrant is necessary for the detection or prevention of serious crime.[11] There is no duty to notify the target. A distinctive but controversial feature of UK law is that it normally prohibits the use of intercepted communications in judicial proceedings.[12]

Canadian law conditions approval of communications surveillance on the judge being satisfied that authorisation would be "in the best interests of justice," and it requires that the target normally be given postsurveillance notification.[13] (In New Zealand, the law was similar until recently.)[14] The normal "last resort" requirement does not apply in the case of terrorism or criminal organisation offences, and the judge may make orders extending the time after which notification must be made for periods of up to three years.[15] Following recent reforms, New Zealand law conditions surveillance warrants on a judge's satisfaction that there are reasonable grounds for believing that surveillance will yield evidence in relation to a serious past, current, or future offence. There is a duty to report to the issuing judge on the outcome of the surveillance, but there is no duty to inform people that they have been the subject of surveillance, unless the surveillance has been in serious breach of the conditions in the warrant or the warrant should not have been issued, and then only if the judge orders disclosure.[16] New Zealand law makes no special provision for terrorism cases.

Australian law makes separate provision for communications interception, bugging, and access to stored communications. Authorisation for interception requires satisfaction that interception would be likely to assist investigation of a serious offence involving either a person likely to use the relevant service or someone with whom that person is likely to communicate.[17] There are no "last resort" requirements, but issuing officers must exercise their discretion on the basis of proportionality-based reasoning, the existence of less-intrusive alternatives being among the matters to be taken into account.[18] Similar rules now govern access to stored communications.[19] The use of surveillance devices is subject to reasonable suspicion of an offence that is being or will be investigated. Surveillance must be necessary for the gathering of evidence, and the issuing authority must also take account of proportionality considerations.[20] There is no requirement to notify people whose communications have been intercepted.

Laws also permit governments to require that third parties divulge business and other records. Insofar as powers are conditioned on judicial approval, the test for their issuance is typically lower than that for search and seizure and interception orders. In the United States, judicial approval is required for orders that service providers disclose customer and subscriber information, but the test to be satisfied by the applicant is relatively undemanding, and the government is not required to provide the customer a notice of receipt of such records.

UK law permits "authorised" government agents to seek access to communications data.[21] In Canada, judicial officers may order a person other than the person under investigation to produce documents relevant to an offence that has been committed or is suspected of having been committed.[22] In addition, financial institutions may be ordered to disclose account details. Such orders may be issued in relation to future as well as past offences and are conditioned on their promise of assisting investigation, rather than yielding evidence.[23] Australian law allows demands for a range of transactional material. Where the request is in relation to a "serious" terrorism offence, an authorised Australian Federal Police officer may require the production of the information or document. For other serious crimes, however, an application must be made to a federal magistrate.[24] New Zealand law makes no provision for such orders, general search warrants being used as a functional equivalent.[25] However, under legislation in effect from April 2014, orders to produce communications data and stored data may be made by issuing officers who are appointed as such, who may, but need not, be judicial officers.[26]

Subject to a prior authorisation, given on the basis that the authorisation was "expedient for the prevention of acts of terrorism," the Terrorism Act 2000 gave the United Kingdom the power to stop and search vehicles, drivers, passengers, pedestrians, and anything they might be carrying.[27] Following a successful challenge in the ECtHR to the exercise of these powers, a review of terrorism legislation recommended that the conditions for exercise of the power be replaced with a far more heavily circumscribed power.[28] In accordance with the Human Rights Act 1998, the home secretary made an order limiting the operation of the act, and that order was, in turn, replaced by legislative amendments that sharply limited the scope of the power. The power to make authorisations is now conditioned on reasonable suspicion that "an act of terrorism will take place" and that the authorisation was necessary to prevent such an act and no greater in its territorial and temporal scope than was necessary to do so.[29] Australian law includes a similar provision, with powers generally conditioned on the person being in an area under the exclusive control of the commonwealth and on suspicion that the person has committed, is committing, or is about to commit a terrorist offence.[30] Its scope is therefore circumscribed, although it could catch people in the relevant geographical area who might not fall within the current UK law. Between 2001 and 2006, and after 2013, Canadian law included provision for the making of orders requiring a person to attend for oral examination if there were reasonable grounds for believing that the examination would yield information about a past or prospective terrorism offence.[31]

Intelligence Gathering

Different statutory regimes govern the gathering of intelligence for national security purposes. Typically, these are far less demanding than the criminal law regimes, the justification being that the information is gathered for a different purpose. It is difficult to think of principled reasons why this should be the case, given that intelligence information can be used to assist police with their inquiries and prosecutions. The interests at stake may be higher, but if so, one might expect that this would be reflected in the rules governing law enforcement surveillance. The explanation for the difference seems to lie in practical politics, and in this respect, the relative invisibility of intelligence surveillance may help account for the content of intelligence surveillance law. But it understandably causes unease.

The United States

In the United States, there is little provision for the gathering of intelligence in relation to purely domestic terrorism. Powers in relation to "international" terrorism are much broader. Various agencies have the power to issue "national security letters" (NSLs), the effect of which is that the recipient must provide relevant information in the recipient's possession. One NSL regime deals with requests for information relating to the leaking of secret government information.[32] The other regimes govern access to various forms of transactional information, including communications transaction records, financial records, and information held by consumer rating agencies about financial accounts. The legislation dates back to 1978. Subsequent legislation expanded the range of information holders who can be asked for and required to provide information, the range of information that can be sought, and the range of people who may seek information.[33] The relevant provisions vary slightly according to the type of records involved.

NSLs do not require judicial authorisation. It is enough that the FBI director or a designated official above a prescribed level certify the existence of facts that would warrant the exercise of the relevant power. The usual requirement is that the records relate to or are sought for "an authorized investigation to protect against international terrorism or clandestine intelligence activities provided that such an investigation is not conducted solely on the basis of activities protected by the first amendment."[34] Other agencies also have the power to require the production of financial records and consumer reports for authorised intelligence-related activities.[35]

Far more important are the powers conferred by the Foreign Intelligence Surveillance Act of 1978 (FISA).[36] Prior to that legislation, the government's power to conduct surveillance for foreign intelligence purposes derived from the president's inherent executive power, the boundaries of which were elusive. FISA was a response to revelations of widespread government surveillance of domestic critics of government policies, coupled with evidence of the misuse of this information. It was predicated on the assumption that it was nonetheless necessary that the United States be in a position to spy on some Americans, either because they were targets or as an unavoidable consequence of the surveillance of non-Americans. Initially, FISA was concerned with communications surveillance. Its scope has been subsequently expanded to permit most of the forms of information gathering open to law enforcement officers.

FISA forbids "electronic surveillance" except as authorised by the act. "Electronic surveillance" is defined to include interception of oral communications, wiretapping, and interception of radio communications. It includes interception of radio communications only in very limited circumstances, and it includes wiretapping and other surveillance only if they impinge on "United States persons" or occur in the United States or if all the senders and recipients are located in the United States.[37] "United States persons" include citizens, permanent residents, and incorporated and unincorporated associations, unless the corporation or association is a "foreign power."[38] The category of "foreign power" is defined broadly. It includes groups engaged in or preparing for "international terrorism."[39] The category "agent of foreign power" is defined to include, inter alia, anyone who engages in or prepares for "international terrorism." Americans are agents only if they do so intentionally. Electronic surveillance (as defined) is permitted only for the purpose of gathering "foreign intelligence information," which means information that relates to the capacity of the United States to protect itself against attack, sabotage, international terrorism, and clandestine activities by foreign powers or their agents. If information concerns US persons, it is "foreign intelligence information" only if it is necessary to the ability of the United States to protect itself against those threats.[40]

The president, through the attorney general, is permitted to authorise surveillance and searches without the need for a court order, but only if there is little likelihood that this will affect a US person.[41] Otherwise, a court order is normally required. The act provides for a special court, the Foreign Intelligence Surveillance Court (FISC), to consider applications for such orders. The FISC comprises district court judges designated by the US chief justice, and appeal lies with a FISA court of review, comprised of three designated federal judges.[42] Applications to install pen registers and trap and trace devices and for access to business records may also be made to a magistrate judge.

Applications must include a variety of details and certifications, depending on the type of surveillance or information gathering involved. One requirement is certification that the information to be yielded by the relevant process be foreign intelligence information. Its collection must be a substantial purpose where communications interception is involved, and for communications interception and searches, the applicant must certify that there are no less-intrusive ways of getting the information.[43]

Applications for interception, search, and production orders must also include details of "minimization procedures." These are intended to ensure that information about US persons is acquired, retained, and disseminated only as is necessary given the need of the United States to gather foreign intelligence. If information is gathered that is not foreign intelligence information, it shall not normally be disseminated. However, procedures may allow for retaining and disseminating information that is evidence of a crime, for law enforcement purposes.[44]

The judge's role is more limited than that of a judge assessing applications for law enforcement warrants. The judge inquires into whether the application satisfies the formal requirements and includes requisite statements of fact and certifications. It is not for the judge to second-guess the applicant, except insofar as the judge may find that certifications are "clearly erroneous" on the basis of the material initially presented and further material presented at the judge's request, but then only in relation to interceptions and searches.[45]

Post-9/11 amendments (discussed later in this chapter) have expanded powers to gather and distribute foreign intelligence information. They have also expanded the potential for situations in which law enforcement agencies are unable to gather particular pieces of evidence and information under criminal justice powers but are able to use material gathered under the less-exacting requirements of FISA. However, these apply only in cases where foreign intelligence is gathered. Terrorists who are not acting for a foreign cause have nothing to fear from FISA, except its misuse.

Amendments in 2008 extended the scope of FISA to cover surveillance outside the United States of non-US targets and expanded the circumstances in which surveillance of US persons from outside the United States might be permitted.[46] The purpose of these amendments was not to protect foreign targets (although it does provide them with limited incidental protection). It was to ensure that surveillance ostensibly targeting foreign targets did not intentionally or unintentionally yield an unacceptable amount of otherwise inaccessible information about US persons who might be parties to such communications.

Surveillance of targets outside the United States may now be jointly authorised by the attorney general and the director of national security, but only if the target is not a US person. That power may not be used for the purpose of targeting a particular known person in the United States or to acquire communications involving a sender and recipient who are both in the United States. The exercise of the power must be consistent with the Fourth Amendment to the US Constitution. Authorisation is subject to targeting and minimisation procedures, guidelines, and certification. Procedures and certification must be submitted to the FISC for ex parte judicial review.[47] The amendments subject surveillance of US persons outside the United States to a regime similar to that governing surveillance within the United States.[48] Orders may be made permitting surveillance both within and outside the United States.[49]

The UK Model

The security services of the United Kingdom, Canada, Australia, and New Zealand are empowered to gather intelligence in relation to both domestic and foreign threats. The Canadian, Australian, and New Zealand services were placed on a statutory footing before their UK counterparts (which are now also governed by statute). Their information-gathering powers are subject to legal regulation and to review. Warrants are required for intrusive information gathering, but the belief requirement relates to the necessity of the warrant for the organisation's performance of its functions, rather than to the likelihood or possibility that those surveilled are engaged in criminal behaviour of which the surveillance might yield evidence. Standards vary according to the type of warrant and cross-nationally. Australian law gives the Australian Security Intelligence Organisation[50] (ASIO) a power not found elsewhere: the power to require people who might be able to provide information about terrorism to answer questions.[51]

There are procedural variations. The issuing authority in the United Kingdom and Australia is the minister (the home secretary in the United Kingdom, the attorney-general in Australia). In New Zealand, warrants require the approval of a warrants commissioner, who must be a former High Court judge, and interception warrants also require the approval of the minister.[52] In Canada, authorisation requires approval from the responsible minister for the making of an application to a judge, as well as authorisation by the judge.[53] In Australia, New Zealand, and the United Kingdom, the process for issuing a warrant is closely monitored by inspectors-general or their equivalent.[54] In the United Kingdom, people who believe that their communications have been wrongly intercepted may complain to the Investigatory Powers Tribunal.[55]

Information gathered by an intelligence service may not be disclosed by the service except in limited circumstances. In Canada and Australia, these include disclosure for criminal justice purposes.[56] In New Zealand, disclosure is permitted in the course of official duties and as authorised by the minister, and the intelligence service's functions include communicating intelligence where this is in the interests of security.[57] These provisions do not expressly permit the use of intelligence information as evidence, but there is Australian and Canadian authority that assumes this to be the case.[58]

Different agencies are responsible for the interception of foreign radio communications and other foreign intelligence. They do not require warrants for intercepting foreign communications, but they do require warrants or authorisation in limited circumstances where a communication involves a citizen or permanent resident.[59]

Surveillance Law and Heightened Fears

Surveillance laws have a complex history. One of their characteristic features is their two-edged nature. To a considerable extent, they both forbid surveillance and permit it. The extent to which they forbid surveillance is not always clear, since statutory prohibitions may coexist with vague constitutional prohibitions and the restraints imposed by other bodies of law, including tort and property law, privacy law, and state or provincial legislation. To a considerable extent, the impetus for recent pieces of surveillance law has come not from panic in the face of apparent emergencies but from abuses of what were arguably government powers. The evolution of surveillance law has also been influenced by technological developments, which have potential both to facilitate and to complicate surveillance. Moreover, much recent surveillance legislation has been developed contemporaneously with attempts to enhance protections for privacy interests.

Nonetheless, terrorism-related concerns have left their mark on the law, especially in the United States and in minor respects elsewhere. Passed in the immediate aftermath of the 9/11 attacks, the USA Patriot Act[60] strengthened the government's information-gathering powers. One of its most controversial amendments related to the FISA powers regarding seizure of business records. Prior to the 2001 amendments, the director of the FBI or a designee was empowered to apply for an order authorising common carriers, accommodation providers, physical storage facilities, and vehicle renters to provide information concerning international terrorism. This was replaced by a power to apply for an order requiring the production of business records for a FISA investigation.[61] While the section heading referred to "business records," the section itself had the potential to apply to almost any record that might be relevant to an investigation, including, notoriously, library records. Concern about these records was not without foundation. In 1970, the Treasury had indeed sought access to library records with a view to finding out which people were reading books on explosives. The American Library Foundation had staged a successful campaign to discourage cooperation.[62]

Other controversial provisions increased the government's powers to acquire, disseminate, and use information under FISA. The most important of these relaxed the certification requirement for FISA surveillance and searches. Under the law as it stood, the attorney general had to certify that the gathering of "foreign intelligence information" was "for *the* purpose of gathering foreign intelligence" (my italics). Courts had held that this requirement was not met unless intelligence gathering was the "sole or primary" purpose. The amendment relaxed the test to require that the purpose be no more than a "significant" purpose.[63] (The administration had argued that "a purpose" should suffice, but concerns about the constitutionality of the proposal led to adoption of the less expansive phrase.)[64] The precise implications of this amendment would depend on how the word *significant* was interpreted, but whatever its full meaning was in this context, it at least meant that there were circumstances where surveillance was authorised notwithstanding that it was the sole or "primary" purpose for the investigation. This revision increased, in turn, the range of circumstances in which law enforcement agencies might be able to use FISA procedures to gain evidence that would not be available under criminal justice procedures.

Other amendments to the FISA powers were less wide-ranging. The power to make ancillary orders in relation to surveillance was expanded so that orders could be made against nonspecified persons when the actions of the target of the surveillance might have the effect of thwarting attempts to determine the person's identity.[65] Unlike similar law enforcement powers, the applicant did not have to specify the target's identity: a description could suffice. Nor was there a requirement that the person subject to surveillance be notified after the expiry of the surveillance. The Patriot Act also expanded the maximum duration of orders.[66]

The act expanded the range of FBI agents who could request transactional records.[67] Providers' powers to disclose stored information were expanded to permit otherwise forbidden disclosure when there was reasonable belief that disclosure was required by "an emergency involving immediate danger of death or serious injury to any person." In 2002, the emergency power was expanded still further.[68]

The act made minor amendments to the law governing criminal investigations. The power to seize stored electronic communications was expanded so that it included voice mail.[69] The details of information that could be subpoenaed were extended to include details of the means and source of payments.[70] The law governing pen registers and trap and trace devices was amended to make it clear that it applied to Internet, as well as more traditional, communications. Requirements for authority to use pen registers and trap and trace devices were changed so that they could have nationwide application and such that the communications to which they related could be defined with less particularity than had previously been the case.[71] The Federal Rules of Criminal Procedure were amended so that search warrants in relation to investigations of domestic and international terrorism could be sought in any district in which activities related to the terrorism might have occurred, for searches both inside and outside the district.[72] Provision was also made for nationwide service of search warrants for electronic evidence.[73]

The act expanded the disclosure powers of law enforcers who had obtained foreign intelligence information in the course of lawful surveillance information, so that they could disclose it to federal officials for the purposes of assisting them in their official duties.[74] Relevant information otherwise obtained in the course of a criminal investigation could be similarly disclosed.[75] The act amended the Federal Rules of Criminal Procedure to permit the disclosure of matters occurring before a grand jury to a variety of federal officials, for the performance of their official duties, in cases involving national security or international or domestic terrorism (as defined in 18 USC § 2331).[76]

One amendment, which has survived in modified form and notwithstanding its apparent unpopularity with the public, allowed a judge to dispense with the requirement that a person whose premises had been searched be notified within a specified time. The FBI had made earlier, unsuccessful attempts to secure this power.[77] Its rationale was clear: to avoid tipping off the subject of the investigation. The power was not confined to terrorism cases.

Several attempts were made in the US House of Representatives and the Senate to delete some of these measures. They failed by sizeable majorities, especially in the Senate.[78] The act was passed by a large majority in the House and with only one dissentient in the Senate. The act and its history exhibit many outward signs of being both a response to heightened fears and a reform that was particularly ill thought through. Its name and timing are suggestive. It was passed in considerable haste in the immediate aftermath of the 9/11 attacks and the even more immediate context of the anthrax scare. Browbeaten by threats that unless it moved quickly, it might well have blood on its hands, the Congress bypassed and abbreviated normal procedures and passed the legislation within a month of being presented with the administration proposals. Members of Congress complained that they had been unable to track down copies of the latest versions of the legislation, much less to study them. (One reason was that following the anthrax attacks, Congress's administrative infrastructure had been temporarily impaired.)[79]

It is useful to disentangle various elements of the "haste" perspective. First, while the legislation was passed in almost indecent haste, neither the executive nor the Congress was completely unprepared for the legislation. Orin Kerr points out that the Department of Justice "had been clamoring for changes to the antiquated surveillance laws for years"[80] and that the Clinton administration had already proposed some of the changes implemented by the act. Indeed, in 1995, following a series of terrorist bombings, the House Judiciary Committee had endorsed, by majority, an act that, if passed, would have included some of what resurfaced later as Patriot Act provisions. Nonetheless, the fact that these proposals had hitherto failed to commend themselves to Congress suggests that the 9/11 attacks provided their proponents with an opportunity to secure the passage of legislation that would normally have been doomed.

Second, post-9/11 emotions notwithstanding, Congress did not give the administration everything it wanted. In the immediate aftermath of the attacks, the attorney general was urging Congress to pass the administration's proposals within a week, notwithstanding that they had not yet been drafted. His major defence of the administration's proposals lay in warnings about the present danger rather than in explanations of why the proposals would avert them.[81] But Congress refused to agree to several of the more objectionable features of the administration's proposals, notably in relation to the use in US courts of material provided by foreign surveillance agencies, the range of officials who might have access to criminal justice and national security information, the ease with which sneak and peek warrants might be obtained and their scope, the conditions for access to business records, and the scope of and accountability for powers in relation to pen registers and trap and trace devices.[82] Moreover, in face of administration objections,[83] most of the Title II Patriot Act amendments to information-gathering powers were subject to sunset provisions.[84]

Further, insofar as there was panic, it was by no means general. The administration's call for almost instantaneous passage of its proposals did not prevail. In the House, the Democratic minority resisted attempts to expedite the passage of a bill that many of them regarded as inferior to one that had received the unanimous support of the House Judiciary Committee. There was some apocalyptic language used to defend calls for urgent passage of the legislation, but it was the exception. Much of the House debate involved Democrats challenging the need for urgency, and many cited past abuses of surveillance powers. In the Senate, defenders of the legislation often combined arguments that it should be passed with awareness of past abuses and took comfort from the thought that the sunset clause would enable reconsideration in calmer circumstances. However, the Democratically controlled Senate voted 98–1 for the legislation, and the House voted 337–97 in favor.

The surveillance provisions faced and continue to face strong opposition. They have been the subject of critical resolutions passed at state, city, and town level. In 2003, the proposed Freedom to Read Protection Act failed by a tied vote to pass the House of Representatives.[85] In 2005–6, Congress once more considered the act. Since most of the Title II provisions had been subject to a sunset clause, they could have been allowed to lapse. Instead, in 2006, the sunset provisions were removed except in relation to the "roving wiretap" and business records amendments, whose expiry date was advanced to 31 December 2009.[86] But the legislation limited the sneak and peek power, by dropping delay to trial as a sufficient ground for such warrants, presumptively limiting their duration to 30 days and renewals to 90 days, and by requiring reports to the Administrative Office of the United States Courts and to Congress.[87] The same legislation limited the range of officials who could apply for certain records, including records relating to library use, book sales, tax, education, medical treatment, and firearms sales. It also made provision for judicial review of production orders and added minimisation requirements.[88]

In late 2009, the expiry date for the business records power was extended until 28 February 2010.[89] There was considerable division within Congress as to whether some or all of the amendments should be repealed, amended, or allowed continued operation and, if so, for how long.[90] The solution was a compromise, suggesting considerable lack of enthusiasm for the amendments: their operation was subsequently extended until 28 February 2011.[91] In February 2011, their operation was extended until May, and it was subsequently extended for another four years.[92] The survival of most of the Patriot Act amendments suggests that their passage cannot be explained simply in terms of temporarily heightened fears, but the uneasy fate of several of the amendments suggests a degree of support for this perspective: their survival has been dependent on their being slightly "weakened" and on the continuation of the sunset clause.

Postattack fears appear to have made little impact on surveillance legislation elsewhere. In the United Kingdom, the power to stop and search suspected terrorists in designated areas predated 9/11. It had its origins in measures designed to deal with the problem of Irish terrorism, but its presence in the United Kingdom's comprehensive Terrorism Act 2000 cannot be understood as a reaction to a particular attack, given the four-year gestation period that preceded the legislation and given that it was enacted in a climate in which the threat of Irish terrorism seemed at last to be ebbing, while the threat of terrorism from elsewhere was diffuse. The Regulation of Investigatory Powers Act 2000 (c 27), which governs most forms of surveillance in the United Kingdom, was prompted by the need to make UK legislation compliant with ECHR standards, although it also permitted surveillance in some circumstances in which it was not permitted under earlier guidelines.[93] The Anti-terrorism, Crime and Security Act 2001 (c 24), which was passed on 14 December 2001, included one surveillance-related innovation. Part 11 of the act made provisions for procedures whereby the home secretary could require telecommunications companies to retain communications data for national and crime control purposes.

Australia's suite of post-9/11 measures included several provisions dealing with surveillance issues. The most controversial related to ASIO's new power to question and require answers from people in possession of terrorism-relevant information. This met considerable resistance and was not passed until 2003, in an amended form.[94] The only other measure relating to surveillance was a bill dealing with stored communication. The issue the bill sought to address had virtually nothing to do with terrorism and was not finally resolved until 2006 (in a manner that differed from that proposed in 2002). Its effect was to strengthen protections for stored communications. A 2008 bill that would have empowered ASIO to apply for warrants to intercept communications involving named persons, without the need to specify the instruments to be intercepted, attracted cross-party opposition in the Senate and was dropped. A compromise relaxed the requirement for warrants for named persons so that a single warrant could specify multiple communication devices. The power to conduct roving wiretaps remains one of the few powers enjoyed by US agencies but not by ASIO.

Following the London 7/7 attacks, the Council of Australian Governments reviewed terrorism legislation. Eight of the nine jurisdictions agreed on a wide-ranging package of measures that included provision for added terrorism-related surveillance powers.[95] The most important of these provided that an authorised Australian Federal Police officer who believed, on reasonable grounds, that a person had transactional records that would assist the investigation of a "serious terrorism offence" could give the person a notice requiring the production of the documents.[96] The other provided for stop and search powers, along the lines of the UK powers, but far more circumscribed in relation to the areas in which they could be exercised.[97] Witnesses before the Senate committee that considered the bill were almost unanimously opposed to the amendments, but the committee recommended its passage subject to minor amendments, including a sunset clause expiring in 5 years rather than 10. The government declined to follow this recommendation. The surveillance measures were passed without further amendment and with little debate, the surveillance issues being overshadowed by far more controversial features of the bill.

General developments in Australia's surveillance law were largely uninfluenced by terrorism-related concerns. Debates, Senate reports, and government papers make no more than occasional, oblique references to terrorism. ASIO's surveillance powers remained almost unchanged during the post-9/11 years.

Canada's post-9/11 legislation amended the requirements for communications interception so that if there was a terrorist offence, the "last resort" requirement did not have to be satisfied, and the target did not have to be notified of the existence of the interception. Further, the target of an interception authorisation did not have to be informed within 90 days of the giving of the authorisation.[98] Potentially more important were provisions for the compulsory questioning of people believed to have information about past or future terrorism offences. Unusually, this legislation was subject to a sunset clause, and expired after the Parliament failed to pass a resolution extending its operation. It was revived in 2013. Otherwise, Canadian surveillance legislation has remained largely unchanged, and there have been no relevant changes to the surveillance powers of the Canadian Security Intelligence Service.

In 2003, New Zealand followed Canada in making special provision for interception of communications in terrorism cases, but the difference between terrorism cases and other cases was negligible.[99] Following a Supreme Court decision[100] whose practical effect was that police lacked the power to gather video evidence except when surveillance was from a public place, the government introduced legislation to validate the use of covert video surveillance from outside an area under surveillance or in conjunction with an authorized search. The legislation applied retrospectively but not to the successful Supreme Court appellants. Its purpose was not to assist the prosecution of suspected terrorists (although it has arisen in a "terrorism" case) but to foreclose the collapse of other pending trials.[101] The following year saw the passage of the comprehensive Search and Surveillance Act 2012, in which the minimal distinction between terrorism surveillance and other forms of surveillance disappeared. Terrorism concerns appear to have been irrelevant to the formulation of the new legislation.[102]

One reason for the different responses of the United States and the other four countries may lie in the particular intensity of the fears and passions unleashed in the United States by the 9/11 attacks, but another may be the many respects in which the other four governments already enjoyed powers conferred by the Patriot Act amendments. Even after the FISA amendments, the FBI's intelligence-gathering powers are narrower in some respects than those of the other countries' security services. In general they are available only for investigations of international terrorism, although this limitation has proved of only limited importance. Many of the FISA powers require judicial approval, whereas security service powers in the United Kingdom and Australia are conditioned on ministerial approval. The new powers to communicate foreign intelligence information to people involved in law enforcement were no greater than those enjoyed by security services elsewhere (although intercept information continues to be unavailable in the United Kingdom as evidence in trials). The controversial power to gain access to business records was already enjoyed by the security services. That said, there are some respects in which US surveillance powers are broader than surveillance powers elsewhere. Unlike the United States, Canada and New Zealand require approval from a judge or retired judge for demands for transaction data in security-sensitive cases, and the United States roving warrant provisions are more generous than the equivalent Australian provisions.

Governments and Surveillance

Surveillance legislation usually involves legislative resistance to proposals to expand government powers, and there appear to be no examples of legislatures conferring greater surveillance powers on the government than the government had sought. Even when voting for the passage of the Patriot Act, legislators were worried about government abuses and cited the well-documented examples of law enforcement agencies' willingness to act with little regard for both law and political proprieties.[103] The United States is not, of course, unique. It was almost an open secret that Australia's largest state police force engaged in phone tapping for more than a decade when it had no authority to do so under the law.[104] The Canadian royal commission investigating the surveillance activities of the Royal Canadian Mounted Police pointed to a long history of improper and illegal surveillance.[105]

The frequency of these forms of deviance is testimony to the avidity with which police and intelligence agencies pursue the acquisition of information. The past is not necessarily a guide to the present. Enhanced surveillance powers may reduce the perceived attractions of deviance. Organisational cultures may change in response to the difficulties of getting away with unlawful surveillance. But intelligence agencies and police continue to press the limits of their legal powers and sometimes still exceed them.

United States

In the United States, there is evidence that the executive has made increasing use of its powers. Despite their expanded powers, officials have engaged in surveillance without complying with prescribed pre-conditions for doing so, but bureaucratic and legal imperatives have set some limits to the level of surveillance.

Use of Powers

The United States provides information about the use of national security letters, the number of applications for FISA interception and/or search warrants, and the number of applications for orders for the production of records and tangible things. These statistics indicate that the use of NSLs has tended to increase since 2001, that there was a steady increase in FISA warrants up to 2007, and that applications for orders for records have been infrequent but sharply increased to 96 in 2010. On the whole, published statistics are unhelpful. They indicate that the likelihood of a randomly selected American being subject to these forms of surveillance is small (about 1 in 20,000 in relation to NSLs), but they leave open the question that matters: whether and to what extent the surveillance provided useful information.[106] Use of roving wiretaps has also been limited. By March 2009, they had only been approved on 147 occasions, but on only one of these occasions does their use seem to have disrupted a terrorist plot.[107]

Exigent Letters

The criteria for issuing national security letters are considerably more relaxed than those relating to the access to content. But between 2002 and 2006, FBI agents in the Communications Analysis Unit (CAU) and (to a lesser extent) the New York Field Division regularly bypassed the statutory requirements, along with guidelines governing requests for call data. A widespread practice involved the use of "exigent letters," requesting call information and stating that formal process would be served subsequently: at least 798 such letters were issued between 2003 and 2006, 722 from the CAU.[108] Investigations by the Department of Justice's Office of the Inspector General found numerous irregularities surrounding this practice. These included the absence of exigent circumstances, the lack of a statutory basis for such letters, their use by people who lacked the power to issue NSLs, their use to gather information for purposes other than national security purposes, failures on behalf of those issuing them to specify time limits to the information sought and to set in motion procedures for ensuring that NSLs would ultimately issue, and failure to monitor their use.[109] Letters were also used to obtain information about subsequent use of communications services.[110] Representatives of the phone companies sometimes prepared NSLs for the FBI.[111]

There was also evidence of exigent letters being issued in the context of the investigation of leaks, requesting call data relating to journalists' phones, without regard to whether this was consistent with the express statutory prohibition on the issue of NSLs in relation to activities protected by the First Amendment and in contravention of the procedures prescribed by regulation.[112] The inspector general also found evidence of informal requests for information by e-mail, phone, and face-to-face communication.[113] A review of a small sample of FISA requests found a number of instances where officials swore that relevant call data had been obtained by NSL when this had not been the case.[114]

Those who signed the letters generally seem to have assumed that the procedure was lawful, guiding their practice by unit folklore and advice from the phone companies rather than by reference to law or to manuals embodying the law. When signatories did express concern, they were assured that "lawyers" had approved the letters. Senior officials were either unaware of the practices or assumed that they were lawful. Service providers were remarkably cooperative, often (but not invariably) taking FBI emergency claims on trust.[115] Even lawyers for the National Security Law Branch (NSLB) seemed unconcerned that exigent letters might be unlawful. They were aware of and concerned about increasing delays in the process of issuing the NSLs promised in exigent letters, but they seem not to have realised that NSLs could not confer retrospective validity on exigent letters. By 2004, doubts were increasing. The NSLB assistant general counsel (AGC) considered that emergency letters might be issued only for periods of up to 48 hours and that applications for subsequent NSLs should not be written to conceal the existence of the prior letters. Despite being aware of these problems, the deputy general counsel continued to apply for NSLs months after the relevant exigent letters and without making reference to their existence.[116]

The NSLB's assumption that there was a power to issue exigent letters was not based on the text of the statute. The AGC's analysis was that "the FBI had 'tried to reconcile the literal interpretation . . . with lots of other policy considerations' that the FBI needs to deal with when 'lots of lives are at stake.'"[117] As late as May 2005, the AGC had not actually seen a copy of an exigent letter.[118] Moreover, given express statutory provision for emergency requests for the provision of data, the assumption underpinning exigent letters seems implausible (and the inspector general found it to be).

Further, in response to providers' concerns about the delay in providing promised NSLs, the CAU issued a series of blanket NSLs. Not only could these not operate retrospectively, but they also failed to meet several of the statutory requirements for NSLs. Some related to crime as well as national security interception. None mentioned that the details had been sought and provided. Most did not include the certification required when NSLs included a confidentiality requirement.[119]

President's Surveillance Program

Unlike some questionable surveillance programs, the President's Surveillance Program (PSP) was conducted with the knowledge and authority of the president. The program was first authorised shortly after the 9/11 attacks, for a period of 45 days, and was subsequently extended by further 45-day extensions.[120] From 25 October 2001, briefings on the program were given to congressional leaders and their staff[121] and to two members of the FISC.[122] Its full scope is still partly classified. One of its elements was the Terrorist Surveillance Program (TSP). Under the program, the National Security Agency (NSA) was purportedly empowered to "intercept the international communications of people with known links to Al Qaeda and related terrorist organizations." Interception was conditional on at least one party to the communication being outside the United States and on at least one party being associated with al-Qaeda or a member of an affiliated organisation. Surveillance took place on a massive scale. Up to 500 phone conversations were simultaneously monitored, and spying extended to millions of Americans' phone calls and e-mails.[123] Its operation was dependent on the voluntary cooperation of telecommunications companies.[124] The TSP was supplemented by "other intelligence activities," details of which remain classified.[125]

Until 2004, the Office of Legal Counsel (OLC) of the Department of Justice (DOJ) advised as to the legality of each successive authorisation, and the attorney general certified as to the legality of the program.[126] Certification required grounds for reconciling the program with the language of FISA. John Yoo, deputy assistant attorney general and the only OLC official read into the program, rose to the challenge, arguing that FISA was to be read as not applying to emergency surveillance and that insofar as FISA purported to do so, it represented an unconstitutional infringement of the president's Article II powers. The only limit on these powers was the Fourth Amendment, and insofar as it was applicable, it required no more than that the surveillance be reasonable. In the circumstances, this requirement was satisfied.[127] In 2003, Yoo resigned, and two other DOJ officials (Patrick Philbin and Jack Goldsmith) were read into the program. They were concerned about flaws in Yoo's analysis, and the deputy attorney general, James Comey (who was also read into the program), agreed. The White House counsel, Alberto Gonzales, disagreed and argued that thousands of lives would be at risk if the program was not recertified. Conflict between the DOJ and the White House culminated in an episode one might expect in a political thriller, the two sides descending on the hospital where the attorney general, John Ashcroft, was recovering from surgery. The White House representatives tried to persuade the ailing Ashcroft to sign the reauthorisation. He refused, citing his reservations and then adding that his views did not matter, since his powers currently lay with his deputy.[128] The solution was a reauthorisation certified by the White House counsel, which the DOJ interpreted as being binding on the entire executive branch, notwithstanding that it was based on a flawed analysis of the law. The White House continued to insist that the law was on its side, but it dropped some of the activities that the DOJ had found to be unlawful.[129]

Surprisingly, the existence of the program was kept relatively secret until about 2005, and the last authorisation expired on 1 February, following a successful application by the government to the FISC for a warrant authorising surveillance of communications of the type authorised under the TSP but subject to the FISA minimisation requirements.[130] Two issues were left to Congress to resolve: (1) whether there should be any protection against legal liability for corporations that had cooperated with the program and (2) the circumstances in which the government might be permitted to intercept communications when the interception took place outside the United States or involved a non-US person as a target.

The initial congressional response was the Protect America Act of 2007.[131] The act amended FISA by excluding surveillance from the definition of "electronic surveillance" if it was "directed at a person reasonably believed to be located outside the United States."[132] This meant that such surveillance was permitted. It also provided a mechanism whereby the government could acquire foreign intelligence information from others who might have access to it.[133] The price for its passage was an extremely short sunset period, on whose passage the legislation lapsed. It was followed by the FISA Amendments Act of 2008,[134] passed with the support of Republicans and a minority of Blue Dog Democrats.[135] This legislation subjected electronic surveillance targeting people outside the United States to a regime subject to FISC supervision. It also made it clear that surveillance was permitted only insofar as it was permitted under FISA or some other statute.[136] The FISA Amendments Act also protected the telecommunications providers from civil liability and state inquiries arising from their cooperation with the government.[137]

United Kingdom, Canada, Australia, and New Zealand

Elsewhere, executive deviance seems to have been more restrained. However, the United Kingdom's use of stop and search powers provides evidence that counterterror powers can be misused or, alternatively, that the purported exercise of those powers is sometimes for improper and therefore unlawful purposes. The stop and search powers were meant to be used in relation to suspected terrorism. By 2010, there was evidence that the power was being used other than for its intended purposes. The areas approved as areas in which people might be stopped included areas where there was no reason to believe that stopping people could serve a counterterrorism purpose. People were sometimes being stopped not for investigative purposes but to produce statistics consistent with nondiscriminatory law enforcement. The annual incidence stoppages in London had increased to 185,086 by 2008–9. While exercise of the power had yielded evidence to ground a small number of convictions for nonterrorism offences and a small number of arrests for terrorism, no terrorism conviction had ever resulted from an exercise of the power. In 2009–10, far fewer people were stopped (80,309 in London), and only 0.5 percent of stops resulted in arrests, none of which were for terrorism offences.[138]

Reports by the interception of communications commissioner provide no information about the number of security-related warrants and only limited details of irregularities relating to security service warrants.[139] They give details of errors reported to the commissioner, which all appear to have involved human error rather than deliberate abuse. They include assurances that inspections of security-related warrants indicate that the agencies have been complying with the act and the code of practice. Reports of the intelligence services commissioner suggest satisfaction with the performance of the secretaries. "Outright and final refusal of [applications] is comparatively rare," according to one report, but senior officials sometimes seek amendments, and the secretaries sometimes require further additional information.[140]

Reports by the Australian inspector-general of intelligence yield similar results. The inspector-general aims to review all warrant requests on their merits, as well as for formal compliance, and to check files to ensure that interception takes place only pursuant to warrant. Annual reports have been positive, although reports mention an average of three cases per year where fault or error led to unlawful interception and a somewhat greater number where there was the unrealised potential for such interception.[141] As in the United Kingdom, these typically involved mistranscriptions and phone numbers that had been reassigned to a person of no security interest, but there were two cases where action purportedly based on a warrant was initiated before the attorney-general had actually signed the warrant.[142] There were no reported cases of deliberate unlawful surveillance. Annual reports from New Zealand's inspector-general give details of the number of warrants issued each year (about 20). They report no irregularities. However, New Zealand's High Court and Supreme Court found that video surveillance of the training camps of suspected domestic terrorists had been unlawful.

Institutional Proclivities: Courts

United States

Underlying the PSP was mistrust of the courts, including the FISC. Jack Goldsmith quotes David Addington, the vice president's counsel, as saying, "We're one bomb away from getting rid of that obnoxious court,"[143] and the reluctance to try to put the PSP on a sound legal foundation reflected this suspicion. However, on the whole, courts have placed few obstacles in the path of government surveillance. FISA applications have almost invariably succeeded. Only about one in a thousand is denied, although FISC made substantive alterations to proposed orders in about 4 percent of cases between 2003 and 2010.[144] Published statistics do not reveal whether judges (or retired judges) in Canada and New Zealand are as cooperative, but statistics relating to criminal justice warrants and approvals suggest a similarly high success rate. Applications for law enforcement warrants succeed in more than 99 percent of cases. Challenges to the legality of surveillance have had some, limited success. In the United States, a long series of Supreme Court decisions had already limited the scope of Fourth Amendment protections,[145] and the Fourth Amendment made little impact on the outcome of post-2001 terrorism surveillance cases.

The Constitutionality of FISA

Challenges to the constitutionality of the FISA legislation have been numerous and, with one arguable exception, unsuccessful. Indeed, prior to the enactment of FISA, there was considerable authority to the effect that the president had inherent (but not unlimited) power to conduct warrantless surveillance for foreign intelligence purposes in certain circumstances.[146] Moreover, while the Supreme Court has not yet pronounced on the validity of the legislation, it has accepted that even if surveillance legislation did not require a warrant on probable cause, "standards may be compatible with the Fourth Amendment if they are reasonable both in relation to the legitimate need of government for intelligence information and the protected rights of our citizens."[147] This observation underlay rulings that FISA, as enacted, was constitutionally valid even if FISA warrants fell short of Fourth Amendment warrant requirements. However, these decisions left open the question of whether the 2001 amendments to FISA were constitutional.

In March 2002, the attorney general approved new "intelligence sharing procedures," following the Patriot Act amendments to FISA, and filed a motion with the FISC seeking an order that it vacate pre-2001 orders in which it had adopted more-demanding minimisation procedures. In May 2002, the presiding judge of the FISC ordered that the new procedures be adopted, with modifications, to apply as minimisation procedures operating in all cases. These precluded law enforcement officials giving recommendations to intelligence officials in relation to FISA searches or surveillance, and the requirement that the FBI and the Criminal Division of the Department of Justice take steps to ensure this. The decision was reissued following argument before all the members then serving on the court. The government then appealed to the Foreign Intelligence Surveillance Court of Review, which allowed the appeal.

In *In re Sealed Case No* 02–001, the court of review held, first, that the FISC's decision had been based on a misconception that there was a dichotomy between law enforcement and intelligence gathering. Information was to be gathered as a means to an end, the protection of US interests, and this end might sometimes be one best achieved by a criminal prosecution.[148] The court found, second, that the conditions imposed by the FISC did not answer the description of minimisation procedures. These were intended to minimise the misuse of information that was not "foreign intelligence information." Since the legislation permitted the retention of information that was not foreign intelligence information if it was evidence of ordinary crimes, using it for this purpose did not constitute misuse. Moreover, the FISC had erred by failing to take account of the implications of the Patriot Act amendments.[149]

The court of review considered that the Patriot Act amendment implied the existence of the very dichotomy that the court had found not to exist under FISA as enacted. But the court interpreted the amended legislation as allowing the use of FISA powers to gain foreign intelligence information except where the sole purpose for doing so was criminal prosecution. This qualification would rarely matter: when the government "commences an electronic surveillance of a foreign agent, typically it will not have decided whether to prosecute the agent (whatever might be the subjective intent of the investigators or lawyers who initiate an investigation)."[150]

Recognising that the broad interpretation of the surveillance powers raised serious questions as to their validity, the court considered two questions: whether the orders constituted warrants for the purposes of the Fourth Amendment and, if not, whether they satisfied the "reasonableness requirement." The court concluded that FISA orders might not be warrants as contemplated by the Fourth Amendment. The probable cause requirement was weaker than for law enforcement warrants, as were important aspects of the particularity requirements. But, it was relevant to satisfaction of the reasonableness requirement that the legislation came close to satisfying the warrant requirement. Also relevant were the public interests at stake, a consideration recognised by the Supreme Court in *United States v United States District Court (Keith).*

The court recognised that there was a Fourth Circuit authority in *United States v Truong Dinh Hung*, to the effect that nothing less than a "primary purpose" requirement could be "reasonable" for Fourth Amendment purposes.[151] *Truong* related to pre-FISA law but had implications for the validity of FISA. The court of review concluded that *Truong* was based on untenable assumptions. The artificial distinctions that it drew generated "dangerous confusion" and created "perverse organisational incentives."[152] It created walls where "effective counterintelligence, we have learned, requires the wholehearted cooperation of all the government's personnel who can be brought to the task."[153] The Supreme Court had approved "apparently warrantless and even suspicionless searches that are designed to serve the government's 'special needs, beyond the normal need for law enforcementn'"[154] The court of review emphasised that the threat facing America could not be forgotten: "After the events of September 11, 2001, though, it is hard to imagine greater emergencies facing Americans than those experienced on that date"; "Our case may well involve the most serious threat our country faces."[155]

Subsequent decisions have almost invariably followed *Sealed Case.* While courts have sometimes preferred to deal with admissibility issues by finding that FISA evidence would have satisfied the "primary purpose" test, their language suggests that they have done so out of caution rather than out of doubts as to whether FISA, as amended, can survive constitutional scrutiny.[156] Others have made positive findings to the effect that the legislation is valid, sometimes in conjunction with findings that the evidence satisfied the "primary purpose" test,[157] but sometimes not.[158]

The one exception is a 2007 decision, *Mayfield v United States*,[159] where Judge Ann Aicken held that the legislation was unconstitutional. According to Aicken's interpretation, the legislation meant that law enforcers could bypass the more rigorous standards that traditionally governed warrants for law enforcement purposes—namely, the requirements of probable cause, notice, specificity, and short duration. Aicken ruled that the *Sealed Case* decision had not been informed by arguments from those affected by the surveillance and was wrong.[160]

The government succeeded on appeal, on the grounds that the plaintiffs lacked standing to raise the constitutionality issue. (The plaintiffs had settled all claims in the action except for the claim for declaratory relief.) This meant that it did not have to address the constitutionality issue.[161] However, the district court's reasoning on the constitutional issue has failed to commend itself to subsequent courts.[162]

National Security Letters

In 2004 and 2005, two district courts held that the legislation governing national security letters was flawed, but not because of Fourth Amendment difficulties. The problem lay in provisions precluding the recipient from disclosing receipt of a "request" to produce. One court held that the legislation was unconstitutional on two grounds: it violated the First Amendment, and the lack of provision for judicial review violated the constitutionally prescribed separation of powers.[163] The other based its decisions solely on First Amendment grounds.[164] The New York District Court held further that section 2709(c) could not be severed from the rest of section 2709. There was therefore no authority for the issuing of NSLs. Before the hearing of government appeals, Congress amended the legislation to remove the blanket ban on disclosure and to provide a rudimentary form of judicial review of nondisclosure orders. In light of this, the court of appeals remanded the case to the district court for reconsideration.[165] While the case was pending, the government withdrew the NSLs, which meant that the only issue before the court related to the validity of the nondisclosure requirement. The district court held that the amendments were not sufficient to save section 2709(c) and that if section 2709(c) could not be saved, the rest of the section had to fall with it.[166] The court of appeals substantially agreed with the district court but concluded that sections 2709(c) and 3511(b) (the judicial review section) could be construed so as to save them from unconstitutionality. So construed, the legislation did not violate the Constitution, nor did partial invalidation of the two sections affect the validity of the remainder of section 2709.[167] The court of appeals remanded the matter for further consideration. In the subsequent litigation, the district court found that the government (which was required to initiate a judicial review application) had made out its case.[168]

The Terrorist Surveillance Program

Revelations about the existence of the Terrorist Surveillance Program provoked a mass of litigation. Despite the general consensus that the TSP was unconstitutional, plaintiffs rarely succeeded, falling victim to a variety of legal hurdles and, ultimately, to legislation aimed at defeating their claims. A challenge to the legality of the TSP by the ACLU and other plaintiffs who claimed to have been injured by the program met with initial procedural and substantive success,[169] but on appeal, the circuit court reversed on procedural grounds.[170] To succeed, the plaintiffs had to be in a position to prove they had standing to sue. The majority held that it was not enough to assert that fears of surveillance meant that the plaintiffs' capacity to perform their various duties was impaired and complicated. They had to prove that the fears were justified, and this would require proof that their communications had been intercepted. Discovery would not assist: the information they needed would constitute a state secret, and state secrets are immune from discovery.

Judge Gibbons dissented, concluding that the plaintiffs had demonstrated harm. The existence of the TSP (which had been acknowledged by the president) meant that the plaintiff's professional obligations precluded them from doing things they otherwise would have done. It also meant that in order for the plaintiffs to perform their professional duties, they would have to use far less convenient means of communication with their clients. This problem would not arise if surveillance were to take place under FISA. In that situation, their professional communications would be protected, so they could freely communicate with their clients, knowing that these communications would be privileged. The Supreme Court denied certiorari.[171]

A claim by the Al-Haramain Islamic Foundation was more successful. Unlike the ACLU, the foundation knew that it had been the victim of warrantless surveillance, having accidentally been shown a document evidencing this, but the court of appeals held that the state secrets doctrine would nonetheless defeat its claim insofar as it was grounded on violation of constitutional rights. It held, however, that a claim for relief under FISA might be capable of being sustained.[172] On remand and after considerable interlocutory skirmishing, the district court held that the state secrets doctrine did not apply to FISA claims, and the plaintiff's claim was made out. But the court of appeals reversed an award of damages and costs against the United States, finding that the relevant FISA provision (50 USC § 1810) did not constitute a waiver of sovereign immunity in relation to claims for damages.[173]

A large number of cases involved challenges by customers to the cooperation of electronic communications providers.[174] Plaintiffs had some procedural successes. In *Hepting v AT&T*,[175] the district court dismissed motions for summary judgment based on state secrets privilege, lack of standing, and absolute and implied immunity. The plaintiffs' status as customers in contractual relations with the companies satisfied the standing requirement. Given what was known about the TSP, it was not clear that the case would turn on matters that constituted state secrets. For these reasons, summary dismissal was inappropriate. It doubted whether common-law immunity survived FISA, and it also concluded that if the plaintiffs' allegations were proved, the factual basis for reliance on the immunities would be unavailable. Following *Hepting*, the Judicial Panel on Multidistrict Litigation made an order that all cases arising from the NSA's alleged wiretapping be transferred to the Northern District of California and consolidated before Judge Vaughn Walker, who subsequently made orders consolidating the cases against the telecommunications companies, where they were handled under the name *In re National Security Agency Telecommunications Records Litigation*.

A further body of litigation related to attempts by state officials in Maine, New Jersey, Connecticut, Vermont, and Missouri to investigate the role of telephone companies in the TPS. Predictably, these activities provoked the telephone companies and the US government to sue, claiming that the states lacked the relevant powers. These proceedings were also consolidated and transferred to the Northern District of California, where the district court denied the government's motions to dismiss.[176]

At this point, the litigation was complicated by the 2008 passage of the FISA Amendments Act (FISAAA). Section 803 of the FISAAA effectively precluded action by the states in relation to electronic communication service providers' "alleged assistance to an element of the intelligence community," and it applied both prospectively and in relation to pending proceedings. On the basis of this provision, the United States moved for summary judgment in the six telecommunications cases. Arguing that the legislation represented an impermissible encroachment on state powers, the states resisted summary judgment, on the basis that some aspects of their inquiries fell outside the section. The district court disagreed, concluding that the legislation did not commandeer the participation of state officials in a federal scheme: it prohibited their participation. The court stated, "Because intelligence activities in furtherance of national security goals are primarily the province of the federal government, Congressional action preempting state activities in this context is especially uncontroversial from the standpoint of federalism."[177]

The legislation also purportedly barred the existing private suits against the communication companies. This led to a further application from the US government and the telecommunications companies for dismissal of the dozens of cases in which the companies had been sued. The plaintiffs challenged the constitutionality of the legislation on the grounds of separation of powers, arguing that it involved congressional usurpation of the judicial role, in that it made the political branches ultimate arbiters of the requirements of the First and Fourth Amendments, impermissibly required the judiciary to decide pending cases in a particular way, and violated the nondelegation principle. The court rejected these arguments.

Constitutional arguments based on the Fifth, First, and Fourth Amendments failed. Creating new immunities does not violate the right to due process. Nor did the special secrecy provisions: there was considerable authority to support the use of ex parte in camera procedures in cases having national security implications. First Amendment rights were not at stake: cases suggesting that there is a First Amendment presumptive right of access to criminal trials are inapplicable in relation to trials involving classified information, and the procedures prescribed by section 802 sufficed to ensure that it did not offend the Constitution.

Following the legislation, but before these judgments, most of the 150 plaintiffs in one of the multidistrict litigation cases, *Anderson v Verizon*, commenced a new case, *McMurray v Verizon*.[178] The District Court of the Northern District of California also dismissed this case. The jurisdictional prerequisites for an action based on the takings clause had not been established, and in any case, no property had been taken: "no property right vests in a cause of action until a final, unreviewable judgment is obtained." Nor did the legislation fall foul of separation of powers or the Fifth Amendment due process clause.[179]

These judgments did not dispose of cases in which the US government and its officials had been sued. One of these had been filed by plaintiffs in *Hepting v AT&T*, which had been remanded by the Ninth Circuit for reconsideration in light of the legislation. Apparently in response to recognition of the hopelessness of their case against AT&T, four of the plaintiffs had filed a fresh claim, this time against the NSA. In January 2010, the district court granted a government motion for summary judgment in this and another NSA case. It found that the plaintiffs lacked standing. In the earlier *Hepting* case, the plaintiffs had standing by virtue of their injury and their contractual relations with AT&T. In the actions against NSA, the plaintiffs were seeking redress for alleged government misfeasance. The parties lacked a sufficient personal stake in the subject matter of the litigation. That they used telecommunications and were broadband Internet subscribers did not distinguish them from Americans in general, since the vast majority of US households had such connections. The court advised that standing was to be approached with particular care when constitutional issues were at stake, especially when

> the constitutional issues at stake in the litigation seek judicial involvement in the affairs of the executive branch and national security concerns appear to undergird the challenged actions. In such cases, only plaintiffs with strong and persuasive claims to Article III standing may proceed.[180]

Amnesty International, civil liberties organisations, media organisations, lawyers, and scholars also challenged section 702 of FISAAA as facially unconstitutional. In the district court, the government succeeded on an application for summary judgment, based on the plaintiffs' lack of standing.[181] The plaintiffs' appeal succeeded, and a motion to have the matter heard en banc failed, by majority.[182] The court of appeals distinguished *American Civil Liberties Union v National Security Agency*, finding that the FISAAA authorised much more than the TSP. *ACLU* was not binding (it applied to a different circuit) and was based on a questionable reading of Supreme Court authority. The Supreme Court disagreed. By majority (five Republican appointees against four Democrat appointees), the Court found that the plaintiffs lacked standing. Threatened injury could ground standing only if it was "certainly impending." There was no evidence that the plaintiffs' communications were being intercepted, nor was there reason to believe that interception was impending, and even if interception were to occur there was no reason to believe that it would be pursuant to § 1881a. Expenses incurred for the purposes of avoiding interception cannot ground standing when the interception has not been shown to be certainly impending, nor when there was a similar incentive to take the precautions under pre-existing legislation. The minority concluded that the plaintiffs' fears were well-founded, and past government practices lent them added credibility. The court had not always insisted that harm be "certainly impending," and applied rigorously, the requirement would be unreasonable. The constitutional standing requirement was closer to a "reasonable" or "high" probability of harm.[183] But even if the plaintiffs had won on the standing issue, their victory might have be Pyrrhic: in rejecting a defendants' Circuit Court application for an en banc hearing, Judge Lynch warned, "[T]here are strong grounds arguments against the plaintiffs' position on the merits."[184]

Stops and Searches

Drawing on nonterrorism precedents, courts have also upheld the use of general and "random" stops and searches at airports, subway stations, and ferry terminals as a counterterror measure, concluding that the relevant programs serve a "special need" and are proportionate, given privacy expectations, the fact that the person could avoid being searched by opting not to use the relevant form of transport, the brevity of the searches, and the preventive and deterrent functions served by such searches.[185] In determining whether the searches serve the legitimate government purpose, considerable deference is given to the government's assessment, and the fact that random searches are less likely to be effective than general searches is immaterial, since random searches also involve less intrusion on privacy interests.[186]

United Kingdom

The only terrorism-related challenge to UK surveillance law involved the stop and search powers under the Regulation of Investigatory Powers Act 2000 (RIPA).[187] A demonstrator and a journalist who were stopped and detained near an "arms fair" challenged the legality of the searches, arguing that the searches were not authorised by the act, that the powers had not been exercised for the purposes of the act, and that the authorisations and the searches were contrary to Articles 5, 8, 9, 10, and 11 of the ECHR. Their argument failed at first instance,[188] in the court of appeal,[189] and before the House of Lords.[190] Moreover, the 10 judges who considered the case were unanimous in concluding against the applicants, who then appealed to the ECtHR, which unanimously held that their Article 8 (privacy) rights had been impermissibly violated.[191]

The House of Lords had obvious reservations about the power but considered that it had a legitimate purpose, "to ensure that a constable is not deterred from stopping and searching a person whom he does suspect as a potential terrorist by the fear that he could not show reasonable ground for his suspicion."[192] The ECtHR agreed that the searches were within the powers conferred by the legislation, but the court found that the exercise of the powers constituted a breach of Article 8: "[T]he use of the coercive powers conferred by the legislation to require an individual to submit to a detailed search of his person, his clothing and his personal belongings amounts to a clear interference with the right to respect for private life."[193] Such searches could therefore be justified only if they were in accordance with the law, pursued a legitimate aim, and were necessary in a democratic society. Since the exercise of the power was largely unconstrained, the legislation failed this test.

One of the ironies of the case lies in the weight that several of the Law Lords attached to the role of intuition.[194] If, as was accepted, police did indeed have a sixth sense for terrorists, there would be much to be said for giving police an unreviewable power to stop terrorists. But the exercise of the stop and search powers put the "hunch" hypothesis to the test. Between 2001–2 and 2008–9, there were more than 540,000 stops in England and Wales under the power. Only 0.9 percent resulted in arrests, and only 0.05 percent resulted in arrests for terrorism offences. None resulted in a conviction for a terrorism offence.[195]

In a challenge to the adequacy of the protections afforded by RIPA to people who claimed to be victims of unlawful surveillance, the ECtHR held that the procedures satisfied the requirements of the ECHR. That the procedures provided for closed hearings by the Investigatory Powers Tribunal was not inconsistent with the convention: it was a proportionate measure, given countervailing security interests.[196]

New Zealand

New Zealand's only "terrorism" prosecutions were prosecuted not as terrorism offences but as firearms and criminal organisation offences. Among the issues to which they gave rise was the question of whether the fruits of covert video surveillance evidence were admissible. The High Court ruled that the evidence was improperly obtained but admissible. The court of appeal ruled that video surveillance could be justified as an extended use of the powers conferred by search warrants.[197] The Supreme Court disagreed: given the relevant legislation, search warrants could not authorise video recording, and the warrants had not purported to authorise it. Nor did the police have any other authority to enter onto the land where they had installed the cameras. Moreover, the Bill of Rights Act prohibited unreasonable searches; the term *search* (in this context) extended to surveillance; and in the absence of authorisation, surveillance was, in the circumstances, unreasonable.

While the Supreme Court had no doubt as to the illegality of the surveillance, it was not unsympathetic to the police. Justice Blanchard recognized that the legal position may not have been altogether clear, but he considered that given the uncertainty, the police should have sought legal advice (but didn't). Blanchard did recognise that the police were caught in a bind.

> They lacked any ability to obtain a warrant for video surveillance because the law did not provide for it, and understandably believed that they could not approach landowners for consent to enter lest the participants in the camps be alerted, and that in person surveillance could endanger members of the police when live rounds were being fired.[198]

In exercising its discretion under section 30 of the Evidence Act 2006 in relation to whether the surveillance evidence might be admitted, the Supreme Court concluded (3–1) that the balance favoured admission in the cases of those charged with serious "criminal organisation" offences but not in the case of those charged only with firearms offences.

In Short

Despite constitutional and quasi-constitutional protections from search and seizure and from invasion of privacy, courts have done little to interfere with government surveillance. The decision in *Gillan v the United Kingdom* is the only authoritative post-9/11 decision to have found surveillance legislation incompatible with Fourth Amendment or privacy rights. In relation to surveillance, courts seem to share some of the nervousness that underpinned the USA Patriot Act, although they have also expressed some of the concerns of its critics. The English courts' decisions in the *Gillan* litigation and the ECtHR's decision in *Kennedy v United Kingdom* display similar deference, which contrasts with a much more assertive stance in other areas of counterterror law. But the deference is not surprising. Privacy carries less weight than freedom from detention.

US courts have been slightly less deferential in relation to executive decisions. In cases challenging the validity of aspects of the TSP, cases that turned on substance resulted in defeats for the government, whereas cases turning on procedure almost invariably went in favour of the government. Most of the cases turned on procedure, and Addington seems to have underestimated the degree to which the law can frustrate not only authoritarians but civil libertarians. New Zealand courts were a little more resistant to executive interests, but the Supreme Court's ruling did not preclude the use of the offending evidence in the cases where the stakes were highest.

Public Opinion: Restraint or Invitation to Opportunism?

Poll data should always be treated with caution, and there are particular reasons for being cautious about polls relating to surveillance. Haggerty and Gazso have argued that people who are particularly concerned about privacy are probably less likely to cooperate with pollsters and that, as a result, poll data may understate privacy concerns, especially where response rates are low.[199] Unfortunately, they do not provide evidence as to the extent of the problem, and reports on polls rarely include evidence of nonresponse rates.

An alternative problem emerges from a finding by Fletcher to the effect that responses to questions about surveillance are subject to assumptions about the conditions for their exercise. "Elites" are relatively supportive of surveillance, but this seems to be largely because their answers are given in the knowledge that powers are subject to judicial supervision.[200] This highlights an inescapable problem: the fact that answers depend on how respondents understand both the question and their answer. Interpreting poll data involves a degree of guesswork.

Nonetheless, post-9/11 polls suggest that the public was somewhat ambivalent towards government surveillance as a counterterrorist strategy and that post-9/11 legislation cannot easily be explained as a response (whether principled or opportunistic) to public receptivity to "tougher" surveillance laws. Polls conducted immediately following the attacks suggested that attitudes towards surveillance varied strongly with the question. Only a quarter of respondents favoured the government being allowed to monitor their personal phone calls and e-mails. Polls relating to surveillance of electronic communications in general typically yielded more disapproval than approval.[201] A poll conducted immediately after 9/11 indicated that a small majority (54 percent) approved of broader government powers to intercept phone calls and that only a bare majority (50 percent, with 5 percent undecided) favoured broader powers to intercept e-mail communications. Far more respondents (68 percent) approved a power to stop people "who fitted the profile of suspected terrorists." A poll conducted a week later yielded similar results. Evidence of ambivalence comes from a contemporaneous Harris poll: more than 70 percent of respondents reported high or moderate concern that increased powers would be associated with increased profiling, the interception of the communications of innocent people, and surveillance of nonviolent government critics; and two-thirds were worried that new powers would be used to investigate nonterrorism crimes.[202] Public concerns about the threat of terrorism do not seem to have been translated into sizeable support for stronger surveillance powers.

In subsequent Harris polls, between 70 and 80 percent of respondents have expressed continuing high or moderate concern about the adequacy of legislative, judicial, and executive supervision of surveillance programs and about the targeting of legitimate political and social groups. Two of these polls also found that 57 percent of respondents thought that law enforcement agencies were using their expanded powers in a proper way.[203]

Polls relating to the Patriot Act suggest that its surveillance provisions commanded majority support, coupled with opposition from a sizeable minority. In polls between 2003 and 2006, bare majorities considered that the act was a "good thing" for America; about a third considered it a "bad thing," and about a tenth volunteered that it was a mixture. Of those who had an opinion, most believed that the surveillance provisions of the act had helped prevent terrorist attacks in the United States, but 41 percent in 2005 and 33 percent in 2006 thought that it had not. Asked whether the provisions should be renewed, most respondents (57 percent) thought they should, but

31 percent opposed renewal. A differently worded question, which included minor change and major change as options, found that only 13 percent favoured no changes and that 50 percent favoured minor changes. Consistent with this is a 2005 poll suggesting that some surveillance provisions commanded far more support than others. There was a very high level of support for allowing the use of foreign intelligence information in domestic crime investigations (81 percent), majority support for government use of communications data (69 percent) and warrants for person-based phone tapping (62 percent), bare majority support for the business records regime insofar as it applied to libraries (53 percent), and opposition to warrantless access to bank records (43 percent support) and sneak and peek search warrants (23 percent support).[204]

In polls conducted following revelations of the TSP surveillance, opinion was evenly divided on the warrantless surveillance of "Americans suspected of terrorist ties," although differently worded questions yielded slightly different approval/disapproval distributions. Slight majorities doubted President Bush's authority to authorise the TSP. A majority thought that communication monitoring was very effective (15 percent) or somewhat effective (48 percent), and a majority were not at all concerned (43 percent) or not very concerned (22 percent) that their own communications might be monitored. Consistent with this lack of concern is a February 2006 finding that only 8 percent of poll respondents thought it likely and 13 percent thought it somewhat likely that their phone conversations had ever been wiretapped; in May 2006, the figures were 9 and 17 percent. Majorities were very concerned (29 percent) or somewhat concerned (33 percent) about losing civil liberties as a result of the administration's counterterrorism measures, but there was slightly less concern about the capacity of such measures to violate "people's privacy." Only 10 percent of poll respondents had a great deal of confidence in the government's capacity to identify correctly those whose phones should be tapped; 46 percent had a fair amount of confidence, and 42 percent had very little or no confidence.[205]

The impact of the TSP revelations on aggregate public opinion seems unclear. A Harris poll provided no evidence to suggest a decline in support for surveillance between June 2005 and February 2006 (indeed, the trend was in the opposite direction, albeit nonsignificantly). While majorities no longer favoured expanded powers to intercept communications, 82 percent favoured expanded undercover penetration of suspected groups; 67 percent, expanded camera surveillance; 64 percent, adoption of a national identification system; and 60 percent, monitoring of Internet discussions.[206] Other series of polls suggest continuing support for monitoring of those regarded by the government as suspicious, but they suggest widespread opposition to sharing data on communications or purchasing patterns with the government.[207]

Poll data relating to surveillance in the other countries is sparse, which probably reflects the limited salience of surveillance issues. In a 2004 UK survey, 69 percent approved police powers to stop and search anyone at any time.[208] Surveillance in public places commands widespread approval (generally more than 80 percent), except when it involves eavesdropping using high-powered microphones (commanding 9 percent approval).[209]

Fletcher's 1989 survey suggested that Canadians were particularly likely to say that the Canadian Security Intelligence Service should have wiretapping powers when the target was "suspected terrorists" rather than mere suspected subversives, support being high among the general public (66 percent) and even higher among a heterogeneous elite sample (81 percent).[210] There appears to be little recent poll data on the subject, apart from a tangentially relevant 2005 poll indicating that 72 percent of Canadians supported video cameras in public places.[211]

A 2007 Australian survey indicated that 39 percent of respondents thought police should definitely have the right to tap the phones of those they suspected of being terrorists, and 38 percent thought they should probably have the right. Only 8 percent thought they should definitely not have the right. There was, however, much less support for a police power to stop and search suspected terrorists in the street: 24 percent thought they should definitely have the right, and 31 percent thought that they should probably have it. Twenty percent thought they should definitely not have the right.[212]

The poll data suggests that there are few votes to be won by advocating stricter surveillance. The public tends to support surveillance of suspected terrorists and seems supportive of video cameras in public places, but it tends to oppose more-intrusive forms of surveillance, indiscriminately applied. At least in the United States, support for some forms of surveillance coexists with scepticism as to whether governments will target surveillance with acceptable precision. Willingness to sacrifice civil liberties does not extend to tolerating a significant risk of one's own private conversations being monitored. In this respect, there is little support for explanations of this area of law in terms of reluctant politicians responding to popular demands for repressive measures. Indeed, the political response is more consistent with public opinion constituting a constraint on repressive measures. Legislators have acted as if they were aware of this: "nongovernment" legislators seem to have never advocated and sometimes resisted greater surveillance powers than those being sought by the government. Taking a civil libertarian stance may sometimes be electorally expedient.

Partisanship and Surveillance

There are several guides to the role of political beliefs as a determinant of stances on surveillance law. One comes from roll call votes. These generally indicate that support for extended surveillance powers tends to come more from Republicans than from Democrats. The few members of Congress to vote against the Patriot Act were all Democrats, and party affiliation has been related to subsequent measures including extending sunset periods and the 2007 and 2008 amendments to FISA. The May 2011 measures involved a degree of leakage. In the House, the yeas included 196 Republicans and 54 Democrats; the nays, 31 Republicans and 122 Democrats. In the Senate, where support for extension was greater, the majority included 41 Republicans, 30 Democrats, and an Independent. The nays included 18 Democrats, 4 Republicans, and an Independent. These latter figures suggest that the impact of political dispositions is largely independent of whether the party supporting the measures is in government—at least in the United States.

Elsewhere, post-9/11 measures have impinged only marginally on liberty and privacy issues, but in Australia, where interception continues to be controversial, partisan positions tend to be related to the parties' rank along a right-left continuum, blurred slightly by the exigencies of being in power. It was, after all, a Labor government that tried to legislate to give ASIO the power to seek warrants for roving interception.

Congressional voting patterns are reflected in the correlates of public attitudes towards surveillance. The reported results for a *CBS News* poll tapping attitudes towards "Bush administration practices" reported an extremely strong relationship between party identification and beliefs about the legitimacy of the TSP. Eighty-three percent of Republicans, 42 percent of Independents, and 33 percent of Democrats approved, but that is what one might expect given the express reference to the Bush administration. A question asking whether the president should have the power to authorise the NSA to monitor communications yielded a similar (but slightly weaker) relationship: 79 percent of Republicans, 49 percent of Independents, and 35 percent of Democrats agreed.[213] Party bore a similar relationship to whether the NSA's analysis of phone call data constituted a necessary tool or went too far in invading privacy.[214] One (unlikely) explanation for this might be that Republicans and Democrats are, politically, two quite different species. Another is that in its selection of professed attitudes, the public relies heavily on cues given by spokespeople with whom they identify. Questions not framed in terms of the Bush administration's actions might have elicited a less-partisan set of responses.

An analysis of the effects of party identification after controls for perceived terrorism threat, authoritarianism (as measured by attitudes towards child rearing), ideology, and demographic variables indicated that party exerted an independent influence on support for warrantless wiretapping but that authoritarianism, ideology, and threat perceptions were also associated with support. It further indicated that among those who were worried about the personal threat posed by terrorism, authoritarianism was unrelated to support for wiretapping. (It did not examine whether this was the case for other predispositional measures.)[215]

In a 2007 Australian poll, the relationship between voting intention and attitudes towards surveillance seems to be weaker. Among Liberal (conservative) voters, 53 percent definitely believed that police should have the power to tap suspected terrorists' phones, and 34 percent thought that they should probably have the power. Among their National (rural) allies, the figures were 45 and 35 percent. There was less support from Labor voters (31 and 41 percent) and Greens (24 and 35 percent). The positions of supporters of other parties were consistent with their stance on the Australian left-right continuum, but only weakly. On the power to stop and search terrorism suspects in the street, Liberals were most supportive (33 percent), followed closely by Nationals (28 percent) and Labor voters (19 percent). Greens were considerably less supportive (10 percent).[216]Again, preferences of voters for other parties corresponded to their general dispositions. The differences are less pronounced than in the United States, probably because government surveillance had not been a major political issue.

Conclusions

While the USA Patriot Act has come to symbolise the evils of counterterrorism law, it is arguably a distraction. Critics of the act (including some of those who nonetheless voted for it) warned that its expanded surveillance powers were unconstitutional. Drawing on a supportive history, they feared abuses. However, even after the passage of the act, the government's powers in relation to domestic terrorism generally fell short of those of the other governments, and its powers in relation to international terrorism were generally more circumscribed. Moreover, later abuses involved not the misuse of powers but acting outside them, and courts have generally upheld the constitutionality of the Patriot Act provisions (except insofar as they purported to permit inadequately reviewable gag orders). Elsewhere, surveillance law has proved less controversial, although the history of the UK stop and search powers highlights both the potential for abuse and the fact that if vagueness were to doom laws to unconstitutionality, bills of rights would be the first casualty. Poll data suggest that the issue is one capable of provoking strong feelings that are based on limited knowledge. Academic disputes, parliamentary debates, and roll calls suggest that being relatively well informed does not resolve those differences. It is therefore not surprising that there is evidence to suggest that stances on the issue are partly bound up with political dispositions.

FIVE

Protecting Government Secrets While Protecting Due Process?

> People hide from government, and government hides from the people, and people and government have both good and bad reasons for hiding from each other.
>
> *Richard Posner*[1]

> [W]here secrecy reigns, we naturally suspect that unsavoury things go on in the shadows.
>
> *Thomas Poole*[2]

The obverse of government interest in others' secrets is a government interest in protecting its own secrets. Laws afford less protection to government secrets than they once did, but they still provide considerable protection for secrets with national security implications, and terrorism has generally been recognised as a threat to national security. Nonetheless, national security interests no longer trump all other interests, and to varying degrees, they must compete against conflicting public and private interests, particularly due process interests. Much of the relevant law predates recent terrorism concerns, but some of it reflects recent attempts by lawmakers to devise arrangements for accommodating the conflicting interests at play.

One area where these conflicts have proved inescapable has been in relation to judicial and quasi-judicial proceedings. The political arms have attempted to devise procedures that protect secrets while affording a degree of due process. Courts continue to recognise governments' interests in keeping secrets, but protecting secrecy normally comes at a price: governments may not normally base their case on evidence unless they are also prepared to disclose it to the opposing party. Moreover, if a secret could help exculpate a criminal defendant, the government may be required to choose between disclosure and discontinuing the prosecution. In US civil cases, the protection of state secrets tends to trump the interests of nonstate plaintiffs. If the success of a nonstate plaintiff requires the disclosure of a state secret, the court will not permit the case to proceed if either the government is unable to defend or the plaintiff is unable to prove its case other than by the disclosure of the secret. In the other four countries considered in this book, security interests are to be weighed against interests in fair trial, but a plaintiff's interest in being able to pursue a meritorious claim may sometimes mean that governments are required either to disclose the secret or to concede the plaintiff's case.

Terrorism concerns have inspired attempts to enhance protections for government secrets, but the relevant post-9/11 legislation has generally been unambitious. It has largely built on pre-9/11 precedents rather than seeking to overturn established principles, and it has aroused far less passion than attempts to enhance governments' surveillance powers. Courts have shown some deference to executive assessments of national security needs, especially in the United States. But deference has coexisted with unwillingness to accept legislative innovations whose effect is to threaten established due process rights, as well as a reluctance to accept government secrecy claims in the absence of evidence to sustain them. This is an area of law where courts tend to get their way, with constitutional norms to draw on and opportunities for executive deviance limited. Political differences have left a limited legacy, with the role of party being mediated by the exigencies of holding office.

Laws

Counterterror measures have generated a large volume of litigation, which typically requires that governments provide evidence to support their claims (when they want to take coercive action) and their defences (when plaintiffs contend that they are entitled to damages as a result of government misconduct). Fairness also dictates that if the government is in possession of evidence that would assist defendants or civil litigants, it should disclose it. This can pose problems for governments. Sometimes the problem is that the evidentiary basis for state action has been flimsy, and sometimes it is that the government does indeed possess information that undermines its case. But sometimes the disclosure of evidence may be objectionable on more-defensible grounds. Evidence may disclose the identity of informants and thereby imperil their security, undermine their capacity to provide further useful information, and encourage other potential informants to have second thoughts. Evidence may throw light on surveillance procedures and capacities, thereby enabling terrorists to take steps to reduce their vulnerability. Apparently innocuous pieces of information may lead to the uncovering of well-kept secrets.

These dangers can be exaggerated and need to be kept in proportion. Successful counterterror activities must almost invariably disclose some information of use to terrorists, and if they leave no mark, this too may be useful information. If every piece of a potential mosaic must be kept secret, this must necessarily be at the cost of the suppression of much innocuous information. Given the ease with which secrets can be stolen and broadcast, there is much to be said for using them while they last. Sometimes the disclosure of information may serve useful purposes. While knowledge of how antiterrorism agencies work may enable terrorists to adjust, it may also discourage timid would-be terrorists who learn, for instance, that the member of the group who advocates militant action may well be the undercover operative assigned to the group or that they have attracted official interest, in which case their value as a terrorist may be limited. Moreover, like antiterrorist agencies, courts need information if they are to do their job properly.

Someone has to decide how to handle these conflicting considerations. Legislatures have made some contribution by devising a variety of arrangements designed to protect interests in both fair trial and security. But on the whole, the relevant law has been developed by or within a framework settled by courts.

What Secrets Are Protected?

In the United States, secrets are protected from disclosure if their disclosure would threaten national security.[3] It is for the court to decide whether a secret involves "matters which, in the interest of national security, ought not be disclosed"; once the court finds the condition is satisfied, the information is privileged.[4] However, though the courts have overriding power, they defer. Writing in 2005, Weaver and Pallitto claimed that there had never been a case "where courts have forced the government to disclose agency-held classified information in any case in which the privilege has been asserted."[5] Yet a secret is not a state secret simply because the executive wants to protect it, Supreme Court authority to this effect being a legacy of Richard Nixon's shenanigans.[6]

In the other jurisdictions, "crown privilege," the equivalent to the state secrets privilege, has generally been subsumed within "public interest immunity." This means that while national security interests carry considerable weight, the national security interest in any given case must be weighed against a countervailing public interest in disclosure, and the logic of the balancing test is that there may be circumstances where a national security interest should be sacrificed in favour of the interest in fair trial. Moreover, courts are concerned not only with the balance between disclosure and secrecy but with whether it is possible to achieve an optimal balance by orders for partial disclosure.[7]

In Canada, Australia, and New Zealand, public interest immunity is now regulated by post-9/11 legislation. In general, this codifies the common law, but it involves slight modifications.[8] Amendments made to the Canada Evidence Act by the Anti-terrorism Act 2001 empower the attorney general to respond to a disclosure order by issuing a certificate prohibiting disclosure in security-sensitive cases. Such orders are reviewable by a single federal judge, but only on the basis that some or none of the information "does not relate either to information obtained in confidence from, or in relation to a foreign entity . . . , or to national defence or security."[9] The legislation means that national security can trump any countervailing interest in disclosure. However, in criminal cases, courts retain the power to determine the consequences of a decision to withhold evidence.[10] As of March 2007, no such certificates appear to have been issued, and a search of CanLII has not thrown up any subsequent examples.[11] Australian legislation maintains the balancing requirement, defines what is entailed in "prejudice to national security," but requires that the court give "greatest" weight to security interests.[12] The New Zealand Evidence Act 2006 specifies categories of state secrets that qualify for protection, but it otherwise codifies the common law.

Procedures for Determining Whether Information Qualifies for Protection

Decisions as to whether alleged secrets should be disclosed require inquiry into whether an alleged secret warrants any protection and, if so, what. Conducting this inquiry in open court and in the presence of all parties would defeat the purpose of the inquiry if disclosure of the alleged secret really would threaten the national interest. Under largely superseded law, the question of whether a secret qualified for protection was generally resolved on the basis of a certificate from a senior official, with minimal inquiry into the basis for the certificate. The government must now show that there is a basis for its claim, usually supported by evidence, though considerable deference is given to government claims.[13] In the United States, courts generally resolve disclosure issues without examining documents embodying the secrets in question,[14] and elsewhere courts may but need not base their decisions on an affidavit rather than on an actual examination of the document.[15]

Insofar as courts take their role seriously, inquiries into whether information should be protected are complex, especially when they also involve taking account of the public interest in a fair trial and the question of what forms of partial disclosure might represent optimal compromises between conflicting public interests. If what turn out to be protection-worthy secrets are to be protected, procedures are needed to ensure that the process that leads to this determination does not simultaneously lead to their disclosure. Preliminary inquiries (and freedom of information inquiries for that matter) are therefore governed by procedures that are far less open than those governing trials.

In several jurisdictions, the handling of disputes about the admissibility of secrets is governed by legislation. In the United States, Canada, and Australia, legislation requires notification to the government of the possibility that protected information will be disclosed in the course of a criminal trial (United States)[16] or a criminal or civil trial (Canada, Australia).[17] The legislation also governs the procedures for determining whether and to what extent secrets will be protected. These procedures are similar to those that apply under the general law in other jurisdictions.

The general rule is that disputes about the admissibility of secret information take place in the presence of all parties except insofar as the protection of potentially secret information requires the absence of parties to the dispute. Courts have a right to full access to the information but potentially lack the assistance that could be provided by nongovernment parties and their counsel. This obviously assists the government. It seems unfair, and it deprives the court of submissions that might enable it to reach a more informed decision, but it is unavoidable if secrets are to be protected. This problem predates terrorism concerns; indeed, it is a problem that can arise in relation to purely private litigation, when commercial and other private secrets are implicated in litigation. Legislatures and courts have adopted a number of partial solutions.

One solution involves the use of security-cleared counsel. Australian law makes express provision for security-cleared counsel, and in the United States, protective orders made under the Classified Information Procedures Act of 1980 may and do make provision for security-cleared counsel.[18] The rationale for requiring security clearance lies in the assumption that security-cleared lawyers will be less likely than other lawyers to disclose state secrets. Security clearance is not lightly granted, and once granted, it is not lightly put at risk.

Another solution involves the appointment of "special advocates." The special advocate procedure appears to have been a Canadian invention,[19] but it first received legislative recognition in the United Kingdom, where legislation provides for its use in relation to several special terrorism jurisdictions.[20] At the suggestion of the Canadian Supreme Court, Canada subsequently legislated to make provision for special advocates in cases involving security certificates in relation to immigrants suspected of constituting security risks.[21] In New Zealand, special advocates were used on an ad hoc basis to deal with the secrecy problems involved in determining whether Ahmed Zaoui had been properly determined to be a security risk (and therefore potentially deportable), and there is now statutory provision for the use of special advocates in immigration matters.[22] Courts in the United Kingdom and Australia have ruled that special advocates can be used in relation to proceedings in the ordinary courts.[23] In Canadian civil litigation, court-appointed security-cleared "amici curiae" have been used in closed hearings to determine whether information should be disclosed,[24] and US and Australian courts have concluded that they could appoint experts to perform a similar function.[25]

Under UK law, special advocates differ from security-cleared advocates in that once they have seen the secret material, they may normally have no further communication with the party whose interests they are representing.[26] This potentially deprives them of information relevant to whether the secret should be disclosed, but it is intended to avoid an alternative danger: namely, that a communication informed by awareness of the secret may inadvertently involve the direct or indirect disclosure of the secret. In Canada, courts may grant advocates leave to question the person on whose behalf they are acting, and the experience of Canadian advocates is that this can sometimes be helpful in uncovering exculpatory information.[27]

Yet another possible solution would involve reliance on the integrity of counsel, whether cleared or not. Given the professional costs of being found to have disclosed confidential information, lawyers will not lightly betray confidences, but politically committed counsel may be tempted to do so, especially in cases where proof of their involvement might be difficult,[28] and politically uncommitted counsel might do so inadvertently.[29] Nonetheless, "uncleared" counsel have sometimes been used in sensitive cases.[30]

The Consequences of Nondisclosure

In criminal law cases, the law is reasonably straightforward and varies little across jurisdictions. If the protected information would otherwise have assisted the government, the government is no longer able to rely on it to prove its case. This means that the protection of secrets may sometimes come at the cost of the government's ability to secure convictions. If disclosure of the secret would strengthen the defendant's case or weaken the case of the prosecution, the government must make concessions that ensure that the defendant is not seriously disadvantaged. If this is not possible, proceedings will be stayed. However, the government can withhold secrets if their exculpatory potential is no more than theoretical.

If it is the defendant who wants to disclose a state secret, a nondisclosure order might mean that the defendant could not present a defence that might otherwise be open. This would be unfair, and a court would normally order a stay. However, it would not do so if it concluded that the order did not materially affect the defendant's capacity to present a defence.

In several jurisdictions, legislation expressly permits partial disclosure in the form of summaries or admissions of facts that the information would tend to prove.[31] In the United Kingdom, Canada, and Australia (but not in the United States), witnesses may give evidence without their identity being disclosed, from behind a screen, or with their voice scrambled, and the duty to disclose seems slightly narrower.[32] However, US courts have managed to devise procedures designed to provide some protection to the interests of witnesses and security, and in certain circumstances, their identity may be kept secret.[33] Moreover, courts recognise that the unfairness associated with non-disclosure of protected information may be slight, in which case a trial may be allowed to proceed, notwithstanding a possibility that unfairness might be occasioned by exclusion of the evidence.

These considerations mean that in criminal cases, the distinction between state secrets immunity and public interest immunity is of limited practical significance. Cases in which disclosure would be ordered under the former but not the latter, system would normally be cases where defendants' interests in a fair trial would be adversely affected, in which case courts would order that proceedings be discontinued on fairness grounds.

In civil proceedings, a finding that information is protected means that if a party can make out its claim or defence only by disclosing a state secret, the claim must be dismissed.[34] If the plaintiff cannot sustain its case without the evidence, the defendant wins. If the defendant is unable to mount a defence that would otherwise be open to it, the claim will be struck out as an abuse of process.[35] The practical consequences of this are potentially unjust, especially in the United States, where the public interest in a plaintiff being able to make out what would otherwise be its case carries no weight in determining whether information can be withheld. Elsewhere, security interests carry considerable weight but are capable of being outweighed by the public interest in plaintiffs being able to pursue their legal interests. It is rare to find cases where governments have succeeded in having cases struck out after having successfully asserted public interest immunity.[36]

In none of the jurisdictions is there provision for disclosure to the court but not to one or more parties, and this seems to be the case even if selective disclosure in a particular case might be in the public interest. In an interlocutory ruling in a UK torture case, the Queen's Bench Division was willing to allow some classified information to be disclosed to the court, with the plaintiffs' interests being protected by a special advocate,[37] but the court of appeal and (with one dissent) the Supreme Court allowed the plaintiffs' appeal, reaffirming the principle that evidence be disclosed to all parties or to none.[38] If there were to be such a departure from tradition, this should be a matter for the Parliament.[39] The Supreme Court was not asked to consider whether parties could agree to a closed procedure, with judges expressing different views.[40] Lord Brown concluded that the problem posed by the case was beyond the courts' capacity to resolve and that such cases either should be tried by a specialist body such as the Investigatory Powers Tribunal (which hears complaints against allegedly unlawful interception of communications) or should not be tried at all. But it was for the Parliament to decide how to deal with the problem, not the courts.[41] Canadian courts have adverted to the question and hinted that closed evidence might be admissible, but in *Canada (Attorney General) v Almalki*, the federal court warned that it could not be assumed that protected information could be disclosed ex parte, citing the UK court of appeal's *Al Rawi v Security Service* decision.[42]

The rules governing public law cases are more complex and vary cross-nationally and by subject matter. There is one important difference between public law and other cases: courts may sometimes rely on secret information, even if this is not communicated to the party seeking relief. In the Guantánamo cases, the courts recognised this principle, subject to the requirement that applicants be provided with enough information to enable them to know the case they had to rebut.[43] In the United Kingdom, the court of appeal in *Al Rawi* assumed that there were circumstances where courts could proceed ex parte in public law cases, but the Supreme Court disagreed.[44] The Supreme Court did, however, recognise that legislation permitting closed hearings in private and public law cases could be compatible with the ECHR. The basis for its decision was that the common law was more exacting than the convention.[45]

Australian legislation dating from 1998 envisaged that courts conducting reviews of ministers' decisions in migration cases might make orders that confidential material be disclosed to neither applicants nor their counsel, notwithstanding that it had been disclosed to the court.[46] The Australian Federal Court based its decision in *Leghaie*[47] largely on secret information that was communicated to the applicant's security-cleared lawyer and not to his client, but this procedure had had the parties' agreement.

The rationale for ex parte use of secrets appears to lie in the fact that it may be the lesser of two evils.[48] The applicant in a security-related public law case may be able to win only if the court has access to the protected information. If so, the applicant is better off if the court receives it ex parte than if it does not receive it at all. If the applicant wins, there is no injustice to the defendant, since the defendant—the government—can be told why it has lost in a classified judgment.

Specialised Courts and Tribunals

Slightly different laws govern specialised courts and tribunals established to deal with terrorism and national security issues. Some of these predate 9/11. In the United States, the Foreign Intelligence Surveillance Act of 1978 includes provisions enabling determinations to be made in relation to whether electronic surveillance has been unlawful, and it includes procedures for dealing with cases where a determination of this issue might involve the disclosure of information when this would be harmful to national security. In these circumstances, the attorney general may file an affidavit that disclosure or an adversary hearing would harm national security. If so, and notwithstanding any other law to the contrary, the question shall be determined by the relevant district court in camera and ex parte. The court may nonetheless disclose to the aggrieved person "portions of the application, order, or other materials," but only if subject to "appropriate security procedures and protective orders" and only "where the disclosure is necessary to make an accurate determination of the legality of the surveillance."[49] In a 2003 decision, the Seventh Circuit reported that it had found no case in which a court had ordered disclosure of FISA materials, and the government brief submitted in a 2008 case asserted that this was still so.[50]

The legislation governing listing decisions under the International Emergency Economic Powers Act of 1977 and the designation of organisations as "foreign terrorist organizations" includes provisions governing the judicial review of designation decisions, including express provision to the effect that for the purposes of in camera and ex parte review, the government might submit classified information used in the making of the designation decision.[51]

The post-9/11 administrative arrangements governing Combatant Status Review Tribunals (CSRTs) and military commissions empowered the relevant bodies to act on information not disclosed to the detainee.[52] Detainees were entitled to attend proceedings, but not when the proceedings involved "testimony or other matters that would compromise national security if heard in the presence of the detainee." Their personal representatives—security-cleared military officers—were permitted to attend all stages of the proceedings except those in which the members of the tribunal deliberated and voted.[53] They were not permitted to share classified information with detainees, but, unlike UK special advocates, they were permitted to communicate with the detainee after having seen confidential material.[54] The order establishing military commissions allowed the accused to be privately represented (at their own expense), but their civilian lawyer had no right to know the contents of classified material. Access to classified material was subject to rules similar to those governing CSRTs.[55] Legislation enacted in the aftermath of

Hamdan v Rumsfeld[56] shifted the balance away from the government. The Military Commissions Act of 2006[57] included provisions for protecting classified information, making it "privileged from disclosure if disclosure would be detrimental to national security."[58] In relevant cases, the military judge might order, as an alternative to the production of sensitive information, partly redacted documents, the substitution of a summary of the relevant evidence, or the substitution of a statement of relevant facts that the evidence would tend to prove.[59] In 2009, these provisions were replaced by provisions modeled on but slightly different to those in the Classified Information Protection Act.[60] The new provisions provide for discovery of classified information or an adequate substitute, if the information "would be noncumulative, relevant, and helpful to a legally cognizable defense, rebuttal of the prosecutor's case, or to sentencing," and the provisions expressly provide that all information admitted as evidence must be disclosed to the accused, who may be ordered not to disclose the information insofar as it is classified.[61] The commission may authorise the government to rely on redacted material, statements, or summaries, but only if these "will provide the defendant with substantially the same ability to make his defense as would disclosure of the original material."[62]

A series of UK acts established courts to deal with a variety of security-related issues, including appeals from immigrants found to pose an unacceptable security risk, appeals by and on behalf of proscribed organisations, employment disputes giving rise to security issues, cases arising under surveillance legislation, and applications for the making or review of control orders and their successors.[63] Proscribed organisation hearings are governed by the same rules of evidence as those governing civil actions.[64] The rules of the Special Immigration Appeals Commission require the tribunal to ensure that information not be disclosed contrary to "the interests of national security, the international relations of the United Kingdom, the detention and prevention of crime, or in any other circumstances where disclosure is likely to harm the public interest," and they provide that parties may be excluded from parts of a hearing.[65] The rules governing employment tribunals, surveillance appeals, and control orders and measures under the Terrorism Prevention and Investigation Measures Act 2011 are similar.[66] In such cases, the relevant minister or a party to the proceeding may request that the attorney-general appoint a special advocate.[67]

Canadian migration legislation provides for special procedures in cases where immigrants are appealing against deportation and detention on security grounds following ministerial certification. As enacted, the legislation required a judge hearing a certificate appeal to hear evidence in camera and ex parte, if the judge concluded that "its disclosure would be injurious to national security or to the safety of any person."[68] A similar provision governed the review of decisions to list bodies as terrorist entities and to certify that charities were making contributions to listed entities.[69]

In migration cases (but not in terrorist entity cases), the judge was to provide the applicant with a summary of the grounds for the certificate, but the summary was not to include any information whose disclosure would, in the judge's opinion, damage national security or threaten any person's safety.[70] There was no provision for anyone to represent the applicant in closed hearings. Following the Supreme Court's decision in *Charkaoui v Canada (Citizenship and Immigration)*, the legislation made provision for the appointment of a special advocate, whose role is almost identical to that of the UK special advocates but whose powers to communicate with the represented person are greater.[71]

Australian law makes many of the commonwealth's administrative decisions reviewable on their merits by the Administrative Appeals Tribunal, a court-like body with a comprehensive jurisdiction. Under pre-9/11 legislation, the attorney-general may certify that information should not be divulged on security grounds, in which case it may be disclosed only to the tribunal.[72] Similar rules govern appeals to the Migration Review Tribunal, but in refugee cases, certification also precludes disclosure to the Refugee Review Tribunal.[73] Certificates are not conclusive: being administrative decisions, they are judicially reviewable.

This contrasts with the position under New Zealand's recently proclaimed *Immigration Act 2009*, which includes provisions designed to protect security-sensitive information while minimally detracting from immigrants' due process rights. While the legislation allows the Immigration and Protection Tribunal and courts to examine classified information that has been withheld from the immigrant, its status may be contested by special advocates and others, and it may be taken into account only if the immigrant whose interests are at stake can be given the gist of the adverse allegation without endangering the secret.[74]

Legislation as a Response to Terrorism?

Secrets laws were clearly modified in response to terrorism concerns, but responses tend not to fit the model of heightened concern. First, many of the post-9/11 responses were neither passed nor introduced in the immediate aftermath of the attacks. Indeed, much of the relevant law predates the 9/11 attacks. Second, much of the post-9/11 legislation was based on legislation passed prior to the attacks.

Canada comes closest to providing prima facie evidence of panic-based legislation. The Anti-terrorism Act 2001 expanded the government's powers to protect its secrets in judicial proceedings, provided for in camera and ex parte hearings in cases challenging terrorist organisation decisions, and included a new official secrets act. It provided for the attorney general to issue certificates prohibiting the disclosure of security-sensitive information. These would be conclusive as against the information and privacy commissioners in relation to whether information fell within the security exemption.

However, despite the speed with which the legislation was passed, it was considered by House and Senate committees that conducted hearings and made or recommended amendments. The Canadian House of Commons Standing Committee on Justice and Human Rights reported the bill subject to amendments that limited the life of the attorney general's certificates to 15 years (under the bill's first reading, they had been indefinite), required publication of certificates, and provided for their judicial review.[75] The Senate committee recommended further amendments (which, however, were not adopted).[76]

Moreover, the legislation has survived reconsideration. Five years after the passage of the legislation, two parliamentary committees inquired into and reported on the legislation. A Senate committee recommended that provision be made for the involvement of special advocates in all cases where the government sought to rely on secret evidence and that the provisions for ministerial certificates be tightened.[77] These recommendations could suggest second thoughts, but they reflect concerns similar to those articulated by the Senate committee that had considered the 2001 bill. The House of Commons subcommittee also recommended a special advocate system (but one that placed more emphasis on counsel's duty to the public than on the applicant/defendant's interest). It had only minor reservations about the ministerial certificate system.[78] But the Parliament adopted almost none of these recommendations, and the one recommendation it did adopt was a response not to the recommendations but to a subsequent Supreme Court decision.

The most important limits on Australian litigants' access to security-related information are those relating to tribunal proceedings, and these predate the 9/11 attacks and have not been amended in response to them. The 2004–5 legislation governing the use of security-sensitive information in criminal and civil trials is procedural rather than substantive, and debates on the bill made few specific references to its implications for counterterrorism.

Most of the relevant UK law predates 9/11, and the only significant post-2001 measures there drew on earlier precedents in which information was kept secret, the effected parties' interests being partly protected by use of special advocates. The US Congress has been even more restrained. While parts of the Military Commissions Acts are controversial, and while the 2006 act was partly enacted against the backdrop of the forthcoming elections,[79] its provisions in relation to the protection of state secrets in commission trials do not suggest either haste or capitulation to short-term heightened concern. It was prompted not by terrorist attacks but by a Supreme Court decision holding that the existing system of military commissions was unlawful. However, reconsideration produced legislation that has slightly increased the protections afforded defendants in cases where secrets are relevant to prosecutions and defences.

Institutional Differences

Courts are necessarily involved in secrecy issues. Terrorism-related trials mean that courts are necessarily involved in the need to make decisions in relation to whether secrets are at stake and with what implications. Moreover, statutory secrets provisions have constitutional implications. In Canada, where legislation gives federal judges the jurisdiction to make admissibility decisions, federalism issues arise when the relevant litigation takes place in provincial courts. Legislation that limits courts' access to otherwise admissible evidence and that directs courts in relation to the weight they are to give to security interests raises issues of separation of powers. Ex parte hearings raise due process issues. Deferential courts may welcome the excuse to dispose of politically controversial cases on state secrets grounds, but even relatively cautious courts may be uneasy about rules of law that stand in the way of their resolving cases on their legal and factual merits.

Courts and State Secrets Claims

Courts have been extremely receptive to state secrets claims by the US government. *Reynolds v United States* continues to live a charmed life, in contrast to other questionable wartime decisions that have either been distinguished (like *Johnson v Eisentrager*) or disowned (like *Korematsu v United States* or the UK analogue *Liversidge v Anderson*, which has been overruled). Weaver and Pallitto found that state secrets claims failed in only 4 out of 58 reported cases in the period 1977–2005—twice because it was obviously inapplicable, once because of failure to follow procedural prerequisites, and once because the court decided to deal with the problem by ordering a secret trial.[80] Post-2005 claims have enjoyed a similar level of success, which has generally assisted the government's substantive objectives. In relation to National Security Agency litigation, the government enjoyed mixed success, winning in a case where the doctrine was found to be fatal to the plaintiffs' standing in a claim for declaratory and injunctive relief,[81] losing in a case where the court held that state secrets privilege was superseded by the special procedures governing FISA damages claims,[82] and losing on a dismissal application on the grounds that it had not shown that the plaintiffs would have to rely on state secrets in order to make out their case.[83] However, the government has been more successful in torture and unlawful rendition cases, including cases where some doubt existed as to whether claims would require the disclosure of state secrets.[84]

Two of the plaintiffs to the US torture litigation were also involved in litigation in the United Kingdom, where they were far more successful. One set of cases related to Binyam Mohamed's application for an order that the United Kingdom produce documents in its possession relating to his mistreatment in the United States, which might assist him in relation to a US habeas corpus application. His application succeeded at first instance, but subject to public interest immunity.[85] Judgment was given in both open and closed forms, the former giving somewhat less detail about the nature of Mohamed's "cruel, inhuman and degrading" treatment in Pakistan. The question of which, if any, documents had to be disclosed was never resolved: the United States subsequently made the documents available, so there was no need for the United Kingdom to do so. However, an ongoing issue related to whether the open judgment should have included the redacted passages. Concerned that full disclosure would mean the disclosure of information provided by American intelligence agencies, the UK government was worried that if the information was disclosed—even under court order—the US would be worried about the precedent this would create and would be more cautious about the kind of intelligence it would provide in future. There was a political principle at stake, notwithstanding that the gist of the information had been disclosed in the judgment. The trial judge was sceptical of this claim and decided that redaction was no longer appropriate.

The court of appeal held, albeit with some hesitation, that the trial judge had erred. He should not have assumed that there was no danger the disclosure would undermine the flow of intelligence simply because, in a communication intended for a court, the Central Intelligence Agency had been tactful in the way it had adverted to possible consequences.[86] He had failed to recognise that "at least on the face of it, the Foreign Secretary, with the benefit of his Foreign Office and SyS and SIS advisers, is better able to assess that risk than a judge."[87] He had not taken into account the secretary's argument that disclosure of the information might also affect the willingness of countries other than the US to provide such information,[88] and he had erred in his handling of information about the US secretary of state's expressed views.[89] Despite these criticisms, the court considered that there were good grounds for being sceptical of the secretary's claims, albeit on grounds not quite sufficient for finding in favour of disclosure.

But since the divisional court's decision, there had been a change in circumstances. A decision by the DC district court had vindicated Mohamed's claims of torture and mistreatment. The information in the redacted passages was now in the public domain and, moreover, had been disclosed by an arm of the government that had supplied the intelligence. It had ceased to be secret, and there was no longer any rational basis for determining that disclosure would threaten national security.

Binyam Mohamed and Al Rawi also succeeded in a claim for rendition-related damages brought in the UK courts, although the precise nature of and basis for this success is unclear. Following the ruling that the government could not rely on secret evidence, the court ordered the first stage of the discovery process, the giving of a list of relevant documents. This did not resolve the question of whether listed documents would attract public policy immunity. That would await inspection of hundreds of thousands of relevant documents, and the government anticipated that this would keep platoons of lawyers at work for years. There are reports that the case has been settled on terms under which the plaintiffs would receive sums of up to around one million pounds. The security service was reportedly fearful lest claims for public policy immunity would fail, so that its secrets would be disclosed.[90] But other plausible hypotheses include fear lest the government lose, fear lest an adverse precedent in relation to liability for complicity be established, and concerns at the cost to a financially straitened government if the case were to proceed. Given the cost of conducting the public interest immunity inquiry, the government was probably better off by 10 to 15 million pounds than it would have been had it fought and won.

In Canada, government claims to public interest immunity have sometimes carried little weight with courts. In litigation relating to whether the Arar Commission's investigation into the treatment of a Canadian who had been subject to extraordinary rendition could disclose information allegedly prejudicial to national security, Justice Noël rejected some of the government's claims, and the information was subsequently released. The justice's unclassified reasons set out the principles governing his decision, though not their application, but their logic is that the government was overclaiming.[91] Following the more-rigorous disclosure requirements prescribed in 2008 by the Supreme Court in *Charkaoui v Canada (Citizenship and Immigration)*, Mr. Charkaoui finally achieved substantive success in his attempt to have an adverse security certificate set aside when the designated federal judge rejected a government claim to public interest immunity and ordered disclosure of the information in question. Rather than disclose its secrets, the government decided that it would not present security-sensitive evidence to the judge.[92] It conceded that the effect of withdrawing the evidence was that there was no longer sufficient evidence to support the certificate, which was accordingly declared void from the date the material was withdrawn.[93] Courts handling Canada's unlawful rendition cases have yet to determine whether any information attracts immunity and, if so, what consequences follow. The plaintiffs will no doubt be encouraged by UK developments. However, the government had one partial success. In *Canada (Attorney General) v Khawaja*,[94] Justice Moseley upheld all its claims to the effect that disclosure of contested information would be prejudicial to national security, although he also concluded that the interests of justice required disclosure of some of the particulars of the protected information.

Australian law is kinder to governments, although not as kind as governments might wish. In a case arising out of adverse security assessments, ASIO failed in a claim that it was not required to provide an affidavit of documents in response to a discovery notice. However, the Federal Court of Australia (in which discovery is discretionary) also observed that circumstances might arise when national security interests might warrant refusal to order the listing of sensitive documents.[95] The court subsequently held that ASIO was not required to produce the documents, even to the applicants' lawyers, and that this was the case notwithstanding that this might make it impossible for the applicants to make out their cases.[96] It subsequently denied the judicial review application.[97] A case of complicity in torture was settled before the Federal Court had an opportunity to make a public ruling on the public interest immunity issues posed by the litigation.

In the only litigation arising out of a New Zealand security risk certificate, the courts effectively resolved the dispute without having to determine whether there were adequate grounds for the certificate. They found that even if there were grounds for the certificate, the subject of the certificate could not be deported if this would entail refoulement to a country where he would be tortured.[98] As a refugee from Algeria, he was safe.

The Validity of Procedures for Deciding Whether Secrets Can Be Withheld

In relation to interlocutory disputes as to whether the information ought to be excluded, courts have accepted that they have no alternative but to handle the dispute in camera and ex parte, but even this practice has caused concern insofar as it may involve the judge becoming aware of facts that are not disclosed to the nonstate party. The ECtHR has ruled that in these circumstances, the ECHR requires that criminal defendants excluded from the inquiry be given notice of the gist of any prejudicial material in cases where the judge conducting the inquiry is also the trial judge, and the court came close to ruling that this was so even in the case of jury trials.[99] Elsewhere, courts have been less concerned about the possibility that exposure to secrets could contaminate judicial minds. In general, however, the problem is mitigated by the role of security-cleared counsel or special advocates.

In Canada, the 2001 amendments to the Canada Evidence Act gave rise to a different issue. On their face, the amendments give the federal court the exclusive jurisdiction to resolve disclosure issues, even in relation to proceedings being litigated before a provincial superior court.[100] This overcomes objections based on judges being prejudiced by virtue of exposure to secret information, but it raised the question of whether the legislation impermissibly interferes with the prerogatives of provincial superior courts by removing their decision-making powers in relation to executive claims that particular evidence is privileged. Several provincial superior courts held that this was the case, at least in some circumstances. The Supreme Court disagreed, ruling that the bifurcated system is constitutionally valid insofar as it applies to criminal cases.[101] A claim based on the Canadian Constitution failed: the Constitution protected only such powers as were vested in provincial courts at the time of its enactment, and in 1867, provincial courts lacked the power to determine issues of crown privilege. The legislation did not interfere with a core judicial function or with the charter right to a fair trial. The basis for its decision in relation to the latter two issues was that, properly interpreted, the legislation required courts to take all steps possible to ensure that privilege decisions did not interfere with a defendant's right to a fair trial and that if, for some reason, a fair trial could not be had, the court could protect the defendant's rights by staying proceedings, a right acknowledged by the legislation. While the need for the federal court to make decisions in relation to evidence in matters being tried in provincial courts might complicate proceedings and render them potentially unfair, it did not interfere with the courts' power to order a stay in such circumstances. The legislation might be unwise, but it did not require that defendants be tried other than fairly.[102]

This reasoning does not necessarily apply to civil law, where the salutary effects of a threatened stay would be irrelevant in cases where the defendant was a government agency or official. Nonetheless, provincial courts have held that the bifurcated system is constitutionally valid insofar as it applies at the interlocutory stage.[103] The Ontario Court of Appeal reversed a ruling by the motion judge that the legislation was invalid in relation to the resolution of evidence issues once trial had begun, but it did so on the grounds that the ruling was premature since the proceedings had not yet reached that stage.[104]

The Validity of Legislative Attempts to Limit the Circumstances in Which Secrets Can Be Disclosed in Judicial Proceedings

Legislation designed to make it easier for the government to exclude secret information raises fairness and accuracy issues. At worst, the legislation dealing with ordinary criminal and civil trials only slightly nibbles away at the principle that as much probative evidence as possible should be admissible, and it has survived judicial scrutiny. Canadian courts have dismissed challenges to the validity of legislation permitting the attorney general to issue a (judicially reviewable) certificate precluding the disclosure of security-sensitive information. The Supreme Court's judgment in *Charkaoui v Canada* included dicta that strongly implied that the Evidence Act provisions were unexceptionable,[105] and in the course of the tortuous *Khawaja* litigation, the federal court[106] and the federal court of appeal[107] rejected challenges to the constitutionality of the legislation. The legislation did not deprive the accused of his right to a trial in accordance with the principles of fundamental justice, which varied with circumstances and might require taking account of state interests as well as individual interests. Moreover, the legislation expressly provided for the dismissal or stay of criminal charges if denial of access to information meant that the defendant could not receive a fair trial.

The Supreme Court's recent decision in R *v Ahmad* seems less deferential. It made it clear that the bifurcated system was valid only because it permits courts to engage in rigorous examination of privilege claims, and there is a hint that section 38.13 (whose validity was not at issue in *Ahmad*) might be constitutionally suspect.[108] Except in relation to the bifurcated decisions issue, courts have not, however, considered the implications of the amendments in the context of civil or public law trials. The logic of *Ahmad* is that there should be no problems as long as the fairness of the trial is unaffected and that constitutional difficulties could arise if the government attempted to use section 38.13 to its advantage.

The Australian National Security Information (Criminal and Civil Proceedings) Act 2004 (NSIA) has survived constitutional challenge, partly because it left the powers of the courts largely unaffected. Although it required courts to give greater weight to security interests than to other interests, this was not held to involve an impermissible interference with constitutionally protected judicial powers.[109] There has, however, been a hint that its definition of "national security" may be overbroad.[110]

The Validity of Measures Allowing the Ex Parte Use of Secrets in Trials and Inquiries

Quite different issues arise where governments want the court to take account of secrets while keeping them concealed from the nonstate parties. To allow this may mean breaching a fundamental principle of procedural fairness, namely, the right of people to know the case they need to meet. Moreover, the lack of an informed response to the secret evidence means that there is a danger that the court will lack some of the information it needs to make an informed decision. Legislation that allows the state to rely on secret information is therefore in danger of falling foul of constitutionally protected due process rights. Anticipating this problem, most statutory regimes attempt to provide some protection for the nonstate party. The United Kingdom relied heavily on special advocates. The United States and Australia rely on security-cleared counsel. Where the secret is such that nonstate parties can be put on notice as to the case they must meet, due process concerns become less serious. The problem is, however, that the essence of the secret may be crucial and may be what the government wants to keep secret. For example, governments naturally want to keep the identity of informants secret, but keeping identity secret means that the subject of the information may not be in a position to advance persuasive reasons for why the tribunal should attach little weight to superficially persuasive evidence. The UK special advocate procedure does not work well in such a situation, given bars on contacts with the nonstate party following examination of the closed material. Security-cleared counsel are in a slightly better position, but their duty not to disclose secrets sets limits to the questions they can ask their clients (and, indeed, to their right to knowingly allow their eyes to light up when their client spontaneously points out that if the adverse information came from a named person, who the lawyer knows to be the confidential source, there are good reasons why it should be treated as lacking in credibility).

Legislation allowing the ex parte communication of evidence to tribunals has survived constitutional scrutiny insofar as it applies to decisions designating groups and individuals as terrorists, but not (except in minor respects) in relation to the determination of combatant status. A USA Patriot Act amendment provided that in judicial reviews of determinations made under section 2003 of the International Emergency Economic Powers Act, classified information might be submitted to the reviewing court ex parte and in camera.[111] Courts have consistently upheld the constitutionality of this amendment, on the basis that the powers are conditioned on the measures being necessary for the protection of national security, and they have also upheld similar restrictions on challenging designation as a "foreign terrorist organization."[112]

In the United States, litigation put in question the legality of the CSRTs and the military commissions. In *Hamdan*, the Supreme Court held that the military commissions were inconsistent with the Uniform Code of Military Justice and the Geneva Conventions and that Congress could legislate to confer the relevant authority.[113] In *Boumediene v Bush*, the Supreme Court left open the question of whether the CSRT procedures satisfied due process requirements, but the majority concluded that "there is a considerable risk of error in the tribunal's findings of fact."[114] It held, however, that the combination of the CSRT procedures and the statutory provisions for judicial review of CSRT decisions[115] fell short of providing the procedural protections needed to justify legislation depriving detainees of their constitutional right to apply for habeas corpus. The Supreme Court's concerns included the detainees' limited access to information about the evidence against them.

However, the procedures designed to deal with subsequent Guantánamo habeas corpus litigation involved acceptance of the need to provide some protection for government secrets. This had been recognised in 2004, when the DC district court recognised petitioners' rights to habeas corpus but made orders to protect government secrets. Following *Boumediene*, the DC district court made a protective order superseding its earlier orders (Protective Order 08),[116] which it amended in January 2009.[117] The government was entitled to refuse to disclose classified information if it could provide a sufficient alternative. If it could not provide a sufficient alternative, it could withhold the information, but if so, the court might make orders in the nature of those provided for under the Classified Information Protection Act.[118] Access to classified information was limited to the government and to security-cleared counsel who had signed the prescribed memorandum of understanding. They were permitted to discuss it with other security-cleared counsel in related cases but were not to disclose it to a detainee except with permission.

UK courts have been wary of allowing courts and specialised tribunals to act on secret information. Most of the relevant litigation has related to whether rights to fair trial for those subjected to control orders are adequately protected by the special advocate system. When the House of Lords first dealt with the question, it concluded that the special advocate system was potentially capable of ensuring a fair trial, notwithstanding that the controlee had not been made aware of the contents of the closed material. However, disclosure to the special advocate would not necessarily mean that a control order hearing would be fair, and the rules had to be read down accordingly.[119]

The ECtHR subsequently took a stricter approach, disagreeing with the decision by the House of Lords insofar as it accepted that failure to disclose the full nature of the government's case was not necessarily contrary to the ECHR's provisions for fair trial,[120] and the House of Lords had no alternative but to follow.[121] These rulings did not require that the party be given access to all confidential information, but they did require that a party subject to a control order be given details of the gist of the case against it, such that it would be in a position to respond to all allegations against it. If this requirement was satisfied, a control order could be made, notwithstanding that the party was not aware of the full details of the evidence produced against it. If it could not be satisfied, the government was not permitted to rely on the evidence.

However, both the ECtHR and the Supreme Court have held that the demands of fair trial were less exacting when liberty interests were not engaged.[122] Among the issues involved in *Kennedy v United Kingdom* was the question of whether the procedures used by the Investigatory Powers Tribunal were consistent with the requirements of Convention Articles 6 (fair hearing) and 13 (right to effective remedy): the restrictions on the applicant's right were both necessary and proportionate.[123] A subsequent Supreme Court case arose from the Home Office's withdrawal of a security clearance. The employee argued that it had discriminated against him on impermissible grounds. Following an application by the Home Office, the Employment Tribunal made an order for a closed material procedure. This meant that some evidence would be heard in the absence of the employee and that the employee might not be given enough details of the evidence to be able to make an effective response. His interests would, however, be represented by a special advocate. The Supreme Court held that this procedure did not contravene the ECHR. There was European authority permitting security interests to prevail over disclosure, even if this came at some cost to the person's capacity to rebut and to their ability to know the precise reasons for an adverse decision. The court was sensitive to the dangers of forcing governments to choose between disclosing information and being unable to sustain a meritorious case, and the court accepted that security vetting was both desirable and dependent on confidential sources. However, the closed material procedure was valid only because of safeguards, which included the tribunal's discretion to determine whether to make the order and the discretion to make orders whose practical effect might be the disclosure of security-sensitive information. But while there was agreement as to the need for balance, there was disagreement as to its extent. Lords Brown and Hope appear to have been particularly sensitive to the need to protect the vetting system. Lord Kerr, who dissented in part, was sensitive to procedural fairness issues, finding that procedural fairness required that the employee be provided with the gist of the closed evidence, even if this might interfere with the effectiveness of the vetting system.

Canadian courts have reached a similar conclusion in relation to legislation governing immigrants suspected of being potential terrorists. In *Charkaoui v Canada*,[124] the Supreme Court unanimously held that section 78 of the

Immigration and Refugee Protection Act infringed section 7 of the Canadian Charter of Rights and Freedoms, which provides that people may be deprived of life, liberty, and security only in accordance with the principles of fundamental justice. The court made it clear that this did not mean that applicants were entitled to access to the evidence, but it did mean that there should be provision for someone to make representations to the court on the applicant's behalf in such matters. The model suggested was the special advocate one, and the legislature duly obliged. In a subsequent decision,[125] the court considered the degree of disclosure required in relation to the issue of a ministerial certificate and held that the charter rights of a person affected by such a decision were such that they should be afforded similar rights to a criminal defendant, subject to public interest immunity considerations. However, a subsequent federal court challenge to the amended legislation was unsuccessful, Justice Noël finding that the new procedure did not offend against the charter's provisions for fair trial and, further, that even if it had done so, it would have been "demonstrably justifiable in a free and democratic society" and therefore saved by section 1 of the charter.[126]

While the Australian Constitution does not include a due process clause, legislative attempts to require courts to follow unfair procedures would contravene the constitutionally based separation of powers. Those affected by administrative decisions have a presumptive right to procedural fairness, but the existence and content of that right is subject to legislation. As a result, in cases where a person's status is affected by adverse security assessments, courts have consistently held that the subject of the certificate has no right to know the nature of the information on which it is based, except insofar as its disclosure would not threaten security interests.[127] High Court litigation relating to the government's right to detain would-be immigrants who had been found to be security risks did not resolve the question of whether legislation could limit the procedural fairness rights of those affected by adverse security assessments. The court found that ASIO had in fact afforded procedural fairness to the plaintiffs in that it had informed them of the gist of the allegations against them and given them an opportunity to reply.[128]

The Executive and Government Secrets

The history of the relevant legislation indicates that government attempts to enhance their secrecy powers are usually watered down in the legislative process and that legislative opposition to secrecy legislation is invariably on the grounds that secrecy should not receive any more protection than it currently enjoys. However, judging by the fate of their legislative proposals, governments generally secured most of what they wanted, which suggests either that their moves for legislation were particularly opportune or that governments and legislatures are broadly agreed as to the advantages of both state secrecy and open government.

But agreement might also reflect government calculations about what might be politically feasible, and in the United States, the government's response to secrecy concerns in relation to counterterrorism tended to take the form of executive unilateralism rather than attempts to extract protective legislation. Its procedures for determining combatant status and guilt of war crimes were designed to ensure that secrets could be both used and kept and that detainees would be hard-pressed to show that they were not properly detained and innocent of the charges against them. Its use of executive powers to protect its secrets was also evidenced by measures designed to limit access to information. In an October 2001 memorandum, Attorney General Ashcroft urged a policy of presumptive nondisclosure in relation to any information that might be confidential, promising the Department of Justice's support for nonrelease decisions other than those that lacked a "sound legal basis" or that frustrated the capacity of other agencies to protect their records. Officials responded by becoming less likely to release information.[129] The government resisted attempts by civil liberties and other organisations to gain access to information relating to details of post-9/11 immigration detention,[130] torture, and unauthorised surveillance, citing national security considerations and drawing on the mosaic theory: that when put together, even innocuous pieces of information could provide information to America's enemies. Its secrecy concerns were also evidenced in its reliance on the state secrets doctrine. Its actions are consistent with a variety of possible motives: a good faith determination to protect the homeland, a belief that the payoff for inroads on procedural fairness would be a higher yield of "true positives," fears lest exposure of errors might undermine the legitimacy of the counterterror program, and fears lest exposure cause personal embarrassment.

However, executive enthusiasm for protecting secrets may have waned. In 2009, the attorney general announced measures designed to limit reliance on the doctrine. Invocation of the doctrine would be limited to cases where disclosure "could be expected to cause significant harm to the national security of the United States." The Department of Justice would not defend its invocation to hide violations of law, inefficiency, or administrative error or to prevent embarrassment. Decisions to invoke the privilege would be made initially by an assistant attorney general and would be reviewed by a State Secrets Review Committee. Final decisions would be made by the attorney general, and the Department of Justice would make periodic reports to Congress on cases in which it relied on the privilege.[131] This has not stopped the government from relying on the state secrets doctrine in rendition and torture cases, but in Al-

Aulaqi v Obama, a claim challenging the alleged authorisation of the targeted killing of a US citizen who was outside the country and apparently deeply involved in anti-US terrorism, the government argued that the court did not have to and should not base its decision on the doctrine. The court agreed and dismissed the case on other grounds.[132]

Elsewhere, executive secrecy concerns were more subdued. One reason is that far less seems to have been at stake. But the governments of the UK, Canada, and Australia all have secrets that they have sought to protect. Another reason is that the courts have generally been receptive to government secrecy claims. Courts are prepared to give terms such as *national security* a reasonably broad interpretation and to give considerable deference to government decisions in relation to whether disclosure would harm national security, although they now require that government claims have a factual basis and adequate evidentiary support.[133] The Canadian decision in *Re Charkaoui* is an arguable exception, but one that is explicable in terms of the wording of the relevant legislation.

Courts have generally acknowledged the validity of standard bases for immunity claims. They have acknowledged the importance of the "third party" rule, especially for countries (such as Canada) that are net importers of intelligence.[134] But the rule does not apply where the government independently acquired the information, where the government has not sought permission to disclose from the provider government, or where the information has been made public by an organ of the provider government.[135] Courts have acknowledged that the disclosure of apparently innocuous pieces of information may be capable of threatening national security (the mosaic theory).[136] They have, however, sometimes been sceptical of attempts to base claims for nondisclosure on the theory, and in several cases, they have insisted that arguments based on the theory must be supported by information as to why disclosure of particular pieces of information might contribute to the construction of a mosaic in a way that would undermine security.[137] Where secrets are inadvertently disclosed, privilege may be claimed in relation to them, but the fact and circumstances of their disclosure is relevant to the balancing exercise required in public interest immunity jurisdictions.[138] Courts have been sympathetic to claims grounded in the need to protect operational secrets, the identities of informants and operatives, and information given in confidence.[139]

Yet there are limits to deference. Judicial consideration of whether information should be withheld often results in subsequent concessions by the government, coupled with a curial decision that other documents be released.[140] However, lack of deference is asymmetrical: courts have never found governments to have erred in cases where they have contended that information should be disclosed.[141]

Insofar as courts have addressed the reasons for the overclaiming, they have attributed it to overcaution and to failure even to consider some factors that have an obvious bearing on whether information should be disclosed.[142] However, courts have also commented on the absence of grounds for suspecting that governments overclaimed in order to prevent disclosure of evidence for improper purposes.[143] But in the UK and Canada, secrecy issues have been the basis for serious conflicts between the security services and the courts.

The UK government fought hard and unsuccessfully to maintain the principle that confidential intelligence from other countries enjoys absolute protection per se. Following the *Al Rawi* decisions, it published a green paper foreshadowing the possibility of legislative changes to enhance the government's capacity to protect its secrets from disclosure in the course of litigation, and in 2013 it secured the passage of legislation to give effect to its proposals.[144] The director of the CSIS was critical of the effects of the 2008 *Charkaoui v Canada* decision: "We were faced with a pretty fundamental dilemma: to disclose information that would have given would-be terrorists a virtual road map to our tradecraft and sources or to withdraw that information from the case, causing a security certificate to collapse."[145] The Australian government has been more successful. Its few applications under the NSIA have enjoyed almost complete success.[146]

The Public and Secrets

Even in the United States, there is little evidence as to public opinion in relation to the issue, which suggests that polling agencies and their users do not regard the issue as particularly salient. A 2002 poll suggests a widespread willingness to sacrifice due process for security. Respondents to a 2002 poll were asked whether they thought an American citizen arrested for planning an al-Qaeda terrorist attack in the United States should be held without trial as a "wartime prisoner" or put on trial in the civilian courts. The 42 percent of respondents who favoured trial in the courts were asked what should happen if the government objected that a trial would jeopardise sensitive intelligence. Two-thirds of these respondents still thought the person should be tried, but 29 percent considered he should be held without trial.[147] In a 2006 poll, 48 percent of respondents considered that if disclosure of evidence could put American lives in danger, it would be better to convict defendants on evidence not shown to them than it would be for the defendant to go free because the government withheld the evidence. The remainder were either unsure (11 percent) or considered the defendant should go free (41 percent).[148] Overall, the data suggest that majorities would not object to abridgement of Sixth Amendment rights but that sizeable minorities would. Given the apparently low salience of this issue, the political capital to be reaped by attacks on the unambiguous constitutional rights at stake would, at most, be minimal, especially given the considerable likelihood that doing so would entail the risk of the legislation being found to be unconstitutional.

Politics and Secrecy

There are scattered pieces of evidence to suggest that the development of the relevant legislation reflects party affiliations, but it is weak. In the United States, the proposed State Secrets Protection Act, which would have narrowed the scope of the state secrets doctrine, was supported in committee by Democrats and opposed by Republicans.[149] In Australia, Labor made attempts to secure amendments to some aspects of the NSIA but generally supported it. The Australian Democrats and the Greens voted against the legislation.

In Canada, the correlates of party were slightly more ambiguous. The Bloc Québécois (BQ) and the New Democrats opposed the Anti-terrorism Act 2001 and dissented from the House of Commons subcommittee report. A proposed amendment to delete the clause by which ministerial certificates could trump freedom of information had the support of the 10 New Democrats and eight BQ members who were present for the vote. It also had support from nine Progressive Conservatives (PCs) and three Canadian Alliance (CA) members of parliament. It was defeated by the votes of 103 Liberals, 33 CA MPs, and a lone PC. There was an almost identical vote in relation to certificates that would trump the Privacy Act. Among the opposition parties, votes roughly reflect their position on a left-right spectrum, but the Liberals' votes are further to the right than one might expect. Moreover, votes on a proposed sunset clause that would have applied to sections of the legislation including the minister's certification power disclosed a somewhat different pattern. The proposal was supported by 10 New Democrats and 16 members of the CA. The government opposed it, supported by seven members of the BQ, eight PCs, and 20 members of the CA. In 2007, a House of Commons subcommittee recommended that a panel of special counsel be established so that entities and charities seeking to challenge their listing or certification could have their interests better represented.[150] The minority, a New Democrat and a member of the BQ, dissented from the report, on the grounds that it should have recommended repeal of the offending provisions (along with the rest of the Anti-terrorism Act).[151] As in other contexts, major parties differ little from each other but consistently from smaller parties to their left.

A more robust test of the relevance of party comes from the effects of changes of government. In the United States, the elections of both Bush and Obama have made a difference, albeit one that may also reflect the different circumstances faced by Clinton and his successors. There have been minor changes in relation to the executive order governing classification criteria and procedures. Executive Order 12958 was made by President Clinton and amended by President Bush. The amendments were relatively subtle, but they facilitated classification by eliminating provisions to the effect that documents were not to be classified or to be classified at a particular level when "significant" doubts existed as to whether they should be. The Bush amendments also made it clear that national defense included defence against transnational terrorism.[152] President Obama's Executive Order 13526 of 2009 restored the rules against disclosure in the event of "significant doubt" and removed the Bush provisions expanding the scope of "national security" in relation to classifiable documents to include defence against transnational terrorism.[153] The order included new provisions designed to discourage overclassification and to accelerate review of classification decisions.[154] The administration also announced that it would place only limited reliance on the state secrets doctrine.[155] However, Democrats did not use their majority in the 111th Congress to pass legislation along the lines of the proposed State Secrets Protection Act.

In Australia, the Labor opposition had promised an overhaul of the NSIA on coming to power. It has indeed made extensive amendments to the act, but these have been of a technical nature. It did, however, abolish ministerial certificates as part of an overhaul of freedom of information legislation. Whether a document falls within the category is now a matter for the information commissioner, the Administration Appeals Tribunal, and the courts, but if disclosure could reasonably be expected to cause damage to the security of the commonwealth, the document continues to be exempt from disclosure, regardless of any public interest in disclosure.

In one sense, the UK government's proposals to amend the public interest immunity laws is consistent with the predispositions hypothesis. It involves a proposal by a Conservative-led coalition to strengthen security at some cost to liberty. Voting was largely along party lines, with Conservatives and their coalition partners and Labour opposing aspects of it. The Conservatives' Liberal Democrat coalition partners generally supported the government bill in the few House of Commons divisions, but in the House of Lords, Liberal Democrats often supported Labour amendments. However, as we shall see in later chapters, the UK Conservatives have often opposed measures to increase antiterrorism powers and, in government, have taken steps to reduce the scope of some of the more controversial counterterror measures. Moreover the Conservatives' junior partners, the Liberal Democrats, have a consistent record of relative liberalism in relation to terrorism issues. It seems more plausible to explain the proposals as a response to the *Al Rawi* decisions and to the exigencies of being in government.

Conclusions

The rules discussed in this chapter have the potential to work badly. The US state secrets rule means that the protection of state secrets may trump the interests of litigants who would have a strong case but for the rule. The public interest immunity rule seems fairer, but its administration may occasionally make it close to unworkable, and the costs of administering it may be such as to deter claims or to force settlements that bear little relation to the legal merits of the case. In any case, the general rule against the ex parte production of evidence means that there will be cases where the protection of secrets will mean that prosecutions are not feasible. One response has been some minor, successful legislative attempts to shift the balance weakly in favour of the government and to devise procedures designed to minimise the risk of disclosure while not prejudicing litigants' legal interests. But there are limits to what the legislation can achieve, assuming that secrets deserve protection and that their disclosure would make decision making more accurate.

The scope of the problem is unclear. Given the rarity of domestic terrorist attacks, it is not a serious one, at least as far as governments are concerned. Moreover, as we shall see in chapter 7, governments have normally been able to achieve convictions in terrorism cases. This does not preclude the possibility of there having been cases where "offenders" could not be prosecuted without disclosure. But if this is so, none of the villains has subsequently committed a terrorist act within the jurisdiction. Nonetheless, perceived problems arising from open trial requirements are among the factors that have encouraged interest in means of bypassing the courts and that have tempted governments to resort to the use of extralegal measures in the fight against terrorism, which themselves become secrets that governments wish to protect.

SIX

Guilt by Association

Terrorism is unlikely to constitute a serious threat unless it is organised. So it is not surprising that governments seek to obstruct terrorist organisations. They do so by imposing penalties on supporters, limiting members' immigration rights, and freezing organisations' assets. Such measures have aroused criticism. First, many of them are predicated on an organisation's having been officially listed as a terrorist organisation, rather than on its having been found by a court to have been engaged in terrorism. Listing decisions are usually judicially reviewable, but the powers of courts are narrower than those of the listing authority. Second, the criteria for listing condition proscription on the organisation's involvement in terrorism, unqualified by consideration of whether its terrorism might have justification. Objections on this ground sometimes involve apologias for relatively vicious groups and are misplaced in that the political element in executive proscription can sometimes provide a safeguard for "good terrorists." But this very possibility raises questions about why laws make no facial allowance for justified terrorism. Third, laws tend to punish involvement regardless of whether the person believes the proscribed organisation engages in terror and even if the person makes the contribution believing that it will be used by the terrorists for nonterrorist purposes, such as those pursued by the organisation's charitable arm. This is deliberate and is intended to make life more difficult for terrorists. But it raises awkward questions about the degree to which the state's political judgments should be allowed to prevail over the conscience of those who disagree with its conclusions.

Given these considerations, one might expect that proscription would encounter resistance from within legislatures and from the courts and that responses to proscription would reflect underlying orientations to authority and to liberty. To some extent, these expectations are borne out. However, controversy tends to surround details rather than proscription itself, which seems to be among the less controversial responses to terrorism.[1] There appears to be considerable cross-institutional support for proscription, and while there is some evidence of a relationship between party allegiance and attitudes towards proscription laws, the relationship is weak and blurred by the impact of whether or not a party is involved in government.

Proscription Laws

Proscription law is complicated by the existence of parallel proscription regimes, best understood as a response to different problems. One of these can loosely be called the "criminal law" regime and is embodied in primary legislation, which builds in some formal political and procedural safeguards. The latter, the sanctions regimes, are more closely tied to duties arising under the United Nations Charter and tend to derive their domestic force from legislation giving domestic effect to the requirements of the charter. Sanctions regimes are subject to relatively weak political and judicial supervision. The two major sanctions regimes are those that proscribe organisations (and people) listed by a UN committee and those that involve listing on the basis of the national government's conclusion that they fall within United Nations Security Council Resolution 1373.

"Criminal Law" Regimes

In all five countries under discussion in this book, legislation makes involvement of a terrorist organisation an element of various offences. In the United Kingdom and the United States, these offences are conditioned on the organisation having been proscribed. In Canada, Australia, and New Zealand, they apply in relation both to proscribed organisations and to organisations that are "objectively" terrorist organisations. However, in the latter case, the prosecution's evidentiary burden is considerably higher.

In the United States, only foreign organisations may be proscribed, but this power extends to permitting proscription of their local alter egos. Proscription requires a finding that the organisation engages in terrorism and is a threat to US security.[2] In the other four countries, the power may be exercised against both domestic and foreign organisations.[3] In the United Kingdom, a number of Irish organisations were proscribed in a schedule to the Terrorism Act 2000, with the home secretary being given the power to add or remove organisations from the banned list. New Zealand legislation now includes all entities listed by the United Nations. Elsewhere the legislation did not list any organisations, but as in the United Kingdom, subsequent proscription decisions required that the relevant official be satisfied that the organisation meets (or no longer meets) the conditions for its proscription. In particular, the organisation must have been (Canada, NZ) or must currently be (UK, Australia) engaged in terrorism. In Canada and New Zealand, the criminal proscription regime also permits the listing of individuals. Unease about "criminal law" proscription was reflected in clauses that limited the life of proscription decisions to two years (United States, Canada), two and later three years (Australia),[4] and three years (New Zealand).[5] In the United States and Canada, the sunset clauses have been replaced by requirements for periodic review.[6]

"Economic Sanctions" Regimes

The five "criminal law" regimes coexist with regimes that impose economic sanctions on designated organisations (and individuals) and that provide for the enforcement of those sanctions. In Australia and Canada, this is done under legislation and regulations giving effect to UN decisions, and this was purportedly the position in the United Kingdom until 2010. There are two different UN sanctions regimes. One (the al-Qaeda regime) implements UN Security Council resolutions relating to the Taliban, Osama bin Laden, and associated entities. These have their origins in Security Council Resolution 1267 (1999), which required the freezing of assets controlled by Taliban-related entities and established a committee (the 1267 Committee) to supervise the process. Resolution 1333 (2000) extended the regime to Osama bin Laden and al-Qaeda and to associated individuals and entities, as designated by the 1267 Committee (par 8(c)). In New Zealand, those listed by the committee are designated both for the purposes of the general criminal law and for sanctioning purposes.[7] In Canada, the relevant regulations apply to all entities on the 1267 list except those listed under the criminal law regime (who are subject to criminal law sanctions for proscribed dealings).[8] Australia incorporates the 1267 list by reference, and it overlaps with Australia's criminal law list.[9] The United Kingdom made regulations to similar effect, but in 2010, the Supreme Court ruled that the relevant regulations were not a valid exercise of the rule-making powers conferred by the United Nations Act 1946 (UK). In response, the government used powers under the European Communities Act 1972 (UK) to make regulations in relation to entities designated in annex 1 to Council Regulation No 881/2002, as amended from time to time.[10] The resolution broadly corresponds to the list of the 1267 Committee and is amended to ensure its continued correspondence.

The other regime (the general regime) has been established to implement Security Council Resolution 1373 (2001), which requires members of the United Nations to take steps to freeze the assets of entities "of persons who commit, or attempt to commit, terrorist acts or participate in or facilitate the commission of terrorist acts; of entities owned or controlled . . . by such persons; and of persons and entities acting on behalf of, or at the direction of such persons or entities" (par 1(c)). Member states must decide for themselves whether a person or entity satisfies these conditions. The United Nations does not maintain a list of those who might fall within the resolution. New Zealand makes no provision for doing so, other than pursuant to the criminal law power, and until 2010, it had made no use of even that power. Canada and Australia permit designation for 1373 purposes, but the Canadian power may be exercised only in relation to those not listed under the criminal law or 1267 regimes.[11]

Following a decision that regulations made to give effect to the resolution were not within the powers conferred by the United Nations Act 1946 (UK), the UK Parliament passed legislation that conferred the power but made it subject to greater safeguards than those afforded by the earlier regulations.[12] It also provides that a designated person for the purpose of the act includes an entity listed for the purposes of General Regulation (EC) No 2580/2001.

The United States imposes economic sanctions on two major classes of terrorists and terrorist organisations.[13] One class consists of "specially designated terrorists" and includes groups declared by President Clinton to be using violence to impede the Middle East peace process, along with foreign persons subsequently designated on similar grounds. The other consists of "specially designated global terrorists," which includes those listed in an order made by President Bush and those subsequently added.[14]

The Consequences of Proscription

Proscription has implications for criminal liability, whether it is under a "criminal law" or a "sanctions" regime. The relevant criminal offences are discussed in more detail in the next chapter. Broadly, if the body is proscribed under a criminal law regime, offences include a wider variety of forms of assistance to the organisation and carry higher maximum penalties. Offences under the "sanctions" regimes are more closely linked to the particular concerns of these regimes, namely, the prevention of economic assistance or the transfer of funds to proscribed entities.

In the United States, there is also an express nexus between immigration and involvement in proscribed organisations. People are inadmissible if they have engaged in terrorist activity or if they are reasonably believed to have done so or to be likely to do so.[15] Terrorist activity includes soliciting funds, recruiting, or providing material support for terrorist organisations.[16] Terrorist organisations include not only designated "foreign terrorist organizations" (FTOs) but also organisations designated by the secretary of state on the request of or after consulting with the attorney general or the secretary of homeland affairs.[17] Also included are groups of two or more people, whether organised or not, which engage in specified forms of terrorist activity.[18] In administering the legislation, limited allowance is made for those who support "good terrorists."[19]

In Canada, permanent residents and foreign nationals are inadmissible on security grounds if they are "members of an organization that there are reasonable grounds to believe engages, has engaged or will engage in [terrorist acts]."[20] That an organisation is listed as a terrorist organisation is relevant to whether reasonable grounds exist for acting on that assumption, as are prior decisions in relation to particular organisations. Thus, while the Mujahedin-e-Khalq (MEK) was still listed in Canada, membership could reasonably constitute grounds for exclusion, even if the organisation had been delisted by the UN Security Council.[21] Under current New Zealand law, a person is ineligible for an entry visa if the person is a member of a proscribed or designated entity, and a member of a group that has engaged in or taken responsibility for a terrorist act may be deported if, for that reason, the person constitutes a threat to public safety.[22] Elsewhere, immigration law makes no explicit reference to involvement in terrorist organisations, whether designated or not, but involvement would nonetheless be relevant to admissibility.

Designation as a terrorist organisation exposes the organisation to the freezing and possibly the confiscation of its assets. Under the sanctions regimes and—sometimes—the criminal law regimes, proscription means that dealings in the entity's assets are prohibited.[23]

Heightened Fears, Opportunism, Symbolism, or Deterrence? Legislative Response to Terrorist Attacks

Proscription laws are self-evidently a response to terrorism and to recent terrorist attacks, but in their current form, they can scarcely be dismissed as a hasty response to either the 9/11 attacks or earlier ones. In the United States, criminal proscription laws had their origins in the Antiterrorism and Effective Death Penalty Act of 1996.[24] The impetus for the act had come from a series of acts of international terrorism, the most recent of which had been the Lockerbie bombing. However, despite the emotions stirred by the attacks (which were evident in the congressional debates), the act was not passed until mid-1996, almost a year after it had been proposed. Moreover, despite the Oklahoma bombing, then recent, the legislation was not extended to domestic terrorist groups. The Patriot Act expanded the range of terrorist activities that could warrant designation but otherwise left the legislation largely unchanged, and these amendments were among the less controversial features of the act.

While the United Kingdom's initial proscription legislation was passed shortly after postwar violence had peaked in Northern Ireland, the 2000 Terrorism Act provisions had been the subject of four years of deliberations.[25] Moreover, prior to the 9/11 attacks, all five countries had passed measures to implement their Resolution 1267 responsibilities.

The criminal proscription laws of Canada, Australia, and New Zealand were passed in response to the 9/11 bombings but, to varying degrees, reflect the UK model. Canada's criminal proscription legislation was enacted with relative haste and included narrower protections than the UK regime. But proposed amendments designed to constrain the exercise of the power and to enhance judicial review rights won the support of all the nongovernment parties, along with a few dissenting government MPs, which suggests that any panic that did exist was confined to the government and that if the government's response was opportunistic, its political wisdom was not apparent to the opposition.

The Australian provisions evolved much more slowly. The original post-9/11 bill provided for listing decisions to be made by the attorney-general, but in a bipartisan report, the Senate Legal and Constitutional Committee recommended that the proscription provisions not be passed in their proposed form, and in any case, it was clear that the Labor and Australian Democrat opposition meant that the government would not have been able to secure the passage of its preferred option.[26] The government had no alternative but to agree to an amendment that limited the proscription power to organisations designated by the United Nations and that provided, in a departure from usual Australian practice, that regulations proscribing organisations did not come into effect until the expiry of the period during which they were subject to disallowance by either house of the federal parliament. The power subsequently underwent further amendment. The "United Nations" limit meant that unless the UN Security Council declared particular bodies to be terrorist organisations, the only bodies that could be banned would be those on the 1267 Committee's list. In 2004, the government was anxious to list the Hizballah External Security Organisation (which was not on the 1267 list). The opposition agreed to ad hoc legislation banning the organisation and later agreed to legislation listing two other organisations.[27] The government and opposition subsequently agreed on a compromise that created a general proscription power but subjected proscription regulations to mandatory review by the joint parliamentary committee responsible for intelligence. The following year, an apparently uncontroversial amendment made proscription regulations operative from the day they were made.[28]

New Zealand's legislation was not passed until more than a year after the 9/11 attacks and after a lengthy consultation process. Unlike legislation elsewhere, it was criticised in the Parliament on the grounds both that it was too narrow and that it was too broad.

Governments and Proscription

Proscription laws can sometimes be understood in terms of governments prising powers from reluctant legislatures, and the Australian experience is particularly consistent with this. However, the New Zealand experience is not, nor are the pre-9/11 experiences of the United States and the United Kingdom. In the United States, the proscription powers contained in the Antiterrorism and Effective Death Penalty Act of 1996[29] were in some ways broader than those sought by the government. President Clinton's proposal for a ban on contributions to terrorist organisations included provision for the establishment of procedures designed to permit the making, in limited circumstances, of contributions to designated organisations for "religious, charitable, literary, or educational purposes."[30] The bill reported by the House Judiciary Committee extended the prohibition to cover the making of many forms of material contributions, and it contained no provision for licensing contributions for worthy causes.[31] The proposed legislation underwent similar changes in the Senate. In the House, the prohibition was later dropped—the resulting bill being, effectively, for an effective death penalty—but it was restored in the conference bill. In the United Kingdom, concerns about the definition of terrorism were inspired partly by concerns at the definition's relevance to proscription, and concerns about the proscription power were also prompted by the fact that it was effectively an executive power rather than one conditioned on prior judicial approval. However, the only proposed amendment—which would have required a prior judicial declaration that proscription was reasonable—was withdrawn.

All five governments have exercised their "criminal law" proscription powers, albeit to varying degrees. Australia currently proscribes only 17 organisations.[32] By contrast, Canada, the United Kingdom, the United States, and, since October 2010, New Zealand have each proscribed 40 or more.[33] Apart from the organisations proscribed in a schedule to the Terrorism Act 2000 (UK), the United Kingdom has not proscribed any domestic organisations. Australia, Canada, and New Zealand have also used their powers only against foreign organisations. Thirteen organisations are listed by all five countries. Ten have been listed by four countries. There is clearly only a rough consensus as to which countries are worthy of "criminal law" proscription. Australian reticence possibly reflects the nonsalience of threats from some Northern Hemisphere groups, along with legislative and quasi-legislative obstacles to proscription.[34]

Deproscription occasionally occurs. In the United States, for example, the Japanese Red Army, the Khmer Rouge, Manuel Rodriguez Patriotic Front dissidents, and the Túpac Amaru guerillas have been dropped from the list of FTOs in recognition of their contemporary irrelevance. In 2008, Australia chose not to renew regulations proscribing the Armed Islamic Group, and it has dropped four other groups. The United Kingdom delisted the People's Mojahedin Organisation of Iran (PMOI), after a successful legal challenge to its continued proscription; but despite its success in securing its deproscription in the United Kingdom and Europe, the organisation was not delisted in the United States and Canada until late 2012.[35] Inertia is frequently warranted: examples of listed groups abandoning their ways are rare. But the outcome in the UK PMOI litigation evidenced government reluctance to consider whether proscription might still be warranted, and in Australia and Canada, statements of reasons for relisting often include no details of developments since the previous listing.[36]

Criminal prosecutions based on involvement in proscribed organisations have been strikingly rare, except in the United States. Indeed, there have been no prosecutions in New Zealand and only a handful in the United Kingdom, Canada, and Australia based on involvement with an organisation listed under the criminal law regime. The lack of prosecutions cannot necessarily be explained in terms of the lack of relevant crimes: there is a degree of support among Kurdish, Tamil, and Irish diasporas for relevant terrorist organisations, and it is unlikely that this never takes extralegal forms. Indeed, the CSIS public reports include periodic reference to the use of extortion by local agents of the Liberation Tigers of Tamil Eelam (LTTE), a listed entity, but this activity has generated only one prosecution.

The "economic sanctions" powers have generally been used to designate a far wider range of organisations and individuals. The US lists are lengthy, with many people and entities listed under several categories. Australia has listed a large number of organisations and individuals pursuant to Resolution 1373. (It includes virtually all the groups proscribed under the criminal law regimes in the other four countries.) It has adopted the al-Qaeda and Taliban lists by reference. In Canada, 36 organisations have been proscribed pursuant to Security Council Resolution 1373, with the al-Qaeda and Taliban lists adopted by reference, subject to exceptions. The UK Treasury's "Consolidated List of Financial Sanctions Targets in the UK" lists 30 organisations and 51 people.[37] New Zealand has adopted the al-Qaeda and Taliban lists by reference and, in October 2010, began a process of listing organisations under the criminal law power in order to satisfy its Resolution 1373 obligations. Other than in the United States, sanctions-related prosecutions have been rare or nonexistent, and the paucity of litigation surrounding assets-related powers suggests that these have rarely been exercised.

Courts and Proscription

Critics of proscription legislation have argued that the relevant legislation is unconstitutional. In the United States, there was a body of promising precedent to draw on: one of the legacies of Cold War persecution of communists is a body of case law to the effect that the first amendment precluded laws forbidding mere membership of organisations that engaged in both lawful and unlawful activities.[38] The Canadian Charter of Rights and Freedoms protects freedom of association, as does the ECHR. *Australian Communist Party v The Commonwealth*[39] is sometimes taken as precluding the banning of organisations, but, read strictly, it is a more mundane decision, to the effect that the federal government lacks the power to make laws with respect to unincorporated associations, except where there is a judicially reviewable nexus between the organisation's activities and a head of commonwealth power.

Scholars have confidently asserted that proscription legislation impermissibly limits freedom of political expression.[40] It tends to involve the imposition of disabilities without the organisation being given a hearing beforehand, and problems could potentially arise from the special provisions governing the judicial review of proscription decisions. Limits (where they exist) on collateral attacks on proscription decisions raise questions about the political branches trespassing into areas belonging to the judicial arm. But for obvious logistic reasons, litigation has been rare,[41] and on the whole, governments have fared reasonably well before the courts.

United States

Under US law, a body designated as a "foreign terrorist organization" has a limited right to apply for judicial review of the listing decision to the US Court of Appeals for the District of Columbia Circuit. Review is to be based on the administrative record, supplemented by any other classified information that is submitted by the government and was used in making the relevant decision. Classified information must be considered ex parte and in camera.[42]

The designation process has raised several due process issues. Organisations have no formal means of making submissions into why they should not be banned. Moreover, the original legislation made no provision for applications for delisting and the making of submissions in relation to this. The original judicial review procedures conditioned redress on errors in the record and did not permit the court to act on such evidence as the organisation might subsequently wish to provide. Furthermore, the narrow statutory standing rules limit the right to challenge listing decisions to the organisation and its agents and preclude collateral attack on listing decisions.

Since "[a] foreign entity without property or presence in [the United States] has no constitutional rights, under the due process clause or otherwise,"[43] a constitutional challenge to the validity of the legislation had to await a situation where a designated body was found to have the requisite presence. This hurdle was overcome in *National Council of Resistance of Iran v Department of State*,[44] where the People's Mojahedin Organisation of Iran was found to have established a presence, but only because the National Council of Resistance of Iran (NCRI) was found to be its alter ego and therefore properly designated, assuming that PMOI had been properly designated. Their due process argument succeeded. While the court conceded that giving notice "might work harm to [US] foreign policy goals in ways that the court would not immediately perceive,"[45] the secretary of state had made no attempt to demonstrate this. Notice was required, as was the chance to present, "at least in written form," "such evidence as those entities may be able to produce to rebut the administrative record or otherwise negate the proposition that they are foreign terrorist organizations."[46] This constitutional minimum was more than was required under the legislation. It followed, therefore, that the designations in question (and all other designations) were flawed.

Despite this, in a June 2001 decision, the court refused relief.

> [W]e also recognize the realities of the foreign policy and national security concerns asserted by the Secretary in support of those designations We further recognize the timeline against which all are operating: the two-year designations before us expire in October of this year.[47]

The court therefore declined to vacate the orders and remanded the questions to the secretary of state, to be considered according to the standards it had laid down. On reconsideration in accordance with the court's orders, the secretary provided the organisations with the unclassified record and considered their replies, along with the unclassified and classified material. Despite the additional information, she redesignated the organisations. PMOI petitioned for review, arguing, inter alia (and notwithstanding the court's earlier decision), that in relying on secret and undisclosed information, the secretary had denied PMOI due process. The court disagreed, saying, once more, that "under the separation of powers created by the United States Constitution, the Executive Branch has control and responsibility over access to classified information and has a 'compelling interest' in withholding national security information from unauthorised persons in the course of executive business."[48] In any case, the decision was supported by the unclassified material and, indeed, by admissions made by PMOI itself.

In 2004, Congress legislated to rectify the procedural defect in the legislation. Notice of an intention to list was still not required, but organisations were permitted to petition for delisting and to provide supporting material that the secretary was required to consider.[49] Organisations have rarely availed themselves of these procedures, and none who have done so have succeeded.

Substantive arguments have also failed. The court in *People's Mojahedin Organization of Iran v Department of State* dismissed an attempt to rely on a variant of the "good terrorist" argument, namely, that "the attempt to overthrow the despotic government of Iran which itself remains on the State Department's list of state sponsors of terrorism, is not 'terrorist activity,' or if it is, that it does not threaten the security of the United States or its nationals."[50] Its rationale (as in previous cases) was that the secretary of state's finding to the contrary was nonjusticiable. A petition from the NCRI seeking review of a 2003 decision by the secretary to leave in place its designation as an alter ego of PMOI failed on constitutional and substantive grounds.[51]

In 2008, PMOI once more sought to be delisted, and its request was once more refused in 2009. An application for review of the decision was partly successful:[52] the decision was made before PMOI had had an opportunity to reply to nonclassified material on which the secretary of state's decision had been based. Changes in legislation did not mean that the secretary's procedural duties were relaxed. Nor was the failure harmless. (The secretary had argued that since the decision was based largely on classified information, further submissions would have made no difference.) The court concluded that the outcome might have been different had the secretary considered responses to nonclassified material, and it further noted the possibility that if had the decision been based solely on classified material, due process might not have been afforded.[53] Almost two years after the decision to remand, the question had not been finalised. The circuit court eventually granted mandamus requiring the secretary to make a decision within four months, failing which the designation would be set aside.[54] On 28 September 2012, the organisation was finally delisted.[55]

The decisions did not address the relevance of flawed designations in cases where people were charged with offences in relation to designated organisations.[56] This issue arose in California, where Hossein Afshari and eight[57] others had been charged with knowingly and wilfully conspiring to provide material support to the Mujahedin-e-Khalq (MEK, another name for PMOI) between 1997 and 2001. The defendants argued that the DC Circuit had effectively found that the MEK designation was a nullity and therefore incapable of serving as a predicate to a charge based on contributing to a designated foreign terrorist organisation. This argument succeeded at first instance but not on appeal.[58] The Ninth Circuit agreed that section 1189(a)(8) did not preclude constitutional collateral attack. If the DC courts had set aside the designation decision, Afshari would have had a defence (although he could have been retried in relation to any contributions made after the nonproblematic "redesignation" in 1999). But the designation had not been set aside and therefore appeared to have legal force, notwithstanding that the designation had been constitutionally defective. An application for a rehearing, en banc, failed on a 6–5 vote, over a spirited dissent by Justice Kozinski.[59] The Supreme Court denied certiorari.[60] An attempt by the defendants to have the issues revisited two years later was unsuccessful.[61]

Listing decisions under the International Emergency Economic Powers Act[62] are judicially reviewable under the Administrative Procedures Act and also reviewable collaterally.[63] Due process arguments have generally failed. Courts have consistently held that the due process clause does not require notice prior to listing[64] and that due process in relation to listing decisions does not preclude reliance on classified information.[65] Even legally inadequate notice is not fatal to the validity of listing decisions, as long as the error can be shown to be harmless.[66] Even if the error cannot be shown to be harmless, the appropriate remedy may be not to quash the decision but to remand the matter for reconsideration.[67] Review is on the "arbitrary and capricious" standard, and designation decisions have satisfied this standard.[68]

However, in two recent decisions, courts have been receptive to the argument that freezing involves the seizure of property and therefore attracts Fourth Amendment protections. In each case, freezing had been achieved by blocking orders pending investigation, followed by designation. There was no suggestion in either case that the Fourth Amendment operated differently depending on whether freezing was achieved by preliminary order rather than by designation. In *Al Haramain Islamic Foundation v Department of the Treasury*,[69] the court held that since seizure was preventive rather than punitive, it was enough that the seizure was "reasonable." The court held that since the government's interest was substantial and outweighed the foundation's Fourth Amendment interest, the reasonableness requirement was satisfied. By contrast, the court in *KindHearts for Charitable Humanitarian Development v Geithner* held that seizure required a warrant, issued for probable cause.[70] It deferred consideration of the remedial implications of this ruling. KindHearts argued that the logic of the finding was that the blocking order was unconstitutional and therefore had to be quashed. The government argued that the court should conduct a post hoc hearing on probable cause. The court agreed that this was the appropriate course of action: the procedure had been accepted in forfeiture cases and, by analogy and on the basis of equitable principles, was applicable in freezing cases, especially given that they implicated Article II powers. The probable cause standard was less exacting in this context than in the criminal context.[71] The court remanded accordingly. In 2012, the government eventually settled on the basis that it would lift the listing of KindHearts and pay its legal costs. With approval from the Office of Foreign Assets Control, KindHearts would transfer its remaining assets to the UN World Food Program, the UN Children's Fund, the UN Relief and Works Agency for Palestinian Refugees, Mercy Corps, and Masjid Saad (physical assets only). This done, it would dissolve itself, but its board members would be free to attempt to establish another charity.[72]

A further set of challenges have targeted the material support legislation on a variety of grounds, including First and Sixth Amendment grounds. First Amendment challenges have been unsuccessful insofar as they relate to the right to associate for terrorist purposes, but the material support offence has been more controversial. The problem is that there is a continuum ranging from providing a nuclear bomb to al-Qaeda, at one extreme, to publicly criticising the Sri Lankan government for discrimination against Tamils, towards the other. The question of where to draw the line has generated years of litigation. In general, courts agreed that financial support was on the wrong side of the line, even if the donor did not intend the gift to be used for terrorist purposes, but there was less agreement in relation to the provision of less-fungible services, as well as some disagreement as to whether Congress intended to and could condition guilt on an intent to contribute in the absence of an intent to assist terrorism. The litigation culminated in a Supreme Court decision that comes close to overruling the freedom of association cases of the post-McCarthyist years and rejects the need to prove specific intent in material support prosecutions.

With considerable success, the Humanitarian Law Project (HLP) and its allies, the Kurdistan Workers' Party (PKK) and the LTTE, had argued that the material assistance legislation impermissibly interfered with some forms of support that the HLP wished to offer to the PKK and LTTE. These included the provision of training in the making of human rights submissions to international bodies, an endeavour no doubt complicated by the two organisations' limited grasp of this concept. They also included advocacy by the HLP on behalf of the organisations. At both the district and circuit levels, courts held that successive versions of the offence were unconstitutional as applied to the plaintiffs' intended activity.[73] However, the government finally sought and was granted certiorari by the Supreme Court, which held, by majority—six Republican appointees against three Democrats—that the court of appeals had erred.

The court rejected the contention that section 2339B required a specific intention to further the organisation's illegal activities: the language and context of the legislation made it clear that it did not. The plaintiffs also could not succeed on a vagueness-as-applied argument. As applied to their activity, the legislation was not vague: it clearly forbade some of their proposed activity while permitting other forms. The former included providing training in dispute resolution skills and in the making of submissions to the United Nations. The latter included independent advocacy on behalf of Kurds and Tamils. For advocacy to fall within the prohibition on providing personnel, it must be done under the FTO's direction or control. That was not what the petitioners had in mind. They therefore knew where they stood.

It followed from the analysis of the legality of advocacy that the legislation applied only to a very narrow category of speech, but it nonetheless did apply to speech and therefore required strict scrutiny and a compelling justification. This was provided both by the fact that "the Government's interest in combating terrorism is an urgent objective of the highest order"[74] and by grounds for believing that any of the proscribed forms of "material contribution" to a terrorist organisation facilitated its criminal conduct. Resources given for lawful purposes would not necessarily be used for those purposes. Even if material support was meant to further peaceable conduct, it could contribute to terrorism by freeing up organisational resources, by lending legitimacy to the terrorist group, and by thereby enabling the group to mobilise additional support. Moreover, tolerating support for foreign terrorism could strain "the United States' relationships with its allies and [undermine] cooperative efforts between nations to prevent terrorist attacks."[75] The majority acknowledged that it was difficult to know whether support would assist terrorists, but it concluded that, for this reason, the court should respect the conclusions of Congress and the government.

> One reason for this respect is that national security and foreign policy concerns arise in connection with efforts to confront evolving threats in an area where information can be difficult to obtain and the impact on certain conduct difficult to assess. The dissent slights these real constraints in demanding hard proof—with "detail," "specific facts," and "specific evidence"—that plaintiffs' proposed activities will support terrorist attacks. . . . That would be a dangerous requirement. In this context, conclusions must often be based on informed judgment, rather than concrete evidence, and that reality affects what we may reasonably insist on from the Government.[76]

The minority argued that, read broadly, the legislation impermissibly interfered with freedom of speech. The government's justifications were not compelling. It had not demonstrated that HLP's activities would free up resources for use in terrorism. Its argument that HLP's proposed activities should be banned because of their potential to lend legitimacy to the PKK and

LTTE ran foul of precedent: the logic of Supreme Court decisions in relation to members and supporters of the Communist Party was that even if an organisation threatened national security, speech that merely lent legitimacy to the body could not warrant interference with membership and support per se. Arguments based on the fungible nature of financial support had merit, but they were irrelevant when the support was clearly not financial and was not clearly convertible into resources that would assist the organisations' terrorist objectives. The constitutional problem would be avoided if the statute were read down so as to require that a defendant know or intend that the resources provided bore "a significant likelihood of furthering the organization's terrorist ends."[77] The dissent left open the question of whether the same test would apply when a person provided support that, of its nature, might well assist its terrorist activities.

United Kingdom

UK courts have rejected arguments that proscription laws are contrary to the ECHR, but they have nonetheless found in favour of plaintiffs in two important cases. UK law provides special procedures for appeals against decisions to proscribe organisations. The first step involves an application to the home secretary, seeking the removal of the organisation from the list of proscribed organisations (Terrorism Act 2000, s 4(1)). Standing rules are broader than the corresponding US rules: both organisations and persons affected by the proscription may apply (s 4(2)). If the application is refused, the applicant may appeal against the refusal to the Proscribed Organisations Appeal Commission (POAC), a body created under the act (s 5(2)). The POAC must allow the appeal if it concludes that the refusal to deproscribe was flawed, "when considered in the light of the principles applicable on an application for judicial review" (s 5(3)). The procedures of the POAC are designed to protect classified information.[78]

The legislation does not, on its face, preclude resort to normal judicial review procedures. Nonetheless, in *R (Kurdistan Workers' Party and Others) v Secretary of State for the Home Department*,[79] Justice Richards dismissed an application for judicial review on the grounds that the POAC was the appropriate forum for considering proscription decisions.[80] One of the applicants in that case, the ubiquitous People's Mojahedin Organisation of Iran, had also lodged an appeal with the POAC. In a preliminary ruling, the POAC dismissed the argument that the decision to proscribe was unlawful on the grounds that PMOI had not been given a prior opportunity to make representations. Since proscription was a legislative decision, rather than a quasi-judicial or administrative one, there was no basis for such a duty in the absence of express legislative provision, and there was no such provision, express or implied, in the legislation. Fairness did not require that an opportunity be given to make representations and be consulted. This would often not be feasible, given the problems of communicating prospective decisions to some organisations and the difficulties, due to the need to protect classified information, of putting them on notice as to the basis of the case against them. Insofar as there was a duty of fairness, it was satisfied by the requirement of parliamentary approval as a condition for the operation of a ban, along with the provision for post-proscription judicial review in the POAC.[81] An appeal against the decision was abandoned, and no action was taken in relation to a further, unsuccessful application for deproscription.[82]

In 2006, three members of parliament wrote to the home secretary to ask yet again that PMOI be deproscribed. Following his refusal of their application, they exercised their right to appeal to the POAC. The ultimate question related to the legality of the refusal to deproscribe, but this raised prior questions, including whether the secretary was required to consult with the organisation prior to refusing to deproscribe, the standard of review to be applied by the POAC, and whether the POAC could rely on evidence that was "available" but not considered by the secretary.

The applicants failed on the fairness issue. Consultation was not required by the legislation and would be difficult to achieve, given the tight timetable set for consideration of applications for deproscription. There were, moreover, procedures to ensure that the overall process was fair: namely, an ongoing duty to reconsider whether proscriptions should remain in force, the right to apply for deproscription, and the procedures for review of refusal decisions.[83] On the standard of review issue, the secretary was less successful.

The commission pointed out that proscription was conditioned on a belief that the relevant body was involved in terrorism. This required more than a suspicion that it might be, and given the nature of the power, the Parliament could be presumed to intend that the exercise of the power should be subject to strict scrutiny.[84] Moreover, since there was no requirement that the secretary consult with the organisation prior to deciding whether to deproscribe, it was reasonable to assume that the applicants should be able to adduce material not before the secretary in order to support their case.[85] The validity of the decision depended on whether there were in fact reasonable grounds for the secretary of state's belief that PMOI "*is concerned in terrorism*."[86]

The outcome did not in fact turn on "standard of review" questions. The commission concluded that the secretary had misdirected himself on the law, by asking whether PMOI had engaged in terrorism, not whether, at the time, it was still doing so. He had failed to consider all the relevant material that was constructively before him. There was, moreover, no evidence that PMOI had been "concerned in terrorism" after 2002.

Given this decision, it was not necessary to consider whether the legislation was inconsistent with the ECHR. The commission nonetheless considered the issue briefly, finding that while the provisions limited the appellants' rights, they did so in a manner that was legitimate and proportionate. National security was the foundation for democracy and human rights, and the law could contribute to it. It did nothing to hinder peaceful and democratic attempts to achieve political change in other states. It did not matter that the government of Iran was undemocratic and repressive. The secretary of state was entitled to conclude that this was not enough to justify terrorism. It was the clear intention of the legislature to support foreign states in the fight against terrorism.[87]

The secretary's application for special leave to appeal to the court of appeal was unsuccessful. The court broadly agreed with the approach the POAC had taken to the review. This was not a case where deference was due.

> The question of whether an organisation is concerned in terrorism is essentially a question of fact. Justification of significant interference with human rights is in issue. We agree with POAC that the appropriate course was to conduct an intense and detailed scrutiny of both open and closed material in order to decide whether this amounted to reasonable grounds for the belief that PMOI was concerned in terrorism.[88]

The only other litigation to canvass the validity of listing decisions related to the validity of listing orders made under the Terrorism (United Nations Measures) Order 2006 (TO) and the Al-Qaida and Taliban (United Nations Measures) Order 2006 (the AQO). The basis for the challenge was that the orders were not permitted by the relevant primary legislation. This argument succeeded at first instance[89] but failed (by majority) in the court of appeal.[90] In January 2010, the newly established Supreme Court ruled that both orders were invalid.

The court held that the United Nations Act 1946 (UK) did not authorise the making of the TO. The power to make orders was a power to make orders that were "necessary or expedient" for giving effect to Resolution 1373. The order allowed listing if the Treasury had "reasonable grounds for suspecting" that a person was or might be a person who fell within a category of persons or entities whose assets the resolution required to be frozen. The Supreme Court unanimously held that the purported power went well beyond what was "necessary" to give effect to the resolution. The resolution required actions against those who fell within the categories, not those who were reasonably suspected of doing so. A fortiori, it did not apply to those whom the Treasury reasonably suspected "may" do so. Nor, given standard principles of statutory interpretation, was it "expedient."[91]

The AQO did not lend itself to that form of attack. It clearly did implement a decision of the UN Security Council, and under the UN Charter, Security Council decisions trumped all other international obligations. In 2008, the House of Lords had accepted that the Human Rights Act was subject to obligations imposed by the UN Charter.[92] A decision by the European Court of Justice striking down European regulations implementing Resolution 1267 was not relevant: since the European Community was not a member of the United Nations, it, unlike the United Kingdom, was not bound by the UN Charter.[93]

This did not mean that the order was valid. By majority, the court held that the act did not confer the power to make the order. Parliament could not have intended that order-making power could be exercised to deprive people of their common-law property rights, without giving them an effective basis for challenging the relevant decision in the courts.[94] It could do so explicitly, but if it did, it would be consciously acknowledging that giving effect to the Security Council resolution should trump basic common-law rights.[95] Lord Brown dissented: given that the United Kingdom was bound under international law to implement Resolution 1267, the act permitted the AQO. That the order was "contrary to fundamental principles of human rights" was not relevant: this was what the resolution required.[96]

The court declared that the TO and Article 3(1)(b) of the AQO were invalid. It would also have suspended the Terrorism (United Nations Measures) Order 2009 if that had been before the court. The logic of the court's reasoning was that clearly drafted legislation could give the government the powers it has assumed it had under the United Nations Act 1946. Instead, to replace the TO, the government introduced an interim bill deeming the terrorism orders to have been validly made and to be within the powers conferred by the United Nations Act 1946. It also provided protection to anyone other than the Treasury who had acted on the validity of the orders between the date of the Supreme Court's decision and the date the legislation was passed. The Treasury's liability was unaffected. The interim bill was passed by the Parliament and given royal assent before the day was out.

It was an interim measure and was superseded, two weeks before its expiry date, by the Terrorist Asset-Freezing (Temporary Provisions) Act 2010 (UK, c 38).[97] The new act was designed to meet some of the Supreme Court's substantive objections to the old sanctions regime. It included provision for notification of interim and final designations, for judicial review of designation decisions, and for the procedures to govern such review.[98] It also broadened the criteria for designation to include a person's past involvement in terrorism.[99] The February legislation did not revive the AQO. Instead, the government made regulations under the European Community Act 1972, giving effect to a European Community directive that, in turn, substantially implements Resolution 1267 but is subject to the protections afforded by European law.[100]

Canada

The first challenge to the validity of the Canadian sanctions legislation was made by a Canadian citizen who had been listed by the 1267 Committee and who had also been listed under the 1373 regime.[101] He faced extradition, but extradition was dependent on the validity of the sanctions regulations. He argued that both sets of regulations were contrary to the Charter of Rights and Freedoms, on the grounds that by designating him, they removed the onus on the Crown to demonstrate that he actually was involved in terrorism. The issue became moot. After inquiries, the government concluded that there was no basis for the plaintiff's listing and removed him from both lists. His removal from the 1267 list was accomplished by an amendment to the Regulations, stating that they did not apply to those listed in a schedule and listing the plaintiff in the schedule. By doing so, Canada was arguably breaching its international obligations,[102] but it subsequently persuaded the Security Council to delist him.[103]

A second case, *Abdelrazik v Canada (Minister of Foreign Affairs)*,[104] involved the question of whether Mr. Abdelrazik was entitled to an order that the Canadian government cooperate with his repatriation to Canada from Sudan. Canada had argued that since Abdelrazik had been listed by the 1267 Committee, assistance with his travel would violate the 1267 sanctions regime. Justice Zinn denounced the 1267 Committee regime as a denial of fundamental human rights but was able to find for the plaintiff without having to determine whether he had been properly listed.[105] In 2010, Abdelrazik commenced a challenge to his listing.[106] On 30 November 2011, he was removed from the list.[107]

Australia and New Zealand

Australian proscription decisions are reviewable according to judicial review procedures, which vary depending on whether a regulation or a refusal to delist is being challenged. There have been no judicial review applications. New Zealand proscription decisions are also reviewable, and originally they were subject to far more intense scrutiny. Section 35 of the Terrorism Suppression Act 2002 (NZ) originally required the approval of the High Court as a condition for extending proscription beyond the initial three-year term and conditioned renewal on the court's satisfaction on the balance of probabilities that the entity satisfied specified conditions. Given that the New Zealand list corresponded to the 1267 Committee list, this would have meant that the government would have had to either breach its UN obligations or prove relevant facts in relation to people in distant lands, which would have been almost impossible. In 2005, it dealt with these problems by amending the legislation so that all designations were extended until two years after the report from a special committee charged with reporting on the Terrorism Suppression Act 2002 (NZ). Before the expiry of this period, the Parliament abolished the requirement for High Court approval.[108] Designation decisions continue to be judicially reviewable, but there have been no applications.

Underlying Beliefs

Proscription poses both liberty and hierarchy issues, and this was manifested in debates about proscription laws. For critics, the legislation aroused memories of earlier attacks on dissident organisations and concerns about the potential of the legislation to catch "good" terrorists as well as bad, and these concerns tended to come from the "left" rather than the "right." They were sometimes reflected in voting. In 1995, 9 Democrat members of the House Judiciary Committee voted to relax the standing requirements for challenging designation decisions and were outvoted by 18 Republicans and a Democrat. In the United Kingdom, Labour MPs seemed slightly less supportive of proscription than members of the opposition Conservatives, and Liberal Democrats were even less supportive. In Australia, Labor voted against the wide proscription powers proposed by the government. In New Zealand, the two conservative parties sought to expand the proscription powers, and the Greens sought to restrict them. In Canada, voting is less easily interpreted. A Progressive Conservative amendment provided that regulations might be made specifying the criteria to be used in listing decisions and that the criteria should be tabled and debated prior to the making of the regulations. This amendment was supported by all nongovernment parties, including the Canadian Alliance, and by a handful of Liberals. However, the amendment would have impaired the government's power only if the government chose to make the regulations.

There is less evidence of changes in partisan balances being reflected in changes to legislation or in the exercise of statutory powers. In the United States, standing requirements remain unchanged. Since coming to power, the Canadian Conservatives have done nothing to amend the criminal proscription regime to conform with the amendment for which they voted in 2001. In New Zealand, the Nationals criticised Labour's failure to proscribe any organisations other than those on the 1267 list, and once in power, they did indeed proscribe a number of additional organisations. The only example of a change of government making a difference consistent with earlier reservations comes from Australia, where Labor's 2010 overhaul of terrorism legislation involved measures that slightly tightened the procedures governing sanctions proscription and the criteria for criminal justice proscription.

Conclusions

Whatever the impact of proscription laws might be, it seems to be small. The targets of the laws lie largely outside the national boundaries of the proscribers, although the case law is testimony to its capacity to impinge occasionally on political organisations, charities, and individuals within national boundaries. Because proscription is necessarily public in outcome, opportunities for executive abuse are limited. However, the opaque processes governing listing for sanctions purposes mean that there is an ever-present possibility of mistakes and that these may not easily be rectified. Cross-institutional conflicts have been slight. In the United States, courts have generally deferred to the executive, and the Supreme Court's decision in *Holder v Humanitarian Law Project* implies that insofar as they have not, they ought to have. In the United Kingdom, the political arms have ultimately deferred to the courts: the legislative response to *R v Ahmad* was not to provide statutory support for the ultra vires orders but to create a new and fairer regime, more in keeping with the values that had underlain the Supreme Court's decision. In the two relevant Canadian cases, the executive gave the plaintiff what he wanted in one case and frustrated him in the other.

The limited salience of proscription may account for the paradox that despite partisan divisions over proscription laws, they have largely survived changes of government and changes in the balance of legislative power. However, another reason for that paradox may be that proscription law implicates issues of internationalism and international law in a manner calculated to arouse a degree of cognitive dissonance for people of both the left and the right. More than most areas of counterterrorism law, proscription law has developed against a backdrop of attempts to internationalise counterterrorism, by both international cooperation and the development of international law. Both practices sit far more easily with the traditions of the left than with those of the right, but their consequences in the counterterror context have obvious appeal to the right. The problem only exists, however, for those who want the world to be simple. The desirability of international cooperation must be assessed against the realisation that just as there may be "good" terrorists, so there are bad states, and since international law may reflect the input of bad states as well as good ones, it, too, will sometimes be imperfect.

SEVEN

Terrorism Offences

> If sentences are imposed which are more severe than the circumstances of the particular case warrants this will be likely to inflame rather than deter extremism.
> *Lord Phillips*[1]

One of the responses to terrorism has been the development of criminal laws that specifically target terrorism. These laws have been criticised on two incompatible grounds. One is that the law already punishes terrorist acts and preparations for those acts.[2] Accordingly, critics of the creation of special terrorist offences have cited their redundancy as evidence that the new offences are no more than window dressing, aimed at reassuring an "anxious public."[3] An alternative criticism is that terrorism offences have gone beyond what the criminal law should proscribe and, "by piling inchoate liability on top of inchoate crimes," run the risk of creating "monstrosities" such as "attempting conspiracies."[4]

The former proposition is clearly correct in relation to completed terrorist acts, and to a considerable degree, preparations for terrorist attacks could also be punished as conspiracies or attempts. In the United States, conspiracy law is extremely wide. It requires an agreement to perform a criminal act, but it does not require that there be agreement as to details of the offence. If people agree that they will acquire the knowledge and material necessary to make a bomb that they will set off somewhere in the hope that this will involve considerable property damage or loss of life, they are involved in a conspiracy to commit relevant offences (such as murder, damage to property, explosives offences). The elements of conspiracy vary somewhat across jurisdictions. A common element is that there must be an agreement to commit an act that, if committed, would constitute a crime, and it is immaterial that a party to the conspiracy subsequently has second thoughts.[5] Some require overt acts evidencing the conspiracy; others do not, although the absence of overt acts may complicate proof of the conspiracy. In the United States, a person can be guilty of conspiracy as long as there is feigned agreement (as, one hopes, is the case where the only other party to the "conspiracy" is with an undercover agent). Elsewhere, there must be an actual agreement.[6] Both in the United States and in the other countries considered in this book, an attempt to conspire to create a substantive offence is not itself an offence.[7]

There are several rationales for the creation of special terrorism offences. First, several activities cannot be caught by substantive offences and conspiracy law. A person may give money to a terrorist organisation under the intent that it be used for charitable purposes or to fund propaganda. This hope may be naive but sincere. If so, the person is not guilty of a conspiracy to do the objectionable things that the contribution facilitates, because the donor does not intend to help the terrorist group achieve its terrorist purposes.[8] However, a government may take the view that people should be discouraged from assuming that terrorist organisations act like good trustees who scrupulously refrain from mingling different funds. Hard-hearted government may conclude that even if the organisation uses funds only for the purpose for which they are donated, this may nonetheless enhance the organisation's capacity to engage in terrorist campaigns.[9] Doing good works is, after all, one way to win hearts and minds, which is why terrorists sometimes kill aid workers whose good works compete with theirs.

Attempt laws may not catch terrorist plans in their early stages. If they involve conspiracies, this will normally be immaterial, but if they involve a lone offender, mere preparation is not enough to constitute an attempt. Making it an offence to prepare for terrorism makes it easier to thwart would-be terrorists.

The UK offence of encouragement of terrorism also expands the scope of the law, especially since encouragement can include "glorification." If the glorification is intended to encourage the commission of a terrorist act, it may well constitute incitement. But if it is merely intended to encourage the creation of an ideological climate in which the commission of terrorist acts becomes more likely, it may fall short of incitement.

A second rationale for special terrorism offences is that they may make it easier to secure convictions. For example, it may be difficult to prove that a person who provides material support to a terrorist organisation knows that the organisation relevantly engages in terrorism or that the money they give for charitable purposes will not be used for uncharitable ones. By making it an offence to contribute to a proscribed organisation, proof may be made slightly easier, although not much: insofar as proof of guilt requires knowledge of proscription, the prosecution might be hard-pressed to prove that the hypothetical little old lady who contributes $20 to Hamas knew that it had been proscribed. More striking examples of facilitated proof are provided by offences whose elements either are satisfied if the prosecution proves that the defendant had reasonable grounds for believing in their existence or cast an evidentiary burden on the defendant.[10]

A third rationale for special terrorist offences is that terrorist crimes may require special treatment. They deserve condign sentences; they might warrant refusal of bail. This belief probably underestimates the degree to which traditional bail and sentencing law allow the requisite pretrial and posttrial detention. Moreover, it does not necessarily require the creation of special terrorism offences. Indeed, US law makes only limited use of freestanding terrorism offences. Rather, it provides that bail should normally be withheld from those charged with "federal crimes of terrorism," and offences may attract a higher sentence if they involved or were intended to promote such crimes. To constitute a federal crime of terrorism, the behaviour must constitute at least one of a number of listed offences. These include but are not limited to offences that are obviously related to terrorism. In addition, however, the offence must be calculated or intended to coerce or intimidate government or to retaliate against government action.[11] The other four countries considered in this book also tend to accommodate terrorist *acts* under the general law, their terrorist offences being largely aimed at precursor activities, and it is hard to see what the Australia and New Zealand achieve via their terrorist act offences that could not be achieved under the general law.

The redundancy argument has some merit, but it underestimates the degree to which the advocates of counterterror laws are seeking to catch those whose conduct would not have brought them within the ordinary criminal law. In particular, it underestimates the degree to which terrorism offences are aimed at catching possible offenders at an early stage of their planning. If there was a risk of particularly serious terrorist attacks, if early intervention could reduce the likelihood of such attacks, and if harm to the innocent was limited, this would be a defensible policy. Critics doubt that any of these conditions are satisfied. They are worried about the use of the criminal law to punish people for what they might do rather than for what they have in fact done, although this is to be blind to the degree to which the criminal justice system looks to the future in nonterrorism cases. They are naturally worried by backdoor relaxation of burdens of proof, since these will necessarily mean more wrongful convictions. They are also worried lest innovations in one area of the criminal law infect other areas of the law, although it is not clear that the likelihood of this is enhanced by special terrorism laws, as distinct from attempts to stretch existing law to accommodate what might be seen as the distinctive needs of terrorism prosecutions.

Legislatures have responded to terrorism to varying degrees and in varying ways, although there has been a general tendency to expand the capacity of the criminal law to perform a preventive function. Governments have tended to use the new offences sparingly, partly because they are conditioned on the existence of offences, which have been in gratifyingly short supply. Courts have generally given governments and prosecutors what they wanted. The new offences have largely survived constitutional scrutiny, and even when they have been given a narrow construction, defendants have generally been convicted on one or more counts. However, convictions come at a cost. To governments, the expense of prosecutions can be massive. Police and prosecutorial errors can detract from the legitimacy governments might accrue from more carefully exercising their powers. A corollary of these costs is that governments make mistakes, and those who pay most for these mistakes are those whose liberty is limited as a result of the exercise of criminal justice powers.

Offences

The appendix at the end of this chapter summarises offences that are defined by reference to some kind of link with terrorism. In the United States, the word *terrorism* is also used in labels applied to groups of offences of a kind that terrorists might commit, regardless of whether the offender intended to coerce governments or sections of the population and regardless of the offender's motives. One bundle of offences is the basis for the offence of material support of terrorists. For the purpose of this offence, a person is a terrorist as long as they relevantly commit any of the listed offences. Another set of offences constitute "federal crimes of terrorism." These include the material support offences. Whether an offence is a federal crime of terrorism is relevant to bail and sentencing decisions.

In other jurisdictions, laws applying generally to "terrorist" acts apply only to offences against terrorism conventions or offences involving a relevant terrorist intent. Many of these offences overlap with conventional criminal offences, but it is also apparent that terrorism offences are designed to catch precursor acts that would otherwise not fall foul of the criminal law. First, there are offences capable of catching preparations that have not yet become "attempts." The most obvious examples of these include the UK and Australian preparation offences. Other examples include the material support and possession offences. Second, there are offences that catch precursor activities that might not amount to a conspiracy. These include contributions to a terrorist organisation that has no current plans for terrorist actions, as well as contributions for the nonterrorist purposes of terrorist organisations. The most wide-ranging of these offences include the UK encouragement and publications offences. Third, there are offences designed to ease proof. These include the UK offences relating to possession of things useful for terrorism.

The countries clearly vary in the scope of their laws. UK law is broadest, and its encouragement, publications, and membership offences would probably fall foul of the US Constitution. Australian law is heavily based on UK law but narrower, in that it does not extend to encouragement and publications. Canada and New Zealand laws are narrower. Importantly, their laws in relation to organisations do not catch people who "participate" in an organisation without intending thereby to enhance its capacity to engage in terrorism. But even UK law basically respects the "reasonable doubt" test, with the quasi-exceptions doing no more than casting an evidentiary duty on the accused.

The United States lacks the United Kingdom's broad encouragement and publications offences, and unlike UK and Australian law, US law does not make it an offence to be a member of a terrorist organisation. But the material support offence would catch anyone whose membership was other than purely nominal, and after taking account of offences that constitute federal crimes of terrorism, there are some respects in which US law is slightly broader than UK and Australian law.

Pretrial and Posttrial Detention

Investigative Detention

UK and Australian law permit the detention of terrorism suspects pending further investigation.[12] Short initial detention periods are permitted, after which judicial approval is required for further periods of detention. In the United Kingdom, the maximum period of detention is currently 14 days. In Australia, the maximum detention period depends on a complex formula. The maximum aggregate time during which an arrestee may be questioned is 24 hours. In addition, detention is permitted during "dead time" during which questioning is impossible, and it is subject to judicial approval for periods when, for other reasons, it is reasonable to delay questioning. The maximum aggregate duration of such periods is now 7 days. Further detention is conditioned on the suspect being charged and is dependent on a court refusing to allow release on bail.[13]

Pretrial Detention

Even if pretrial detention were permitted solely for the purpose of ensuring a person's presence at trial, it also serves as de facto preventive detention functions insofar as defendants charged with terrorism offences constituted a flight risk.[14] The heavy penalties associated with terrorism offences mean that those charged might be tempted to try to flee the country or go into hiding, and insofar as alleged terrorists have links with terrorist networks, their prospects for being able to go into hiding might be enhanced. Moreover, in the United States, bail legislation requires taking account of the "danger" the arrestee poses to the community, which would also count against release in terrorism cases.[15]

Legislation in the United States, Canada, and Australia requires that pretrial detention decisions take account of whether the defendant is charged with a terrorism offence. In the United States, detention must be ordered if the judicial officer finds that no condition or combination of conditions will ensure appearance at trial and guarantee the safety of any other person and the community. There is also a rebuttable presumption that when a person is charged with particular offences, no conditions will satisfy the appearance and safety requirements. Since 2004, these offences have included those that would also constitute federal crimes of terrorism, regardless of whether they satisfy the requirement of intent to coerce.[16] Since 2006, a judicial officer determining the adequacy of possible conditions for release is also required to consider matters that include whether the offence is a federal crime of terrorism.[17]

Canadian law creates a strong presumption in favour of conditional release, but the presumption is reversed if the accused is charged with specified offences. Since 2001, these have included terrorism offences.[18] Australian law prohibits the granting of bail in the case of terrorism offences, save in exceptional circumstances where a person is charged with terrorism offences and other specified offences and where the "physical element" involves death or the risk of death.[19]

Sentencing

Under ordinary sentencing principles, terrorism offences could be expected to attract heavy sentences. Terrorism offenders seem to have slightly better prior records, and once one discounts for their involvement in terrorism, they are sometimes people of relatively good character. In relation to very serious offences, however, priors and character generally play a relatively minor role. Moreover, those charged with terrorism offences may be hard-pressed to argue other mitigating factors, such as remorse, although some have done so, with some success.[20] The heavy maximum sentences that apply even in relation to precursor offences also mean that sentences determined according to ordinary sentencing principles may be considerable, even for middle-level examples of the relevant offence. However, legislatures evidently do not consider this to be enough. In the United States, federal sentencing guidelines provide for an increased sentence if the offence was intended to promote a federal crime of terrorism.[21] UK law now expressly requires courts to take into account whether the offence has a "terrorist connection," an aggravating factor for sentencing purposes, and Canadian law is similar.[22] Australian law requires that in terrorism cases (inter alia), the nonparole sentence be at least three-quarters of the head sentence.[23]

The Development of the Law

Some of the laws have a long lineage, and many predate the 9/11 attacks. The United Kingdom's uniform and symbols offence had its ancestry in the Irish troubles of the nineteenth century, and other UK terrorism offences tend to have their origins in laws targeting Irish violence. Their rationale was given close consideration, however, in the years leading up to the passage of the Terrorism Act 2000. Parliamentary concerns about the offences were based largely on objections to their implications, given the breadth of the definition of terrorism, rather than on the contention that they would be inappropriate, even given a narrower definition. The only relevant attempt to amend the offences provisions of the Terrorism Bill 2000 in the House of Commons related to the substantive provision of reverse onus in relation to the offence of possession of articles for terrorism, which was opposed by the Liberal Democrats and two Labour MPs.

The US offence of providing material support to terrorists predates the attacks that prompted the Antiterrorism and Effective Death Penalty Act of 1996 (AEDPA). AEDPA added the offence of providing material support to a terrorist organisation, an innovation sharply criticised in a dissent to the report of a bill including the provision.[24] The 7 dissenters were all Democrats but comprised only a minority of the 15 Democrats on the committee.[25]

Pre-2000 offences have survived largely unchanged, but new offences have been added in all five countries. In the United States, the 9/11 attacks left little direct mark. The Patriot Act expanded the definition of "material assistance" to include "expert advice or assistance," increased the maximum sentences for material support and other terrorism-related offences, and added the harboring offence.[26] The Intelligence Reform and Terrorism Protection Act of 2004 amended bail legislation to raise the hurdles to the granting of bail in cases involving federal crimes of terrorism.[27]

In the United Kingdom, post-9/11 measures have been more widespread and more controversial. While investigatory detention was uncontroversial, attempts to extend the maximum detention period aroused considerable resistance, even from the government's back bench. (This issue is discussed in more detail in the next chapter.)

The Terrorism Act 2006 also added the encouragement, publications, and training offences, along with the preparation offence. These were more controversial than the 2000 offences. Despite some early amendments to the bill, the encouragement, publications, and training offences were the subject of a critical report by the Joint Committee on Human Rights, with three of the four Labour MPs dissenting in relation to the encouragement and dissemination offences. (The committee was satisfied of the need for the preparation offence.)[28] All opposition parties and a considerable minority of government backbenchers supported proposed amendments that would have tightened the intention requirements and eliminated the glorification element of the encouragement offence, and the opposition parties also sought to tighten the requirements of the training offences. The bill was later amended to take account of some of the committee's concerns in relation to encouragement and dissemination.

Canadian, New Zealand, and Australian terrorism offences were a response to the 9/11 attacks, although, to varying degrees, they drew on UK precedents. As in the United Kingdom, concerns about the offences was primarily a response to fears based on excessively broad definitions of terrorism, rather than on the grounds that the relevant conduct ought not be criminal even assuming a narrower definition. In Canada, there was debate in committee about the operation of provisions dispensing with any need to prove that activity was oriented towards a particular act, but the doubters seem to have been reassured. Indeed, there was a rare nongovernment attempt to expand the scope of the legislation. A Canadian Alliance amendment would have made membership per se an offence and would have precluded parole for those sentenced to life sentences. At the report stage, there were no attempts to amend the bill's criminal law provisions, except for the organisation offences, although there was debate about the details.

The original Australian proposals included relaxed knowledge and intention requirements and, in several cases, reverse onus provisions. In the face of committee objections and political realities, the government tightened the knowledge requirements, although not sufficiently to satisfy the Australian Democrats and the Greens.

New Zealand's 2002 legislation was opposed in its entirety by the Greens, who also sought (unsuccessfully) to make it lawful to finance well-intentioned liberation movements. For their part, the conservative parties sought to remove the requirement in the participation offence that the defendant intend to enhance the group's capacity to engage in terrorism.

In Canada, the legislation has survived almost unchanged. In New Zealand, engaging in terrorism was made an offence in 2007. The amendment was opposed only by the Greens and the Māori Party. In Australia, the 2002 offences have been left intact, but there have been changes to procedural and substantive law. In 2004, Australia legislated to provide for investigatory detention. The result was poorly drafted legislation, which was subsequently amended in 2010 to make it less opaque. The offence of associating with a terrorist organisation was also introduced in 2004.

Prosecutions

Pleas, Trials, and Convictions

Despite the paucity of terrorist attacks, there have been numerous terrorism trials, especially in the United States and the United Kingdom. Statistics exist, but the heterogeneity of terrorism cases means that the statistics are not always easy to interpret. The unit of analysis may be a case (with multiple defendants) or a defendant. Statistics are based on a variety of definitions of what makes a case a "terrorism" case: for instance, US authorities use at least three definitions, and analysts of US data use yet further definitions and samples.[29] The Center on Law and Security (CLS) follows cases arising from arrests that were justified on the grounds of the defendant's involvement in terrorism. Zabel and Benjamin have reported comprehensively on cases involving Islamic terrorists.[30] Chesney has provided data in relation to material assistance cases.[31]

The CLS data disclose a sharp decline in the average number of terrorism indictments, from 127 in the year following 9/11 to an annual average of 30 in recent years. Most "terrorism" cases do not involve "terrorism" charges,[32] although reliance on terrorism charges has increased over time. The CLS estimate is that fewer than one in three "terrorism" defendants faced a terrorism charge, with another 12 percent charged with "national security" offences (under the International Emergency Economic Powers Act, or IEEPA) and hostage-taking offences. It found that more than 80 percent of charges in terrorism cases involve "nonterrorism" offences, including general criminal conspiracy, general fraud, racketeering, immigration violations, and national security violations. Zabel and Benjamin broadly agree, noting that one reason for this is that would-be terrorists are likely to commit numerous other offences in the course of their preparations.

Robert Chesney's analyses highlight two matters that do not emerge from the other studies. First, although material support legislation predates the 9/11 attacks, there were very few material support prosecutions prior to 2001. There were two section 2339A prosecutions, one involving a domestic militia; and there were four section 2339B prosecutions, two involving Hezbollah supporters and two involving supporters of the Mujahedin-e-Khalq. There were no IEEPA prosecutions.[33] This changed after 2001. The other striking finding to emerge from his data highlights a matter not mentioned in other studies, namely, the numerical importance of "uncompleted" offences.[34] Slightly more than half of the 108 section 2339B prosecutions in his sample involved charges of conspiracy only (30), conspiracy coupled with attempt (24), or attempt only (5). Thirty-eight involved a conspiracy and a contribution charge, and only 11 involved contribution only. The lack of charges based on terrorist acts is not surprising given the paucity of actual terrorist attacks, yet it is striking that even would-be contributors to terrorist organisations are so often apprehended before making their contribution.

The CLS study highlights the importance of distinguishing between conviction rates by charge and conviction rates by defendant. Almost 90 percent of defendants were convicted, and fewer than 4 percent were acquitted. (In the remaining cases, all charges were dismissed.) By contrast, more than a third of charges are dealt with by acquittal or dismissal. One reason is that, on the whole, terrorism defendants do not seek to transform their cases into political trials: about 80 percent plead guilty. In exchange or because of redundancy, some of the charges against them are dropped. Acquittals by juries are extremely rare, comprising only 1.7 percent of resolved indictments. Appeals make little difference: guilty verdicts were vacated or reversed in nine cases, but guilty verdicts on some charges survived in five of these. Zabel and Benjamin report similar conviction rates in connection with their sample of trials involving terrorism related to al-Qaeda, although their sample had a considerably higher rate of not guilty pleas (more than 40 percent).[35]

In Great Britain, between 2001–2 and 2007–8, proscribed organisation charges were the principal charge in 31 cases. (The statistics are silent in relation to the extent to which other cases included organisation charges.) In other terrorism cases, the most frequent principal offence charges were possession of an article for terrorist purposes (71), fund-raising (34), provision of information relating to a terrorist inquiry (20), collecting information useful to a terrorist act (15), inciting terrorism overseas (10), preparation for terrorist acts (10), training offences (9), and other offences (8).[36] In addition, there were 118 terrorism-related cases where the principal offence was not a terrorism offence. Principal charges included conspiracy to murder (36), acting with intent to cause an explosion (20), conspiracy to commit armed robbery (8), Firearms Act offences (6), and theft (6).[37]

The Home Office statistics indicate that 58 percent of those charged with terrorism-related offences were convicted. The conviction rate for those tried was considerably higher, 91 percent in 2007 and 80 percent in 2008. Conviction rates among those charged were much higher where the principal charge was a nonterrorism offence than when it was a charge under terrorism legislation (80 percent compared with 46 percent).[38] Otherwise, the Home Office data throw only limited light on whether particular charges are relatively easily proven. Trial outcomes are tabulated by reference to the principal conviction charge (which is the charge for which the defendant received the heaviest sentence). Since this is not necessarily the principal charge (which is the charge carrying the maximum possible sentence), it is impossible to know whether discrepancies between charge and outcome data reflect acquittals or sentencing.

Thirty-eight people have been charged under Australian counterterror laws, of whom 22 were arrested for their alleged involvement in relation to a loose conspiracy involving 13 defendants from Melbourne and 9 from Sydney. In Melbourne, 1 defendant pleaded guilty and provided evidence against the other 12, 6 of whom were convicted on the 136th day of their trial, with a seventh convicted shortly afterwards. Four were acquitted, and the jury was unable to agree in one case.[39] (The defendant subsequently pleaded guilty.) Five of the Sydney defendants pleaded not guilty, and after a trial that lasted for 10 months, followed by four and a half weeks of jury deliberation, the five defendants were convicted of conspiring to commit acts in preparation for a terrorist act, four others having earlier pleaded guilty to related offences.[40] Three Tamils had originally been charged with membership of and providing funds to a terrorist organisation. While the Tamil Tigers was not a listed organisation, the prosecution was based on the unproblematic assumption that the organisation nonetheless was a terrorist organisation. The defendants eventually pleaded guilty to the lesser offence of providing money in contravention of the UN Charter of the United Nations Act 1945.[41] Five defendants were charged with having planned an armed attack on a Sydney army barracks; Three were convicted.[42] In other cases, four other defendants were convicted, three on nonterrorism charges.[43] In two other cases, charges were dropped. One case became unsustainable after the trial judge ruled that evidence of admissions was inadmissible on the grounds that they had been made after the defendant had been wrongly led to believe that he was required to answer questions put to him by ASIO officers.[44] In the other, charges were dropped after it became clear that they could not be sustained.

In Canada, there have only been three relevant trials or sets of trials. One trial involved a single defendant who was found to have been involved to a limited extent in a multinational terrorist plot, a set of trials arose out of two related Toronto conspiracies, and a third trial arose from a defendant's fundraising activities on behalf of the Liberation Tigers of Tamil Eelam (LTTE). The first trial resulted in a conviction, following a trial by judge alone.[45] The conspiracies resulted in 18 arrests and charges against 17 defendants, 5 of whom were minors. Charges related to involvement in a terrorist organisation (which consisted of parties to the conspiracies in question), and other precursor offences. The prosecution dropped the charges against four of the minors and three adults. Of the remainder, six pleaded guilty (generally only shortly before their trials were due to commence), two were convicted after trial by jury, and two were convicted by judge alone.[46] The third trial was resolved by a guilty plea.[47] In 2011, an alleged al-Shabaab supporter was charged with terrorist group offences.[48] The case has yet to come to trial.

Following a raid on a group of Māori militants, arrestees were charged with terrorism offences, but on the advice of the solicitor-general, these were almost immediately dropped. Other charges against 13 of the 18 people arrested were dropped after the Supreme Court ruled that video surveillance evidence had been illegally obtained. One defendant died, and of the remaining four, who were tried on firearms and criminal organisation offences, convictions resulted for only three and only on firearms charges.[49]

Sentences

Courts seem sympathetic to the sentiments that underlie the legislature's decision to impose heavy maximum sentences for precursor terrorism offences.[50] They attach little weight to the fact that a defendant was arrested before having had an opportunity to give effect to his or her terrorist intentions. What matters are defendants' intentions prior to their arrest.[51] Courts also do not attach much weight to the fact that most of those convicted of terrorism offences have had no prior convictions or to the fact that some of them would have been people of excellent character but for their involvement in terrorism.[52] Lack of remorse and evidence of commitment to terrorism count in favour of a long sentence and are taken as suggesting little likelihood of rehabilitation.[53]

In serious cases, even remorse may not count for much: in a Canadian case involving a conspiracy that, if effected, would have caused massive loss of life and property damage, the ringleader was sentenced to the maximum sentence ("life"[54] imprisonment) on the more serious count, notwithstanding a (late) guilty plea and some evidence of remorse.[55] A US circuit court held that a district court erred in not recognising terrorists as unusual in that their likelihood of recidivism did not decrease with age.

> Although recidivism ordinarily decreases with age, we have rejected this reasoning as a basis for a sentencing departure for certain classes of criminals, namely sex offenders. . . . We also reject this reasoning here. "[T]errorists[,] [even those] with no prior criminal behavior[,] are unique among criminals in the likelihood of recidivism, the difficulty of rehabilitation, and the need for incapacitation."[56]

Dissenting, Judge Barkett objected that the majority had misread the cases it cited, that the government had not challenged the lower court's sentence on the ground that it had underestimated the likelihood of recidivism, and that there was no evidence cited to warrant the conclusion that terrorists' risk of recidivating did not decrease with age.[57]

In relation to US charges, the CLS has been unable to find much information on the frequency with which sentencing enhancements have been imposed. It reports practitioners' claims that they are frequently imposed, especially in material support cases, but its own research, complicated by inadequate records, disclosed only 24 instances, all but 4 of which were "terrorism" or "national security" cases.[58] However, its continuing importance is documented in Zabel and Benjamin's summary of recent federal appeals decisions and by the egregious decision in *United States v Jayyousi*.[59]

There is better evidence in relation to the sentences actually imposed. Although the relevant terrorism offences have rarely involved actual participation in a terrorist act, those convicted in "terrorism" cases have almost invariably been sentenced to terms of imprisonment, usually to lengthy ones. Sentences in the United States varied according to whether the prosecution included terrorism charges (median 10–14 years), national security or hostage taking (median 5–9 years), or neither of these categories of offence (median less than 1 year).[60] Zabel and Benjamin found that almost 90 percent of those sentenced for offences involving terrorism related to al-Qaeda received prison sentences, the remainder receiving either probation or time served.[61]

Data from the UK Home Office also throw only limited light on sentencing patterns, beyond suggesting that defendants convicted of terrorism offences almost invariably receive custodial sentences of at least one year and that among those receiving custodial sentences, the sentences are not as long for those convicted of terrorism offences as for those convicted under nonterrorism legislation.[62] In Australian terrorism cases, convicted defendants have almost invariably received custodial sentences, and while several of these have been for time served, the defendants had spent three or four years in custody prior to their conviction. However, the three Tamils escaped imprisonment. In their plea in mitigation, they argued that they had intended that the money be used for charitable purposes. Accepting that the defendants had acted on the basis that contributing the funds was the only way to help the Sri Lankan Tamil community, the judge sentenced the defendants to prison terms but released them on good behaviour bonds.[63]

In Canada, where there have been relatively few terrorism trials, all of those convicted have been sentenced to custodial terms, including one life sentence (with a nonparole term of 10 years from the date of arrest).[64] In several cases involving people with relatively minor roles in the Toronto conspiracies, the defendants were effectively sentenced to time served (which, by the time of their sentencing, was between three and four years). The effective sentences imposed on the conspirators were generally shorter than those imposed on the Australian conspirators, but the Canadians had generally pleaded guilty and had generally shown some signs of remorse.[65] The LTTE fund-raiser received a six-month sentence for raising between two and three thousand dollars.[66]

Pretrial Detention

In Great Britain, suspected terrorists are generally arrested pursuant to the investigatory detention power, rather than under the general law. The detention period is typically two days or less, and even after the extension of the maximum period to 14 and then 28 days, only 6 percent of arrests resulted in detention for periods of 14–28 days. Those detained for 14 days or more were more likely to be charged with an offence than were other arrestees (59 percent compared to 39 percent). Since 2007, no suspect was detained for more than 14 days. In Australia, the power has been used only once. Depending on the outcome of the investigation, further detention will depend on whether the defendant is charged and on the outcome of the subsequent bail application.

Of the 289 defendants in Zabel and Benjamin's sample, 157 were ordered detained without bail.[67] UK statistics are elusive. The defendants in the Sydney and Melbourne conspiracy trials served lengthy periods in pretrial detention (in conditions considerably worse than those to which ordinary criminal defendants were subjected), and those detained included defendants who were acquitted. However, there have been other Australian cases where defendants were released on bail pending trial. (In one case, the defendant was subsequently acquitted, and in the other, charges were dropped.) The convicted defendants in the Toronto conspiracy cases had all been detained from the time of their arrest to the time of their sentencing. (But at least one of those against whom charges were dropped was released on bail prior to the dropping of charges.) The alleged al-Shabaab supporter was released on bail of $200,000 and subject to strict conditions.

Restraints

Criminal law tends to be the public face of law. It has the potential to empower governments by lending legitimacy to the detention of people who might otherwise pose a threat to society. It may cause risk-averse dissidents to turn towards forms of political dissent that are less violent. It may reassure the public that terrorism is under control and that evil gets its just deserts.

However, legitimation is dependent on the government being on its best behaviour. This means closely complying with prescribed procedures and being able to sustain a story capable of convincing judges and jurors that the defendant is guilty. It also means recognising that trials are a form of theatre and that a successful trial is one from which the audience learns the lessons the government wants it to learn. This means concentrating not on the question of whether the accused is guilty but on whether and how others can be convinced of this. Such a focus has obvious implications. It means that it will usually be unwise to prosecute weak cases. It also means that it will usually be unwise to prosecute cases where the evidence justifies conviction but where jurors or members of the public are likely to sympathise with the accused and to consider that the prosecution ought not to have been brought.

Governments appear to take these considerations seriously. High conviction rates indicate both recognition of the importance of having a strong case and the capacity to recognise when one does have such a case and when one doesn't. Legislation almost invariably survived constitutional attack. While US district and circuit courts found aspects of the material support legislation unconstitutional, they almost invariably accepted that knowing financial support of listed terrorist organisations was an offence, even if the person intended the contribution to be used for the group's peaceful activities. Moreover, the concerns expressed in some lower courts were, in the end, not shared by the Supreme Court. The only situation in which a Canadian court has struck down legislation in the context of a criminal trial was one where the decision had the effect of broadening the scope of Canadian counterterrorism offences to include cases where the intent to coerce or intimidate did not coexist with an ideological purpose.

UK courts have read down offences to ensure that the legislation is compatible with the ECHR. *Attorney General's Reference (No 4 of 2002)* related to a charge of belonging to a proscribed organisation. The defence was that the person had joined the organisation before its proscription but had taken no subsequent part in its activities. At issue was whether the defendant had to prove inactivity or whether the obligation was simply to produce evidence sufficient to raise reasonable doubts as to his subsequent involvement. The court of appeal unanimously held that the burden of proof lay on the defendant. The House of Lords held, in a 3–2 decision, that this was the Parliament's intention but that compliance with the ECHR necessitated that the requirement be read down so that the defendant was required to do no more than raise reasonable doubts as to whether he was subsequently active.[68] In cases involving possession of things useful to terrorism, their reading down appears to have involved orthodox statutory interpretation, rather than a response to the ECHR.[69]

However, success comes at a cost. Terrorism trials have often proved extraordinarily complex. In Canada, Mr. Khawaja was charged and denied bail in 2004. Interlocutory disputes continued for years. One related to the pretrial discovery of 1,500 pages from the 90,000 pages of material in the Crown's possession. In 2008, the trial judge lamented that such trials were nearly impossible, although Khawaja was eventually convicted and sentenced.[70] The UK trial of Mr. Khawaja's associates was completed more quickly, but it lasted for a year, and the jury took a month to deliberate.[71] Investigations and trials arising out of the 2006 plane conspiracy came to 35 million pounds.[72] The Melbourne terrorist conspiracy case took 136 days before it yielded a verdict,[73] and the Sydney case (which involved fewer defendants) lasted for 10 months and was followed by more than a month of jury deliberations.[74]

Moreover, prosecutions can sometimes cast the government in a bad light. Unsustainable claims can backfire. When first apprehended, José Padilla was alleged to be involved in a plot to unleash a dirty bomb somewhere in the United States,[75] but the subsequent charges involved far more mundane types of terrorist support: recruitment, soliciting and transferring money, providing communications equipment, and seeking training. When Nuradin Abdi was indicted by a grand jury, the government press release announced that the indictment was "for plotting with other members of an Al Qaeda cell to bomb a Columbus Ohio-area shopping mall,"[76] but the indictment made no mention of the bombing, and it turned out that while Abdi may have boasted of his intention, he had not chosen the mall and had not acquired any explosives.[77] After a plea bargain, Abdi was convicted of providing material assistance to al-Qaeda and of providing information about possible targets for attack. Iyman Faris, who had provided information about Abdi's threat, had been involved in a plan to destroy the Brooklyn Bridge, but after examining the feasibility of doing so, he had concluded that it was impracticable and advised al-Qaeda accordingly.[78] Brendon Mayfield was detained after a poorly conducted fingerprint analysis had wrongly been taken as indicating that he had been involved in bombings in Madrid.[79] There has also been one case where convictions were dismissed as a result of a prosecutor's failure to comply with disclosure obligations. In 2004, a US district court ordered a new trial of defendants convicted of terrorism-related offences after the government conceded that the prosecutor had failed to disclose exculpatory material and evidence impeaching the character of a jailhouse informer.[80]

In the United Kingdom, a series of cases involving people charged with involvement in IRA bombings resulted in initial convictions, which were eventually set aside on the basis of flawed forensic evidence, failure to disclose exculpatory material, and coerced or otherwise flawed confessions.[81] Lessons seem to have been learned, but post-9/11 trials have sometimes seen elaborate plots evaporate in the face of evidence. One such trial involved the ricin plot. Raids in January 2003 were followed by an announcement that ricin had been found on the premises and that the police had closed down an al-Qaeda terror laboratory. The truth was more mundane: 22 intact castor beans (which contained ricin) were found, as were scales, acetone, rubber gloves, and instructions on how to make ricin. But the provenance of the instructions was American rather than from al-Qaeda. Nine people were charged, but only one was convicted, and that conviction was for an offence that had nothing to do with ricin.[82]

Australia and New Zealand have also yielded examples of apparent terrorism cases that have rapidly unraveled. Dr. Haneef, who worked in a Queensland hospital, was a second cousin of two brothers, one of whom had been involved in the attempted 2008 bombings in London and Glasgow.[83] On the basis of information suggesting his possible involvement, he was arrested and detained for investigation for the next 11 days. He was then charged and shortly afterwards released on bail. His visa having been cancelled, he was once more detained, notwithstanding that the director of public prosecutions (DPP) had decided to drop charges and despite a favourable ASIO report. An inquiry into the circumstances of his arrest and detention reported misunderstandings of evidence, with the effect that the Australian Federal Police (AFP) overestimated the strength of the case against him; defective AFP advice to the DPP (with the effect that the case seemed stronger than it was), failure by the AFP to comply with legal requirements in relation to Haneef's entitlement both to access to legal advice and to communicate with his family, and failure by the DPP's office to apply the proper test in advising whether Haneef should be charged. New Zealand's only terrorism trial ended as a trial for nonterrorism offences. Despite the massive resources devoted to the surveillance that had prompted the arrests, the trial turned out to be a trial of the police as well as the defendants. It ended with a hung jury on the organisation offences. Some of the jurors evidently distinguished between the defendants' violent statements and interest in mastering weaponry, on the one hand, and their actual intentions, on the other.[84]

Conclusions

Authoritarians are wary about the power of the criminal law in the fight against terrorism. They fear that trials will require or involve the disclosure of state secrets; they are concerned that insofar as secrets are protected, the price will be difficulties in securing convictions; and they are mindful of the fact that proof beyond reasonable doubt means that guilty people must sometimes be acquitted. High conviction rates and the severe sentences imposed on convicted defendants suggest that these problems are not insuperable, but these statistics are by no means conclusive. They might, after all, reflect no more than the fact that prosecutors prosecute only those cases they expect to win and that, as a result, there is a reservoir of people who might well be terrorists but cannot be convicted. These might include people who might possibly be terrorists, but it may also include people who quite probably are but cannot be shown to be, given the criminal justice system's exacting standards.

This wariness is questionable. First, the paucity of terrorist attacks in the past 10 years indicates that very few terrorists have escaped the clutches of the criminal justice system. Second, revelations of terrorist plots have almost invariably been accompanied by prosecutions. Indeed, with one possible and contested exception, there have been no cases where reported post-9/11 plots in the United States have not resulted in prosecutions and, insofar as they have been concluded, convictions.[85]

These findings point to a paradox. The requirement of proof of guilt beyond reasonable doubt means no more than that people can be detained as terrorists if the government can prove beyond reasonable doubt that they have committed a precursor offence. There is no additional requirement that the government prove that the precursor offence does in fact foreshadow a considerable likelihood that the offender will, if not restrained, go on to engage in or facilitate an actual terrorist attack. Precursor offences mean that as long as their elements can be proved, people who may pose a relatively small risk may nonetheless be convicted and detained. But governments are not content to rely solely on the criminal law, especially when nonnationals are suspected of constituting an unacceptable risk. When this is legally and politically feasible, states sometimes find it tempting to resort to preventive detention, grounded on standards that are less demanding than those required by the criminal justice system.

Appendix: Terrorism-Related Crimes, by Jurisdiction

US	UK	Canada	Australia	New Zealand
Offence: Material support for terrorism and possession of things connected with terrorism				
Provision of material support, knowing or intending that it be used for specified offences including related inchoate offences: 18 USC § 2339A(a); material support includes property, training, services; personnel (including oneself) Provide or collect property, intending or knowing that it will be used for a terrorist act: 18 USC § 2339C(a) (applies to offences within and outside the United States, but in each case only in limited circumstances)	Solicit, receive, or provide property intending or reasonably suspecting that it will be used for purposes of terrorism: s 15 Use or possession of property for purposes of terrorism: s 16 Dealing to make property available for terrorism: s 17 Possession of things such as to give rise to a reasonable suspicion that the thing is to be used in connection with terrorism, subject to a defence that this was not the person's purpose: s 57 Possess record or information likely to be useful for acts of terrorism, but not if person has reasonable excuse for possession: s 58	Provide or collect property, intending or knowing that it will be used for a TA: s 83.02 Soliciting property or financial services to benefit person facilitating terrorist activity or knowing terrorist group will use benefit: s 83.03 Use or possess property for a TA: s 83.04	Provide or collect funds, reckless as to whether they will be used for a TA: s 103.1 Intentionally make funds available to another, or collect funds for another, reckless as to whether the other person will use them for a TA: s 103.2 Collecting funds, making documents known to be connected with a terrorist act: s 101.5(1) (and s 101.5(2) (reckless)) Possess thing known to be connected with a terrorist act: s 101.4 (and s 101.4 (reckless))	Provide or collect funds, intending or knowing that they are to be use to carry out a TA: s 8(1)
Offence: Terrorism				
		Facilitate a TA, thereby being guilty of an indictable offence. Person need not know it is a particular act: s 83.19 Knowingly instruct a person to carry out a TA: s 83.22 (but no need for knowledge that a particular act involved)	Engage in terrorist act: s 101.1	Engage in a terrorist act: s 6A

(continues)

US	UK	Canada	Australia	New Zealand
Offence: Preparation				
Insofar as it involves providing material support: 18 USC § 2339A Harboring people involved in specified offences: 18 USC § 2339	Preparation: TA06 s 5	Insofar as it involves providing or collecting property: s 83.03	Acts in preparation or planning for a terrorist act: s 101.6	
Offence: Giving or receiving training				
18 USC § 2339A (giving)	Provide, receive, or solicit the participation of others in particular training, it being a defence that the training was not for a purpose related to terrorism: s 54 Provide, receive specified training for purposes of terrorism: TA06 s 8	Only if terrorist group involved	Training that is known to be connected with preparation for, engagement, or assistance of person in terrorist act: s 101.2(1) (and s 101.2(2)(reckless))	
Offence: Encouragement				
	Encouragement: TA06 s 1 Dissemination of terrorist publications: TA06 s 2			
Offence: Harboring terrorists				
Harboring people involved in specified offences: 18 USC § 2339.				Knowingly or reckless harbouring a person who has or intends to carry out a TA, to enable the person to escape apprehension: s 13A

Offences: In relation to terrorist organizations				
Provide material support for foreign terrorist organisation, knowing it is an FTO: 18 USC § 2339B(a)(1) Material support is defined in § 2339A(b) Receive military training from an FTO, knowing it to be an FTO: 18 USC § 2339D.	Directing: s 56 Membership: s 11 Inviting support for: s 12 Wear clothing or display symbol suggestive of support: s 13	Participation or contributing to ability of terrorist group to carry out a TA for the purpose of enhancing this ability: s 83.18 Participation or contributing includes: providing or receiving training; providing expertise at group's direction; recruiting a person to commit a terrorist act; entering another country for a terrorist group; making self available at behest of group, for terrorist activity Commit indictable offence for terrorist group: s 83.2 Knowingly instruct a person to do something for purpose of enhancing the group's capacity to carry out a TA: s 83.21(but no need for knowledge that a particular act involved)	Knowingly directing: s 102.2(1); reckless: s 102.2(2) Knowing membership: s 102.3(1); reckless: s 102.3(2) Knowingly recruiting for: s 102.4(1); reckless: s 102.4(2) Knowingly training or receiving training from: s 102.5; reckless: s 102.5(2) Knowingly getting funds to or from: s 102.6(1); reckless: s 102.6(2) Intentionally providing support or resources knowing that the donee is a terrorist organisation: s 102.7(1); reckless: s 102.7(2) Associating: s 102.8	Knowingly recruiting for a terrorist entity: s 12 Knowing or reckless participation in a terrorist entity, for the purpose of enhancing the entity's capacity to carry ort or participate in a TA: s 13 Provide or collect funds for terrorist organisation, intending or knowing they will benefit an entity involved in TAs: s 8(2) Dealing with property of a designated entity: s 9 Making property or financial services available to a designated entity: s 10

Note: Except where otherwise stated, United Kingdom references are to the Terrorism Act 2000 c 11; see too Terrorism Act 2006 c 11 (TA06). Canadian references are to Criminal Code Act RSC 1985, c C-46; TA means "terrorist activity." Australian references are to Criminal Code Act 1995 (Cth). For all offences, it is irrelevant that the terrorist act does not occur and that the behaviour does not relate to a specific terrorist act. New Zealand: references are to Terrorism Suppression Act 2002 (NZ).

EIGHT

Detention without Conviction

> Let the terrorists among us be warned: If you overstay your visa—even by one day—we will arrest you. If you violate a local law, you will be put in jail and kept in custody for as long as possible.
>
> *Attorney General John Ashcroft*[1]

> To deny extremists one of their most potent recruitment tools, we will close the prison at Guantánamo Bay.
>
> *President Barack Obama*[2]

The counterterrorist's dream is that of a government with the capacity to track down prospective terrorists and lock them away before they are able to execute their plans. The criminal law permits various forms of de facto preventive detention, but posttrial detention is usually possible only after a court is satisfied that the detainee has committed a crime; that the evidence proves the defendant's guilt; and that on the facts before the court, a custodial sentence is warranted. Otherwise defendants must go free, regardless of whether they pose a high actuarial risk. Further, in cases where proof of the relevant crime would require the disclosure of state secrets, proof of guilt might be difficult if the government wishes to protect secrets from disclosure.

For reasons set out in the previous chapter, the seriousness of these problems can be exaggerated, especially given the recently created precursor offences and the courts' willingness to impose long sentences on people who did little to give effect to their plans. Moreover, if there is insufficient evidence to support a conviction for a precursor offence, this may be because there is little evidence that the suspect is indeed a potential terrorist. In addition, there are costs involved in detaining the innocent. These include costs to the detainees, but even if one is indifferent to these, there are others. Detention is expensive. Detention of the innocent is wasteful and involves the use of resources that could be used more profitably elsewhere: in January 2012, detention at Guantánamo Bay cost $800,000 per detainee, and guarding each detainee required an average of 17 soldiers.[3] Ill-tailored preventive detention can sometimes have the effect of generating more terrorism than it prevents, by delegitimating governments and their counterterror policies.

Yet the craving for certainty means that the authoritarian's dream is capable of weaving its seductive web. There are precedents for the detention of people based on nothing more than attributes that mean that they are slightly less unlikely to constitute a threat than those without the attribute. An obvious example is provided by the wartime detention of enemy aliens, some of whom no doubt hoped their homeland would win, but few of whom ever seem to have done anything to further this end, either before or on release from detention. These precedents rightly stand as a warning as to the dangers of barely regulated detention. It is probably a warning heeded by modern governments and their judiciaries, but more by judiciaries than by governments.

Preventive detention is not the only reason for detention without conviction. In addition to the detention of suspected criminals, detention may also be used (legally or otherwise) against prospective deportees and people who might otherwise refuse to provide evidence to those entitled to demand it.

In wars on terror, the enemy lurks both within and without. Yet detention without conviction generally involves the enemy without, and this is reflected in the laws of the five countries discussed in this book. However, law and practices differ. In the United States, relatively restrictive laws have coexisted with strained executive interpretations, widespread illegal detention, and considerable, but belated, judicial resistance. Elsewhere, laws are sometimes repressive, but executive compliance with law is higher. In the United Kingdom and Canada, there has been statutory provision for the detention or house arrest of suspected terrorists, and the governments have made some use of these powers. But the legislation has fallen foul of the courts. Australian law is similar, but powers created by post-9/11 legislation have rarely been used, although their use has survived judicial scrutiny.

In this chapter, I outline detention regimes in the five countries, arguing that while detention laws have developed in response to heightened concerns about terrorism, their scope has been circumscribed, especially in relation to domestic detention. With some exceptions, they do not appear to have been enacted in haste, and despite evidence of public support for such laws, proposals to extend detention powers have aroused considerable political resistance. Institutional considerations are reflected in practices and, to a lesser degree, in law. Responses to detention regimes generally seem to be related to preexisting beliefs. To a considerable extent, civil libertarians have been substantively (if not symbolically) successful.

Detention Regimes

Preventive detention is governed by a variety of legal regimes. One set of regimes governs those captured in theatres of war, particularly Afghanistan and

Iraq. Prisoner-of-war regimes are formally concerned with preventing participation in armed conflicts rather than preventing terrorism. However, in both conflicts, the "enemy" included terrorism against civilians among its tactics. Taking prisoners therefore had the potential to serve antiterrorism functions as well as preventing armed attacks on service personnel. While the UK, Canada, Australia, and New Zealand accepted that the detention of prisoners was governed by the international law governing armed conflict, the US government argued that the nature of the Afghanistan conflict was sui generis and governed by a distinctive body of law.

Different bodies of law govern the detention of suspected terrorists who are not involved in "armed conflict." Such laws potentially include people living both outside and within a country's borders, but their operation is limited in practice to those within national borders. Moreover, the relevant powers to detain are highly circumscribed, both by legislation and by judicial supervision. Their importance is symbolic rather than substantive.

United States

The United States has detained thousands in its War on Terror. A 2005 Amnesty International report estimated that a total of 70,000 had been detained, the vast majority of whom had been released. Most were taken prisoner in Afghanistan and Iraq, but a small number had been captured elsewhere, including some who had been kidnapped in Europe. Of those still in detention in 2005, more than 10,000 were detained in prisons and bases in Iraq, and about 550 were detained at bases in Afghanistan. Moreover, despite arrangements for transferring prisoners into the custody of the Afghanistan government, the Bagram detention facility in Afghanistan has been expanded so that by December 2009, it could accommodate 1,200 detainees.[4]

A substantial number of those captured in Afghanistan and elsewhere in the immediate aftermath of the 9/11 attacks were transferred to Guantánamo Bay Naval Base in Cuba. At its peak, Guantánamo contained up to 800 prisoners, of whom 520 remained in custody as of April 2005. By January 2009, 234 people remained there, and one of the first orders issued by President Obama was an inquiry into the status of those remaining and the closure of the base within 12 months.[5] His target has not been met, closure being complicated by congressional prohibitions on the appropriation of money to bring Guantánamo detainees to the United States.[6] As of 13 May 2011, the Guantánamo facility still contained 172, and two years later, the figure was 166. More than half have been cleared to leave but remain in custody either because no country is willing to accept them, because there is no guarantee that their human rights would be respected in those countries that are willing to accept them, or because of lingering doubts about whether possible destination countries could ensure that they would not constitute threats to security. In May 2013, following a months-long hunger strike by detainees, Barack Obama announced the lifting of a moratorium on the release of Yemeni prisoners and other measures aimed at reducing the number of detainees.[7]

Various paths led to Guantánamo. Most detainees had been captured by US and allied forces in Afghanistan, but others had been captured elsewhere. The Guantánamo detainees had generally been taken prisoner in Afghanistan or Pakistan, and their detention was justified partly as pretrial detention pending trial before military commissions and partly on the grounds that those kept in custody were "unlawful enemy combatants" who could be detained as if they were prisoners of war. In practice, a major purpose of detention has been for interrogation. The choice of Guantánamo was based partly on doubts about the security of Afghan facilities and partly on the calculation that, not being an area over which the United States exercised sovereignty, prisoners would not be able to avail themselves of the rights enjoyed by those kept prisoner on US soil. In particular, they would not be able to apply for judicial review of their custody status.[8]

If the relevant "enemy combatants" had the decency to wear uniforms, prisoner-of-war regimes could operate reasonably easily. Since they do not, countries that take prisoners are confronted with the problem that their right to do so depends on whether they have adequate grounds for believing that the person is indeed a participant in the relevant conflict. While not acknowledging that the Geneva Conventions applied to the Afghanistan conflict, the United States established procedures for determining whether prisoners qualified for detention. On the basis of these procedures and on the basis of representations by a number of governments on behalf of their nationals, a substantial number of prisoners were eventually released. However, the procedures provided only rudimentary due process, and even when release was recommended, the recommendations were sometimes disregarded.[9] Provision was also made for military commissions to try prisoners for war crimes. These also fell far short of the procedures governing ordinary criminal trials in the United States, notwithstanding that the commissions were empowered to impose the death penalty.

Within months of the first arrivals at Guantánamo, lawyers acting on behalf of prisoners at Guantánamo and elsewhere challenged their detention. One issue related to whether the government had the power to detain "enemy combatants" and, if so, whether this power extended to the detention of US citizens who had been captured in Afghanistan. A potential obstacle to the detention of US citizens was 1971 legislation that forbade the imprisonment or detention of US citizens except pursuant to an "Act of Congress."[10] In *Hamdi v Rumsfeld*,[11] a case involving an alleged US citizen who had been captured in Afghanistan and transferred to the United States, a majority of justices held that Congress's Authorization for Use of Military Force[12] provided authority for the detention of US citizens. Justices Scalia and Stevens dissented: if US citizens took up arms against their country, they should be prosecuted under the criminal law. It was constitutionally impermissible that they be otherwise detained. Justices Souter and Ginsburg dissented on different grounds: the Authorization for Use of Military Force was not an "Act of Congress" for the purposes of the 1971 legislation. But if US prisoners could be detained as enemy combatants, it followed, a fortiori, that enemy combatants who were aliens could also be so detained, and there has been no dissent from this position in later cases.

However, the right to detain did not necessarily mean a right to detain unfettered by judicial accountability. In 2004, the Supreme Court ruled that detainees at Guantánamo had a statutory right to petition for habeas corpus.[13] Congress responded by amending the relevant legislation.[14] The court ruled that the amendment did not operate to deprive petitioners who had already begun proceedings of their habeas corpus rights.[15] Congress amended the legislation yet again.[16] This time, its intention was clear. The petitioners therefore enjoyed a right to petition for habeas corpus only if they possessed a constitutional right to the writ. In *Boumediene v Bush*, the court held that they did.[17] Crucial to its ruling was a finding that the statutory procedures established for the determination of prisoners' status fell short of those needed to afford due process. The court left open the question of what procedures might satisfy these requirements,[18] and in the years following *Boumediene*, the DC district and circuit courts have developed standards and procedures for resolving habeas corpus cases. They have accepted that it is for the government to show that detention is warranted. The standard of proof required of the government is lower than the criminal standard but similar to the civil standard. Probative evidence is admissible notwithstanding that it would be inadmissible in a criminal trial. In limited circumstances, the government may rely on classified information without being required to disclose it to the petitioner, but the petitioner must be made aware of its gist. Judicial expositions of the law have varied somewhat, partly as a result of the facts of the case and partly as a result of differences as to the rigour of the standards to be imposed before detention is upheld.[19] Initially, petitioners had considerable success despite these differences and the role of classified information; and while more-recent petitions have failed, the overall success rate still exceeds 60 percent.[20] Litigation has largely related to detention at Guantánamo, and while an application by prisoners in Afghanistan for the writ had some success before the district court, the government successfully argued on appeal that the writ did not lie in relation to detention in a theatre of war.[21]

In addition to those detained in Iraq, Afghanistan, and Guantánamo Bay, a smaller number of prisoners have been detained as part of the US extraordinary rendition program.[22] Some of these have been taken to prisons run by the Central Intelligence Agency.[23] Some were taken by the United States to third countries.[24] Some were taken from custody in third countries into CIA custody, and in some cases, prisoners were taken from third-party or CIA custody to Guantánamo. In many cases, they have been released by the third country or by the CIA and returned or allowed to return to their country of citizenship.[25] While one rationale for extraordinary rendition has been the extraction of information, preventive detention has been another—especially when rendition has been to countries whose interrogation techniques are unlikely to yield reliable information.[26] Practical considerations have meant that even if and when the victims of extraordinary rendition would have been legally entitled to apply for habeas corpus,[27] neither they nor those who would have wished to sue on their behalf were in a position to initiate habeas corpus proceedings. However, kidnapping exposes those who engage in it to criminal prosecutions in the country where the kidnapping occurs, and following an Italian investigation, twenty-two CIA employees were convicted in absentia for their involvement in the rendition of Abu Omar.[28]

US law confers limited powers to detain people other than prisoners of war within the United States. These include the power to detain for the purposes of deportation, and in October 2001, the de facto power to detain was extended by a rule providing that at the instance of a district director, an order by an immigration judge releasing a person from custody might be stayed pending the outcome of an appeal.[29] This power was used to justify the detention of at least 1,200 people from Arabic backgrounds in the immediate aftermath of the 9/11 attacks.[30] The power to detain was conditioned on the detainees' being illegally present in the United States and is for the purposes of facilitating deportation. Nonetheless, detainees were also questioned at length and sometimes detained for far longer than was needed in order to arrange their repatriation.[31] They were also mistreated, although not to the extent of the Guantánamo Bay inmates. Their attempts to seek legal redress were generally unsuccessful, except insofar as claims of mistreatment or detention for longer than the permitted period could be sustained.[32] By majority, the Supreme Court rejected a claim that the ethnically based arrest policy was improperly discriminatory: as far as the majority was concerned, it made perfect sense to target Muslim Arabs, since Muslim Arabs had been responsible for the 9/11 attacks.[33]

Yet there are limits to the use of immigration detention. Detention for more than six months is normally impermissible when an alien has entered the country and has subsequently become subject to a removal order but cannot or must not be deported to another country.[34] Detention may, however, be permitted for longer periods on security grounds.[35] The USA Patriot Act of 2001 made additional provision for preventive detention of aliens if the attorney general certified, on reasonable grounds, that the alien fell into one or more specified categories, including involvement in various terrorism-related activities.[36] This legislation has never been invoked: the powers were heavily circumscribed, and preexisting immigration law has meant that they have been unnecessary.[37]

The government has also made use of a power to detain "material witnesses." This power was designed for use in cases where there was a danger that a possible witness in criminal proceedings might flee before giving evidence. Since 2001, it has also been used to detain and investigate people suspected of involvement in terrorism.[38] Between 2001 and 2005, at least 70 people, some of whom were US citizens, had been detained under this legislation, often in circumstances where the possibility of their being called on to testify has been no more than a pretext for their detention.[39] The use of the power as the basis for de facto preventative detention has provoked surprisingly little litigation. In a claim against former attorney general Ashcroft and others, a divided Ninth Circuit Court of Appeals held that pretextual detention could ground a claim under *Bivens v Six Unknown Agents of Federal Bureau of Narcotics*[40] claim for damages, but in an appeal by Ashcroft, the Supreme Court unanimously reversed, finding that since, at the time of the arrest, there was little or no authority suggesting that pretextual detention of material witnesses would be unconstitutional, the appellant enjoyed qualified immunity. Four justices also held that the reasonableness of detention under a warrant based on individualised suspicion turned on objective criteria—namely, whether the arrest would have been lawful if it had been for its proper purpose—and that the reasonableness had not been contested. Four other justices—Kennedy, Ginsburg, Breyer, and Sotomayor—doubted that the warrant had been validly obtained. Ginsburg, Breyer, and Sotomayor doubted whether a warrant would be properly obtained when the issuing authority was not told that its purpose was not to secure the target's presence at trial, and they further doubted whether the terms of the detention could be justified even if the detention itself could be.[41]

The case was remanded. A magistrate judge recommended summary judgment in favour of the plaintiff against one of the FBI agents, on the basis that the affidavit supporting the warrant application recklessly omitted relevant information and included misleading information. It would therefore have been defective even if its purpose were to secure its ostensible purpose. The district court adopted the report against the author of the misleading application and granted summary judgment (based on qualified immunity) in favour of the other defendant. There was no appeal.[42]

United Kingdom

Historically, the United Kingdom has not been averse to the use of preventive detention. During World War II, it interned most of the German nationals present in the United Kingdom, notwithstanding that most of those detained were refugees whose lives were at particular risk in the event of a German victory.[43] It also made intermittent use of internment as a response to Northern Irish terrorism, its last such use proving a disaster: the internees were chosen from lists that had long since ceased to be up to date, and the result was the arrest of hundreds of nonterrorists, with a minimal yield of current activists.[44] This unnecessarily alienated the Catholic community and was belatedly recognised to have been a self-defeating strategy. The Terrorism Act 2000 made no provision for internment. Post-2001 legislation has made only limited provision for preventive detention, and attempts to introduce even limited forms of preventive detention have encountered considerable political and judicial resistance.

Unlike the United States, the United Kingdom at any given time detained only a handful of people, and those were detained only for very brief periods.[45] Its arrangements with the government of Afghanistan provided that people detained by UK forces would be transferred as soon as possible to the Afghanistan government or, if that was not possible, to a facility approved by the International Security Assistance Force. Prisoners transferred to the Afghan authorities were not to be transferred outside the country without UK approval.[46] The United Kingdom was a detaining authority in Iraq, under a variety of legal arrangements.[47]

The UK government has been critical of the US government's analysis of the Geneva Conventions and of US procedures for determining combatant status, and it (successfully) sought the repatriation of UK nationals held at Guantánamo.[48] It had also been critical of the proposed military commissions.[49] However, aware that the Geneva Conventions could pose problems for its own powers to detain,[50] it declined to accept general responsibility for nonnationals who had enjoyed refugee status in the UK.[51] It was criticised by a House of Commons committee for not doing more to help nonnationals,[52] and it eventually agreed to their transfer to the UK.

The government has made only limited use of statutory powers permitting the detention of suspected terrorists. In the immediate aftermath of 9/11, the United Kingdom legislated to enable the detention of immigrants who seemed to constitute a security risk and whose deportation was impractical.[53] (The power supplemented a preexisting power to detain for the purposes of deportation, a power whose exercise sometimes involves lengthy custody, especially when suspected terrorists are resisting deportation to countries with poor human rights records.) The power was used sparingly,[54] official policy being that it be reserved for cases where prosecution for an offence commensurate with the risk posed by the person was not possible. This might be because the only incriminating evidence was either inadmissible or, if admitted, would involve the disclosure of confidential material.[55] The legislation was the subject of a highly critical report,[56] and the House of Lords ruled in 2004 that the legislation was incompatible with the ECHR.[57] Detention was replaced by a system of "control orders" under which the controlee was subjected to a form of house arrest, mitigated by limited daytime freedom of movement.[58] As of 3 February 2011, shortly before their replacement by measures based on the Terrorism Prevention and Investigation Measures Act 2011 (TPIMs, discussed further shortly), 48 people had been subject to control orders, and eight orders were currently in force.[59]

In principle, the rationale for the orders is clear: if people really are quite probably dangerous, restrictions on their freedom of movement might be justified even if their dangerousness could not be proved beyond reasonable doubt. However, Metcalfe points out that in 2006, seven of those under control orders had absconded. The home secretary had said that he "did not believe the public was at risk."[60] But it is hard to see how those orders could then be justified, especially as one would expect that those who complied with the orders would, if anything, be even less dangerous.

The ECtHR's decision in *A v United Kingdom* has meant that the government is now required to provide details of the gist of adverse allegations to the controlee,[61] but while the system survived this ruling, there have been cases where the government has concluded that the costs of disclosure outweigh the advantages of seeking continued controls, even when the person appears to the government to constitute an ongoing security risk.[62] In January 2011, the Conservative–Liberal Democrat government announced plans to introduce a less intrusive system.[63] The Terrorism Prevention and Investigation Measures Act 2011 (c 24) replaced control orders with TPIMs, which were substantially similar except that a TPIM could last for no more than one year (but was renewable). Measures were conditioned on reasonable grounds to "believe," rather than "suspect." Curfew hours were limited. There was no longer a power to order that a person relocate.

UK law also makes provision for detention pending investigation (see chapter 7).[64] The power is strictly for investigative purposes. It may not be used as a form of preventive detention[65] and would, in any case, be of little use for that purpose.

Canada

Canada has a history of using mass detention in response to emergencies. Like other British dominions, it interned thousands of German and Italian nationals during World War II, and like the United States, it interned tens of thousands of people of Japanese descent. In 1971, it arrested more than a thousand people suspected of links with the Front de libération du Québec. However, these potential precedents have acquired the status of cautionary tales, and their legislative foundation has been repealed.

Canada has been involved in the Afghanistan War since 2001, having accepted that the conflict was an international armed conflict. Under the Canadian Task Force's Theatre Standing Order 321A, the power may be exercised on "reasonable belief" that detainees are, inter alia, "persons who are themselves not taking a direct part in hostilities, but who are reasonably believed to be providing support in respect of acts harmful to the CF/Coalition Forces."[66] Canadian practice is to transfer prisoners to the Afghan authorities within 96 hours of capture, but there is a discretion to detain for longer periods,[67] and between 5 November 2007 and 26 February 2008, transfers were suspended on the grounds that transferred prisoners were being ill-treated.[68]

The Canadian government has also been implicated, to a limited degree, in the foreign detention of Canadians and aliens. One instance of this involved a victim of the US extraordinary rendition program. The others involved Canadians who were initially detained by the Syrian authorities. Maher Arar, a citizen of Canada and Syria, was apprehended in New York, transported by the United States to Syria via Jordan, and detained there for a year. Canada's involvement in his fate was peripheral. His treatment was the subject of a commission of inquiry that found that it may have been prompted by the provision of unduly prejudicial material to the American authorities and that it may have been prolonged by the failure of Canadian government agencies to present a united front in relation to his release.[69]

Three other Canadians with dual citizenship were detained in Syria for various periods,[70] and one of them was subsequently transferred by Syria to Egypt (where he was detained for a further two years). An internal inquiry was unable to conclude whether Canada was responsible for the initial detention of one of the three, Abdullah Almalki, but it concluded that the sharing of "information" probably contributed indirectly to the detention of the other two,

Ahmad Abou-Elmaati and Myayyed Nureddin.[71] As in Arar's case, the information was highly prejudicial (and had been communicated to the Syrians). In addition, while details of the detainees' travel plans were not communicated to Syria, they were communicated to the United States, with the risk that they would be passed on.

Canadian courts found that the government failed to take adequate steps to ensure the release and repatriation of Canadians detained abroad. One was Omar Khadr, a Guantánamo detainee. Such subsequent steps as the Canadian government took were a qualified success. Khadr was not released but was tried before a military commission. He eventually pleaded guilty and was sentenced to 20 years imprisonment, but he will serve his sentence (less remissions) in Canada. The court also came to the rescue of Abousfian Abdelrazik, who had been arrested and later released in Sudan, where he subsequently sought refuge in the Canadian consulate. The court ordered that the Canadian government arrange and pay for his repatriation. (The Sudanese government had no objections to this, but Canada had argued that sanctions laws precluded it from making the requisite arrangements.)

The taking of prisoners by Canadian forces in Afghanistan appears to have been legally nonproblematic, but their release to Afghan police units has been politically controversial, given claims that this exposed the prisoners to near-certain torture. The government, however, doubted whether its arrangements with the Afghan authorities permitted the long-term detention of prisoners.[72]

Under legislation antedating the 9/11 attacks, there is provision for the detention of nondeportable immigrants suspected of constituting a threat to security.[73] In 2007, the Supreme Court ruled that aspects of the legislation were unconstitutional.[74] First, it failed to ensure that the subjects of certificates were adequately informed of their basis. Second, it concluded that the discrimination between permanent residents and foreign nationals exposed the latter to arbitrary detention. The Parliament amended the legislation to accommodate the decision. Most of the instances where the legislation has been used predate the 9/11 attacks,[75] but five people were arrested or rearrested and then subsequently detained under this legislation in or after 2001. By 2010, all had been released from detention after long periods of imprisonment, but three were still subject to conditions akin to the UK control orders. Their fate has generated more than 150 interlocutory or final orders.

Canada's post-9/11 counterterrorism legislation amended the Criminal Code by making limited provision for detention without conviction,[76] but this was subject to rigorous review procedures. The relevant powers were never used, and they lapsed when the Parliament refused to extend them following the expiry of a relevant sunset period.[77] However, despite the fact that the detention power (and a power to arrest for investigatory purposes) were never used while they were available, Canada's Conservative government attempted to secure their restoration, finally succeeding in 2013.[78]

Australia

During World War II, Australia interned a higher proportion of German and Italian aliens than Canada or the United States, most being released within a year of their initial detention. It detained only a small number of nonaliens, and when Australians list injustices done in the name of national security, they rarely list wartime internment. Cold War plans envisaged the internment of prominent communists in the event of a war between the Soviet Union and the West, but in the absence of the war, nothing came of these plans. (The Korean War did not count.)

Although Australia was a participant in both the Iraq War (2003–9) and the Afghanistan War (2001–2, 2006–13), it did not maintain its own prisons, transferring those it detained into the custody of other governments. However, two Australians were among those detained at Guantánamo, both of whom were parties in *Rasul v Bush*. One, Mamdouh Habib, was detained in Pakistan, transported to Egypt and then to Guantánamo via Afghanistan, and released in 2005, following representations by the Australian government. The other, David Hicks, was seized in Afghanistan in December 2001, transferred to Guantánamo in January 2002, and not released from there until 2007. Unlike the UK government, the Australian government did not have a firm policy of seeking the release of its citizens.[79] Indeed, in February 2007, the prime minister rashly stated that while he could secure the release of Hicks at any time, he chose not to do so. His reasoning was that, given Hicks's alleged conduct, he should be tried, but trial in Australia would be pointless because the alleged behaviour was not, at relevant times, an offence under Australian law.[80] Hicks was eventually released from Guantánamo under a plea bargain whereby he pleaded guilty before a military commission in exchange for a seven-year sentence (with all but nine months suspended) for making a material contribution to terrorism. (The basis for this was contributions to and having received training from terrorist organisations.)[81] A conviction having been achieved, the United States and Australia agreed that Hicks could serve his nine-month nonsuspended prison sentence in Australia.

Australia has followed the United Kingdom by legislation providing for control orders in relation to suspected terrorists.[82] Only two such orders have been made, both on conditions far less onerous than those imposed in the United Kingdom. One involved David Hicks on his release from custody and was lifted on the expiry of his parole period. The other involved a defendant in a terrorism case who had been released on bail following a successful appeal against a terrorism conviction, and the order was lifted after he was released following a retrial, which ended with a conviction and a sentence of time served, for presenting false documents.

Australia makes limited provision for detention for questioning by ASIO.[83] There is also provision for preventive detention, conditioned on reasonable grounds to suspect involvement in a proposed terrorist act or on a need to preserve evidence of an attack that has taken place within 28 days. Its duration is limited to 48 hours.[84] Neither the detention for questioning nor the preventive detention powers have been exercised.

Immigration legislation permits detention pending deportation and has been held to permit the indefinite detention of people who cannot be deported in the foreseeable future. In a case involving a nonrefugee, the High Court held that the relevant legislation did not infringe on the constitutional separation of powers.[85] The operation of the legislation depends on the person's immigration status, but would-be immigrants who are assessed as being involved in terrorism may become deportable and therefore detainable under the power to exclude people constituting a threat to national security. Until recently, cases involving the use of these powers in relation to suspected terrorists were rare, but a considerable number of suspected members of the Liberation Tigers of Tamil Eelam have been refused entry and detained under these provisions, their deportation to Sri Lanka not being feasible, given the risk of torture. In March 2011, there were "about 14" people in detention following adverse ASIO assessments.[86] By the end of 2011, the figure had swelled to 54.[87] Responses to this increase have included both political pressures to relax the law and litigation. A parliamentary committee inquiring into immigration detention has recommended that those subject to adverse ASIO assessments be subject to periodic internal reviews and that they have a right of appeal to the Security Appeals Division of the Administrative Appeals Division.[88] A recent High Court challenge to the detention regime succeeded, in part, on the grounds that relevant regulations were inconsistent with provisions of the Migration Act governing the refusal or cancellation of protection visas.[89] The decision did not address the question of whether it would be constitutionally open to the Parliament to amend the act to permit the making of the offending regulations.

New Zealand

Like other countries, New Zealand law makes provision for the detention of immigrants pending deportation, and this includes the detention of those who face deportation on security grounds.[90] Under current legislation, a judge must order that a person who is a security risk be released on conditions, if this would not be contrary to the public interest. Detained immigrants must normally be released on conditions once they have been in detention for a period of six months, dating from the later of their initial detention or their exhaustion of appeal rights or—in some circumstances—the determination of a claim for refugee status. This precludes the lengthy periods of detention potentially available elsewhere.

Heightened Concerns?

The timing of legislation is sometimes consistent with the model of heightened concern. Detention legislation can sometimes be explained as a reaction to heightened concerns. Moreover, after experience of their operation, governments and legislatures have sometimes recognised the desirability of curtailing the scope of the powers. That said, timing of relevant legislation poses some problems for both the panic and opportunism perspectives.

The Patriot Act's provisions relating to the detention of immigrants suggest a degree of panic and would-be opportunism on the part of the administration, and there is poll data suggesting that the climate was temporarily ripe for repressive detention legislation. In the administration's bill, the power would have been indefinite.[91] Moreover, at the time, there seems to have been considerable public support for preventive detention. In a September 2001 poll, 54 percent of respondents said they strongly favoured giving the government the power to detain indefinitely a legal immigrant suspected of a crime, and another 28 percent said they would accept that it was necessary.[92] In November 2001, 86 percent thought that the dragnet detentions in the immediate aftermath of the 9/11 attacks were justified.[93]

But Howell argues that these detention powers were among the provisions to the Patriot Act where Congress made important inroads into what the administration had originally proposed.[94] Indeed, the government has subsequently made no use of these powers, having evidently concluded that existing powers were sufficient. Moreover, subsequent legislation scarcely suggests that legislators have become more tolerant of people who might pose a threat. Most relevant post-9/11 legislation has been passed in response to the Supreme Court's Guantánamo Bay decisions and has involved a mixture of resistance and reluctant accommodation. More than 10 years after the 9/11 attacks, the National Defense Authorization Acts have been used to frustrate attempts to close Guantánamo, and a provision in the 2011 act was found by a New York district court to have (impermissibly) expanded the government's detention powers.[95]

The timing of the United Kingdom's Anti-terrorism, Crime and Security Act 2001—introduced on 12 November 2001 and granted royal assent on 14

December 2001—is consistent with heightened concerns, panic, and opportunism, and the legislation was criticised accordingly. But its detention provisions were subject to a sunset clause[96] and supported only by members from the governing Labour Party. The Conservatives abstained, and all other parties voted against them, as did 12 Labour rebels.

The legislation establishing the control order system is not so easily characterised: it was a response not to a terrorist attack but to a judicial ruling whose practical effect had been to strike down the 2001 detention legislation. It had been foreshadowed in a review of the 2001 legislation. Moreover, potential critics of the legislation resisted with some success, and the legislation that emerged included accountability procedures lacking in the original bill, as well as a requirement of annual renewal by an order approved by each House. While its repeal is consistent with its having been an overreaction, the 2011 legislation that abolished control orders simultaneously established a regime that was only slightly less rigorous than the regime it replaced.

The history of investigatory detention also suggests a high level of parliamentary resistance to detention without trial. In 2005, following the 7/7 attack, the government introduced a bill to extend the detention period to a maximum of 90 days but suffered a rare defeat in the House of Commons when a substantial number of backbenchers joined opposition parties to ensure that the extension was limited to 28 days. A subsequent attempt to extend the period to 42 days succeeded in the House of Commons but failed in the House of Lords, and the government decided against resubmission of the bill. But it may have taken the 7/7 attack to secure even the extension to 28 days. The 28-day extension has not survived. It was subject to a requirement that its operation be periodically affirmed by order, and the Conservative–Liberal Democrat coalition allowed it to lapse in January 2011 when the July 2010 order expired. A 2012 amendment gave legislative force to the 14-day limit.[97]

Poll data suggest that preventive detention nonetheless enjoyed considerable public support, even at a time when it aroused widespread parliamentary dissent. Following the bombing of commuter trains in Madrid in 2004, 66 percent of a national sample favoured the detention of asylum seekers until they could be assessed as not being terrorist threats, 63 percent favoured the indefinite detention of British terrorist suspects, 62 percent favoured the indefinite detention of foreign terrorist suspects, and 58 percent favoured the indefinite detention of people associating with terror suspects.[98] In response to a 2005 poll conducted prior to the 7/7 attacks, 61 percent of respondents said they regarded the detention of suspected terrorists without trial as acceptable, and 73 percent considered that placing suspected terrorists under house arrest was acceptable.[99] In 2006 (in the aftermath of a thwarted plot to bomb transatlantic aircraft), 69 percent of respondents said that it should be possible to detain terror suspects who had not been charged with any offence for up to 90 days.[100] Such findings would be consistent with the hypothesis that the government was behaving in an electorally opportunistic manner, but if so, they raise the question, why did the opposition and substantial numbers of government backbenchers vigorously support apparently unpopular policies rather than trying to outflank the government on the right?

Canada's immigration detention regime predated the 9/11 attacks and was amended only to ensure that it conformed to the Supreme Court's decision in *Charkaoui v Canada (Citizenship and Immigration)*. The preventive detention provisions of the Anti-terrorism Act (SC 2001) received considerable opposition, were sunsetted, and expired after the government's failed attempt to secure a resolution extending the life of the legislation but were re-enacted in 2013.

Australian immigration law's provisions for immigration detention also predated 9/11 and targeted immigrants ineligible for entry, regardless of whether they were security risks. Post-9/11 legislation provides little evidence to suggest that heightened concerns of terrorism played a major role in its form and passage. The original suite of counterterror bills introduced in 2001 included a proposal for detention for the purposes of questioning by ASIO. It evidenced executive hunger for expanded powers but was strongly opposed by the nongovernment parties, and the detention for questioning legislation was not passed until 2003, after extensive amendments designed to protect questionees.[101] Legislation giving police a limited investigative detention power was not introduced until 2004. A bipartisan Senate committee recommended greater judicial supervision of extended detention. The government accepted the recommendation, and the legislation[102] passed with support from the opposition Labor Party. The 2005 measures for preventive detention and control orders followed the London 7/7 bombings but also implemented decisions of a conference of heads of government (a majority of whom were Labor state and territory premiers and first ministers).[103] The legislation nonetheless elicited considerable opposition and, in any case, becomes salient for preventive purposes only in the exceptional circumstance where ordinary arrest powers are inadequate.

The 2007 defeat of the Howard government made little difference to the relevant legislation, except insofar as legislation was later passed to provide greater safeguards for those subject to investigatory detention in connection with criminal justice proceedings. In New Zealand, the only relevant post-9/11 legislation tightened the standards for immigration detention.

Institutional Concerns

Detention law can partly be understood as the outcome of interinstitutional conflict. The executive seeks broader detention powers. The legislature generally limits executive proposals. Courts set limits on what the political arms can do. But institutional considerations play out much more visibly in relation to the detention of aliens than in relation to the detention of citizens. Conspicuous features of detention regimes are the narrowness of the laws permitting the detention of citizens and the rarity with which powers are used against citizens. Powers of preventive detention in a context outside criminal law are either nonexistent or so rudimentary as to be of little practical relevance, and when they are potentially intrusive, they are usually used against noncitizens. Governments and parliaments generally appear to be content to rely on the criminal law to achieve preventive detention of citizens and permanent residents. Noncitizens enjoy far less protection. Relevant laws are typically initiated by the executive and encounter mild resistance from the legislature (but Congress was prepared to strip Guantánamo detainees of habeas corpus rights), and governments or coalitions with parliamentary majorities have introduced legislation to curtail detention powers.

The record of the courts can be viewed in two ways. First, it is clear that they did more to protect human rights than did the other two branches of government. The Guantánamo litigation established the right of aliens to seek habeas corpus if detained by the United States. It established, first, that the government had to demonstrate that it had evidence to justify detention and, second, that detainees had a right to know the content of the case against them. It affirmed the (partial) application of the Geneva Conventions to unconventional wars. It has resulted in the freeing from detention of people who ought not to have been taken or kept prisoner.

The decision by the House of Lords in *A v Secretary of State for the Home Department* (no 1, 2004)[104] went even further, striking down the 2001 immigration detention regime on the grounds that the secretary's order on which its operation depended was discriminatory (against nonnationals) and unreasonable (since if measures were needed to deal with nonnational threats, they must also be necessary to deal with the threat posed by nationals). (But, basing its decision on the different language of the Canadian Charter, the Canadian Supreme Court rejected a similar argument in relation to the corresponding Canadian legislation.[105])

Decisions in UK and Canadian cases have also insisted on the existence of a firm evidentiary foundation for detention decisions and have tended to expand detainees' rights to know the details of the case against them, even if this might come at some cost to security. They have, moreover, been willing to use the writ of habeas corpus to require governments to take steps to secure the release of people in the custody of foreign states. In Canada, the relevant detainee was a citizen. In the United Kingdom, the duty was grounded in the detainee's having been detained by UK forces, coupled with memoranda of understanding that governed rights in relation to prisoners transferred to another party to the memoranda. In 2004, the detainee had been transferred from Iraq to Afghanistan, without the consultation required by the memoranda. The courts proceeded on the basis that the detention was unlawful. The Geneva Conventions applied, and the war was over. There were steps the secretary could take that might secure the detainee's release, and those steps should be taken.[106] But they were in vain. The United States denied that the continued detention was unlawful and made it as clear as diplomatic language could that it was not going to agree to the detainee's release. The court of appeal concluded that the secretaries had done all they could. That was sufficient compliance with the writ.[107]

However, these decisions cannot be understood simply in terms of courts' devotion to the rule of law. Like other political actors, judges disagree about what the law means. In every detention case to reach the highest court, there have been dissenting decisions and disagreement between the highest court and courts lower in the hierarchy. This is partly a reflection of the obvious: cases that find their way to final courts of appeal tend to be cases where the law is unclear, but this implies, in turn, that in relation to many important detention-related issues, law yields only slightly better results than tossing a coin. The plaintiffs in *Rasul* lost before both the district court and the court of appeals,[108] before succeeding by majority[109] before the Supreme Court. Following *Rasul*, two sets of detainees' cases yielded different results at first instance.[110] *Hamdan v Rumsfeld* succeeded at first instance, but the government succeeded on appeal.[111] Following *Hamdan* (in which Justices Scalia, Thomas, and Alito dissented), the court of appeals ruled in *Boumediene v Bush* that Congress had successfully stripped the courts of their habeas corpus jurisdiction,[112] and the Supreme Court's subsequent decision in *Boumediene* provoked dissents from Chief Justice Roberts and Justices Scalia, Thomas, and Alito. However, the litigation finally went some way towards settling the law (at least for the time being). The aftermath has been ambiguous. Initially, applicants enjoyed considerable success: detainees won 38 out of 52 cases decided between 2008 and July 2010. Since then, the position has changed: between July 2010 and November 2011, five detainee successes were reversed on appeal, and none of the 11 cases heard by the district court resulted in a win for the detainee.[113] In one sense, only 6 percent of detainees owe their release to litigation, but this underestimates the political and legal effects of the litigation.

UK courts were less divided. Cross-tier and intracourt unanimity was achieved in litigation relating to the validity of a control order involving house arrest for 18 hours a day, and there was almost as much judicial consensus when the House of Lords (overruling a single judge) upheld the validity of orders lasting 12 to 14 hours.[114] There was, however, slightly less agreement in *A v Secretary of State* (no 1, 2004),[115] but only 3 of the 13 judges who dealt with the case found for the government. In the Canadian *Charkaoui* litigation, the government succeeded at first instance and in the federal court of appeal, only to fail before a unanimous Supreme Court.[116]

In assessing the role of courts in counterterror cases, it is also important to note that justice sometimes comes slowly and that practical obstacles may stand between detainees and their legal rights. While *Boumediene* was a substantive triumph for liberty, it was not a procedural one. The time taken to resolve the question meant that by the time of *Boumediene* and its progeny, the government had been able for a considerable time to detain those it suspected of being terrorists. While prisoners at Guantánamo had formal access to the courts, staff at the prison sometimes sought to subvert trust between prisoners and counsel (by using people pretending to be lawyers as interviewers) and to obstruct effective representation (by limiting contact between counsel and their clients).[117]

In the United Kingdom, the plaintiffs in *A v Secretary of State* (no 1, 2004) had succeeded before the Special Immigration Appeals Commission in July 2002. The court of appeal found for the government in July 2003, and the House of Lords gave its decision in December 2004. Yusuf Rahmatullah was detained in 2004, but it was not until 2010 that habeas corpus proceedings became possible, and it was another 21 months before they were (unsatisfactorily) resolved. Litigation involving control orders is faster, but the UK Parliament's Joint Human Rights Committee concluded, "[T]he slow service of evidence, the need for the special advocates to be able to do their job, the secret hearings to consider closed evidence, these all mean that it is an extraordinarily prolonged process with no immediate remedy."[118] Delay means that courts effectively give governments what they want in the short run, although they may have to pay in the end.[119]

Moreover, courts were sometimes highly deferential to the executive. In the Guantánamo litigation, the government had generally succeeded before the lower courts. Indeed, in a post-*Boumediene* decision, *Al-Adahi v Obama*,[120] the DC Circuit Court of Appeals suggested that the government was not required to meet a preponderance of evidence standard in habeas corpus cases, but the court noted that the government had argued for a more rigorous standard. In *Ashcroft v Iqbal*, the Supreme Court itself had proved remarkably tolerant of the government's post-9/11 roundup of immigrants from Arab countries. Deferential courts summarily dismissed *Bivens* claims by José Padilla and Maher Arar, based on their alleged unlawful detention and torture.[121]

Deference seems to have played a more limited role in the UK and Canadian litigation and a complex one in Australia. In *A v Secretary of State* (no 1, 2004), one of the conditions for the exercise of the relevant power was the existence of a "public emergency threatening the life of the nation." The majority concluded, first, that this question was such that great weight should be given to the judgment of the political arms of government and, second, that the possibility of future terrorist attacks could fall within this rubric. (Lord Hoffman disagreed.) But deference was not required in relation to whether the response to the emergency could be justified as proportionate. Moreover, UK courts have intervened in areas where US courts still seem reluctant to intervene, notably in relation to inquiring into the seedy practices of foreign governments. In the security certificate cases in Canada, the legislation required something akin to merits review, thereby limiting the role for deference. In cases involving detainees abroad, Canadian courts, like their UK counterparts, have treated constitutionally protected rights as prevailing over traditional executive prerogatives.

In a challenge to the validity of Australia's legislation on control orders, the plaintiff's arguments included the contention the criteria governing the making of control orders were such that legislation was purporting to invest federal courts with non-judicial powers. The basis for this argument was that the assessment of the risk posed by potential controlees was outside the expertise of judicial officers. The High Court majority held that the power was of a judicial character.[122] However, Justice Hayne, dissenting, concluded that the findings it required could properly be made only by the executive and that the legislation therefore impermissibly purported to confer executive powers on the judiciary. A condition for the validity of the legislation was, paradoxically, lack of deference. However, complicating Justice Hayne's dissent was his finding that conferring the powers on the executive would probably constitute an impermissible violation of the judiciary's near monopoly over the right to make detention orders. (He concluded that a section analogous to the (then inoperative) section 83.3 of the Canadian Criminal Code was needed.)

Also suggestive of lack of deference is an interlocutory decision in relation to an application by David Hicks for judicial review of the government's decision not to seek his release from Guantánamo. A government application for summary dismissal was unsuccessful,[123] which suggested that even in the absence of a human rights act or a charter, Australian courts might be willing to intervene in foreign policy decisions. But Australian courts are reluctant to accede to summary dismissal applications. The case suggests only that Hicks might have succeeded if the case had proceeded further. It did not, because it became moot on his repatriation.

The ability of courts to play an active role was also limited, to some extent, by practical obstacles to effective litigation. People aggrieved by their detention can litigate only if they are in a position to initiate litigation. This requires a degree of cooperation from captors, who must, at the very least, be willing to allow the prisoner to communicate to a court or (less fancifully) someone who can initiate litigation on their behalf. Effective litigation also requires the capacity to obtain and contact legal advisers. For those detained outside the United States, this may not be easy, and even those detained at Guantánamo were often hard-pressed to pursue their legal rights. Even those detained within the United States as material witnesses or in immigration detention were sometimes unable to contact counsel and were kept so ill-informed as to the basis for their detention as to leave them unable to contest it.[124] Practical obstacles to litigation elsewhere seem to have been weaker, partly because the governments engaged in far less extraterritorial detention, partly because detention regimes condition detention on a judicial order, and partly because the governments seem to have been less ruthless in obstructing access to the courts.

Underlying Beliefs

The US experience is consistent with the importance of underlying beliefs as a determinant of receptivity towards detention without trial. Typically, congressional responses to the more controversial features of detention-related issues have been strongly along party lines. An attempt to amend the proposed Military Commissions Act so as to preserve the right to habeas corpus failed narrowly, but largely along party lines, and the final votes on the passage of the Military Commissions Act were also strongly along party lines. This cannot be dismissed merely as an artifact of partisans supporting their government and opposing governments of the other party. One of President Obama's first measures was to initiate plans to close down the Guantánamo prison, and resistance has come from the Republicans, consistent with their earlier enthusiasm for detention. Moreover, under Obama, the government has predicated its resistance to habeas corpus applications on the government's having to meet a higher standard than that previously adopted by the DC Circuit.[125]

Poll data suggest that a similar phenomenon is to be found among the population at large. In response to a May 2009 Gallup poll, 68 percent of Republicans, 36 percent of independents, and 22 percent of Democrats believed that the prison had strengthened US security.[126] Given this finding, it is not surprising that numerous polls have yielded a similarly strong relationship between party identification and beliefs about whether the prison should be closed,[127] and self-identification as a conservative or a liberal is also strongly related to attitudes towards the prison's closure: 68 percent of liberals polled in January 2009 wanted the prison closed, while 61 percent of conservatives wanted it kept open.[128]

The preventive detention regime in Australia was also the subject of partisan division. It was passed when the Liberal-National coalition enjoyed a rare majority in both houses: the Parliament voted strictly along party lines, the coalition in favour and Labor and the other nongovernment parties against. Similar divisions also characterised the initial proposals in relation to ASIO's powers to detain for questioning, but legislation conferring more-limited powers was later passed with Labor support, as was legislation providing for detention for the purposes of criminal investigation. (The Australian Democrats and the Greens voted against the legislation at the Senate third reading.) The 2010 amendments to the legislation also received cross-party support.

Poll data disclose a relationship between party preference and support for the propositions, first, that the government should have the right to detain terrorist suspects for as long as they liked without putting them on trial and, second, that police should have the power to detain a person they suspect of planning a terrorist attack, until satisfied otherwise. In a 2007 poll, Liberals were strongly supportive of detention without trial (40 percent definite and 29 percent probably), as were Nationals (39 and 26 percent). Labor voters were evenly divided (22 and 26 percent), and Greens were opposed (12 and 15 percent). In response to the second question, the vast majority of Liberals strongly agreed or agreed (53 and 36 percent), as did Nationals (50 and 31 percent). Labor voters were less enthusiastic (30 and 33 percent), and Greens were considerably less so (18 and 28 percent). In each case, the attitudes of voters for smaller parties were consistent with their party's rank on a right-left continuum.[129] But it is difficult to separate out the role of being in opposition and the role of beliefs. Complicating beliefs-based explanations is the fact that when in power, Labor has done little to amend the relevant measures.

Canadian evidence is also equivocal. Preventive detention legislation has been the subject of partisan conflict, but the partisanship seems to be a surrogate for the effect of being in office. The Liberals introduced preventive detention but sunsetted it. When an incoming Conservative minority government sought a resolution extending the operation of the section, the Liberals joined the New Democrats and Bloc Québécois to ensure its defeat, notwithstanding that the Liberal members of a committee reviewing the act had earlier agreed that the power should remain. It was restored in 2013.

The United Kingdom provides even messier findings. In 2000, the Conservatives had unsuccessfully moved to amend the Terrorism Bill to provide for preventive detention, arguing that, properly administered (as it had not been in Northern Ireland), the power might prove valuable. They abstained on the 2001 legislation that established a regime for detaining immigrants certified to be a security risk. The Liberal Democrats opposed it. The opposition parties also opposed attempts to extend the maximum investigatory detention period, and they were joined by enough Labour backbenchers to ensure the defeat of 2005 proposals to extend the period to 90 days or, failing that,

60 days. Consistent with this opposition, the recently elected Conservative–Liberal Democrat government legislated to replace control orders with orders that were slightly less intrusive.

A second manifestation of the limited relevance of party allegiance comes from the reports of parliamentary committees. Reports from the House of Commons Foreign Affairs Committee and from the Joint Committee on Human Rights have been critical of the government's position in relation to the treatment of prisoners at Guantánamo.[130] More important, the reports have generally been unanimous, as have committee reports on preventive detention laws.[131]

Finally, poll data suggest that public attitudes towards detention measures also bear no obvious relationship to preference for one of the major parties over the other. In response to a 2005 poll, Conservatives were at most only slightly more likely than Labour voters to approve of detention of suspected terrorists without trial (62 percent compared to 59 percent), although Liberal Democrats are far less likely to do so (38 percent). House arrest was most likely to be approved by Labour voters (81 percent) and less likely to be approved by Conservatives (67 percent) and Liberal Democrats (66 percent).[132] However, in 2010, there was a change of government, Labour being replaced by an uneasy Conservative–Liberal Democrat coalition. Respondents to a 2011 YouGov poll were asked whether the government should have the power to use control orders. Eighty-five percent of Conservatives said that it should, as did 69 percent of Liberal Democrats. Only 65 percent of respondents intending to vote with the Labour Party agreed. Fifty-one percent of Conservatives were also more likely to believe that reducing the constraints imposed as part of control orders would put people at greater risk of terrorism, as compared with 35 percent of Labour voters and 28 percent of Liberal Democrats.[133] Among Conservatives and Labour voters, attitudes towards control orders vary according to whether one's party is in power. But there is a complication to what would otherwise be an elegant hypothesis: there were indeed proposals to limit the scope of control orders. They came from the coalition. But the pressure for them seems to have been one of the rewards given to its junior partner by the Conservatives.

Conclusions

Preventive detention is designed to fill gaps left by the criminal law by virtue of both the law's requirement of proof beyond reasonable doubt and the rigorous procedural standards it ostensibly requires. But advocates of preventive detention face two major obstacles. First, the logic of preventive detention is that the law should be willing to countenance the detention of people who are probably innocent in order to protect the interests of those who remain free. Poll data suggest that the public may be willing to accept this, but questions rarely put the issue so starkly and in relation to imprisonment at Guantánamo, which squarely posed this issue, American opinion tended to be evenly divided. Moreover, official rhetoric suggests recognition that detaining the innocent is not electorally appealing. Ashcroft's message was to "terrorists." Detention at Guantánamo was defended on the grounds that it housed the "worst of the worst," rather than on the more honest basis that it housed people who might pose a risk to American troops if released and that since it was difficult to determine who were and were not risks, it was wiser to err on the side of caution. Furthermore, a striking feature of preventive detention regimes is that they have typically involved nonnationals. This makes limited sense from a preventive perspective unless the threat is largely external, and even if that is the case, the logic of preventive detention is that legislation should at least permit it if a citizen is planning to embark on an attack. It makes some sense politically, but not as much as one might expect on the basis of crude analyses based on widely shared prejudice against the "other" or on the others' inability to vote and lack of political resources. The interests of the others coincide with the economic and ideological interests of people with far more political resources. The post-9/11 roundup was exceptional. It suggests executive panic. It soon came to a halt, and it was not replicated elsewhere. Low-intensity harassment continues, but it is not reflected in indiscriminate detention, at least within national borders.

Second, insofar as the rationale for preventive detention rests on mistrust of traditional criminal procedures, it meets political and judicial resistance. One reason is that traditional procedures are designed to avoid the detention of the innocent, but another is that they have the potential to increase the likelihood of well-informed decision making, regardless of whether the standard of proof is beyond reasonable doubt, on the balance of probability, or something lower. Courts have a constitutional and quasi-constitutional basis for insisting on rigorous standards, but these are not determinative. For instance, "due process" is the process that is due, and this is potentially highly malleable. But courts have proved reluctant to depart from exacting procedural standards. Except in the United States in relation to habeas corpus rights, legislatures have either agreed or recognised that it would be futile to legislate if the legislation will only be struck down.

The upshot is laws that allow limited scope for preventive detention other than pursuant to criminal law.[134] These have frustrated governments, but except in the United States, this has self-evidently done them no harm, even when their consequence has been the release of people regarded by the executive as dangerous. Indeed, no one who has absconded from house arrest or been released in order to protect secrets has been involved in any kind of subsequent terrorist attack. Prisoners released from Guantánamo have sometimes fought against US and allied forces.[135] But these include both those released by Combatant Status Review Tribunals and those released later, and while they can be taken as evidence that preventive detention may have saved American lives, this conclusion is valid only if detention at Guantánamo also did little to stimulate terrorism among those who were detained and among others angered by their detention. Its relevance to the wisdom or otherwise of preventive detention is also complicated by the degree to which detention was accompanied by torture and mistreatment.

NINE

Torture and Coercive Questioning

> We do not torture.
>
> *President George W. Bush, 2005*

> We also have to work the dark side, if you will, the shadows, in the intelligence world. . . . It is a mean, nasty, dangerous and dirty business, and we have to operate in that area.
>
> *Vice President Richard Cheney, 2001*[1]

> Human rights is a very flexible concept. It depends on how hypocritical you want to be on a particular day.
>
> *Michael Scheuer, former head of the CIA's Bin Laden Unit, 2005*[2]

> I assumed that if they were doing things out of the ordinary or outside the guidelines, someone would have said something. Also the wing belongs to MI [the Military Intelligence Corps] and it appeared MI personnel approved of the abuse.
>
> *Abu Ghraib corporal*[3]

As far as international law is concerned, official torture can never be justified. It is prohibited by customary international law, and the prohibition binds both states and individuals. The Geneva Conventions govern the treatment of those seized in the course of armed conflict. Convention expectations vary according to whether the conflict is an "international" armed conflict and, if it is not, according to whether the Second Protocol to the conventions applies. Even if the conflict is neither "international" nor governed by the Second Protocol, Common Article 3 of the conventions applies and forbids the torture and ill-treatment of those taken prisoner in the course of armed conflict and of nonparticipants. The conventions do not apply to conflict that falls short of constituting "armed conflict."

Article 7 of the International Covenant on Civil and Political Rights (ICCPR) absolutely forbids "torture or cruel inhuman or degrading treatment or punishment." The Convention against Torture and Other Cruel, Inhuman or Degrading Treatment or Punishment (the "Torture Convention") came into effect on 26 June 1987. It prohibits "torture," which is defined to involve the intentional infliction of severe injury by public officials. Its prohibition on torture is subject to no exceptions.[4] The convention also prohibits "cruel, inhuman or degrading treatment," but signatories' duties in relation to this are less exacting. As of mid-2012, there were 150 parties to the Torture Convention, a sizeable number of which have nonetheless engaged in or been complicit in torture or something closely resembling it. The discrepancy between norms and practice should come as no surprise: the exacting standards of international law owe their existence to national governments' capacity for hypocrisy; and, less cynically, the need for most forms of proscriptive law arises from the existence of the behaviour it proscribes. What is more interesting is how countries handle the strain between the apparent unacceptability of torture and the temptation to resort to it, and that is the subject of this chapter.

But first, I offer a caveat. Even when the term *torture* is defined, it may not always be clear whether a particular form of brutality falls within its rubric.[5] One of the more controversial elements of the US "torture memoranda" related to precisely this issue. Part of the problem with the memoranda lay with the point at which they drew the line, but part of the problem also seems to lie in understandable revulsion at the thought of lawyers calmly deciding and giving advice to the effect that some forms of very painful treatment should be denied the label "torture." Nonetheless, international law implies that lines must be drawn and that they have important consequences. The Torture Convention implies a distinction between "torture" and lesser (but nonetheless unacceptable) forms of ill-treatment.[6] The UN special rapporteur on torture has concluded that for the purposes of the Torture Convention, torture and inhuman treatment are distinguished not by severity of harm but by the fact that inhuman behaviour is covered by the convention regardless of whether it involves official conduct.[7] This view is contentious,[8] however, and has been expressly rejected by the Court of Appeal of England and Wales.[9] For the purposes of this chapter, I shall use the term *torture* loosely to include "inhuman" treatment.

Torture and Ill-Treatment: Use and Complicity

United States

The United States is a party to the Geneva Conventions, the ICCPR, and the Torture Convention, and it has passed legislation to give effect to the obligations it assumed by its 1994 ratification of the Torture Convention. However, Senate ratification was subject to a narrow definition of what was entailed in "severe mental pain or suffering." It also limited US obligations in relation to cruel, inhuman, or degrading treatment to "the cruel, unusual and inhuman treatment or punishment prohibited by the Fifth, Eighth, and/or Fourteenth Amendments to the Constitution." In anticipation of the ratification of the Torture Convention, Congress had earlier legislated to prohibit the use of torture. Its definition anticipated the Senate's subsequent reservation.[10]

Coercive interrogation has nonetheless been used by the United States in its War on Terror. It was widely used at Guantánamo[11] and Afghanistan[12] and has been used by the Central Intelligence Agency in prisons maintained by the agency.[13] The notorious use of torture at the Abu Ghraib prison in Iraq took place in a context in which the military police involved had been requested to "set physical and mental conditions for favorable interrogation of witnesses."[14] In addition, the CIA has outsourced interrogation to countries whose governments are notorious for their use of torture.[15] Because the United States takes law seriously, the agencies responsible for the use of potentially inhuman interrogation techniques were concerned about their legality and anxious to know how far they could go. In a series of controversial memoranda (here called the "torture memoranda"), lawyers in both the Department of Justice and the Department of Defense advised that they could go a very long way.

The torture memoranda advised that, for the purposes of US criminal law, "torture" involved the infliction of a higher degree of pain than was usually involved in coercive interrogations and gratuitously inflicted violence.[16] To be "severe," it was necessary that, at the very least, torture involve the infliction of lasting physical or mental harm. The memoranda also advised that an official might be able to rely on the defences of necessity and even self-defence. They also argued that insofar as the torture legislation purported to limit the power of the president as commander in chief, it was unconstitutional. The memoranda also cast doubt on whether the use of "lesser" forms of violence and humiliation for intelligence-gathering purposes was illegal under US law.

Other memoranda addressed and approved the use of particular methods of interrogation.[17] While the CIA continued to use "enhanced techniques" that had been specifically approved, it did not take full advantage of the broader powers postulated in the memoranda.[18] The use of violence and degradation in military facilities was less constrained and more widespread and was manifested both in violent interrogations and in the gratuitous mistreatment of prisoners, both at Guantánamo and in other prisons, including, notoriously, Abu Ghraib.[19] However, like the CIA, the Defense Department did not authorise the full exercise of the powers implicit in the two general memoranda.[20]

Under the Detainee Treatment Act of 2005 and onwards, the powers of the military have been restricted so as to preclude use of interrogation methods other than those listed in the army's field manual on intelligence interrogation,[21] which itself was amended so as to impose tighter standards than those required by the Geneva Conventions.[22] However, the legislation also provided considerable protection to interrogators who had used techniques on the basis of assurances that the techniques were legal.[23] But while the Detainee Treatment Act extended the prohibition on torture and inhuman treatment so that it applied to anyone in the physical custody of the United States, regardless of where, it did not subject the CIA to the field manual.

The Supreme Court decision in *Hamden v Rumsfeld* meant that, contrary to the administration's view, prisoners at Guantánamo were also entitled to the protections afforded by Common Article 3 of the Geneva Conventions.[24] Congress responded by narrowing the scope of the relevant legislation (18 USC § 2441(3)(c)) and limiting the circumstances under which officers and service personnel could be prosecuted under the section for offences committed between 2001 and 2005.[25]

A bill that would have subjected the CIA to the field manual restraints was vetoed by President Bush and failed to secure the congressional majority needed to overcome the veto.[26] President Obama's executive order of 22 January 2010 banned the use of torture by the CIA.[27] However, it provides no protection against a subsequent president's issuing of a fresh and inconsistent order.

An alternative to the use of torture by US agents is its use by foreign governments on behalf of or with the connivance of the United States. In some cases, this involved the capture of suspects outside the torturing state and their transfer to countries where they have been subjected to lengthy periods of torture and ill-treatment.

The focus of this section has been on torture for the purposes of interrogation, but the boundary between torture for interrogation and its expressive use can be vague, and in any case, it is clear that torture or inhumane treatment was not limited to its use in the context of interrogation. Practices developed for ostensibly instrumental coercion were reflected in noninstrumental mistreatment. Abu Ghraib was its visible face, and it was far less atypical than one would wish. Moreover, complicity in torture was not confined to the victims of extraordinary rendition. While there is some evidence that US personnel sometimes tried to prevent the use of torture by the Iraqi government, recently disclosed US Army field reports have disclosed a general failure to investigate reports of abuse by Iraqi authorities.[28]

United Kingdom

Historically, the United Kingdom has not been averse to the use of coercion as a means of gathering information from suspected terrorists. It was used in the course of the attempts to control anticolonial insurgencies in the 1950s.[29]

The United Kingdom's treatment of suspected Irish terrorists may not have involved torture, but it did involve the use of highly coercive tactics, to the point where it violated the ECHR.[30] However, the United Kingdom is a party to the Torture Convention, its accession not having been subject to any reservations. It has passed legislation to give effect to its obligations under the convention.[31] Its governments have unequivocally denounced torture. Its security services have claimed that "coercive interrogation techniques were alien to the Services' general ethics, methodology and training."[32]

In keeping with this stance, UK officials expressed concerns about the US treatment of detainees. However, committees of members of parliament have been critical of the government's failure to do more. The Intelligence and Security Committee (which consists of parliamentarians appointed by the prime minister) was critical of the instructions given to UK officials following the expression of concerns. These advised that officers should "consider" reporting ill-treatment to a senior US officer; they should have advised that officers were obliged to do this. The committee also complained that the UK government did not always follow up on its concerns.[33] It was also critical of failure to ensure that some of those involved in interrogation were unaware of their obligations under the Geneva Conventions and under the relevant standard operating instructions.[34]

Moreover, while the UK government has emphasised its abhorrence at the use of torture and its refusal to resort to it, abhorrence has coexisted with willingness to use the fruits of torture by foreign intelligence agencies.[35] Some ambiguity surrounds what UK interrogators are permitted to do and the extent to which there is compliance with these instructions. A 2002 "guidance document" emphasised the importance of not condoning or being party to the ill-treatment of interviewees and warned that servants of the Crown who engaged in inhuman or degrading treatment of prisoners would be criminally liable under UK law. A subsequent document was issued in 2004, after it "became clear to SIS and the security service that their existing Guidance to staff on dealing with foreign liaison services was insufficiently detailed given the increasing requirement to cooperate with foreign services in counterterrorism operations." But apart from brief extracts, the documents enjoyed classified status, and the government argued against their disclosure in the litigation of *Al Rawi v Security Service*.[36] The government has, however, finally released its *Consolidated Guidance to Intelligence Officers*.[37] This document precludes interrogation where the person knows or believes that torture will take place, and it permits interrogation where the person believes there is a lower-than-serious risk of cruel, inhuman, or degrading treatment. In other circumstances, senior personnel must be consulted. Cruel, inhuman, and degrading punishment is defined to include use of stress positions, sleep deprivation, hooding, physical abuse, and degrading treatment. The guidance document is misleading insofar as it implies that interrogation may legally proceed if there is a real risk of torture or inhuman treatment, provided a senior officer or the relevant minister or ministers approves it.[38] But its standards are far more exacting than those that governed interrogation at Guantánamo, and they clearly encompass the activities alleged in the torture litigation cases. Insofar as similar guidance applied prior to 2010, the government was purporting to authorise torture and inhuman treatment only in cases where the relevant minister or ministers or a senior officer was willing to take responsibility for doing so.

Claims that UK soldiers have been involved in the torture or mistreatment of prisoners in Iraq have been the subject of public inquiries (and still are), as well as of a representative action before the UK courts seeking damages and/or judicial review remedies on behalf of more than 140 Iraqis.[39] An inquiry into the circumstances surrounding the death in custody of Baha Mousa documented not only the brutality with which Mousa was treated but the systematic use of ostensibly prohibited procedures, including hooding and the use of stress positions. There is also evidence of UK complicity in torture and ill-treatment elsewhere. Issues of complicity have arisen in a number of contexts. In early 2002, the UK government had been advised that British citizens were possibly being tortured in a US prison in Kabul, but it did little to try to prevent this.[40] The UK's intervention on behalf of prisoners at Guantánamo was less than wholehearted, and the UK cooperated with the extraordinary rendition program.[41] It was involved in the 2004 rendition of people associated with the anti-Gaddafi Libyan Islamic Fighting Group to Libya, where they were tortured.[42] It has sometimes handed over prisoners to the Afghan National Security Directorate and to the Iraqi authorities in circumstances where they faced a serious risk of torture or death.[43] Like their US counterparts, UK forces in Iraq have sometimes failed to investigate reports of abuse of detainees by Iraqi authorities.[44] Moreover, there can be little doubt that the security services have provided information that has been the basis for subsequent rendition and interrogation.[45] UK forces working with US forces in Afghanistan and Iraq have been responsible for arrests of people who have subsequently been transferred to US prisons.[46] UK agents have interviewed people whom they knew had been ill-treated during detention, although officers had been instructed by 2009 that they were forbidden from conducting any further questioning of a detainee after being informed by the detainee that the detainee had been tortured.[47]

The government also accepts that there might be circumstances in which the use of tainted evidence for intelligence purposes might be justified.[48] In *A v Secretary of State for the Home Department (No 2)*, the home secretary stated that it was not his policy to rely on information that he knew to have been obtained by torture,[49] but he argued that he was entitled to make detention decisions based on evidence obtained from foreign intelligence sources, notwithstanding that the foreign agency had in fact used torture to extract it. He further argued that a court considering the reasonableness of continued detention was required to treat the evidence as admissible, provided it was probative.[50]

Canada

Canada is a party to the Torture Convention and has passed legislation to give effect to its obligations under the convention.[51] There is no evidence that Canadian officials have been directly involved in torture. There is, however, evidence that Canadian officials have indirectly caused people to be subjected to torture and that Canadians have handed prisoners to Afghani police in circumstances where they could assume that there was a serious risk that prisoners would subsequently be subjected to torture.

There have been four cases where Canadian inquiries have found that Canada indirectly contributed to the torture of its citizens in Syria and Egypt. Canadian involvement included the provision of unduly prejudicial material to the American authorities, but the commission of inquiry concluded both that Canadian authorities had not anticipated that Arar would be transported to Syria and that Arar was subjected to no further torture once Canadian authorities were aware of Arar's detention there.[52] The Iacobucci inquiry concluded that Canadian officials had indirectly contributed to torture of three Canadians by directly or indirectly passing on information to foreign governments, by failing to pass allegations of torture on to superiors and other interested government agencies (in two cases), by failing to visit detainees speedily and frequently (in two cases), by sending questions to be asked by the Syrians without inquiring into the circumstances in which these questions would be asked (in two cases), and by communicating concern to a foreign government about the possibility that one of the detainees might be released (in one case).[53] In *Abdelrazik v Canada (Minister of Foreign Affairs)*, a federal court judge found, on the evidence before the court, that the CSIS had recommended the imprisonment of Mr. Abdelrazik—a Canadian citizen—by the Sudanese authorities and that Canada knew that conditions would be harsh but did not know, until after his release, that Mr. Abdelrazik had in fact been tortured.[54] Canadian courts also found that Omar Khadr, a Canadian citizen detained at Guantánamo, had been interviewed by CSIS officials, who sought to question him still further in 2004, notwithstanding that they knew he had been subjected to sleep deprivation with a view towards making him more compliant.[55]

More recently, there have been allegations that Canadian forces in Afghanistan have been handing prisoners to Afghani police units, knowing that this was likely to result in their being tortured. The latter allegations have been the subject of hearings before the Canadian House of Commons Special Committee on the Canadian Military Mission in Afghanistan. In evidence before the committee, a senior Canadian diplomat reported that Canada did little to monitor the fate of those it transferred to Afghan custody, that it was dilatory in reporting transfers to the International Committee of the Red Cross, and that its record keeping was poor.[56] There is, in short, no evidence that Canadian officials directly participated in or intentionally encouraged torture. But there is evidence of elements of complicity. However, in 2009, the Canadian government has directed CSIS to "not knowingly rely upon information which is derived from the use of torture" and to take "all reasonable measures to reduce the risk that any action on the part of the Service might promote or condone, or be seen to promote or conduct the use of torture, . . . when sharing information with foreign agencies."[57] A 2010 directive dealt with the case where a foreign agency has provided information whose source cannot be determined, but such that ignoring it would constitute an "unacceptable risk to public safety." In such cases, public safety is paramount, and the information may be shared.[58]

Australia

Australia is a signatory to the Torture Convention and has passed legislation broadly consistent with its convention responsibilities.[59] Moreover, while the Australian government argued that the Afghanistan conflict was a noninternational armed conflict, its expressed policy was to treat prisoners as if they had been captured in the course of an international armed conflict.[60] Australia has not maintained any prisons in Afghanistan, and it transferred detainees to allies in the conflict or to the Afghan government. A Defence Department inquiry found a complaint of ill-treatment of a detainee (made by a member of the Afghan National Army) to be largely unfounded. (There was no medical evidence to sustain claims of abuse, and the Dutch—to whom the detainees had been transferred—had not noted anything untoward.)[61]

Although Australia participated in the Iraq War, its role was a marginal one,[62] and there appear to have been no reported instances of Australian involvement in torture and mistreatment of prisoners, perhaps partly because Australia did not maintain its own prisons and transferred such people as it apprehended to its allies. But a Senate committee found that its monitoring of their treatment was imperfect. Reports from Defence Department personnel about their own and the Red Cross's concerns were poorly followed up and did not come to the attention of senior officers or the government.[63] Moreover, the Australian government's failure to establish processes for monitoring the treatment of prisoners by transferee governments was in breach of its Geneva Convention responsibilities.

While Australian authorities appear generally to have complied with the requirements of the legislation, Mamdouh Habib, a victim of extraordinary rendition and a former detainee at Guantánamo, has claimed (in a book about his experiences[64] and in a claim before the Australian Federal Court),[65] that agents of ASIO and other commonwealth officials were, in various ways, party to his torture, their contributions including the provision of information to interrogators, their knowledge that torture was taking place, their presence at interrogations where torture was used, their suggestions that release would be dependent on confessions, their failure to take steps to ensure secure his release, and their knowing use of the fruits of torture. The case was scheduled to be tried in mid-2011 but was settled on undisclosed terms (reported to have involved a payment of damages) in early 2011.[66] A subsequent report by the Australian inspector-general of security and intelligence concluded that while Australian officials could and should have done more to look after Mr. Habib's welfare, they had not been complicit in his mistreatment.[67]

New Zealand

New Zealand's involvement in the Afghanistan War has been slight, but it has been enough to give rise to concerns that it may have been or may be in danger of being implicated in torture. In 2002 (when New Zealand was governed by a Labour-led coalition), New Zealand forces handed over a number of detainees to US forces, without recording their names, although it did record other details.[68] More recently, after New Zealand's Special Air Service (SAS) was once more sent to Afghanistan (this time under a National-led coalition), concerns were expressed that the SAS was working with Afghan authorities in operations where those taken prisoner are at risk of being detained and tortured.[69] The government has acknowledged the cooperative activity but has argued that the Afghans are the lead authority in the relevant exercises and that the SAS therefore does not take and hand over prisoners.[70] Government supporters have, predictably, expressed confidence that the SAS did not and will not assist torture.[71] Green MPs do not share this confidence. The SAS's activities have generated no litigation.

The Development of the Law

Unlike in the other areas of law already discussed in this book, terrorist concerns have made almost no impact on the legislation governing torture. There have been virtually no attempts to water down antitorture legislation, and insofar as there have been statutory developments, these have involved tightening the relevant prohibitions. The only relaxation of legal prohibitions on torture has been the statutory protection afforded to members of the US intelligence community, and that was retrospective. Indeed, insofar as post-9/11 legislation has addressed the use of torture and ill-treatment, it has narrowed the range of permissible coercive techniques. It represents a response not to terrorism but to abuses committed in the name of counterterrorism.

Institutions and Torture and Inhuman Treatment

Differences between executive and legislative priorities are only tenuously reflected in the development of legislation. They are reflected more dramatically in the contrast between the law as interpreted by the executive and the law as understood by the courts. However, while courts have generally proceeded on the basis that torture and inhuman treatment are abhorrent, their decisions sometimes suggest that their abhorrence is qualified.

Torture and the Executive Arm

For those charged with the protection of national security, there may be circumstances where torture seems justified. One justification is that the infliction of pain as a counterterror measure is necessary to avert a greater evil. Some argue that interrogators may need to use the infliction of pain as a means of extracting information that can be used to take effective action against would-be terrorists. Whether this argument is correct is highly controversial, but claims by governments and others that coercive interrogation has yielded useful information[72] may generate and reinforce beliefs to this effect. Popular culture may do its bit,[73] and bad logic may be persuasive: terrorists' manuals tell terrorists how to resist interrogation, and if a person refuses to give information about his or her involvement in terrorism, an interrogator may reason that the person is a terrorist and that he or she will respond only to force.[74] Moreover, use of ill-treatment may increase the interrogator's determination to extract admissions, since the lack of admissions leaves open the worrying possibility that the interrogator has been ill-treating an innocent person. Governments are likely to want to believe that torture has not been in vain and are therefore inclined to believe that it can often be instrumentally effective.

However, whatever the instrumental attractions of inflicting pain might be, it is also clear that there are powerful restraints against doing so. First, within the executive arm, there was considerable resistance to the use of torture. This is evidenced by arguments in relation to the status of the Geneva

Conventions. The torture memoranda tended to dismiss the conventions as irritating irrelevancies that either did not apply, given the nature of the War on Terror, or, if they did apply, conferred rights and duties on states only. This interpretation was welcomed by the president but rejected by the State Department and regarded with concern by the Defense Department lawyers and by the Joint Chiefs of Staff.[75] A narrower issue is related to the use of torture and some less-painful forms of coercive questioning, whether by the armed forces or the CIA. The utility of coercive questioning was accepted within the CIA and (to some extent) within the armed forces,[76] but not by the FBI or the State Department.[77]

One reason for both restraint and its lack lies in the logic of the Geneva Conventions. The vast majority of those subjected to ill-treatment were people captured in the course of armed conflict, whose treatment was governed by the conventions. But as a matter of practice, the effective operation of the rules of war depends partly on reciprocity.[78] Ideally, unilateral compliance will be its own reward, and this is what the conventions require, if necessary—with the defaulting parties being dealt with later as war criminals. Well-disciplined armies may engage in unilateral compliance most of the time, but the strains will be considerable. They tend to be particularly acute in the context of unconventional wars, where insurgents tend not to reciprocate. Nonetheless, it is striking that even in the context of the Afghanistan and Iraq wars, the US Joint Chiefs of Staff and Defense Department lawyers were uneasy about suggestions that the conventions could be disregarded.

Stances on torture also appear to reflect agency priorities. One would expect the State Department to be concerned at policies that would have negative ramifications for the international standing of the United States, and consistent with this was its objections to the Department of Justice's arguments for a narrow reading of the obligations imposed by the Geneva Conventions. The FBI's doubts about the efficacy of coercive questioning may be partly explicable in terms of its institutional reasons for collecting information. Given its role in criminal prosecutions,[79] the FBI had no choice but to base its operating procedure on the need to ensure that its evidence was noncoercively acquired. Conversely, the CIA was accustomed to operating outside the law, given the exigencies of operating in hostile countries and its subjection to the different imperatives of gathering intelligence rather than proof and of averting attacks rather than responding to them.

But those disposed to favour the use of coercive interrogation were also concerned about the legality of doing so, as evidenced by the fact that the CIA and armed forces sought clarification of the legality of proposed interrogation techniques.[80] The advice of the torture memoranda was reassuring. This was not surprising: those who were asked to give it tended to be people sympathetic to the view that the law conferred sweeping powers on the executive in times of national emergency.[81]

If law is what the courts are likely to say it is, the advice of the memoranda was flawed. Even lawyers sympathetic to the government soon concluded that the memoranda were seriously flawed. Jack Goldsmith, who had considerable respect for John Yoo, nonetheless concluded that the memoranda had to be withdrawn. In a 2009 report, the Department of Justice's Office of Professional Responsibility (OPR) concluded that the memoranda had been flawed in that they, first, had inadequately addressed material that was contrary to their conclusions and, second, had misused sources in order to reach tendentious conclusions.[82] The OPR concluded that Professor Yoo must have known "that his view of Commander-in-Chief power was a minority view" and that he should have advised his client "that his analysis was a novel and untested one."[83] However, while critical of some of the reasoning used in a 2005 memorandum giving advice in relation to the legality of methods employed by the CIA, the OPR concluded that its flaws did not rise to the level of professional misconduct.[84] The OPR's report was submitted to David Margolis, an associate deputy attorney general, for the purposes of determining whether it should be referred to the disciplinary authorities of the relevant state bar associations. He decided against doing so, but not on the grounds that the memoranda represented a balanced assessment of the law.[85]

The advice of the torture memoranda proved politically sound. There have been no prosecutions of CIA or military interrogators. A major reason for this is that advice from the Office of Legal Counsel has a quasi-constitutive effect. It is authoritative within the executive arms, and its effect is such as to make it politically impractical to punish those who relied on it.

Courts

As a prediction of how courts would react to torture, the advice of the torture memoranda was less prescient. Executive powers in security cases are not as broad as the memoranda assumed, and torture encompasses a wider range of practices than the memos assumed. But insofar as the memos suggested that harsh techniques could be used with impunity, their authors have largely been vindicated. The only cases in which people detained outside the United States have had much success in relation to torture and ill-treatment claims against the United States have been habeas corpus cases where petitioners have succeeded on the basis of claims that admissions, confessions, and hearsay evidence adverse to their claims were obtained through torture or ill-treatment.[86] The courts' rejection of evidence tainted by torture and coercion is unsurprising, and as a corollary, courts have been willing to order discovery of documents relating to the likelihood that evidence adverse to habeas corpus applicants has been obtained by torture.[87]

Otherwise, torture-based claims have had little success. US courts have attached finality to government certificates in relation to whether Guantánamo detainees face the risk of torture if returned to their country of citizenship or sent somewhere else, as well as in relation to whether detainees in foreign countries face torture if transferred to the custody of the foreign government.[88] To date, alleged victims of extraordinary rendition have been unsuccessful in attempts to recover damages from the United States and from a corporation that allegedly assisted in the plaintiffs' transfer. In each case, the state secrets doctrine has proved fatal to some claims, albeit by the narrowest of margins in one case.[89]

Other cases failed on the basis of narrow interpretations of the circumstances under which people have a right to damages for harm suffered in consequence of breach of their constitutional rights (*Bivens* claims). Maher Arar had far less success before the US courts than in Canada.[90] In an en banc hearing, the Second Circuit decided by majority (7–5) that Arar's *Bivens* claim could not be sustained, its reasoning being that there were "special factors counseling hesitation" against extending the tort to cover the alleged wrongs. These included both the fact that it involved issues relating to foreign relations and the fact that it would potentially involve state secrets and required that proceedings be partly closed. The dissenters argued that this reasoning was flawed and that if the case did indeed require the disclosure of state secrets, it could and should be dismissed on this ground, given the normal rule that courts should not consider constitutional issues if a case could be disposed of on nonconstitutional grounds. The minority favoured remanding the case for a decision on the state secrets issue.

Afghan and Iraqi citizens who were held by US military forces were also unsuccessful in a suit alleging mistreatment by the US military. The district court dismissed a *Bivens* claim, on the grounds that the claimants were not entitled to the protection of the Fifth and Eighth Amendments: they were "nonresident aliens who were injured extra-territorially while detained by the military in foreign countries where the United States is engaged in wars."[91] The court determined that even if constitutional rights had been violated, the defendants could rely on special immunity (since the status of the rights had not been clear at relevant times) and on "special factors." In a split decision, the court of appeals found it unnecessary and undesirable to resolve whether *Boumediene v Bush* meant that the district court's analysis of the constitutional position was correct. Dismissal was nonetheless warranted on the grounds of qualified immunity (given the uncertain state of the law) and the undesirability of disrupting and hindering "the ability of our armed forces 'to act decisively and without hesitation in defense of our liberty and national interests.'"[92] Other avenues were blocked. The plaintiffs had failed to exhaust the administrative remedies on which claims based on the Federal Court Claims Act were predicated, and the Alien Tort Statute did not create substantive rights.

By contrast, a *Bivens* claim by José Padilla against John Yoo, based on his alleged contribution to the plaintiff's imprisonment, survived an application for summary dismissal in the district court.[93] The court held that *Bivens* claims extended to Yoo's conduct and that the law was not sufficiently unclear to ensure that Yoo would be able to rely on a defence of qualified immunity. In a related case in South Carolina, *Lebron v Rumsfeld*, the plaintiffs failed on both issues. The district court held that there were "special factors" counting against extending the scope of the tort. These included the probable scope of the pretrial discovery process, which

> would require the devotion of massive government resources, which by necessity would distract the affected officials from their normal security and intelligence related duties. Moreover, [a] trial on the merits would be an international spectacle with Padilla, a convicted terrorist, summoning America's present and former leaders to a federal courthouse to answer his charges. This massive litigation would have been authorised not by a Congressionally established statutory cause of action, but by a court implying an action from the face of the American Constitution.[94]

Given the outcome of the litigation surrounding Padilla's habeas corpus applications, it could not be said that the unlawfulness of his detention and his subsequent treatment had been clearly established.[95] The court of appeals affirmed, agreeing that it was not a case where a *Bivens* action could be maintained. It related to matters that were properly the prerogative of the political branches.[96]

By the time the Ninth Circuit Court of Appeals eventually heard Yoo's appeal, a Supreme Court majority had ruled that plaintiffs in a *Bivens* action had to show that "every reasonable official" would have understood that the behavior in question would violate the plaintiff's constitutional rights.[97] The court concluded that the plaintiffs could not meet the exacting standards required by this decision.[98] Unlike the district court in *Lebron*, it made no reference to political justifications for its decision. Indeed, it inclined to the view that the facts alleged by Padilla would, if true, mean that he had been tortured.[99]

Two *Bivens* claims against Donald Rumsfeld and others arising out of the alleged ill-treatment of American civilians detained in US prisons in Iraq succeeded at first instance. One failed before the DC Circuit Court of Appeals.

The other, which involved the alleged mistreatment of whistle-blowers who had previously reported details of corruption to US authorities, survived before the Seventh Circuit Court of Appeals, only to be vacated pending a hearing en banc, and subsequently reversed.

In each case, the alleged basis for Rumsfeld's liability was that he was responsible for the policies that had caused the plaintiffs' ill-treatment. The district courts dismissed summary dismissal applications based on "special factors" and qualified immunity. The cases did not involve the courts interfering with the conduct of military activities. If the cases threatened the disclosure of state secrets, this could be dealt with at a later stage. The relevant law was clear, and the government had not argued that the conduct in question would not amount to torture. In each case, the courts regarded it as relevant that the plaintiffs were Americans and entitled to correspondingly greater constitutional protection from the US government.[100] Similar reasoning underlay the decision of the Seventh Circuit panel.[101] (The decisions predated the court of appeals decisions in *Padilla v Yoo* and *Lebron*.)

The DC Circuit Court of Appeals disagreed, arguing, "The Supreme Court has never implied a *Bivens* remedy in a case involving the military, national security or intelligence." There was no appellate authority for permitting *Bivens* actions in such cases. (The Seventh Circuit decision in *Vance v Rumsfeld* had been vacated.) In providing limited relief to the victims of torture, Congress had implicitly decided not to create "a cause of action for detainees to sue federal military and government officials in federal court for their treatment while in detention." The court did not decide whether Rumsfeld could rely on qualified immunity.[102] In its en banc decision, a majority of the Seventh Circuit Court of Appeals agreed.[103] The majority opinion concluded that *Bivens* actions were not available against soldiers and others in the military chain of command, and that in any case, Rumsfeld's alleged involvement in the plaintiffs' mistreatment was too tenuous to justify his being held personally liable. A seventh judge disagreed with the majority on the availability issue, but agreed with the tenuous link argument. Three judges dissented.

The upshot of these cases is that no victim of brutal treatment by US officials outside the United States has yet managed to win a damages case against the US government. This is not because the alleged conduct does not amount to torture: none of the relevant decisions have been based on this ground. In part, it is a result of the nature of federal torts law. But it is clearly also a result of judicial choice. While the decisions have tended to bear out advice that ill-treatment could be engaged in with impunity, they also coexist with interpretations suggesting that cases could easily have gone the other way, at least at the summary dismissal stage. Detainees mistreated within the United States have had somewhat more success. In a suit brought by a handful of those detained in the Metropolitan Detention Center, the US eventually settled the claims of five plaintiffs for $1.26 million, and several of those responsible for their mistreatment were prosecuted.[104]

UK courts have given the government limited leeway in relation to the use of evidence tainted by the circumstances surrounding its collection. However, the courts have granted applications for judicial review of decisions to refuse to hold inquiries into alleged mistreatment by UK troops in Iraq. UK courts have also proved much more sympathetic than their US counterparts to torts claims with an obvious potential to involve state secrets.

In *A v Secretary of State for the Home Department (No 2)*, two members of the House of Lords expressly distinguished between torture and ill-treatment, concluding that the latter, when engaged in by state officials, was prohibited neither by the Torture Convention nor by ius cogens.[105] In *R v Ahmed*, the court of appeal followed these dicta,[106] applying this decision in a case where the government did not depend on evidence derived from torture or ill-treatment but where the prior investigation had been assisted by intelligence from a state known to engage in torture. In doing so, the court expressly rejected the opinion—held by a special rapporteur for the United Nations and by the Joint Parliamentary Human Rights Committee—that such behaviour constituted complicity in torture.[107] With varying degrees of enthusiasm, the House of Lords considered that the home secretary was entitled to rely on information both notwithstanding that it came from a government that had used torture to obtain it and provided that it was probative despite its tainted source. But it also ruled that the quasi-judicial commission responsible for review of the secretary's decision was precluded from doing so, regardless of whether the evidence was probative.[108]

In civil claims brought by plaintiffs claiming to be victims of torture, judicial rulings have tended to favour the plaintiffs and have involved findings to the effect that the Security Service (MI5) must have known that the plaintiff was being subject to torture, that it had misled the Intelligence and Security Committee, and that it had indirectly caused the foreign secretary to mislead the court.[109] The High Court has been prepared to prohibit UK forces in Afghanistan from delivering prisoners to particular agencies after having found, on the evidence, that there would be a real risk that prisoners would be tortured if they were transferred.[110]

Article 3 of the ECHR creates a duty on member states to hold inquiries into credible allegations of breaches of the convention and such systemic issues as arise from these. In *(R) Mousa v Secretary of State for Defence*,[111] the court of appeal held that the secretary had erred in concluding that it was proper to delay an inquiry into systemic issues until the findings of three current inquiries were reported. Consideration of one of the current inquiries was flawed insofar as there was an institutional relationship between its investigators and those doing the investigation into systemic issues.

The UK courts have also been prepared to adjudicate claims for damages arising out of the UK's failure to take adequate steps to prevent the mistreatment of British nationals detained at Guantánamo Bay. They did not regard the likely complexity of the litigation or the sensitivity of the issues as grounds for not allowing the case to proceed, notwithstanding estimates that resolving the issues of public interest immunity would require the services of 60 lawyers over three years.[112] (The case was finally settled.)[113] The High Court has also held that questions of whether a person is likely to be tortured in another country are to be resolved by the courts, even if this means finding that the government has erred in assuming that it might be possible to gain a worthwhile diplomatic undertaking from foreign governments.[114]

Australian and Canadian courts have had only limited occasion to adjudicate torture-related cases. In Habib's claim for damages arising out of his mistreatment, an application by the government for summary judgment was successful in relation to a number of claims, but at first instance and on appeal the federal court found that, as a matter of law, the Criminal Code provisions applied to commonwealth officers, regardless of where the alleged torture took place, and that commonwealth officers were therefore under a legal duty not to aid, abet or counsel torture or ill-treatment, and if they did so, would be acting in breach of their lawful authority. The fact that the claim rested on proof of the alleged misconduct of officers of foreign states was not a bar: the act of state doctrine did not apply when the act of state involved torture.[115] The court did not, however, address the overall merits of the case, except insofar as it found against Habib in relation to the fact relating to one of the factual issues underpinning his claim.

Canadian courts addressed torture-related issues in a number of cases. One involved Omar Khadr's application for judicial review of the government's failure to take adequate steps to ensure his release from Guantánamo. As noted earlier, the courts found evidence of Canadian officials being complicit in his mistreatment by US officials.[116] Claims arising from the mistreatment of Abou-Elmaati, Almalki, and Nureddin are currently before the courts, with trial not due to start until late in 2012.[117] The government appears not to have sought summary dismissal except in relation to a limitation defence, pleaded in response to claims by relatives and a former employer of Mr. Almalki for losses suffered as a result of their having been wrongly suspected of being terrorists.[118] Courts also addressed whether Canada was obliged under the Charter of Rights and Freedoms to refuse to transfer detainees in its custody to the Afghan authorities in circumstances where this would expose the detainees to a substantial risk of torture. The trial judge and the federal court of appeal held that the charter did not apply and that the application failed.[119]

Public Opinion

Both the reluctance of governments to admit to using or even being complicit in torture and the strict requirements of antitorture legislation suggest that governments and legislators doubt that there is much popular support for torture. If they do, their perceptions are largely borne out. US poll data suggest ambivalence and that tolerance of torture is sensitive to question wording and to response categories. In eight polls since 2004, the Pew Research Center has asked US respondents whether the use of torture "against suspected terrorists in order to gain important information" was "often," "sometimes," "rarely," or "never" justified. Responses have been relatively stable: on average, 16 percent said that torture might be justified "often," 31 percent "sometimes," 21 percent "rarely," and 29 percent "never."[120] Similar results have been reported in polls with slightly different response categories.[121]

Fifty-eight percent of respondents considered torture justified if it "might lead to the prevention of a major terrorist attack."[122] However, apparent willingness to condone torture must be understood in the light of the question, which assumes the utility of torture: only a third of respondents were prepared to support torture if it made it more likely that Americans might be tortured, and almost three-quarters considered that the recent allegations of torture had hurt America's image "a lot" or "somewhat."[123] When told that members of the US military were "required to abide by the Geneva Convention standards which prohibit the humiliating and degrading treatment of prisoners," a comfortable majority (57 percent) said that the CIA, when interrogating a person believed to have information about possible terrorist plots against the US, should comply with the conventions, rather than use measures that are more forceful.[124] Consistent with this ambivalence are the results of a December 2005 poll conducted for *ABC News* and the *Washington Post*, in which only a third of respondents said they regarded the use of torture against suspected terrorists as an acceptable part of the US campaign against terrorism.

Polls where respondents are asked to choose between "sometimes" and "never" justified yield a higher proportion of "never" responses than polls where, as in the case of the Pew polls, respondents are given four possible response categories. In a 2006 poll, 56 percent of respondents opted for the "never" category over "sometimes." Answers were strongly related to party, but even among the Republicans, only half said torture was "sometimes" justified. Differently worded polls giving a choice between never using torture and sometimes doing so have yielded similar results.[125]

Only 40 percent of respondents to a 2007 poll said that they thought "waterboarding" (which was briefly described) should be allowed; a differently worded 2009 poll yielded a similar result; and in a 2010 poll, 39 percent strongly or moderately approved of the practice.[126] In a 2009 poll asking respondents whether they approved or disapproved of the "harsh interrogation procedures" used by the Bush administration, 50 percent said they approved, and 46 percent said they disapproved.[127] In a 2010 poll asking respondents whether they thought the use of these techniques by the military and intelligence agencies was justified, 26 percent thought this was always justified, 31 percent that it was justified most of the time, 19 percent that it was sometimes justified, and 15 percent that it was never justified.[128] Given the vagueness that surrounds what constitutes "torture," the poll figures should be interpreted with care, but they suggest that attitudes towards the use of torture have been stable over the last five years and that many Americans are willing to accept the use of torture in some circumstances, despite the negative connotations of the word.

Elsewhere, polls tapping attitudes towards torture have been less frequent. In a 2005 UK poll, only 20 percent considered that it was acceptable to allow evidence obtained abroad by the use of torture to be used in British courts.[129] However, this does not reflect blanket opposition to the use of torture. Questioned about whether torture could be justified on rare occasions, British respondents were only slightly less likely than Americans to consider that it could be justified.[130] By contrast, most Australians either strongly agreed (28 percent) or agreed (31 percent) that the use of torture to prevent a terrorist attack was never justified. The percentage that neither agreed nor disagreed was 16.7, and 20.7 percent disagreed or strongly disagreed. (The remainder admitted not knowing.)

In a 25-nation poll on torture, respondents were asked to choose between two alternatives. One was that "clear rules against torture should be maintained because any use of torture is immoral and will weaken international human rights standards against torture." The other was that "terrorists pose such an extreme threat that governments should now be allowed to use some degree of torture if it may gain information that saves innocent lives." The Australian, Canadian, and UK responses were almost identical: three-quarters (75 percent of Australians, 74 percent of Canadians, and 72 percent of UK respondents) opted for the former alternative, and 22 percent of Australians and Canadians and 24 percent of UK respondents opted for the latter. US respondents were rather less hostile to torture: 58 percent favoured the first position, and 36 percent the second.[131]

The data suggest that there is little political capital to be gained by advocating torture but that if governments do wish to engage in torture, they should justify it in terms of its necessity. They also suggest the possibility of a relationship between national involvement in torture and national acceptance of torture. They leave open the reasons for the relationship.

Underlying Beliefs

Like other issues relating to the control of terrorism, interrogation policy involved party-related splits. The Detainee Treatment Act, passed in the aftermath of the revelation of the abuses occurring at the Abu Ghraib prison in Iraq, received widespread bipartisan support. However, the nine Senators who voted against it were all Republicans, and President Bush had threatened a presidential veto in response to Congress's failure to include an exception for national security emergencies.[132] His signing statement indicated that his administration would interpret the measure in accordance with "the constitutional authority of the President to supervise the unitary executive branch." The Senate Select Committee on Intelligence split along party lines over a 2005 inquiry into the CIA's role in rendition to torture and its detention practices, and its response to the Church Report on interrogations involved a similar split.[133] Following the Democrats' successes in the 2006 elections, Congress passed a bill to impose restrictions on CIA questioning that were similar to those imposed on the armed forces under the Treatment Act. An attempt to override the president's veto failed, with the nays largely drawn from the Republicans. Voting on the Intelligence Authorization Act of 2008 and on whether it should pass, despite the president's veto, was heavily partisan. On the latter issue, in the House of Representatives, only 5 Republicans out of 190 voted "aye," while only 3 out of 223 voting Democrats voted "nay."[134] The Obama years have not yielded torture-related legislation, but they have yielded executive orders consistent with the proposition that tolerance of coercive torturing is not simply an institutional response but a response reflecting decision makers' general political beliefs.

Similar results emerge from poll data. In response to a November 2005 *Newsweek* poll, 59 percent of Republicans, 42 percent of independents, and 36 percent of Democrats thought torture could sometimes to be justified to gain important information from terrorists,[135] and in September 2006, 50 percent of Republicans, 32 percent of independents, and 25 percent of Democrats thought that torture was "sometimes" justified (the alternatives were "never" or "depends"). In a 2010 poll, 52 percent of Republicans, 32 percent of independents, and 34 percent of Democrats considered the use of torture against suspected terrorists to be always justified or justified most of the time. Tolerance of use of enhanced interrogation techniques was also considerably higher among Republicans (77 percent) than among independents (60 percent) and Democrats (48 percent), as was strong or moderate approval of waterboarding (58 percent of Republicans, 42 percent of independents, and 30 percent of Democrats).[136] In a multivariate analysis of 2006 data, Hetherington and Suhay found that support for the use of torture was related to party identification and also to ideology and a measure of authoritarianism. They found that as worry about the threat posed by terrorism increased, the relevance of authoritarianism decreased. Their analysis does not report whether there was a similar interactive effect between worry and other "dispositional" variables.[137]

In the United Kingdom, there were no relevant House of Commons divisions, but poll data suggest a very weak relationship between party preference: Conservatives were slightly more likely to regard the use of evidence obtained by torture as acceptable (22 percent) than were Labour supporters (17 percent) and Liberal Democrats (16 percent).[138] In Australia, where there were also no relevant parliamentary votes, analysis of a 2007 poll showed that distaste for torture bears a moderate relationship to voting intention. Disapproval of torture was lowest among those intending to vote National (56 percent) or Liberal (54 percent), higher among Labor voters (64 percent), and highest among Greens (78 percent). In a logistic regression analysis, the relationship continued, after controls for the perceived risk of a terrorist attack.[139]

Conclusions

Poll data suggest that the general public is unwilling to countenance torture but that there are some circumstances where sizeable minorities and even majorities consider that it might be justified. Neither heightened concern nor a perception that it might sometimes be necessary have moved legislators even to consider relaxing statutory prohibitions on torture, although Congress provided limited statutory protection for past sins. Courts have unequivocally condemned torture, citing a proud history of judicial resistance to the use of coerced evidence in judicial proceedings. Governments disown torture and proscribed forms of ill-treatment.

Yet it is self-evident that governments are sometimes willing to countenance the use and threat of pain against their prisoners. Their willingness is strongly related to context. First, the use of torture has been largely directed against those captured in the course of armed conflict. Second, its post-9/11 victims have usually—but not invariably—been nonnationals, and when nationals have been victims, they have typically been outside the country.

Courts denounce torture, but US courts have generally proved unhelpful to those claiming to be victims of torture. To a considerable extent, this reflects general legal principles and, in particular, the limited circumstances in which victims of official misfeasance may sue either the US government or

US officials. These limits are reflected in the ease with which *Bivens* claimants are able to satisfy the requirement that there are no alternative avenues for redress. They also reflect the *Bivens* requirements themselves. It is not enough that an official acted unlawfully. The remedy is available only if there was a breach of constitutional duties and if, at the time of the breach, it was settled law that the conduct in question did indeed amount to a breach. There must also be no "special factors" counseling against the availability of damages as a remedy. Moreover, there is ample judicial authority to suggest that special factors include the possibility that permitting a cause of action could interfere with the protection of national security. The relevant decisions suggest that these principles are sufficiently vague to allow judges to base their decisions on varied assessments of what, if anything, national security requires in particular cases, as well as on the dangers of allowing victims of torture to sue those responsible in the US courts, as compared with the dangers of not allowing them legal redress. Courts elsewhere have a better record, but this is partly explicable in terms of different legal contexts: laws that have removed crown immunity and give full effect to the Torture Convention, quasi-subordination to the ECtHR (in the case of the UK courts), and cultural contexts that seem less tolerant of torture.

Law probably has the potential to discourage torture, but it may be difficult to disentangle the effect of law on torture from the impact on law of those factors that prompt torture. In particular, the nexus between the Afghanistan and Iraq wars and the use of torture suggests that if one wants governments to abstain from torture, one should oppose their involvement in wars. If war is a necessity, the best one can hope is that governments will recognise the dangers of tolerating torture, that well-trained troops will be sufficiently disciplined to keep its incidence to a minimum, and that law will provide some redress when discipline breaks down.

Conclusion

Terrorism has stimulated a variety of responses ranging from concessions to war, and including law. This book has examined some of the ways in which law has responded and some patterns underlying legal responses. In relation to the areas of law discussed earlier, the main conclusion to be drawn is that while there are some important differences, the substantive law tends not to vary markedly from country to country.

New Zealand law is almost certainly less illiberal than the law of the other four countries. New Zealand attaches relatively few consequences to terrorism per se and relies solely on the general law to address terrorism in the context of surveillance, state secrets, and migration. Moreover these general laws tend to provide greater protection than the equivalent laws in the other jurisdictions.

Canadian law goes a little further. It recognises two sanctions regimes. Its range of terrorism-related criminal offenses is slightly broader than New Zealand's. It provides governments with slightly expanded powers in the context of surveillance, evidence, and migration, when terrorism is involved, but the scope of these provisions has been qualified by Supreme Court decisions whose effect has been to condition the imposition of negative consequences upon the affected person's being afforded a substantial degree of procedural fairness.

Overall, UK legislation has tended to be less liberal than Australia's (which has drawn on UK models for much of its counterterror law). Its definition of terrorism is broader. It criminalises "glorification" of terrorism, whereas Australia doesn't. Its legislation in relation to stopping and searching suspected terrorists was far broader than Australia's. Its standards for control orders were slightly less rigorous than Australia's, and its provisions for investigatory detention are still a little broader than Australia's. But Australian law includes powers unavailable to their UK counterparts, including ASIO's (rarely used) detention and questioning powers and its very limited and never-used preventive detention powers. But Australian immigration laws have been interpreted in a manner that has been used to justify the lengthy detention of people believed by the government to constitute security risks.[1] Moreover, the effects of decisions by the UK courts and by the ECtHR have curbed many of the more egregious UK powers, while Australian courts (acting within a different legal framework) have so far done little to limit the scope of Australian laws.

In some respects US law is less illiberal than Australian and UK law. This is particularly so where the terrorism in question is largely domestic. Unlike the other four countries, the United States makes no provision for the proscription of groups not engaged in international terrorism, and the surveillance powers of its intelligence agencies are far more attenuated where the target is within the United States or when it is a US citizen or resident. Unlike Australia and the United Kingdom, it makes no provision for control orders. Unlike the United Kingdom, it has not criminalised the glorification of terrorism. In relation to international terrorism, the differences are more attenuated, and there are some respects in which US legislation has been considerably more illiberal than elsewhere. None of the other jurisdictions has attempted to limit the courts' powers to engage in the judicial review of detention decisions. Nor have any of the other jurisdictions legislated to protect officials who engaged in torture or inhumane treatment. The effects of some measures have been qualified by rulings by US courts, notably in relation to detention at Guantánamo Bay. But in other contexts, US courts have been less interventionist than UK and even Australian courts. Court rulings mean that the state secrets doctrine provides considerably greater protection for the government in civil litigation than the public interest immunity rules that apply in the other jurisdictions. The use of "material witness" powers as a pretext for detaining suspected terrorists would be unlawful, per se, in the other four jurisdictions, as would the use of immigration powers as a pretext for investigatory detention. Yet US courts have been prepared to countenance these tactics in at least some contexts. But generalizations about US courts are complicated by intracourt and cross-court variations and by decisions in which majorities dispose of constitutional issues on procedural grounds while hinting that they might agree with the minority on the substantive issues, but not necessarily. The indeterminacy of US case law complicates any attempt to rank US law in terms of its relative illiberalism. In some respects it is more liberal; in some, less; and in others the state of the law is such that it could be developed in either direction, depending on the composition of the Supreme Court and other courts.

The development of the law throws considerable light on the degree to which it can be understood as a response to attacks; as a reflection of the distinctive interests of the executive, the legislature, and the courts; and as a reflection of lawmakers' underlying political beliefs. It also suggests possible explanations for cross-national differences and similarities.

My analysis provides ample evidence of rapid responses and of pressures on legislators to pass complex legislation within exceptionally short periods. But it also cautions against assuming that counterterror law is typically the product of haste and therefore ill considered. It concludes that counterterror laws enacted in haste often differ relatively little from laws enacted after longer deliberation and that post 9/11 innovations have tended to survive political and judicial review, notwithstanding that the perceived threat posed by terrorism appears to have declined.

The Patriot Act is an almost perfect example of legislation enacted in haste and passed in highly emotional circumstances. The 9/11 attacks had led to enhanced fears of further attacks, and at the time of its passage, these fears had barely begun to evaporate. In pressing for rapid enactment, the administration has resorted to moral blackmail (if you delay, the blood of those killed in future attacks will be on your hands). Congress agreed to fast track the legislation (notwithstanding that the legislation is extraordinarily hard to understand without access to the legislation it amends). It was passed within a month, its title highlighting the emotional context in which it was considered and enacted.

The effects of the attack were not confined to the United States. Canada responded almost as quickly, passing a complex bill before the year was out. The United Kingdom responded with a raft of additional measures (which included the ill-fated power to detain immigrants with terrorist proclivities), securing the passage of the legislation within weeks.

But passage of post 9/11 measures was not always so fast. The Australian government announced that it recognised the need for urgent action, but it was not until March 2002 that it was able to present a bill to the House of Representatives. The government insisted that passage was urgent, and used its numbers to ensure rapid passage of the legislation by the House, but it lacked the numbers to do so in the Senate, and the slightly watered-down legislation was passed only after lengthy committee hearings and debate. New Zealand was already considering legislation to give effect to recent counterterrorism conventions and decided to incorporate these into comprehensive counterterrorism legislation, but passage was slow and delayed by public hearings on the bill.

However, terrorist attacks are not a sufficient condition for wide-ranging amendments. The most obvious example of a failed quest for enhanced powers comes from the legislative response to the post-Oklahoma legislation. This got off to a good start, with bipartisan support and tear-jerking speeches mobilizing memories of those who had died in Oklahoma and over Lockerbie, but was derailed following an FBI raid on an armed religious sect, which had had a bloody ending. Conservative Republicans, who decided that the FBI was not to be trusted, and whose denunciation of the federal government occasionally suggested that they were not particularly outraged by violent attacks on government targets, combined with Democrat civil libertarians to scuttle most of the proposals to increase the government's powers in relation to domestic terrorism. Nor did Canada and New Zealand (or the United States) initiate or pass additional counterterror measures in response to the London 7/7 bombings, and Australia responded only after discussion with state and territory governments. (And more recently, and for different reasons, Norway seems to have reacted with remarkable stoicism to Anders Breivik's twin attacks.)

A more compelling problem for the "haste" hypothesis is provided by the content of counterterror legislation enacted without the spur of a recent attack. The UK Terrorism Act 2000 was such an act. While the Canadian legislation was passed in haste, it relied heavily on the UK act, yet in important respects it limited government powers and the scope of the criminal law to a greater degree than the UK legislation. Moreover Australia continued to expand government counterterrorism powers well after the initial shock of the 9/11 attacks. After Australia failed in 2002 to secure the passage of legislation giving ASIO the power to require people to provide information relating to terrorism, such legislation was passed in 2003, albeit with much greater safeguards. Government powers to proscribe terrorist organisations were expanded in 2004. Legislation governing use of security sensitive information in civil and criminal trials was passed in 2004–5. In 2007 New Zealand amended its legislation to transfer the power to extend proscription periods from the courts to the prime minister. Moreover, as noted in chapter 4, governments other than the US government had enjoyed surveillance powers about as wide as and in some respects wider than those conferred on the US government under the Patriot Act amendments. Legislation permitting immigration detention antedated the 9/11 attacks.

Further, if the civil libertarian version of the haste argument were correct, one would expect that legislators would have second thoughts. To a limited degree this expectation has been borne out. The controversial "library records" provision was amended when the relevant sunset clause required that the amendment be once more ratified by Congress if it was to survive. Despite government efforts, the Canadian provisions relating to compulsory questioning and binding suspected terrorists to keep the peace were not renewed on expiry. In addition to amendments necessitated by court rulings, the United Kingdom has reduced the period during which suspected terrorists can be detained for questioning and tightened the rules governing what were formally called control orders. After a 2006 review of its counterterrorism legislation, Australia belatedly limited the circumstances in which police could detain suspected terrorists, and the duration for which they could do so. It also provided procedures for review of proscription decisions by the foreign minister (but retained the status quo in relation to other decisions). But these amendments have generally involved little more than tinkering, and legislation apparently passed in haste has generally survived remarkably well.

One reason why the haste perspective does not receive more support may be that haste does not necessarily denote cursory consideration. For instance in Canada, where the legislation was introduced and passed within a period of a little more than two months, committees of both houses conducted hearings and prepared recommendations, and professors from the University of Toronto managed to produce and publish a book providing a comprehensive evaluation and critique of the bill in time to contribute to legislative deliberation.[2] Moreover while deliberation on the Patriot Act was hectic, the issues surrounding some of the controversial amendments had already been before Congress in other contexts.[3]

Another reason may be legislative inertia. Consistent with this is the fact that provisions subjected to sunset clauses seem to have been a little more vulnerable than other provisions. However most sunset clauses have survived, and nonsurvival may reflect not procedural vulnerability but the fact that such clauses would not have been sunsetted but for their controversial nature, which in turn makes them more vulnerable to repeal. It may also be that controversial clauses survive because they appear to do no harm. The appearance may be misleading, but there is some evidence to suggest that where powers do appear to be misused, they may become vulnerable. Sometimes, notably in the United Kingdom, courts step in. Sometimes, legislatures see fit to curb executive powers. The Snowden and Wikileaks revelations about the level of surveillance by US government agencies have also prompted both litigation and legislative proposals for limiting surveillance powers insofar as they expose Americans to surveillance. Little can be said about either at this stage. Two district courts have ruled, and they have disagreed. The time that has elapsed since the revelations indicates that outrage does not always prompt hasty legislation and this raises questions about the salience of surveillance-related concerns and the ease with which they can be translated into effective political action. Changes seem inevitable. Their nature is less clear.

Governments and civil libertarians tend to agree on one thing: governments want wide-ranging powers, and other institutions—and courts in particular—sometimes stand in their way. Given this consensus, it seems almost trivial to conclude that the expectation is borne out. But coexisting with the obvious conclusion is evidence that suggests that the relationship is not always particularly strong and that it may vary cross-nationally.

The most consistent finding to emerge from this analysis is that support for wide-ranging counterterrorism laws is most pronounced within the executive and in particular its military, police, and security agencies. The political executive may share the agencies' concerns but does not necessarily do so. Several bodies of evidence bear out this unsurprising conclusion. First, in hearings before legislative committees, the support for broader executive powers is largely confined to the bodies that will exercise those powers and to people with obvious links to those bodies. Opposition comes from numerous nongovernment organisations, but one usually looks in vain for submissions from nongovernment organisations committed to the enhancement of government powers. Second, proposed legislation is almost always watered down in its progress through the legislature. Indeed, there are almost no examples of proposed counterterrorism legislation being amended to enhance government powers, and only rarely have there even been attempts to amend the legislation in order to expand government powers.

Exceptions arguably include the US Appropriation Act amendments that precluded the movement of prisoners from Guantánamo to the United States, but these also reduced government powers by precluding the Obama administration from exercising powers in the way it thought best. The few unsuccessful attempts by opposition parties to expand government powers included a Conservative amendment which would have made provision for preventive detention under the *Terrorism Act 2000* and proposals by the New Zealand Nationals to tighten the definition of terrorism to include "eco-terrorism." However, Conservative enthusiasm for preventive detention soon eroded, and the Nationals may have been primarily concerned with annoying the Greens. The rarity of legislative pressures for tougher laws is such as to constitute a potential puzzle, but it is one that can be resolved. If, as is sometimes contended, the proponents of "tough" legislation are motivated by a desire to win votes rather than to protect their country, one might expect a few attempts to embarrass governments by opportunistic amendments whose rejection could be the basis for proclaiming the government to be soft on terrorism. The lack of such amendments suggests that nongovernment politicians doubt that there are votes to be won by giving governments powers they don't want. Poll data suggest that their assessment may correct.

Third, distinctive institutional interests are evidenced by executive "deviance" and the secrecy surrounding it. Secrecy may reflect sound assessments of its necessity, but it may also reflect recognition that aspects of executive conduct are legally and/or politically unacceptable. Deviance seems to reflect a sense that powers are too narrow and that there is no prospect of their being broadened.

However, these generalisations require some qualification. First, the executive branch includes agencies with diverse views about how best to deal with terrorism, and the responses of the political arms may take account of these. The arguments within the Bush administration over the status of the Geneva Conventions and the permissibility of acts that arguably constituted torture highlight the degree to which even "tough minded" agencies can differ, depending on their particular institutional interests, and on how institutions with conflicting interests go about resolving them. Goldsmith's account of his period in the Department of Justice points to the importance of personal differences as determinants of institutional output. And modern executives usually include niches that provide a home for institutional tendermindedness: proposals for relaxed surveillance laws meet resistance from privacy commissioners, especially in Canada, New Zealand, and Australia, and the New Zealand commissioner has published several searing critiques of counterterrorism law.

Second, while post-9/11 legislatures never gave governments more powers than they were seeking, they frequently gave the government all or almost all the powers it wanted. Indeed, sympathetic critics of the Bush administration's response to terrorism have argued that its powers might actually have been enhanced had it sought to work with the legislature, rather than relying on the president's alleged inherent powers.[4] Indeed, legislative responses to executive deviance suggest a considerable degree of sympathy towards executive interests, even in the face of arguable illegality. The statutory protection for the communications companies that assisted in the Terrorism Surveillance Program and for those involved in the interrogation of US detainees also indicates congressional reluctance to permit criminal and civil proceedings against organisations and people who have acted in good faith but illegally.

Those aggrieved by counterterror laws and their execution have had some success in challenges to the legislation or behaviour in the courts. The net effect of judicial decisions is almost necessarily to frustrate governments and legislatures. Even if courts were sympathetic to strong counterterror laws, it would require extraordinary imagination to extract from constitutions implied executive obligations to pursue terrorists with more vigor than governments are inclined to use and by mechanisms that legislatures have chosen not to sanction. Courts have almost never shown such imagination and instead have tended to rely on more orthodox forms of judicial reasoning based on bills of rights, separation of powers, the language of legislation, and the desirability of evidence to justify measures likely to impinge adversely on people and organisations. The effect of this has been that courts have tended to provide more protection for civil libertarian values than governments or legislatures.

But they have done so unevenly. The areas of greatest intervention have involved two related issues: prolonged preventive detention and government attempts to rely on evidence kept secret from the nongovernment party. In the United States and the United Kingdom, prolonged preventive detention itself raises constitutional problems, except in cases where it involves detention pending deportation, where deportation is a practical possibility. In the United Kingdom control orders have been found to infringe the ECHR when their duration exceeds sixteen hours daily. In the United States, the United Kingdom, and Canada, courts have also held that insofar as detention is not, per se, impermissible, detainees must be given an opportunity to reply to the government case. In Australia, in the context of litigation relating to the legality of the prolonged detention of immigrants found by ASIO to be security risks, the High Court, in its current mood, may find that the detention regime is inconsistent with the courts' powers to determine who may be incarcerated.

Due process concerns mean that if the government intends to rely on secret information, it may do so only if the affected party has sufficient notice of its content to be able to respond effectively to it. Provisions for special advocates may not suffice. These requirements have evoked government criticism, and in the United Kingdom, even some members of the Appeals Committee of the House of Lords were critical of the ECtHR's ruling in relation to the validity of the control order procedures.

Other areas of counterterrorism law have fared remarkably well. An attempt to challenge the legality of the targeted killing of suspected terrorists failed on standing grounds, in circumstances that suggested that this obstacle was not insuperable, so long as the claim was brought by the target himself, and that this might not require his presence in the United States. But it also failed on the basis that the issue was a nonjusticiable "political question."[5] The Patriot Act has survived judicial scrutiny almost unscathed.[6] The only surveillance power to have fallen foul of metalegal constraints has been the United Kingdom's much abused stop and search power, and even that survived all the way to the ECtHR. US, Canadian and Australian legislation governing the use and nonuse of state secrets in ordinary judicial proceedings has so far survived almost intact (except in Canada, insofar as it purported to require hearings from which the public but not the parties were excluded). Proscription legislation has generally survived constitutional challenge (but the UK sanctions regimes were struck down on the grounds that the relevant acts did not permit the relevant subordinate legislation). Constitutional challenges to the validity of laws creating special terrorism offences have almost invariably failed.

Governments have also had considerable success in criminal cases, winning around 80 percent of cases resolved by plea or verdict. Moreover, pretrial detention and heavy sentences for precursor offences have meant that the criminal law system provides the basis for de facto preventive detention of many potential terrorists. Courts have generally allowed applications for control orders or their equivalents. In the United States, governments and government officials have generally—but not invariably—been successful in defending themselves in civil actions arising out of their counter activities. Elsewhere, civil claims for counterterrorism related activities have been rare, but governments have been less successful, and in both the United Kingdom and Australia, governments have concluded that it was necessary to settle cases brought by former Guantánamo detainees for sizeable amounts of money.

Governments' successes can be attributed to a variety of considerations. In the United States, procedural obstacles have played a major role in thwarting attempts to raise constitutional and even civil claims. Courts have relied on standing rules and state secrets immunity to thwart attempts to challenge, or seek redress in relation to, allegedly unlawful surveillance, torture, and targeted killing, thereby enabling them to dispose of cases summarily. But elsewhere, standing rules have played almost no role in counterterror decisions, public interest immunity has rarely thwarted suits against the government in relation to counterterror measures, and attempts to rely on summary disposition almost invariably have failed.

Governments have also been able to rely on a degree of judicial deference. Again, this has been most explicit in the United States, where there is ample authority for the proposition that courts should defer to government judgments in cases involving questions of national security. Elsewhere, courts are more wary of the language of deference. In *A v Secretary of State for the Home Department*, Lord Bingham was critical of suggestions that courts might owe a duty of "deference" to the political authorities, preferring the idea that the demarcation of powers be guided by "relative institutional competence," with the courts' potential role being greatest when the relevant question involved considerable legal content.[7] Rejections of the language of deference are an assertion that courts do not defer, but the logic of recognising "relative institutional competence" is that there will be cases calling for de facto deference. Indeed in the A litigation, all but one of the judges who considered the issue concluded that the question of whether the threat of terrorism constituted a "'public emergency threatening the life of the nation" was largely a political question and that the Secretary's decision that it was a public emergency could stand. Control order cases have generated undeferential decisions, but in *Secretary of State for the Home Department v AF*, in which the House of Lords held that a decision of the European Court of Human Rights gave controlees the right to know the gist of the case against them, several speeches were critical of the ECtHR decision's potential to undermine what the Lords regarded as a valuable counterterrorism tool.

In Canada, judges have rejected the language of deference, but in the context of legislation that made judges responsible for determining the relevant substantive issue. In other contexts, judges have exhibited signs of de facto deference by giving considerable weight to government assessments of what national security demands. In Australia, the lack of a constitutionally entrenched bill of rights reduces the range of circumstances in which deference issues might arise, and a functional equivalent of deference is arguably provided by the messy logic of the constitutional separation of powers. But, as in Canada, Australian courts have been prepared to give considerable weight to government evidence in decisions as to whether the disclosure of information would endanger national security.[8]

Moreover, very occasionally, US courts have hinted that the government has underestimated its powers and its obligations. The state secrets doctrine may mean that a court must forbid the disclosure of a secret even if the government is willing to do so. And there have been suggestions that the standard of proof required of the government in habeas corpus cases may be more relaxed than that accepted by the government. But these examples are exceptional.

The passions generated in debates about the proper scope of counterterror laws would seem to suggest that legislation would reflect the politics of the legislators. To some extent it does, but the relationship between beliefs and votes is complex. For one thing, the beliefs that matter are not the beliefs of individual legislators but the beliefs adopted by the parties to which they belong. In Australia and New Zealand, this is a trivial observation: parliamentarians almost invariably vote strictly by party, whether the issue is terrorism or the control of sheep diseases. In the United Kingdom and Canada, party is a very good predictor of vote, but in each country there are instances of MPs from the larger parties voting against their party. In the United States, party is a strong predictor of vote, but nonparty voting is more extensive than in the parliamentary democracies.

The relevance of party seems to reflect two distinct mechanisms: responses reflective of the different political beliefs of those attracted to different parties; and responses to the exigencies of being, or not being, in power. There is evidence consistent with the former explanation. When there are divisions on terrorism issues, party preferences generally reflect the party's position on a left-right continuum. This is particularly the case in the United States, Australia, and New Zealand. Parties of the right (Republican, Liberal-National, National) are more supportive of expanded counterterror powers than parties of the Centre (Democrat, Labor, Labour) and, a fortiori, parties of the Left (Green/s), and there are no exceptions to this. Canadian parliamentary divisions yield results that are weakly consistent with this analysis. The New Democrats take a predictably leftist stance, as to some extent does the Bloc Québécois. Conservatives have tended to favour "tougher" stances than the Liberals (Centre), but during the passage of the *Anti-terrorism Act*, the Progressive Conservatives sometimes outflanked the Liberals on the left, and the more conservative Canadian Alliance also joined the leftist parties on some issues.

But if beliefs mediated by party were a powerful explanation of parliamentary votes, one would expect that on coming to power, parties would change counterterrorism laws in a direction consistent with their prior politics. There is, however, little evidence of this. In Australia, Labor, on coming to power in 2007, made a large number of minor amendments to counterterror legislation. Some of these slightly limited government powers, a few expanded them, and most simply clarified ambiguities. Labor did not repeal any legislation it had earlier opposed. Under New Zealand's National government, its terrorism laws have remained largely unchanged, and in some minor respects (migration law, warrants), they have been liberalised. The Nationals have, however, expanded New Zealand's list of proscribed organisations, consistent with their earlier criticisms of the then government's failure to do so. Canada's minority conservative government tried to save the sunsetted provisions of the *Anti-terrorism Act*, and after winning a House of Commons majority, it restored them, albeit subject to a sunset clause, and in conjunction with legislation to respond to judicial findings in relation to the unconstitutionality of provisions for the mandatory closing of courts to the public in cases where courts were hearing disputes about the use of security-sensitive information.

A further expectation would be that party would also be related to attitudes to counterterror measures among the general public. There is some evidence from Australia and Canada consistent with this explanation. US polls have generally borne out this expectation, but several 2013 polls have suggested that Republicans are slightly less supportive than Democrats of large-scale surveillance and only slightly more supportive of the use of drones to assassinate suspected enemies when this is done under a Democratic administration.

The role of party is even messier in the United Kingdom. If the political beliefs model explained voting, Conservatives would tend to support "tough" measures. Labour would do so with reservations and muttering from the left. The Liberal Democrats would oppose. The Liberal Democrats and to some extent the Labour left behave as predicted, and the Conservative amendment proposing the restoration of preventive detention powers in 2000 was consistent with its position on the right. Since 2000, however, the Conservatives have shifted to the "left" on counterterror measures. They abstained on the preventive detention of immigrants in 2001, but they opposed longer investigatory detention and sought more rigorous intention requirements in relation to the new 2006 terrorism offences. Moreover, the Conservative-Liberal Democrat coalition has allowed the investigatory detention period to revert to its 2003 level. It has slightly relaxed the control order regime. This may reflect the influence of the Liberal Democrats. It would be a relatively cost-free sop to compensate them for the humiliation of having to be complicit in the Conservatives' unpopular cost-cutting program. But it is also consistent with the Conservatives' stance on counterterror measures prior to having come to power. But complicating matters still further is the coexistence of liberalisation with proposals for limitations: limits on the circumstances in which litigants can require the production of information in cases where governments fear that disclosure will undermine national security; and limits on the circumstances in which the ECtHR can hear objections to the decisions of United Kingdom courts.

Consistent with this is the fact that the relationship between party support and UK voters' attitudes to counterterror measures also takes a different form in the United Kingdom. Most polls suggest that the relationship is weak and by no means consistent from item to item. There is, however, one poll that has yielded a strong relationship between party and terrorism-related attitudes. Voters were asked about whether they thought Labour had been effective in controlling terrorism and were also asked whether they thought the coalition would be effective. Party preferences were strongly related to the answers to the two questions in the predicted directions. There was, however, one surprising finding. Respondents were also asked whether they thought that the threat of terrorism had increased or decreased over the past five years. Labour voters were only slightly more likely to think it had decreased, and there was almost no difference in the percentages of Labour voters and Conservatives who thought the risk had increased. Where questions relate expressly to the performance of governments, they are much more likely to arouse partisan responses than when they lack the relevant cues. It is possible that Labour and Conservative partisans were torn in two directions: by party-related beliefs and by cues given by their party's stance on counterterrorism.

UK exceptionalism is not easily explained. A tentative explanation takes as its starting point the Blair government's willingness to play an important role in the deeply unpopular Iraq war, a decision that suggests a government uncharacteristically indifferent to its traditional supporters' political beliefs. If so, it is understandable that the same might have been the case in relation to the government's counterterror measures. Assuming that supporters would normally have been disposed to scepticism in relation to wide-ranging counterterror laws, the discrepancy between political dispositions and party loyalty could be partly resolved by following the government line (which received considerable publicity). Conversely, the Conservatives' stance could be expected to encourage a shift in Conservative voters' attitudes. The result would be the observed blurred relationship between party and attitudes. This analysis may not withstand reanalysis of relevant UK poll data, but it suggests limits to explanations in terms of party-related political dispositions and also suggests that the exigencies of being in government may sometimes trump such beliefs as the members of the government brought with them to government.

Judges vote too, and one of the striking features of judicial responses to counterterrorism laws is the lack of unanimity. The US Supreme Court terror cases all involved split decisions, and all involved rejection of decisions of district or circuit courts and sometimes both. In the United Kingdom, complete unanimity is rare. There are several exceptions, notably *Gillan* and *Al Jedda*, but these led to appeals to the ECtHR, which found—unanimously in *Gillan*, with one dissent in *Al-Jedda*—that the UK courts had erred. In other cases, there was usually either intracourt disagreement, cross-court disagreement, or—usually—both. But there was almost invariably a sizeable majority for the "winning" position and usually no more than a single dissenter in the House of Lords/Supreme Court. In Canada, *Charkaoui* (No. 1) involved a unanimous Supreme Court overruling a unanimous Federal Court of Appeal that had upheld the first instance decision.

If legal materials provide an imperfect guide to judges, they must rely on something else, but that "something else" seems to be more important in the United States than in the United Kingdom, and its nature is sometimes elusive. In the United States, it is apparent that judges tend to be reasonably consistent in their relative propensity to answer terrorism-related questions in favour of the government, although Justice Scalia's judgment in *Rasul* indicates that judges' responses are sometimes too nuanced to be predicted on the basis of rank along a single dimension. However, in the House of Lords/Supreme Court, differences of judicial opinion are expressed more subtly, and voting patterns provide no evidence consistent with general dispositions to favour the government. Typically there were no more than one or two dissents, and different judges dissented in different cases. Lord Hoffmann dissented in favour of the government in relation to control orders but was also the only judge in *A v Secretary of State* to find that terrorism did not pose a threat to the nation. Lords Rodger and Carswell held that a reverse onus provision cast a legal as well as an evidentiary burden but that this was not incompatible with the ECHR. (They also found that, on the facts, this did not matter since, given the evidence, the defendant had discharged this burden.) Lord Brown dissented in relation to whether the Al Qaeda Order was validly made. This evidence is inconsistent with explanations of decisions in terms of the assumption that decisions of the House of Lords and its successor, the Supreme Court, can be understood in terms of their relative rank on a hypothetical civil libertarian dimension, although it does not rule out the possibility that UK judges are politically more homogeneous than their US counterparts. Moreover, the fate of UK decisions before the ECtHR suggests that UK judges are more deferential to perceived security interests than the Strasbourg judges. This may be for attitudinal reasons, but it may also reflect institutional culture. The fate of UK decisions might have been different if appeals went instead to a hypothetical and improbable European Security Court.

The analysis throws only limited light on the reasons for cross-national differences, although it is suggestive. Prior to 9/11, the laws of the five countries seemed to reflect national experiences of terrorism. In the United States, where the threat had typically come from international rather than national terrorism, the law reflected this, and UK law had evolved in the context of Northern Irish terrorism. In Australia, Canada, and New Zealand, where the paucity of terrorist attacks suggested that terrorism was not a serious threat, terrorism was relevant only in isolated circumstances, which tended to reflect the tendency for threats to be international rather than domestic. But this account works imperfectly. The Oklahoma City bombing highlighted the fact that that it was not only foreigners who resorted to terror. The Air India bombing highlighted the fact that terrorist attacks could be arranged on Canadian soil. And while Australian law made no provision for terrorism, this was to some extent a matter of expression rather than substance. ASIO enjoyed considerable surveillance powers in relation to politically motivated violence, which largely subsumed terrorism.

The intensity of the US response to 9/11 is not surprising. The attack not only cost thousands of lives. It demonstrated the potential vulnerability of a country that had rightly come to think of itself as the world's sole superpower. It called not only for countermeasures but also for revenge. But while the United States waged both actual and symbolic war on terrorists, it was far more hesitant in seeking draconian legal powers to do so. While the government sought more powers than it probably needed, the legal outcome was one in which liberties were bruised rather than destroyed, and the Patriot Act even included a statement that the sense of Congress was that American Muslims were making a valuable contribution to the country, a sentiment not reflected in the government's response to the many Muslim non-Americans who, for reasons that had nothing to do with a desire to resort to terrorism, had allowed their visas to lapse. War reflected anger and humiliation (and the hope that it would transform Afghanistan for the better). Law seems to have been constrained by a degree of recognition of the instrumental and moral value of a proportional response to the threat and recognition that America's legitimacy derives partly from its being a country bound by law. What best reflects the enormity of the attack is not the legal response but the strain between temptation and law. Elsewhere, 9/11 was interpreted as calling for a response. In the United Kingdom, the response reflected a perception that the new threat was to a considerable extent external. The Canadian, Australian, and New Zealand responses highlight the fact that one response to pressures to legislate quickly is to draw on "foreign" laws. The UK Terrorism Act 2000 provided an attractive precedent, having been designed for the kind of terrorist threats likely to face liberal democracies in the 21st century, and its definitions, proscription provisions, and crimes provided a basis for Canadian, Australian, and New Zealand law. Australia and, more particularly, New Zealand drew on Canadian law. But imitation goes only some way towards explaining their post 9/11 legislation.

During the 2000s UK law continued to develop, developments being prompted by further attacks; near attacks; the need to adapt the law to judicial rulings; and, recently, second thoughts about the need for wide-ranging laws. Australia, which was free from attacks on home soil, tended to follow UK innovations, while adding a few of its own. By contrast, after the initial response to the 9/11 attacks, Canadian and New Zealand law remained largely unchanged.

Australia's response is perhaps the hardest to understand. It may be explicable in terms of politics: unlike Canada and New Zealand, Australia was governed by a conservative coalition with a majority in the lower house, and—for three years—both houses. Expansion of the scope of counterterror laws largely ceased under Labor (from 2007 onwards). And while Australia was free of domestic terrorist attacks, Australians comprised more than 40 percent of the 202 people killed in the Bali bombings in October 2002. But the nexus between the attacks and later legislation is not apparent, and many of the more controversial pieces of legislation were enacted in 2004–5. Nor can the later legislation be explained in terms of Australia's lack of a constitutional bill of rights. On the whole the new powers are subject to sufficient constraints to ensure that they would probably survive constitutional challenge even if Australia were to adopt, say, the Canadian Charter. The legal basis (insofar as there is one) for the most vulnerable and draconian feature of Australian counterterror responses—indefinite immigration detention—predates the 9/11 attacks.

In short, national laws bear some relationship to national experiences of terrorism, but the relationship is tenuous. Laws may be transplants. They may reflect politics. And their worst features may not be a response to terrorism but a response to quite different problems, formulated in different times.

In one important respect, this analysis suggests that law will tend to restrain governments, first because legislators are rarely willing to give governments all the powers they would like and second because courts are sometimes unwilling to accept legislators' assumptions that laws are within their constitutional powers, or that the law and the facts are such as to warrant particular executive responses to terrorism. Law may operate reactively. It may also influence choice. Lawmakers are likely to, and indeed may be required to, take account of whether proposed legislation is likely to survive constitutional scrutiny, and executive actors are clearly sensitive to the question of whether their conduct is lawful. Courts are in a slightly different position. Lower courts are likely to be constrained by the possible reaction of higher courts. But if law is what the highest court in the judicial hierarchy says it is, the judges of that court are potentially not restrained by law, and if the highest court's statements are not necessarily law, the rule of law is potentially capable of requiring noncompliance.

This conundrum does not cause major problems. While courts may not be constrained by law given the Holmesian definition, they are constrained to try to act as if they were, given that the legitimacy of their decisions is predicated on the assumption that they are indeed bound by law. If they want their decisions to become embedded in "the law," they must use justifications calculated to legitimate those decisions in the eyes of future judges whose perspectives may nonetheless differ from their own. But even if judges try to act according to "law," frequent judicial dissensus necessarily means that the relevant law is indeterminate and that judicial decisions are sometimes no more than selections from a range of defensible possibilities. And if law is indeterminate, judges must necessarily base their decisions either on guesswork or on extralegal criteria, including the overall rightness of a particular measure.

Indeterminacy does not mean that law will not constrain. Its effects will depend on the probability of different outcomes, their cost, and the risk aversiveness of the relevant political actor. Likely outcomes are capable of constraining behaviour, although not to the same extent as extremely likely outcomes. However, the impact of law may be seriously weakened by indeterminacy in conjunction with wishful thinking. The US Department of Justice's memoranda and other advice on the legality of the use of coercive interrogation techniques appear to provide an example. Law proved sufficiently ambiguous to enable its use as a form of delinquency neutralisation and a basis for securing the de facto protection of people who relied, in good faith, on the advice.

Law's future capacity to constrain will depend partly on the lessons to be learned from the response to executive deviance in the years following 9/11. For civil libertarians, there is an optimistic story to be told. The lesson of those years is that deviance is hard to conceal. Secrets will out. Those who thought they could safely violate human rights will find themselves enmeshed in litigation, and governments that countenance this will find themselves politically embarrassed and forced to pay millions of dollars in damages to those they implied were dangerous terrorists. Law is civilising war, and the costs of waging war will increasingly include the legal costs associated with the infringements of rights that inevitably accompany this. This may yield benefits: Machiavelli notwithstanding, it may be better to be loved than feared. And even if the subjection of armed conflict to the rule of law means that war becomes harder to wage than was once the case, this may be no bad thing. On the whole, wars end in tears for those who initiate them. Even when wars are fought with the best intentions, the intended beneficiaries are rarely grateful. And balancing budgets requires that scarce resources be carefully husbanded, so wars should not be embarked upon lightly.

There is also a more pessimistic viewpoint. At least in the United States, deviance on behalf of one's country goes almost unpunished. (In this respect the torture memoranda were prescient, although to some extent self-fulfillingly so.) Wars are occasionally necessary or desirable, and law has a nasty habit of accommodating the exigencies involved in the waging of war. If law gets in the way of national security, laws will be changed, both by legislatures and by courts. While decisions such as *Boumediene* indicate a preparedness to regulate some aspects of the conduct of hostilities, the decisions of US courts suggest that they sometimes feel torn between the duty to protect constitutional rights and the duty to protect national security and national honour.

There is also an agnostic outlook. Terrorism tends to encourage "tough" measures, both legal and nonlegal, but in the absence of major attacks, governments are generally content to respond to the diffuse threat of terrorism by and within the law. If terrorist plots and attacks continue to be as rare as has been the case in Canada, Australia, and New Zealand it is likely that governments will gradually devote fewer resources to enforcement of counterterrorism laws and to related investigations. It is even possible that, like New Zealand, they will reassimilate some aspects of counterterrorism law to the general law. If, on the other hand, there were to be an upsurge in terrorist attacks, the experience of the five countries suggests the near certainty of governments seeking and gaining added powers and of courts doing their bit to ensure the punishment of probable terrorists and the control of others. Moreover while courts can currently devote months to the handling of terrorism cases, it is not so apparent that they could deal with the case loads generated in the event of a sharp increase in the number of people suspected of involvement in terrorism, nor that governments would tolerate the burdens associated with prosecutions and the defence of civil actions. Indeed the discovery burden in the *Al Rawi* litigation and its consequences have already encouraged the UK government to explore the feasibility of limiting the scope of the country's public interest immunity laws. It follows that insofar as people are committed civil libertarians, they should welcome measures that have the potential to reduce the terrorist threat or at least keep it at its current level.

Notes

INTRODUCTION

1. Those who regret this omission should read Donohue 2007.

2. Human Rights (Parliamentary Scrutiny) Act 2011 (Cth), s 8. (Failure to do so does not invalidate legislation.)

CHAPTER 1

The epigraphs at the beginning of this chapter are from United States Department of Defense, Office of the Assistant Secretary of Defense (Public Affairs) 2002; and O'Sullivan 2006.

1. Kahneman, Slovic, and Tversky 1982, 163–78, 465–66.

2. Sunstein 2007, 523.

3. Ibid.

4. Marks 2006, 584.

5. Roach and Trotter 2005, 1033.

6. Vermeule 2005.

7. Mueller 2006, 13–48.

8. Lord Lloyd of Berwick 1996, 2:90.

9. United States, FBI 2002.

10. United States, FBI 2006, 4; Global Terrorism Database nd, GTD Ids 200202040010, 200607280004.

11. Global Terrorism Database.

12. United States, Department of State, 2003, 2004, 2006, 2007, 2008. Statistics for 2004 and earlier are derived from a different methodology and use a different definition ("international terrorism") to the methodology and definition ("terrorism") used in 2005 and subsequently: see United States, Department of State, 2007.

13. Torrance 1986, 243–44; http://www.start.umd.edu. The two indeterminate cases involved attacks from unknown sources on one government and one private target.

14. Major 2010, 2:547–85.

15. CSIS 2009, 8.

16. For example, there were bomb attacks against gas pipelines and wellheads, but such acts were noteworthy for their rarity (ibid., 8).

17. CSIS 2006, 1; 2007, 2.

18. The motives for a 1984 attack that killed the wife of a family court judge are not known, but if it was intended to intimidate the court (which seems unlikely), it would be the most recent attack (see K. Baker 2006, 308). The Global Terrorism Database

lists several other incidents, none of which seem to fall within the broad category of "public violence." One was an indiscriminate gun massacre. The database reports an incident in which six Turks were allegedly killed by an anti-Turkish group, but that incident turns out to have been an explosion in a post office in which no one was killed, and it was possibly not even deliberate. The killing of a Greek consul that is among the incidents listed was treated by the police as nonpolitical. There were two fatal attacks on police, neither of which was accompanied by any statement by the perpetrator or by police claims that it was political. The other incidents involved private individuals and unknown motives.

19. K. Baker 2006, 214.

20. Lord Lloyd of Berwick 1996, 2:108. A different source, Conflict Archive on the Internet, gives slightly different figures ("Northern Ireland Violence" 2009).

21. Lord Lloyd of Berwick 1996, 2:11–12.

22. "Northern Ireland Violence" 2009.

23. Ibid. Estimates in the annual editions of *Patterns of Global Terrorism* are similar but slightly different.

24. Donohue 2007, 184.

25. Ibid., 207 (21 deaths in Birmingham); Lord Lloyd of Berwick 1996, 1:1 (22 Birmingham deaths).

26. A thirteenth incident listed in the database was a fire at a nightclub, which caused 37 deaths but does not appear to have had any "collective interest" element.

27. In one of these, a gunman at the Libyan embassy responded to an anti-Gaddafi demonstration by shooting at the demonstrators, injuring several and killing a police officer.

28. Lord Lloyd of Berwick 1996, 2:29. The incident is included in the Global Terrorism Database as an incident involving no deaths. (The hostage was killed before British forces attacked the embassy in their successful attempt to free the hostages, and when listing number of deaths, the database does not include terrorists who have died in an attack.)

29. United Kingdom, Security Service, 2013b.

30. United States, Department of State, 2004, 56.

31. United Kingdom, Security Service, 2013a.

32. United States, Federal Bureau of Investigation, 2006.

33. For a comprehensive list, see Difo 2010.

34. *United States v Reid* 02-cr-10013 (D Mass 2003), Government's Sentencing Memorandum.

35. See complaint in *United States v Abdulmuttalab* 2:09-mj-30526, document 1.

36. *United States v Shahzad* 1:10-mj-00928, document 1.

37. See, e.g., *United States v Abu Ali* 528 F 3d 210, 221–26 (4th Cir 2008); *United States v Shareef* 06-cr-00919 (ND Ill), affidavit of Jared Ruddy; *United States v DeFreitas* cr-00543 (ED NY), document 1 (complaint), [28]; United States, Department of Justice, 2009.

38. Manningham-Buller 2011.

39. Australian Broadcasting Corporation 2008; Sturcke 2009 (7 aircraft). Manningham-Buller (2011) gives the number as "up to a dozen"; Difo (2010, 20) gives the figure of "up to 10."

40. *R v Ibrahim* [2008] EWCA Crim 880, [4], [11]–[15]; "London Glasgow Terrorist Attacks" 2008.

41. Details of the planned attacks on infrastructure are provided in a case involving a Canadian who had been involved in the plan, albeit at the periphery: see R *v Khawaja* [2008] OJ No 4244; 2008 ON C LEXIS 4226; R *v Barot* [2007] EWCA Crim 1119, [5].

42. Friscolanti, Gatehouse, and Gillis 2006.

43. See, generally, the account of the plot in R *v Khalid* [2009] OJ No 3513; 2009 ON C LEXIS 3117.

44. Mohammed Mansour Jabarah, one of those involved, later pleaded guilty, with the plea and sentence remaining secret until the government rescinded the cooperation agreement (Center on Law and Security 2010, 45).

45. See R *v Benbrika* [2009] VSC 21; (2009) 222 FLR 433; R *v Kent* [2009] VSC 375; R *v Touma* [2008] NSWSC 1475; Munro 2010, 1.

46. Keenan 2008, 18–28; Cumming and Masters 2012.

47. R *v Barot* [2007] EWCA Crim 1119, [5]. See Cumming and Masters 2012 for a discussion of the New Zealand trial, which turned on the question of how far behaviour and intercepted conversations were to be taken at face value.

48. Barros and Proença 2005, 299–300; Enders and Sandler 2005, 261–62; Masters 2008.

49. Enders and Sandler 2005.

50. Reinares 2004 (examining the changing backgrounds of ETA terrorists); Pape 2003 (describing suicide bombers as once young, uneducated, socially isolated, and male but more recently better educated, older, more likely than earlier to be married, integrated, and female).

51. For example, compare the conclusions as to the nature of Islamic terrorism that were drawn by Barros and Proença (2005) on the basis of a sample of observations from 1979–2002 with the finding by Enders and Sandler (2005, 275) that in response to post-9/11 attacks on al-Qaeda, there had been a substitution effect whereby bombings were replacing hostage taking.

52. Enders and Sandler 2005, 261, 262.

53. OECD 2005, 19, 35.

54. Ibid.

55. Ibid., 35; United States, General Accounting Office, 2004, 22.

56. OECD 2005, 19, 22. In Australia, some insurers offer insurance for residential housing (which is not covered by the government compensation scheme) subject to a CBRN exemption, but residential housing is not otherwise subject to a terrorism exemption (Australia 2006, 60–61).

57. See, e.g., United States, General Accounting Office, 2004, 14–15 (on the US Treasury's conclusion that there was no need to bring group life insurance within the Terrorism Risk Insurance Act of 2002).

58. OECD 2005, 19, 40; Australia 2006, 26–27.

59. OECD 2005, 41 (citing two studies yielding slightly different estimates); Australia 2006, 25–26.

60. Australia 2006, 27

61. Terrorism Risk Insurance Act of 2002, 15 USC § 6701 note. For details of rules implementing the TRIA, see United States, General Accounting Office, 2004; Terrorism Insurance Act 2004 (Cth).

62. United States, General Accounting Office, 2004, 27–30; OECD 2005, 14, 33–34, 36–37. The authors of the report emphasise the problems posed by the dynamic

nature of modern terrorism. They may, however, underestimate the degree to which terror becomes institutionalised. After all, the 9/11 attack reflects the union of two prior bin Laden obsessions.

63. OECD 2005, 32–33.

64. Use of the term *free* here is not intended to imply that such markets are to be preferred to those in which there has been government intervention. Indeed, the persistence of apparently reluctant government involvement in the provision of terrorism insurance suggests that some kind of government role is essential if terrorism insurance is to be provided.

65. Australia 2006, 8.

66. United States, General Accounting Office, 2004, 25–26.

67. Ibid.

68. OECD 2005, 42–43; Australia 2006, 9 (providing a more recent—and therefore slightly different—summary to that provided by the OECD report).

69. Australia 2006, 2–4 (Australia: A$10 billion), 8 (Belgium: €2 billion), 10 (Germany: €10 billion; Netherlands: €1 billion), 13 (the US government is responsible for 85 percent of losses in excess of insurers' responsibilities).

70. United States, General Accounting Office, 2004, 24.

71. Australia 2006, 35.

72. Ibid., 40.

73. Goldsmith 2007, 71–74.

74. Ibid., 74.

75. Manningham-Buller 2011.

76. Mueller 2006, 35–36.

77. United Kingdom, *House of Commons Hansard*, 14 December 1999, col 157.

78. United States, House of Representatives, Judiciary Committee, 2001, 289.

79. Canada, *House of Commons Hansard*, 16 October 2001, [10.15].

80. Phil Goff, in *New Zealand Parliamentary Debates* 603, 1062.

81. Darryl Williams, in Australia, *Commonwealth Parliamentary Debates*, 12 March 2002, 1040–42.

82. Homeland Security Presidential Directive-3, http://www.dhs.gov/xabout/laws/gc_1214508631313.shtm.

83. United States, Homeland Security Advisory Council, 2009, appendix C.

84. United Kingdom, Home Office, 2012.

85. United Kingdom, Security Service, 2012.

86. An inquiry by the United Kingdom Intelligence and Security Committee into the 7/7 attack acknowledged that threat alerts could be based only on information available to MI5 and that MI5 had had no evidence about the intentions of the group responsible for the attacks. It recommended that the meaning of alerts be clarified so that it was clear that they were based only on information before MI5 (United Kingdom, Intelligence and Security Committee, 2006). In its 2006–7 *Report to Parliament*, ASIO, also noting the problems posed by unstructured extremist groups, reported that in addition to following up leads (the "knowns"), it was also devoting resources to identify the unknowns (ASIO 2007, 23).

87. ASIO 2007, 3.

88. Ibid., 3.

89. ASIO 2003, 3; 2004, 24.

90. United Kingdom, Security Service, 2013.
91. CSIS 2003.
92. Ibid.
93. ASIO 2006, 18.
94. NZSIS 2002, 5.
95. NZSIS 2004, 11.
96. NZSIS 2005, 6, 10–11.
97. NZSIS 2006, 6, 11, 12.
98. ASIO, Director-general, 2007 (bullet points and references omitted).
99. *ABC News* poll, September 2001, terror10.
100. *Fox News*/Opinion Dynamics polls, October 2001, June 2002, terror9, 8.
101. Harris Interactive poll, June 2007, http://www.angus-reid.com/polls/index.cfm/fuseaction/viewItem/itemID/16244.
102. EKOS/*CBS News* polls, February–March 2003 (available from www.ekos.com).
103. Angus Reid poll, November 2010.
104. COMPAS poll, July 18, 2005, 4, 5 (available from www.compas.ca).
105. Newspoll, January 2003.
106. ANU Poll 2009.

CHAPTER 2

1. Bush 2010, 128.
2. Canada, *House of Commons Hansard*, 16 October 2001, 10.15 am.
3. See Mueller 2006, 35–36, for some egregious examples.
4. Lum et al. 2006.
5. See, for instance, Roach 2009, 131–34.
6. Huddy et al. 2002, 420, 431.
7. Ibid., 420, 431.
8. Viscusi and Zeckhauser 2006, 103–6.
9. Pew Research Center survey, September 2001, terror10 (55% necessary, 33% unnecessary); *CBS News/New York Times* poll, September 2001, terror10 (74% give up, 21% no); *Newsweek* poll, September 2001 (63% necessary, 32% not necessary); *Los Angeles Times* poll, August 2002, terror7 (49% necessary to give up, 33% government will go too far); *Fox News*/Opinion Dynamics polls, July 2005, January 2006, May 2006, terror4 (64, 61, and 54% willing to give up some personal freedom). Cf. Pew Research Center polls, September 2006, December–January 2006, terror3; Ipsos/McClatchy poll, January 2010, terror.
10. Pew Research Center survey, September 2001, terror10; *CBS News* polls, November 2002–August 2006, terror3; *CBS News/New York Times* poll, September 2008 (see also November 2006), terror2.
11. Associated Press poll, August 2002, terror7; Associated Press poll, September 2003, terror6; *CBS News* poll, January 2006; *Fox News*/Opinion Dynamics poll, January 2006, terror4 (two-thirds concerned lest liberties be restricted).
12. YouGov/*Daily Telegraph* poll, July 2005, http://www.angus-reid.com/polls/index.cfm/fuseaction/viewItem/itemID/8049.
13. YouGov poll, June 2008, http://www.angus-reid.com/polls/32480.
14. Shapiro and Steinzor 2006, 100–102; Obama 2010, 19; United Kingdom, Privy

Counsellor Review Committee, 2003; Varghese 2003. Cf. Walker 2006, 1142–44 (with qualifications); Whitaker 2003, 263 (some pro-security measures facilitated by 9/11 attack, but they were in the pipeline anyway).

15. Powe 2009, 348.
16. Ramraj 2009.
17. Boyne 2004, 67–72.
18. Roach 2008, 17–18.
19. Schwartz 2009, 426.
20. Converse 1964.
21. Alford et al. 2005; Haidt 2012.
22. Alford et al. 2005; Hatemi et al. 2011. See generally Haidt 2012.
23. Eysenck 1954.
24. Gastil et al. 2005.

CHAPTER 3

1. Cited and translated in Gewald 2007, 91–92.
2. Evidence of qualified enthusiasm for freedom fighters comes from Article 2(a) of the Arab Convention for the Suppression of Terrorism, adopted by the Council of Arab Ministers of Justice (Cairo, April 1998): "All cases of struggle by whatever means, including armed struggle, against foreign occupation and aggression for liberation and self-determination, in accordance with the principles of international law, shall not be regarded as an offence. This provision shall not apply to any act prejudicing the territorial integrity of any Arab state." Palestinian freedom fighters are praiseworthy; Kurdish ones are not.
3. The convention was adopted at New York on 9 December 1999.
4. Convention for the Suppression of Unlawful Seizure of Aircraft, adopted at the Hague on 16 December 1970; Convention for the Suppression of Unlawful Acts against the Safety of Civil Aviation, adopted at Montreal on 23 September 1971; Convention on the Prevention and Punishment of Crimes against Internationally Protected Persons, including Diplomatic Agents, adopted by the General Assembly of the United Nations on 14 December 1973; International Convention against the Taking of Hostages, adopted by the General Assembly of the United Nations on 17 December 1979; Convention on the Physical Protection of Nuclear Material, adopted at Vienna on 3 March 1980; Protocol for the Suppression of Unlawful Acts of Violence at Airports Serving International Civil Aviation, supplementary for the Convention for the Suppression of Unlawful Acts against the Safety of Civil Aviation, adopted at Montreal on 24 February 1988; Convention for the Suppression of Unlawful Acts and the Safety of Maritime Navigation, adopted at Rome on 10 March 1988; Protocol for the Suppression of Unlawful Acts against the Safety of Fixed Platforms Located on the Continental Shelf, adopted at Rome on 10 March 1988; International Convention for the Suppression of Terrorist Bombings, adopted by the General Assembly of the United Nations on 15 December 1997.
5. See, e.g., Cassese 2006; Watkin 2004, 14–17. Di Filippo (2008) assumes that there is still considerable disagreement but that this does not pose an insuperable obstacle to agreeing on a core definition.
6. For a comprehensive discussion of this issue, see Saul 2006.

7. Geneva Conventions Act 1957 (Cth); Geneva Convention Act, RSC 1985, c G-3; Geneva Conventions Act 1957 (NZ); Geneva Conventions Act 1957 (UK), c 52. The United States legislation did not reproduce the conventions but made it an offence to commit a grave breach of the conventions (18 USC § 2441).

8. "'Terrorism' means the use of violence for political ends and includes any use of violence for the purpose of putting the public or any section of the public in fear." For a discussion of earlier emergency legislation aimed at Irish political violence, see Donohue 2007.

9. For details of the successive emergency acts, see Donohue 2007, chapters 5 and 6.

10. It was loosely based on a definition used in the United States by the FBI (Lord Carlile of Berriew 2007, 3). Legislation governing insurance against the risk of terrorism antedates the 2000 act and contains a different definition: "'Acts of terrorism' means acts of persons acting on behalf of, or in connection with, any organisation which carries out activities directed towards the overthrowing or influencing, by force or violence, of Her Majesty's government in the United Kingdom or any other government de jure or de facto" (Reinsurance (Acts of Terrorism) Act 1993 (UK), c 18, s 2(2)). The combined effect of Article 12 of Council Directive 2004/83/EC and the European Communities Act 1972 (UK, c 68) is that terrorism is grounds for refusing refugee status only insofar as it falls within Article 1F of the Refugee Convention. For the purposes of the Immigration, Asylum and Nationality Act 2006 (UK, c 13, s 54), *terrorism* must be read accordingly and (more or less) limited to "the use for political ends of fear induced by violence" (*Al-Sirri v Secretary of State for the Home Department* [2009] EWCA Civ 222, [13]–[18], [28]–[32]).

11. 25 October 1978, PL 95–511, § 101(c), 92 Stat 1783, 1784, codified at 50 USCS § 1801(c).

12. See also other, almost identical definitions: 44 USCS § 921(22) (relaxes standards for proving profit when disposer of firearms supplies them to terrorists: definition of "terrorism" substantively identical except that it applies only to people who are not US nationals or permanent residents); 49 USCS § 44703(g)(3) (airman certificates: definition of "acts of terrorism" substantively identical except for lack of geographical limitations). See, too, EO 13224, 66 FR 49079 § 3(d), and 31 CFR § 594.311 ("terrorism" for the purposes of the Global Terrorism Sanctions Regulations), each of which defines terrorism to also include acts dangerous to property or infrastructure. Section 2331 of Title 18 of the United States Code (29 October 1992, PL 102–572, § 1003(a)(3), 106 Stat 4521; amended by, 26 October 2001, PL 107–56 § 802, 115 Stat 376 (adding definition of "domestic terrorism")) includes a definition similar to but slightly broader than the FISA definition, for the purposes of legislation giving victims of international terrorism the right to sue; domestic terrorism is defined slightly more narrowly. Section 3077 of Title 18 provides that for the purposes of chapter 204 (Rewards for Information Concerning Terrorist Acts and Espionage), "'act of terrorism' means an act of domestic or international terrorism as defined in section 2331." This definition of "act of terrorism" is itself incorporated by reference elsewhere: see, e.g., 6 USCS § 488f (protection from civil liability for reporting a reasonable belief that a person seeking to purchase or transfer ammonium nitrate for an "act of terrorism"). The Homeland Security Act of 2002 included a definition of terrorism that was substantively identical except in that it extended to acts destructive to infrastructure or key resources (Act, 25

November 2002, PL 107–296, § 2, 116 Stat 2140; 6 USCS § 101). See also 6 USCS § 1104 (immunity for reports of "covered activity," which includes (§ 1104(d)(2)(B)) "an act of terrorism" as defined by 18 USCS § 3077).

13. 22 December 1987, PL 100–204, Title I, Part B, § 140, 101 Stat 137, codified at 22 USC § 2656f(d). Subsequent amendments to the act have not affected the definitions. The definition of terrorism coincides with a definition adopted by the State Department in 1984: see Schmid 2005, 376.

14. 29 November 1990; PL 101–649 § 601(a), 104 Stat 5011; am by Act, 26 October 2001; PL 104–32 § 411(1), 115 Stat 345; 8 USCS § 1182(a)(3)(B)(iii).

15. 29 October 1992, PL 102–572, § 1003(a)(3), 106 Stat 4521; am by Act, 26 October 2001, PL 107–56 § 802, 115 Stat 376 (adding definition of "domestic terrorism"); 18 USCS § 2332.

16. 24 April 1996, PL 104–132, § 702, 110 Stat 1293; 18 USCS § 2332b(g)(5)(A).

17. 26 October 2001, PL 107–56, § 802, 115 Stat 376; 18 USC § 2331(5).

18. 26 November 2002, PL 107–297, § 102, 116 Stat 2322; am by Act, 22 December 2005, PL 109–144, 119 Stat 2660; 26 December 2007, PL 110–160, 121 Stat 1839.

19. Australian Security Intelligence Organization Act 1979 (Cth), s 4.

20. Customs (Prohibited Imports) Regulations 1956 (Cth), reg 4a(1a), as amended by the Customs (Prohibited Imports) Amendment Regulations 1983 (Cth) (SR 331/1983).

21. Australian Security Intelligence Organization Act 1979 (Cth), s 4, as amended by the Australian Security Intelligence Organization Amendment Act 1986 (Cth), s 3(e).

22. Customs (Prohibited Imports) Regulations 1956 (Cth), reg 4a(1a), as amended by the Customs (Prohibited Imports) Amendment Regulations 1983 (Cth) (SR 403/1995), reg 3, item 3.4.

23. Criminal Code 1995 (Cth), s 100.1, added by Suppression of the Financing of Terrorism Act 2002 (Cth), Sch 1, item 2.

24. International Terrorism (Emergency Powers) Act 1987 (NZ), s 4. "International terrorist emergency" means "a situation in which any person is threatening, causing, or attempting to cause" death or serious injury to a person or the destruction of or serious damage or serious injury to property, the environment, or "any animal" "in order to coerce, deter, or intimidate" governments or bodies of people "for the purpose of furthering, outside New Zealand, any political aim."

25. Immigration Act, RSC 1985, c I-2, ss 19(1)(e)(iv)(C), 19(1)(f)(ii), (iii)(B) (am 1992, c 49, s 11(2)). In *Suresh v Canada (Minister of Citizenship and Immigration)* (2002 SCC 1; [2002] 1 SCR 3), the Canadian Supreme Court acknowledged the ongoing debate about what "terrorism" meant, but it concluded that the definition in Article 2(1)(b) of the International Convention for the Suppression of Terrorism caught "the essence of what the world understands by 'terrorism'"(at [98]) and that, interpreted thus, the term was not unconstitutionally vague. The current immigration legislation leaves the term undefined (Immigration and Refugee Protection Act SC 2001, c 27, s 35). For a summary of judicial interpretations of what the term meant, see Bhabba 2003, 103–9.

26. Criminal Code, RSC 1985, c C-46, s 83.01, added by Anti-terrorism Act, SC 2001, c 41, s 4.

27. Criminal Code, RSC 1985, c C-46, s 83.01, definition of "terrorist activity," par (a). An act falls within this paragraph if it "is committed in or outside Canada" and, "if committed in Canada," if it "is one of the [listed] offences." The offences are confined

to offences that are "referred to" in section 7 of the code and that have varying degrees of extraterritorial effect under that section.

28. The discussion that follows is based on the definitions in the comprehensive counterterror legislation passed since 2000. New Zealand's two pre-2000 definitions remain in force in relation to "international emergencies" and immigration, and the United Kingdom's insurance-related definition of terrorism is still in force. Given their narrow range of application, these definitions are not discussed in the text.

29. Australia, s 100.1(2)(a), (ba), (c); Canada, par (b)(ii)(A), (B); New Zealand, s 5(3)(a); United Kingdom, s 1(2)(a), (c). These and subsequent references are to the standard definitions. Canadian references refer to the paragraph in the definition contained in the definition section of the relevant legislation, namely, section 83.01(1) of the Criminal Code (definition of "terrorist activity"). Australian, New Zealand, and UK references are to the relevant sections of the Criminal Code Act 1995 (Cth), the Terrorism Suppression Act 2002 (NZ), and the Terrorism Act 2000 (UK, c 11).

30. Australia, s 100.1(d); Canada, par (b)(ii)(C); New Zealand, s 5(3)(b); United Kingdom, s 1(2)(d). There is one respect in which the definitions appear to vary. Unlike the UK, Canadian, and Australian definitions, the New Zealand definition does not expressly include behaviour that endangers life, except insofar as it provides that serious interference with infrastructure constitutes a terrorist act if it is likely to endanger life (Terrorism Suppression Act 2002 (NZ), s 5(3)(c)). An indiscriminate violent attack that endangered life would fall within the "serious risk to the health or safety of a population" category, but it is not clear that a targeted attack would do so.

31. For example, as a result of the combined effect of Criminal Code, RSC 1985, c C-46, ss 83.01 (definition), 7(3) (referring to specified violent offences including those in section 66, where the victim is an internationally protected person) and 266 (making assault an offence), assault, even when triable summarily, can constitute a terrorist activity if committed against an internationally protected person. Similar reasoning would apply in New Zealand.

32. Australia, s 100.1(2)(b), (e); United Kingdom, s 1(2)(b), (e).

33. Compare, however, the very broad definition of situations capable of constituting an international terrorist emergency, in International Terrorism (Emergency Powers) Act 1987 (NZ), s 2. For the purpose of the Immigration Act 1987 (NZ), the category "act of terrorism" included acts involving the use of explosives or incendiary devices that cause or are likely to cause damage to buildings, installations, or vehicles (s 2(1), definition of "act of terrorism," par (b)).

34. Canada, par (b)(ii)(D); NZ s 5(2)(c).

35. Canada, par (b)(ii)(E); NZ ss 5(2)(d), 5(2)(e).

36. Article 3 of the Terrorist Bombing Convention provides that the convention shall not apply to the commission of one or more offences as set forth in the convention where the offender and the victims are nationals of the state in which the offence takes place and the alleged offender is present in that state and where the state was the political target of the attack. Under section 4(1) of the Terrorism Suppression Act, the category "act against a specified convention" extends to an offence against a convention only if the convention "applies" in relation to it.

37. United Kingdom, s 1(1); Australia, s 100.1.

38. Canada, s 83.01, definition of "terrorist activity," par (b).

39. 50 USCS § 1801(c).

40. See, e.g., Douglas 2010, 299–301.
41. 18 USCS § 2332b(5)(A).
42. Terrorism Act 2006 (UK), c 11, s 34.
43. Australia, s 100.1(1), definition of "terrorist act," par (c).
44. Canada, par (b)(i)(B).
45. Canada, s 83.01(1)(b)(i)(B).
46. New Zealand, s 5(2)(b).
47. Terrorism Act 2000 (UK), c 11, s 1(c), amended by Counter-terrorism Act 2008 (UK), s 75(1).
48. Criminal Code, s 83.01(1), definition of "terrorist activity," par (b)(i)(A); Terrorism Suppression Act 2002 (NZ), s 5(2); Criminal Code Act 1995 (Cth), s 100.1, definition of "terrorism," par (b). Unlike the other three definitions, the Australian definition requires that the act be done with the intention of advancing a cause. Little turns on this: under the Code's definition of intention, people have the requisite intention if they act, believing that their conduct will have a particular effect in the ordinary course of events, notwithstanding that they who would also prefer that it didn't: s 5.2(c).
49. Canada, par (b)(ii)(E).
50. Australia, s 100.1(2A).
51. New Zealand, ss 5(3)(d), 5(5).
52. As to whether and when terrorism might constitute "armed conflict" and as to what activities international law might permit, see, e.g., Watkin 2004.
53. This is the result of the combined effects of Criminal Code sections 83.01(1) para (a) (definition of "terrorist activity") and 7(3.72) (which refers to ss 431.2 and 431.2(3), exempting such acts in the same manner as the proviso to the general definition).
54. Terrorism Suppression Act 2002 (NZ), ss 4(1), 5(1)(c), 5(4).
55. Lord Bach, in United Kingdom, *House of Lords Hansard*, 16 May 2000, col 241.
56. Ibid., col 244.
57. Ibid., col 244.
58. Quoted in *R v Gul* [2012] EWCA Crim 280, [11].
59. See ibid., [27]–[60].
60. Australia, Senate, Legal and Constitutional Legislation Committee, 2002, 103.
61. *R v Khawaja* 2006 OJ No 4245; (2006) 214 CCC (3d) 399, [58].
62. [2007] JSCC No 31776, *Bulletin of Proceedings* 502 (5 April 2007).
63. *United States v Nadarajah* [2009] OJ No 946; (2009) OR (3d) 514.
64. *R v Ahmad* 2009 CanLII 84774; 257 CCC (3d) 135, [94]–[136].
65. *R v Khawaja* 2011 ONCA 862; 103 OR (3d) 321, [118]–[135].
66. *United States v Sriskandarajah* 2010 ONCA 857; 109 OR (3d) 680; *United States v Nadarajah* 2010 ONCA 859; 109 OR (3d) 662.
67. *R v Khawaja* [2011] JSCC No 34103 (special leave); 2012 SCC 69; *Sriskandarajah v United States* [2011] JSCC No 34009, 34013 (special leave); 2012 SCC 70.
68. See the speeches of Scott Reid (CA) and Peter MacKay (PC/DR) in Canada, *House of Commons Hansard*, 26 November 2001, 12.25 and 1.30 pm.
69. Michel Bellehumeur, in Canada, *House of Commons Hansard*, 26 November 2001, 12.45 pm ("The numerous witnesses who appeared before the committee, some 60, 70 or 80 of them, and a number of groups, told us that [the definition] was too broad"); Australia, Senate, Legal and Constitutional Legislation Committee, 2002, 32–39; Keith

Locke (Green), in *New Zealand Parliamentary Debates*, 8 October 2002, 1071 ("virtually all of the 150 public submissions oppose the bill").

CHAPTER 4

1. Quoted in Weaver and Pallitto 2005, 86.
2. Herman 2006, 73.
3. Quoted in N. V. Baker 2006, 152.
4. Crimes Act 1914 (Cth) (hereinafter CAA), s 3E(1), (2); 3F(1)(d). As to the difference between these standards, and for examples of New Zealand's use of multiple standards, see New Zealand Law Commission 2007, 56–59.
5. Terrorism Act 2000 (UK), c 11, Sch 5, cl 1(5).
6. Donohue 2008, 187–95, 201–5.
7. 18 USC § 2518(3), (5).
8. 18 USC § 2518(8)(d).
9. 18 USC § 2518(7) (emergencies), (11) (impracticality).
10. 18 USC § 2703(a)–(d).
11. Regulation of Investigatory Powers Act 2000 (UK), c 23 (hereinafter RIPA), s 5.
12. RIPA, s 17.
13. Criminal Code, RSC 1985, c C-46 (hereinafter CCC), ss 186(1)(a), 196; on the legislation's antecedents, see Rahamim 2004.
14. Crimes Act 1961 (NZ), ss 312C(1), 312CB(1), 312CD(1).
15. CCC ss 185(1.1), 186(1.1), 196(5).
16. Search and Surveillance Act 2012 (NZ), ss 51(a), 53, 59, 61(1)(c), (2), (3).
17. CAA, ss 3E(1), (2); 3F(1)(d) (CA); Telecommunications (Interception and Access) Act 1979 (Cth) (hereinafter T(IA)A), ss 46(1)(d) (interception of a service), 46A(1)(d) (named person).
18. T(IA)A, ss 46(2), 46A(2).
19. T(IA)A, s 116.
20. Surveillance Devices Act 2004 (Cth), ss 14(1), 16.
21. RIPA, s 22.
22. CCC, s 487.012.
23. CCC, s 487.013.
24. CAA, ss 3ZQL-3ZQP.
25. New Zealand Law Commission 2007, 291, 294–95.
26. Search and Surveillance Act 2012 (NZ), ss 70, 71, 108.
27. Terrorism Act 2000 (UK), c 11, ss 44–45.
28. May 2011, 15–19.
29. Terrorism Act 2000 (Remedial) Order 2011, SI 201/631. Inelegantly, the order achieved its purposes by providing that the act was to have effect as if sections 44–47(g) had been repealed and as if several new sections had been added. The Protection of Freedoms Act 2012 (c 9, ss 59–63) repealed the order and amended the Terrorism Act 2000 so that the narrower powers are now part of that act. Section 47A of the amended act limits the circumstances in which authorisations may be made.
30. CAA, ss 3UB-3UK.
31. CCC, s 83.28.

32. 50 USC § 436 (authorized investigative agencies may obtain financial information for investigations, inquiries, and security determinations).

33. 12 USC § 3414 (1978) (financial institutions); 18 USC § 2709 (1986) (communications service providers); 50 USC § 436 (1994) (financial, consumer credit, or travel agencies, in relation to government employees with access to classified information); 15 USC § 1681u (1996) (consumer credit agencies); 15 USC § 1681v (1996) (consumer credit agencies).

34. 12 USC § 3414(a)(5)(A); 15 USC §§ 1681u(d)(1); 18 USC § 2709(b)(1) .

35. 12 USC § 3414(a) (financial records); 15 USC § 1681v (consumer reports).

36. Foreign Intelligence Surveillance Act of 1978, PL 95–511, 92 Stat 1783 (FISA).

37. 50 USC §§ 1809(a) (prohibition), 1801(f) (definition). On the significance of the general exclusion of radio communications, see Wittes 2008, 234–35, 241–42.

38. 50 USC § 1801(j).

39. 50 USC § 1801(a).

40. 50 USC § 1801(e).

41. 50 USC §§ 1802(a) (communications interception), 1822(a)(1) (searches), 1842(a)(1) (pen registers etc.)

42. 50 USC § 1803. As to the court, see Wittes 2008, 219–20, 226–27.

43. 50 USC §§ 1804 (interception), 1823(a) (searches), 1842(c) (pen registers), 1861(a) (business records).

44. 50 USC § 1801(h).

45. 50 USC §§ 1805(a) (interception), 1824(a) (searches), 1842(d) (pen registers, trap and trace devices), 1861(c) (business records).

46. The circumstances of the amendments are discussed later in this chapter. See generally Schwartz 2009, 412–17.

47. 50 USC § 1881a.

48. 50 USC §§ 1881b, 1881c.

49. 50 USC § 1881d.

50. Apparent inconsistency in this book in my spelling of *organization* in relation to the name of the ASIO is deliberate. Following an amendment to the early legislation, it is now spelled with an *s* in that name, in line with modern Australian usage.

51. Sections 25(1) and 25A of the Australian Security Intelligence Organisation Act (hereinafter ASIO Act) "will substantially assist the collection of intelligence . . . in respect of a matter that is important in relation to security" (search warrants, computer access warrants). In relation to warrants for named persons, the attorney-general must be satisfied that "the person is engaged in, or reasonably suspected by the Director-General of being engaged in, or of being likely to engage in, activities prejudicial to security" and that interception "will, or is likely to assist the Organisation in carrying out its function of obtaining information relating to security" (T(IA)A, s 9A(1)). See also T(IA)A, ss 9, 10 (telecommunications interception), 11A–11C (interception to gather foreign intelligence), 109 (stored communications), 175–79 (communications records); ASIO Act, ss 26(3) (listening devices), 26B(2), 26C(2) (tracking devices), 27(2), 27A(3) (postal articles), 34A–34ZZ (questioning); Canadian Security Intelligence Service Act, RS 1985, c C-23 (hereinafter CSIS Act), s 21(2) (warrant "required to enable the Service to investigate a threat to the security of Canada or to perform its functions"; also a "last resort" requirement and details of previous applications to be given and taken into account); New Zealand Security Intelligence Service Act 1969 (NZ) (hereinafter NZSIS Act), s 4A(3) (warrant necessary "for the detection of activi-

ties prejudicial to security" or for "gathering foreign intelligence material essential to security"; "last resort," proportionality, and minimisation requirements exist (ss 4F, 4G); Government Communications Security Bureau Act 2003 (NZ), s 7(2) (use of interception device to intercept foreign communications); Security Service Act 1989 (UK), c 5, s 3 (warrants for entry and interference with property needed and may be issued if the secretary thinks they are "necessary to obtain information which . . . is likely to be of substantial value in assisting the Service to discharge any of its functions"). Surveillance is governed by RIPA.

52. NZSIS Act, ss 4A, 5A.

53. CSIS Act, s 21.

54. The inspector-general of security and intelligence (Australia, New Zealand) or intelligence services commissioner (United Kingdom).

55. For more details, see *Kennedy v United Kingdom* [2010] ECHR 682; (2011) 52 EHRR 4, [21]–[98].

56. ASIO Act, s 18(3)(a) ("information relates or appears to relate to the commission . . . of an indictable offence"); CSIS Act, s 19 ("may be used in the investigation or prosecution of an alleged contravention").

57. NZSIS Act, ss 12A(1), 4(1)(a).

58. *Parkin v O'Sullivan* [2006] FCA 1413; (2006) 162 FCR 444; *Charkaoui v Canada (Citizenship and Immigration)* 2008 SCC 38; [2008] 2 SCR 326 (a charter-based decision).

59. See Laberge 2009, 111–12; Intelligence Services Act 2001 (Cth), ss 6–10A (minister may authorise Australian foreign intelligence agencies); National Defence Act, RSC 1985, c N-5, s 273.65 (minister may authorise the Communications Security Establishment to intercept "private communications" in the course of targeting foreign entities located outside Canada); Government Communications Security Bureau Act 2003 (NZ), ss 14–24 (minister may authorise); Intelligence Services Act 1994 (UK), c 13, ss 5–7 (secretary may authorise).

60. 26 October 2001, PL 107–56, 115 Stat 272 (hereinafter USAPA). The original short title of the act—"Uniting and Strengthening America by Providing Appropriate Tools Required to Intercept and Obstruct Terrorism (USA PATRIOT ACT) Act of 2001"—was later amended to permit the act to be cited as the USA Patriot Act (PL 109–177, Title 1, § 101, 120 Stat 194).

61. USAPA § 215.

62. Donohue 2006, 1090–91.

63. USAPA § 218.

64. McCarthy 2002, 443–45.

65. USAPA § 206.

66. USAPA § 207.

67. USAPA § 505.

68. USAPA § 212, further amended by the Homeland Security Act of 2002, PL 107–296, § 225(d)(1), 116 Stat 2157.

69. USAPA § 209.

70. USAPA § 210.

71. USAPA § 216. As to its implications, see Ashdown 2006, 795–97.

72. USAPA § 219. As to the implications of this, see Ashdown 2006, 790.

73. USAPA § 220.

74. USAPA § 203(b).

75. USAPA § 203(d).

76. USAPA § 202(a)(1).
77. Donohue 2006, 1107.
78. Howell 2004, 1170–71.
79. N. V. Baker 2006, 150–51.
80. Kerr 2003, 672.
81. Howell 2004, 1152, 1159–66.
82. Contrast sections 103, 352, 156, and 155 of the administration's draft bill "to combat terrorism and defend the Nation against terrorist acts, and for other purposes," the Anti-Terrorism Act of 2001, with sections 203, 213, 215, and 216 of the Patriot Act. Section 105 of the Anti-Terrorism Act did not appear in the Patriot Act, even in an amended form. For more details, see Howell 2004, 1179–99.
83. Howell 2004, 1179–1200.
84. USAPA § 224.
85. Herman 2006, 82–85.
86. USA Patriot Improvement and Reauthorization Act of 2005, 9 March 2005, PL 109–177 (hereinafter PIRA), Title I, § 102(a), 120 Stat 194.
87. PIRA, Title I, § 114, 120 Stat 210.
88. PIRA, Title I, §§ 102(b), 106(f)(2), 106(g), 120 Stat 194, 195, 198.
89. 19 December 2009, PL 111–118, Div B, § 1004(a), 123 Stat 3470.
90. Henning and Liu 2009, 6–7, 14–15.
91. 27 February 2010, PL 111–141, § 1(a), 124 Stat 37.
92. PATRIOT Sunsets Extension Act of 2011.
93. Donohue 2008, 201–2.
94. Australian Security Intelligence Organisation Legislation Amendment (Terrorism) Act 2003 (Cth).
95. See Australia, Senate, Legal and Constitutional Legislation Committee, 2005, 3–6 (citing rationales given for the bill).
96. CAA, s 3ZQN, added by Anti-Terrorism Act (No 2) 2005 (Cth), Sch 6, item 1.
97. CAA, ss 3UA–3UK, added by Anti-Terrorism Act (No 2) 2005 (Cth), Sch 5, item 10.
98. Anti-terrorism Act, SC 2001, c 41, ss 5–8.
99. Crimes Amendment Act (No 2) 2003 (NZ), s 8.
100. *Hamed v* R [2011] NZSC 27.
101. Video Camera Surveillance (Temporary Measures) Act (NZ) 2011; Cumming and Masters 2012.
102. See, e.g., New Zealand, House of Representatives Justice and Electoral Committee, 2010, which makes no references to the possible relevance of terrorism to the bill or vice versa.
103. Donohue 2006, 1075–77, 1080–88.
104. Grabosky 1989, 47–65.
105. Canada, Commission of Inquiry, 1981, 1:363–95.
106. Assistant Attorney General to Majority Leader, US Senate, 14 May 2009, 30 April 2010, 29 April 2011.
107. Difo 2010, 3.
108. United States, Department of Justice, Office of the Inspector General, 2010, 12–16, 26.
109. Ibid.
110. Ibid., 81–89.

111. Ibid., 33.
112. Ibid., 89–104.
113. Ibid., 45–50.
114. Ibid., 122–29.
115. Ibid., 34–43.
116. Ibid., 137–55.
117. Ibid., 156.
118. Ibid., 166.
119. Ibid., 165–85.
120. United States, Offices of Inspector General, 2009.
121. Ibid., 7, 16, 23.
122. Ibid., 17.
123. Seifert 2007, 18–21; Michaels 2008, 910.
124. Michaels 2008, 911–17.
125. United States, Offices of Inspector General, 2009, 6; see Aid 2009, 287–88, 290, 292–95, for details.
126. United States, Offices of Inspector General, 2009, 6–7.
127. Ibid., 10–14.
128. Ibid., 19–23.
129. Ibid., 27–30.
130. Ibid., 30–31.
131. 5 August 2007, PL 110–55, 121 Stat 552.
132. PL 110–55, § 2, 121 Stat 552, adding § 105A (50 USC § 1805a).
133. PL 110–55, § 2, 121 Stat 552, adding § 105B (50 USC § 1805b).
134. 10 July 2008, PL 110–261, 122 Stat 2436.
135. In the final Senate vote, there were 60 yeas (43 Republicans, 16 Democrats, 1 independent) and 28 nays (all Democrats); see also Aid 2009, 292–95.
136. FISA Amendments Act of 2008, PL 110–261, § 112, 122 Stat 2459, coded as 50 USC § 1812.
137. FISA Amendments Act of 2008, PL 110–261, § 202, 122 Stat 2467, coded as 50 USC § 1885–1885a.
138. Lord Carlile of Berriew 2009, 28–31; United Kingdom, Home Office, 2010, 41–42.
139. Donohue 2008, 197–198.
140. Gibson 2010, 9, 11.
141. Australia, Inspector-General of Intelligence and Security, *Annual Reports* 2001–2002—2008–2009.
142. Ibid., 2001–2002, 35; 2004–5, 19 (no interception had actually taken place).
143. Goldsmith 2007, 181.
144. Electronic Privacy Information Center 2007; Assistant Attorney General to Majority Leader, US Senate, 14 May 2009, 30 April 2010, 29 April 2011. In 2008, substantial modifications were required in only two cases.
145. Ashdown 2006.
146. See, e.g., the authorities cited in *In the matter of Kevork* 634 F Supp 1002, 1012 (CD Cal 1985).
147. *United States v United States District Court (Keith)* 407 US 297, 322 (1972).
148. *In re Sealed Case No 02–001* 310 F 3d 717, 722–28 (FISCR 2002); for a critical review of the case, see Hoffman 2003.

149. *In re Sealed Case No 02–001*, 728–34.
150. Ibid., 735.
151. *United States v Truong Dinh Hung* 629 F 2d 908 (4th Cir 1980).
152. *In re Sealed Case No 02–001*, 743.
153. Ibid., 743.
154. Ibid., 745 (citing *Vernonia School District 47J v Acton* 515 US 636, 653 (1995)).
155. Ibid., 746.
156. *United States v Hammoud* 381 F 3d 316, 334 (4th Cir 2004); *United States v Warsame* 547 F Supp 2d 982 (D Minn 2008).
157. *United States v Holy Land Foundation* 2007 US Dist LEXIS 50239, 21 (ND Tex 2007); *United States of America v Mubayyid* 521 F Supp 2d 125 (D Mass 2007); *United States v Islamic American Relief Agency* 2009 US Dist LEXIS 118505 (WD Mo 2009).
158. *United States of America v Abu-Jihaad* 531 F Supp 2d 299 (D Conn 2008), aff'd *United States v Abu-Jihaad* 630 F 3d 102 (2d Cir 2011) (a material assistance case); *In re Directives Pursuant to Section 105B of the Foreign Intelligence Surveillance Act* 551 F 3d 1004 (FISCR 2008); *United States v Schnewer* 2008 US Dist LEXIS 112001 (D NJ 2008); *United States v Ahmed* 2009 US Dist LEXIS 12007, 30 (ND Ga 2009); *United States v Kashmiri* 2010 US Dist LEXIS 119470 (ND Ill 2010).
159. 504 F Supp 2d 1023 (D Ore 2007).
160. The court had, however, received briefs filed by the ACLU and the National Association of Defense Lawyers, as amici curiae: see *In re Sealed Case No 02–001* 310 F 3d 717, 719 (FISCR 2002).
161. *Mayfield v United States* 599 F 3d 964 (9th Cir 2010).
162. See *United States v Abu-Jihaad* 630 F 3d 102 (2d Cir 2011) and the cases cited therein.
163. *Doe v Ashcroft* 334 F Supp 2d 471 (SD NY 2004).
164. *Doe v Gonzales* 386 F Supp 2d 66 (D Conn 2005).
165. *Doe I v Gonzales* 449 F 3d 415 (2d Cir 2006).
166. *Doe v Gonzales* 500 F Supp 2d 379 (SD NY 2007).
167. *John Doe Inc v Mukasey* 549 F 3d 861 (2d Cir 2008).
168. *John Doe v Holder* 665 F Supp 2d 517 (SD NY 2009).
169. *American Civil Liberties Union v National Security Agency* 438 F Supp 2d 754 (ED Mich 2006).
170. *American Civil Liberties Union v National Security Agency* 493 F 3d 644 (6th Cir 2007).
171. *American Civil Liberties Union v National Security Agency* 128 S Ct 1334 (2008).
172. *Al-Haramain Islamic Foundation v Bush* 507 F 3d 1190 (9th Cir 2007).
173. *In re National Security Agency Telecommunications Records Litigation* 564 F Supp 2d 1109, 1121 (ND Cal 2008); *In re National Security Agency Telecommunications Records Litigation* 595 F Supp 2d 1077 (ND Cal 2009); *In re National Security Agency Telecommunications Records Litigation* 700 F Supp 2d 1182 (ND Cal 2010), rev'd, 2012 US App LEXIS 16379 (9th Cir 2012).
174. There were dozens of such cases, including *Jewel v National Security Agency* 2010 US Dist LEXIS 5110, 4 (ND Cal).
175. 439 F Supp 2d 974 (ND Cal 2006).
176. *In re National Security Agency Telecommunications Records Litigation* 630 F Supp 2d 1092, 1094 (ND Cal 2009).
177. Ibid., 1102 (ND Cal 2009), motion for leave to file motion to dismiss denied; *In*

re National Security Agency Telecommunications Records Litigation 2009 US Dist LEXIS 62640 (ND Cal 2009).

178. 2009 US Dist LEXIS 64621 (ND Cal, 2009).

179. Ibid., 10–13, aff'd, 669 F 3d 928 (9th Cir 2011).

180. Ibid., 25.

181. *Amnesty International v McConnell* 646 F Supp 2d 633 (SD NY 2009).

182. *Amnesty International v Clapper* 638 F 3d 118 (2d Cir 2011), reh'g, en banc, denied, 667 F 3d 163, 172 (2d Cir 2011).

183. *Clapper v Director of National Intelligence* 133 S Ct 1138 (2013).

184. *Amnesty International v Clapper* 667 F 3d 163, 172 (2d Cir 2011).

185. See *MacWade v Kelly* 460 F 3d 260 (2d Cir 2006) (subways); *Cassidy v Chertoff* 471 F 3d 67 (2d Cir 2006) (ferries).

186. *MacWade v Kelly*, 273–75 (2d Cir 2006); *Cassidy v Chertoff*, 84–87.

187. In a nonterrorism case, *Kennedy v United Kingdom*, the ECtHR found that RIPA was consistent with the ECHR, given its provisions for independent adjudication and supervision.

188. *R (Gillan) v Metropolitan Police Commissioner* [2003] EWHC 2545 (Admin).

189. *R (Gillan) v Metropolitan Police Commissioner* [2004] EWCA (Civ) 1067; [2005] QB 388.

190. *R (Gillan) v Commissioner of Police of the Metropolis* [2006] UKHL 12; [2006] 2 AC 307.

191. *Gillan v the United Kingdom* [2010] ECHR 28; (2010) 50 EHRR 45.

192. Ibid., [35], Lord Bingham, with whom Lords Hope, Scott, Walker, and Brown agreed.

193. Ibid., [63].

194. See, e.g., ibid., [67] (Lord Scott), [78]–[81] (Lord Brown).

195. See United Kingdom, Home Office, 2010, 37; *Gillan v the United Kingdom*, Application 4158/05, unreported 12 January 2010, [45]: there were 46 arrests for terrorism offences of people in vehicles in 2005–6, 14 in 2006–7, and 34 in 2007–8, compared with about 250, 246, and 665 arrests for other offences.

196. *Kennedy v United Kingdom* [2010] ECHR 682; (2011) EHRR 4

197. *Hunt v R* [2010] NZCA 528.

198. *Hamed v R* [2011] NZSC 101, [196].

199. Haggerty and Grazso 2005.

200. Fletcher 1989.

201. Huddy et al. 2002, 419, 428–29.

202. *Los Angeles Times* poll, 13–14 September 2001, terror11; *Newsweek* poll, September 2001; Harris poll, September 2001, terror10.

203. Harris poll, February 2006 (reporting earlier polls), terror5.

204. Center for Survey Research poll, August 2005, terror5; CNN/*USA Today*/Gallup poll, January 2006; *Fox News*/Opinion Dynamics poll, January 2006, terror4.

205. *Fox News*/Opinion Dynamics poll, May 2006; *USA Today* poll, May 2006; *ABC News/Washington Post* poll, March 2006; *CBS News* poll, February 2006; Harris poll, February 2006; CNN/*USA Today*/Gallup poll, February 2006; *CBS News/New York Times* poll, January 2006—all at terror4.

206. Harris poll, February 2006, terror4.

207. *CBS News* poll, May 2006, terror4.

208. ICM/BBC poll, 26 May 2004, http://www.angus-reid.com/polls/24381.

209. YouGov/*Sun* poll, October 2010.
210. Fletcher 1989.
211. Strategic Counsel poll/CTV/*Globe and Mail* 14 August 2005, http://www.angus-reid.com/polls/16395.
212. ASSDA, Australian Survey of Social Attitudes (2007), v123, v124, weighted by v656.
213. *CBS News* poll, February 2006; *Fox News*/Opinion Dynamics poll, February 2006, terror4.
214. *Newsweek* poll, May 2006, terror4.
215. Hetherington and Suhay 2012.
216. ASSDA, Australian Survey of Social Attitudes (2007), cross-tabulation of v123 and v124 with v539, weighted by v656.

CHAPTER 5

1. Posner 2008, 246.
2. Poole 2010, 92.
3. *Reynolds v United States* 345 US 1 (1953). See generally Chesney 2007b, 1270–97.
4. But the state secrets doctrine applies much more broadly in relation to civil than criminal cases: see *Mohamed v Jeppesen Dataplan* 614 F 3d 1070, 1077 (n 3) (9th Cir, en banc, 2010), cert denied, 131 S Ct 2442 (2011).
5. Weaver and Pallitto 2005, 87.
6. *United States v Nixon* 418 US 683 (1974).
7. *Conway v Rimmer* [1968] UKHL 2; [1968] AC 910; *Sankey v Whitlam* [1978] HCA 43; (1978) 142 CLR 1. See also *Canada (Attorney-General) v Ribic* 2003 FCA 246; [2005] 1 FCR 33.
8. Canada Evidence Act, RSC 1985, c-5 (hereinafter CAE), s 37 (after objection on public interest grounds, the court shall prohibit disclosure unless (1) disclosure would not encroach on the specified public interest (s 37(4.1)) or (2) disclosure would encroach but "the public interest in disclosure outweighs in importance the specified public interest," in which case, "after considering both the public interest in disclosure and the form of and conditions to disclosure that are most likely to limit any encroachment upon the specified public interest resulting from disclosure," the court may order disclosure of all or some of the information, in various forms and subject to conditions (s 37(5)). See also Evidence Act 2006 (NZ), s 70 ("information that relates to matters of State must not be disclosed in a proceeding if the Judge considers that the public interest in the communication or information being disclosed in the proceeding is outweighed by the public interest in withholding the communication or information").
9. CAE, s 38.13. The validity of this section insofar as it applies to nonfederal courts is unclear: see *Canada (Attorney General) v Almalki* 2010 FC 1106, [23], [46]–[51] (summarising the state of the relevant constitutional litigation, but proceeding on the basis that the legislation was constitutional).
10. CAE, s 38.14.
11. Canada, House of Commons, Standing Committee on Public Safety and National Security and Subcommittee on the Review of the Anti-terrorism Act , 2007.
12. National Security Information (Criminal and Civil Proceedings) Act 2004 (Cth) (hereinafter NSIA), ss 31(8), 38L(8). Disclosure is likely to prejudice national security

only if "there is a real, and not merely a remote, remote possibility" that disclosure will have this effect (s 17).

13. *R v Lodhi* [2006] NSWSC 571, [109]; (2006) 163 A Crim R 448; *Watson v AWB* [2009] FCA 1047, [51]; (2009) 259 ALR 524; *Canada (Attorney General) v Almalki*, [70].

14. Weaver and Pallitto 2005, 101.

15. See Rosenthal 2003, 189, 198; Zuckerman 1994, 705, 718–19 (but cf. criminal cases, discussed at 720–22); *Sankey v Whitlam* (1978) 142 CLR 1, 46 (Gibbs CJ, generally limiting inspection to cases where there has been a provisional decision that the document should be disclosed), 96 (Mason J, inspection when "appropriate"), 110 (Aickin J, concluding that courts should inspect), 110 (order, declaring court had read documents); *Burmah Oil v Bank of England* [1979] UKHL 4; [1980] AC 1090; *Air Canada v Secretary of State for Trade* [1983] 2 AC 394; *Goguen v Gibson* [1983] 2 FC 463; 7 DLR (4th) 144 (FCA: inspection will depend on the likelihood that it would alter the court's view of where the public interest immunity balance lies). In *Canada (Attorney General) v Khawaja* 2007 FC 490; [2008] 1 FCR 547, Justice Mosely read the redacted sections in the 1,700 pages of contested documents, at [29]; see also *Parkin v O'Sullivan* (2009) 260 ALR 503, where Justice Sundberg read the documents at issue).

16. Classified Information Procedures Act of 1980, PL 96–456 (hereinafter CIPA), § 3, 94 Stat 2025, codified in 18 USC App, as amended by PL 100–690, Title VII, § 7020(G), 102 Stat 4396.

17. CAE, s 38.01 ("sensitive" or "potentially injurious" information); NSIA, ss 24, 25, 38D, 38E (national security information defined at ss 8–11; see also s 17).

18. NSIA, ss 39, 39A. As to the US, see CIPA, § 5 (the act applies only to material that has been classified, according to § 1(a)). The procedures established under the act provide that "the government may obtain information by any lawful means concerning the trustworthiness of persons associated with the defense and may bring such information to the attention of the court for the court's consideration in framing an appropriate protective order pursuant to Section 3 of the Act" (Security Procedures Established Pursuant to PL 96–456, 94 Stat 2025, by the Chief Justice of the United States for the Protection of Classified Information (2012), par 5). In noncriminal cases, protective orders may require that counsel for nongovernment parties be security-cleared: see, e.g., the protective order issued in *Bismullah v Gates* 2007 US App LEXIS (DC Cir 2007). See generally Turner and Schulhofer 2005, 25–28.

19. It was used by the Security Intelligence Review Committee in its review of security decisions: see Forcese and Waldman 2007, 7–10 (for its operation).

20. Special Immigration Appeals Commission Act 1997 (UK), c 68 (hereinafter SIAC), s 6; Terrorism Act 2000 (UK), c 11, Sch 3, cl 7 (hereinafter TA); Proscribed Organisations Appeals Commission (Procedure) Rules SI 2001/1286 (hereinafter POAC), rr 9–10; Employment Tribunals (Constitution and Rules of Procedure) Regulations 2004 2004/1861 (hereinafter ETR), Sch 2, r 8; Civil Procedure Rules SI 1998/3132 (hereinafter CPR), rr 76.23–76.25 (control orders), rr 80.19–80.21 (notices according to the Terrorism Prevention and Investigation Measures Act 2011).

21. Immigration and Refugee Protection Act, SC 2001, c 27 (hereinafter IRPA), ss 85–85.6 (as amended by An Act to Amend the Immigration and Refugee Protection Act (Certificate and Special Advocate) and to Make a Consequential Amendment to Another Act, SC 2008, c 3, s 4).

22. Forcese and Waldman 2007, 49–50; Immigration Act 2009 (NZ), ss 263–70.

23. *R v H; R v C* [2004] UKHL 3; [2004] 2 AC 134. See also *Secretary of State for the*

Home Department v AHK [2009] EWCA Civ 287, [97]–[99] (providing examples, but emphasising that the procedure is adopted as a last resort); *Al Rawi v Security Service* [2010] EWHC 1496 (QB) (for purpose of a public interest immunity inquiry in civil claim arising out of alleged torture); *R v Lodhi* [2006] NSWSC 586 (where the court nonetheless considered that such an order was not required in the circumstances of the case).

24. *Canada (Attorney General) v Khawaja* 2007 FC 463; [2008] 1 FCR 621, [47]–[57]; *Canadian Security Intelligence Service Act (Re)* 2008 FC 300; [2010] 1 SCR 44, [3]; *Canada (Attorney General) v Almalki* 2010 FC 1106, [29]. But in *Harkat (Re)* 2010 FC 1242, Justice Noël considered that special advocates provided better protection (at [155]).

25. *Hepting v AT&T* 439 F Supp 2d 974 (ND Cal 2006); *Leghaei v Director-General of Security* [2005] FCA 1576, [84] (in the absence of an application from counsel, no appointment was made).

26. The court may permit such communications, but this power is rarely used, partly because of doubts that permission would be forthcoming and partly lest such an application "give away to the opposing party the parts of the closed evidence in relation to which the controlled person does not have an explanation" (United Kingdom, Parliament, Joint Committee on Human Rights, 2007, 53). Most communications seem to have been one-way communications from the advocate (Forcese and Waldman 2007, 35).

27. *Almrei (Re)* 2009 FC 1263; [2009] FCJ No 1579, [487]; *Harkat (Re)* 2010 FC 1242, [67], and see [79] and [139] for other respects in which the Canadian system allows greater powers to special advocates and therefore greater disclosure. See generally Forcese (n.d., chap. 10).

28. See, e.g., *United States v Sattar* 395 F Supp 2d 79 (SD NY 2005) (a case where a radical lawyer was found to have communicated confidential information to her client).

29. See, e.g., *R v Khazaal* [2006] NSWSC 1061, [34]. See also *R v Khazaal* [2006] NSWSC 1335, for an example of how even honest lawyers can make mistakes that lead to their not recognising that information is confidential.

30. They have normally been used in Australian terrorism prosecutions: *R v Khazaal* [2006] NSWSC 1061, [34]; *R v Thomas* [2006] VSC 18, [7]; *R v Benbrika (Ruling 1)* [2007] VSC 141, Order 5. As to their use in Canada, see *Harkat (Re)* 2010 FC 1242, [77].

31. CIPA, §§ 4 (pretrial discovery; also redacted document), 6(c)(1) (evidence); CAE, s 38.06(2); NSIA, ss 26(2), 31(2), 38F(2), 38L(2). As to applications of the CIPA procedure, see Turner and Schulhofer 2005, 20, 23, 24–25.

32. Townley 2007, 223–27; *R v Lodhi* [2006] NSWSC 571; (2006) 163 A Crim R 448.

33. Turner and Schulhofer 2005, 41–45.

34. *United States v Reynolds* 345 US 1, 11 (1953); *General Dynamics v United States* 131 S Ct 1900 (2011).

35. *Carnduff v Rock* [2001] 1 WLR 1786 (CA); but cf. *Secretary of State for the Home Department v A* [2010] EWHC 42 (Admin), an administrative law case, where Justice Silber observed that his decision would mean that the government would be exposed to a damages claim. In defending the claim, it would not be permitted to rely on the closed evidence, since this would interfere with the claimants' right to a fair trial and would be inconsistent with the decision in *Secretary of State for the Home Department v AF* [2009] UKHL 28; [2010] AC 269. He took comfort from the fact that the damages that would be awarded would be small, since the government had acted in good faith. He did not advert to the possibility that the claim might be dismissed as an abuse of process, on

the grounds that its commitment to protecting national security would mean that the government would be unable to present its defence.

36. *Al Rawi v Security Service* [2011] UKSC 34, [50] (Lord Dyson).

37. *Al Rawi v Security Service* [2009] EWHC 2959.

38. *Al Rawi v Security Service* [2010] EWCA (Civ) 482; [2011] UKSC 34.

39. *Al Rawi v Security Service* [2011] UKSC 34, [44] (Lord Dyson), [74] (Lord Hope), [78] (Lord Brown).

40. Ibid. [75] (Lord Hope, doubtful), [84] (Lord Brown, disagreeing), [98] (Lord Kerr, doubtful), [112]–[113] (Lord Mance (with whom Lady Hale agreed, concluding that it should be possible).

41. Ibid. [86]–[87].

42. *Canada (Attorney General) v Almalki* 2010 FC 1106, [64].

43. "Protective Order and Procedures for Counsel Access to Detainees at the United States Naval Base in Guantanamo Bay, Cuba," *In re Guantanamo Bay Detainee Litigation* Case 1:08-mc-00442-TFH, document 409, filed 09.11.08 (Protective Order 08).

44. *Al Rawi v Security Service* [2010] EWCA Civ 482; [2010] 3 WLR 1069, [33] (cases "where a wider public interest is engaged"); see also, to similar effect, [59], [61], [64], [65]. Cf. *Al Rawi v Security Service* [2011] UKSC 34; [2012] 1 AC 531, Lord Dyson at [62] (but recognising, at [63]–[64], that there might be cases where departure from the general rules would be justified as being in the interests of justice, e.g., wardship, commercial secrets cases); Lords Hope [76] and Kerr [88] (agreeing with Lord Dyson); Lord Clarke [169]–[171] (rejecting the distinction).

45. *Al Rawi v Security Service* [2011] UKSC 34; [2012] 1 AC 531, Lord Dyson [68], Lord Hope [74], Lord Brown [85], Lord Clarke [138], [152], Lord Bingham [192].

46. Migration Act 1958 (Cth), s 503(1)(d).

47. *Leghaei v Director-General of Security* [2005] FCA 1576, appeal dismissed, *Leghaei v Director-General of Security* [2007] FCAFC 56, special leave refused, *Leghaei v Director-General of Security* [2007] HCATrans 655.

48. See, e.g., *Home Office v Tariq* [2011] UKSC 35, [40] (Lord Mance, with whom Lords Hope, Dyson, Phillips, and Clarke and Lady Hale agreed), but cf. [110] (Lord Kerr, who considered that where a fair trial was not be possible, it was better that none be held).

49. 50 USC § 1806(f). "'Aggrieved person' means a person who is the target of an electronic surveillance or any other person whose communications or activities were subject to electronic surveillance" (50 USC § 1801(k)).

50. *In re Grand Jury Proceedings in the Special April 2002 Grand Jury* 347 F 3d 197, 203 (7th Cir 2003); *United States v Abu-Jihaad* 531 F Supp 2d 299, 310–11 (D Conn 2008) (the court followed the line of authority).

51. 50 USC § 1702(c); 8 USC § 1189(c)(2).

52. See generally Turner and Schulhofer 2005, 55–58.

53. United States, Deputy Secretary of Defense, 2004, par (g).

54. Ibid., par (c).

55. United States, Department of Defense, *Military Commission Order No 1*, 21 March 2002, par 6(B)(3).

56. 548 US 557 (2006).

57. 17 October 2006, Pub L 109–336, 120 Stat 2600.

58. 10 USC § 949d(f)(1)(A); see also § 949d(f)(2)(B) (evidence that might disclose classified intelligence-gathering methods).

59. 10 USC § 949d(f)(2).

60. Military Commissions Act of 2009, 28 October 2009, Pub L 111–84, Title XVIII, 123 Stat 2574.

61. 10 USC §§ 949p-4(a)(2), 949p-1(b).

62. 10 USC § 949p-6(d)(1).

63. SIAC, s 1; TA, s 5; ETR, Sch 1, r 54, and Sch 2, rr 8, 10; Regulation of Investigatory Powers Act 2000 (UK) c 23 (hereinafter RIPA), s 65 (as to the "intelligence services" jurisdiction, see R *(A) v* B [2009] UKSC 110); Prevention of Terrorism Act 2005 (UK), c 2, Sch 7; CPR, Pt 76; Terrorism Prevention and Investigative Measures Act 2011 (UK), c 23, Sch 4; CPR Pt 80.

64. POAC, r 35(4) (evidence disclosable if would be admissible in civil proceedings).

65. Special Immigration Appeals Commission (Procedure) Rules (UK), SI 2003/1034, r 4(1).

66. RIPA, s 69(6) (which also includes "the economic well-being of the United Kingdom" but does not include a reference to international relations); ETR, Sch 1, r 54; Investigatory Powers Tribunal Rules 2000 (UK), SI 2000/2665, r 6; CPR, rr 76.28, 80.18.

67. See note 20.

68. IRPA, s 78(b), (e), (g) (as enacted).

69. Criminal Code, RSC 1985, c C-46, s 83.05; Charities Registration (Security Information) Act, SC 2001, c 41, s 113, ss 4–8.

70. IRPA, s 78(h) (as enacted).

71. Ibid., ss 83(1)(b), 83(1.2), 85–85.2, 85.4.

72. Administrative Appeals Tribunal Act 1975 (Cth), ss 36(1)(a) (documentary evidence, general appeals), 39A, 39B (evidence, security assessment appeals). Other provisions govern oral evidence in nonsecurity cases and qualifications to the right to reasons in security cases.

73. Migration Act 1958 (Cth), ss 357, 375A, 437.

74. Immigration Act 2009 (NZ), ss 241–44, 256, 259 (use in proceedings), 263–70 (special advocates and special counsel).

75. Canada, House of Commons, Standing Committee on Justice and Human Rights, 2001, 21–24.

76. Canada, Senate, Special Committee on the Subject Matter of Bill C-36, 2001, 4.

77. Canada, Senate, Special Committee on the Anti-terrorism Act, 2007, recs 7–9, 13–15.

78. Canada, House of Commons, Subcommittee on the Review of the Anti-terrorism Act, 2007, 44–45, 75–81.

79. Wittes 2008, 140–41.

80. *Johnson v Eisentrager* 339 US 763 (1950); *Korematsu v United States* 323 US 214 (1944); *Liversidge v Anderson* [1942] AC 206; Weaver and Pallitto 2005, 101–2, 109.

81. *American Civil Liberties Union v National Security Agency* 493 F 3d 644 (6th Cir 2007), rev'g *American Civil Liberties Union v National Security Agency* 438 F Supp 2d 754 (ED Mich 2006).

82. *Al-Haramain Islamic Foundation v Bush* 507 F 3d 1190 (9th Cir 2007).

83. *Hepting v AT&T* 439 F Supp 2d 974 (ND Cal 2006).

84. *El-Masri v United States* 479 F 3d 296 (4th Cir, 2007), cert denied, 2007 US LEXIS

11351; *Mohamed v Jeppesen Dataplan* 614 F 3d 1070 (9th Cir, en banc, 2010), cert denied, 131 S Ct 2442 (2011), rev'g 563 F 3d 992, 1007 (9th Cir, 2009).

85. R *(Gillan) v Metropolitan Police Commissioner* [2004] EWCA (Civ) 1067; [2005] QB 88; see also R *(Aamer) v Secretary of State for Foreign and Commonwealth Affairs* [2009] EWHC 3316 (Admin).

86. R *(Mohamed) v Secretary of Foreign and Commonwealth Affairs* [2010] EWCA Civ 65; [2011] QB 218, [146] (Lord Neuberger MR).

87. Ibid., [144] (Lord Neuberger MR), and see [288] (Sir Anthony May).

88. Ibid., 65, [147] (Lord Neuberger MR, and see further at [173]), [288] (Sir Anthony May).

89. Ibid., [148]–[151] (Lord Neuberger MR), and see [289] (Sir Anthony May).

90. Patrick Wintour, 2010.

91. *Canada (Attorney General) v Commission of Inquiry into the Actions of Canadian Officials in Relation to Maher Arar* 2007 FC 766; [2008] 3 FCR 248. See also Roach 2008, 37, who argues that the decision suggests that the desire for secrecy was prompted more by a desire not to embarrass the government and its allies than by concerns to protect information providers' anonymity or national security.

92. *Charkaoui (Re)* 2009 FC 342; [2010] 3 FCR 67. See also *Charkaoui (Re)* 2009 FC 175; [2010] 4 FCR 448.

93. Ibid.

94. *Canada (Attorney-General) v Khawaja* 2007 FC 533; [2007] FCJ No 724.

95. *Parkin v O'Sullivan* [2006] FCA 1413; (2006) 162 FCR 444; *Parkin v O'Sullivan* [2007] FCA 1647; *O'Sullivan v Parkin* [2007] FCAFC 98.

96. *Parkin v O'Sullivan* [2009] FCA 1096, [32] ("this consequence . . . is not exceptional").

97. *Sagar v O'Sullivan* [2011] FCA 192; (2011) 193 FCR 311.

98. *Attorney-General v Zaoui* [2005] NZSC 38; [2006] 1 NZLR 289.

99. *Jasper v United Kingdom*, Application 295052/95, 16 February 2005; cf. *Edwards v United Kingdom* ([2003] ECHR 381), where the court dismissed, by a 9–8 majority, an appeal made on the grounds that the relevant decision was made by a jury (which had not seen the prejudicial material).

100. The rationale for this messy procedure was that the federal court was a particularly appropriate tribunal for dealing with security issues. It possessed special facilities for keeping information safe. In addition, the federal judiciary included 10 designated judges who dealt with national security issues. They were specially trained, met regularly, and had developed expertise in the area. See *R v Ahmad* [2009] OJ No 6166; (2009) 257 CCC (3d) 135 (citing the crown privilege argument).

101. R *v Ahmad* 2011 SCC 6; [2011] 1 SCR 110, rev'g R *v Ahmad* [2009] OJ No 6166; (2009) 257 CCC (3d) 135.

102. R *v Ahmad* 2011 SCC 6; [2011] 1 SCR 110, [61]–[80].

103. *Abou-Elmaati v Canada (Attorney-General)* 2010 ONSC 2055; (2010) 101 OR (3d) 424, appeal by government allowed, cross-appeal dismissed, *Abou-Elmaati v Canada (Attorney General)* 2011 ONCA 95.

104. *Abou-Elmaati v Canada (Attorney General)* 2011 ONCA 95, [36]–[42].

105. *Charkaoui v Canada (Citizenship and Immigration)* 2007 SCC 9; [2007] 1 SCR 350, [77].

106. *Canada (Attorney-General) v Khawaja* 2007 FC 533; [2007] FCJ No 724.

107. *Canada (Attorney-General) v Khawaja* 2007 FCA 388; (2007) 289 DLR (4th) 260.

108. *R v Ahmad* 2011 SCC 6; [2011] 1 SCR 110, [23]–[24].

109. *R v Lodhi* [2006] NSWSC 571; (2006) 163 A Crim R 448; *R v Lodhi* (2007) 179 A Crim R 470.

110. *Thomas v Mowbray* [2007] HCA 33; (2007) 233 CLR 307, [124]–[126] (Gummow and Crennan JJ).

111. USAPA § 106(c).

112. *Global Relief Foundation v O'Neill* 315 F 3d 748 (7th Cir 2002), reh'g, en banc, denied, 2003 US App LEXIS 6708 (7th Cir 2003), cert denied, 2003 US LEXIS 8207 (2003); *People's Mojahedin Organization of Iran v United States Department of State* 327 F 3d 1238, 1242 (DC Cir 2003); *Holy Land Foundation for Relief and Development v Ashcroft* 333 F 3d 156 (DC Cir 2003), cert denied, 158 L Ed 2d 153 (2004).

113. *Hamdan v Rumsfeld* 548 US 557 (2006).

114. *Boumediene v Bush* 553 US 723, 785 (2008).

115. On which, see Detainees Treatment Act of 2005, PL 109–148, Title X, § 1005(e), 119 Stat 2741, codified as 10 USC § 801 note.

116. "Protective Order and Procedures for Counsel Access to Detainees at the United States Naval Base in Guantanamo Bay, Cuba," *In re Guantanamo Bay Detainee Litigation* Case 1:08-mc-00442-TFH, document 409, filed 09.11.08 (Protective Order 08).

117. *In re Guantanamo Bay Detainee Litigation* Case 1:08-mc-0442-TFH, document 1496, filed 01.09.09, Exhibit 1.

118. *In re Guantanamo Bay Detainee Litigation* 634 F Supp 2d 17, 23–25 (D DC 2009).

119. *Secretary of State for the Home Department v MB and AF* [2007] UKHL 46; [2008] AC 40.

120. *A v United Kingdom*, [2009] ECHR 301; (2009) EHRR 29.

121. *Secretary of State for the Home Department v AF* [2009] UKHL 28; [2010] AC 269.

122. *Home Office v Tariq* [2011] UKSC 35.

123. *Kennedy v United Kingdom* [2010] ECHR 682; (2011) 52 EHRR 4, [171]–[191].

124. *Charkaoui v Canada (Citizenship and Immigration)* 2007 SCC 9; [2007] 1 SCR 350.

125. *Charkaoui v Canada (Citizenship and Immigration)* 2008 SCC 38; [2008] 2 SCR 326.

126. *Harkat (Re)* 2010 FC 1242.

127. See *Leghaei v Director-General of Security* [2005] FCA 1576, appeal dismissed; *Leghaei v Director-General of Security* [2007] FCAFC 56; special leave refused, *Leghaei v Director-General of Security* [2007] HCATrans 655; *Sagar v O'Sullivan* [2011] FCA 192.

128. *Plaintiff M47 v Director General of Security* [2012] HCA 46; (2012) 292 ALR 243.

129. Shapiro and Steinzor 2006, 117.

130. Amnesty International 2002, 7–8, 9 (but its requests yielded some information); Tumlin 2004, 1193–97, 1206–10.

131. United States, Attorney General, 2009; see also the emphasis on openness in Obama 2010, 37.

132. *Al-Aulaqi v Obama* 727 F Supp 2d 1, 53–54 (D DC 2010).

133. See, e.g., *Canada (Attorney-General) v Ribic* 2003 FCA 246; [2005] 1 FCR 33; *Canada (Attorney General) v Khawaja* 2007 FC 490; [2008] 1 FCR 547, [64] (but executive opinions must have a factual basis established by evidence: see [65]); *Canada (Attorney General) v Almalki* 2010 FC 1106, [68]–[78] (national security), [79]–[80] (injury to international relations); *R v Khazaal* [2006] NSWSC 1061, [31]–[37]; *Parkin v O'Sullivan* [2009] FCA 1096, [30].

134. *Canada (Attorney General) v Khawaja* 2007 FC 490; [2008] 1 FCR 547, [138]–[145];

Canada (Attorney General) v Commission of Inquiry into the Actions of Canadian Officials in Relation to Maher Arar 2007 FC 766; [2008] 3 FCR 248.

135. *Canada (Attorney General) v Khawaja* 2007 FC 490; [2008] 1 FCR 547, [146]–[154]; *Canada (Attorney General) v Commission of Inquiry into the Actions of Canadian Officials in Relation to Maher Arar*, [73], and see [80] (importance of consideration depends on the relevant intelligence relationship).

136. *Henrie v Canada Security Intelligence Review Committee* [1989] 2 FC 229; 1988 FC LEXIS 321, [29]–[30]; generally see Weaver and Pallitto 2005, 103–5.

137. *Canada (Attorney General) v Khawaja* 2007 FC 490; [2008] 1 FCR 547, [136]; *Canada (Attorney General) v Almalki*, [115]–[118]; *Canada (Attorney General) v Commission of Inquiry into the Actions of Canadian Officials in Relation to Maher Arar*, [82]–[84]. Cf *Mohamed v Jeppesen Dataplan* 614 F 3d 1070, 1082 (9th Cir, en banc, 2010), cert denied, 131 S Ct 2442 (2011). In *Watson v AWB* (2009) 259 ALR 524; [2009] FCA 1047, at [65], the court rejected a mosaic argument on the grounds that disclosure of the relevant documents to the court would not create a danger that a vital piece of information would fall into wrong hands.

138. *Canada (Attorney General) v Khawaja* 2007 FC 490; [2008] 1 FCR 547, [104]–[111].

139. Ibid., [117]–[134], [137]–[162]; *Canada (Attorney General) v Almalki*, [120]–[170] (but the government must usually have made reasonable attempts to secure the foreign government's consent to disclosure).

140. Turner and Schulhofer 2005, 32–34.

141. The issue arose in *A v Hayden* [1984] HCA 67 (where the court held that the information should be disclosed); (1984) 156 CLR 532. See also *Almrei (Re)* 2009 FC 240 (where the court noted that the designated judge's obligation in a security certificate case was to ensure nondisclosure of information that would injure national security even if the minister was willing to allow disclosure); [2010] 2 FCR 165.

142. *Canada (Attorney General) v Almalki*, [108]–[109] (noting that a CSIS witness had conceded that the CSIS review of documents did not consider their age, whether the operating techniques they disclosed were still employed, whether the information they disclosed was now in the public domain, and whether use of aliases would protect sources).

143. *Harkat (Re)* 2009 FC 1050; [2010] 4 FCR 149 (failure of CSIS to disclose information capable of casting doubt on the credibility of a CSIS source was not the result of an intention to deceive but was attributable to poor training and failure of witnesses to recognise their obligations to the court); *Canada (Attorney General) v Almalki*, [112].

144. United Kingdom 2011; Justice and Security Act 2013 (UK), c 18.

145. Cited in *Benatta v Canada (Attorney General)* [2009] OJ No 5392; 2009 ON C LEXIS 4688, [124].

146. Several involved applications for closed court hearings, for which the legislation provided. These were treated as nonproblematic. In Canada, they have fallen foul of the charter.

147. ABC News.com poll, June 2002, terror7.

148. *USA Today*/Gallup poll, September 2006, terror3.

149. United States, Senate, Committee on the Judiciary, 2008; for analysis of the legislation, see Chesney 2008.

150. Canada, House of Commons, Subcommittee on the Review of the Antiterrorism Act, 2007, 75–81.

151. Ibid., 123–26, 128–29.

152. Cf. Executive Order 12958 of 17 April 1995 (60 FR 19825), §§ 1.2, 1.3, 1.4, with Executive Order 13292 of 25 March 2003 (68 FR 15315), §§ 1.2, 1.3, 1.4.

153. Executive Order 13526 of 29 December 2009 (75 FR 707), §§ 1.1(b), 1.2(c), 1.4(e), (g).

154. Ibid., §§ 2.1(d), 3.7.

155. United States, Attorney General, 2009.

CHAPTER 6

1. There appears to be little relevant poll data (which itself is suggestive). In a 2002 poll tapping attitudes towards possible counterterror measures and their correlates, respondents were asked whether it should be a crime "to belong to or contribute money to any organization that supports international terrorism" or whether "a person's guilt or innocence should not be determined only by who they associate with or the organizations to which they belong." Seventy-one percent opted for the first alternative and 29 percent for the latter, and this item attracted a higher proportion of "pro-security" responses than items tapping attitudes towards racial profiling, warrantless searches, communications interception, preventive detention, and national ID cards (Davis and Silver 2004). Moreover, respondents were (probably unwittingly) endorsing an expansion of the law into unconstitutional territory.

2. 8 USC §1189(a)(1).

3. For the powers, see Terrorism Act 2000 (UK), c 11, s 3; Criminal Code, RSC 1985, C-46, s 83.05; Criminal Code 1995 (Cth), s 102.1; Terrorism Suppression Act 2002 (NZ) (hereinafter TSA), ss 20, 22.

4. Three years has been the limit since 2010 and it was previously two years.

5. TSA, s 35(1).

6. PL 108–458, Title A, § 7119, 118 Stat 3801 (United States); Department of Public Safety and Emergency Preparedness Act, SC 2005, c 10, s 18(3) (Canada).

7. TSA, s 3 (definition of designated terrorist entity).

8. United Nations Al-Qaida and Taliban Regulations (Can) SOR/99-444, s 1 (definitions).

9. Charter of the United Nations (Terrorism and Dealing with Assets) Regulations 2002 (Cth), reg 6A, made under Charter of the United Nations Act 1945 (Cth), s 18.

10. Al-Qaida and Taliban (Asset-Freezing) Regulations 2010 (UK), SI 2010/1197.

11. Listing is by regulation: Regulations Implementing the United Nations Resolutions on the Suppression of Terrorism (Can) SOR/2001-360, ss 1 (definition of "listed person"), 2(1), Sch. The Australian foreign minister has exercised powers conferred under Charter of the United Nations (Terrorism and Dealing with Assets) Regulations 2002, reg 6, made under Charter of the United Nations Act 1945, s 15: for the list, see http://www.dfat.gov.au/icat/UNSC_financial_sanctions.html.

12. Terrorist Asset-Freezing etc Act 2010 (UK), c 38.

13. On the antecedents of these decisions, see Chesney 2005, 4–12.

14. President Clinton's Executive Order 12497 listed entities and imposed sanctions and was issued under the authority of the International Emergency Economic Powers Act of 1977 (IEEPA) (codified at 50 USC §§1701ff; for an analysis, see *United States v Lindh* 212 F Supp 2d 541, 558–560 (ED Va 2002). President Bush's Executive Order 13224 was made under the IEEPA and the United Nations Participation Act of 1945

(on the basis of Resolutions 1214, 1267, 1333, and 1363). Annexes to the orders listed individuals, groups, and groups associated with those listed. The orders delegated rule-making powers. (The act permits this (50 USC § 1704), and this has been held not to constitute an impermissible delegation of legislative power: see *United States v Dhafir* 461 F 3d 211 (2d Cir 2006).) Regulations made pursuant to the delegated powers have permitted subdelegation. Part 595 of Title 31 of the Code of Federal Regulations supplements, Order 12947; Part 594 of Title 31 supplements, Order 13224.

15. 8 USC § 1182(a)(3)(B)(i).

16. 8 USC § 1182(a)(3)(B)(iv)(IV)(bb), (cc); (V)(bb), (cc); (VI)(cc), (dd).

17. 8 USC § 1182(a)(3)((B)(i)(I), (II).

18. 8 USC § 1182(a)(3)((B)(i)(III). This is not so if the person could demonstrate by clear and convincing evidence that they could not reasonably have known that the group was a terrorist organisation.

19. Martin 2009,15–17; McCarthy 2002, 451–52.

20. Immigration and Refugee Protection Act, SC 2001, c 27, s 34(1)(f).

21. *Motehaver v Canada (Minister of Public Safety and Emergency Preparedness)* 2009 FC 141; [2009] FCJ No 190, [18]. The court judgment suggests that it had been delisted, but it had never been listed, and the court may be confusing UN delisting with the organisation's recent delisting by the Council of the European Community.

22. Immigration Act 2009 (NZ), ss 16(1)(b), 73(1)(c).

23. 31 CFR §§ 594.201, 594.202 (SDGTs), 595.201, 595.204 (SDTs). See also 8 USC § 1189(a)(2)(C) (the secretary of the Treasury may require institutions to block dealings in organisation's assets on notification, on notification to congressional leaders of the intention to designate), and 8 CFR § 597.201 (FTOs); Al-Qaida and Taliban (Anti-Freezing) Regulations 2010 (UK), SI 2010/1197, s 3; Charter of the United Nations Act 1945, s 20; United Nations Al-Qaida and Taliban Regulations, SOR/99-444, ss 4, 4.1; Criminal Code, s 83.08; Regulations Implementing the United Nations Resolutions on the Suppression of Terrorism, SOR/2001-360, s 4; TSA, s 9. Until 2007, the TSA had applied only to organisations designated under the act, while the United Nations Sanctions (Afghanistan) Regulations 2001 (NZ) governed entities designated under the al-Qaeda/Taliban regime.

24. 24 April 1996, PL 104–132, § 302(a), 110 Stat 1248; am by Act, 30 September 1996, PL 104, §§ 356, 671(c)(1), 110 Stat 3644, 3733; 26 October 2001, PL 107–56, § 411(c), 115 Stat 349; 17 December 2004, PL 108–458, § 7119(a)–(c), 118 Stat 3801, codified at 8 USC § 1189(a)(1). While it was passed in the aftermath of the Lockerbie and Oklahoma bombings, it could trace its ancestry to legislation drafted in response to the 1993 bombing of the World Trade Center: see Martin 2006, 211–12.

25. See Donohue 2007, 100–105, 147–51, 218–20, 236, 242, 253, 288–89.

26. Australia, Senate, Legal and Constitutional Legislation Committee, 2002, 45–58.

27. Criminal Code Amendment (Hizballah) Act 2003 (Cth); Criminal Code Amendment (Hamas and Lashkar-e-Tayyiba) Act 2003 (Cth).

28. Criminal Code Amendment (Terrorist Organisations) Act 2004 (Cth); Anti-Terrorism Act (No 2) 2005 (Cth).

29. On the AEDPA, see, e.g., Chesney 2005, 15–18.

30. Omnibus Counterterrorism Act of 1995, HR 896, s 301 (adding proposed 18 USC § 2339B).

31. United States, House of Representatives, Judiciary Committee, 1995, 3.

32. See http://nationalsecurity.gov.au/Listedterroristorganizations/Pages/default.aspx (20 April 2014).

33. See http://www.osfi-bsif.gc.ca/Eng/fi-if/amlc-clrpc/atf-fat/Pages/default.aspx for a complete list of listed organisations and individuals; http://www.publicsafety.gc.ca/cnt/ntnl-scrt/cntr-trrrsm/lstd-ntts/crrnt-lstd-ntts-eng.aspx for criminal law listings (Canada: 50 organisations); https://www.gov.uk/government/publications/proscribed-terror-groups-or-organisations--2 (United Kingdom: 55 international and 14 Northern Irish organisations proscribed under Terrorism Act 2000 (UK), 2 under the Terrorism Act 2006 (UK)); http://www.state.gov/j/ct/rls/other/des/123085.htm (United States: 58 organisations). Prior to 2010, New Zealand had not proscribed any organisations other than those listed by the 1267 Committee. Since then, it has proscribed 19 additional entities, so its list corresponds closely with the criminal sanctions lists of Canada, the United Kingdom, and the United States. See http://www.police.govt.nz/advice/personal-community/counterterrorism/designated-entities#anchor3. Numbers and URLs are as at 20 April 2014.

34. See Lynch et al. 2009, 6–7.

35. On the murky politics surrounding ongoing attempts to secure its delisting, see Bennett-Jones 2012.

36. Ibid., 9.

37. http://www.hm-treasury.gov.uk/d/terrorism.htm.

38. *Yates v United States* 354 US 298 (1957).

39. (1951) 83 CLR 1.

40. E.g., Beall 1998, 699–705; Cole and Dempsey 2006, 198–201, 204–5.

41. See Lynch et al. 2009, 16.

42. 18 USCS § 1189(a)(3), 1189(c).

43. *People's Mojahedin Organization of Iran v United States Department of State* 182 F 3d 17, 22 (DC Cir 1999).

44. 251 F 3d 192 (DC Cir 2001).

45. *National Council of Resistance of Iran v Department of State* 251 F 3d 192, 208 (DC Cir 2001).

46. Ibid., 209.

47. Ibid.

48. *People's Mojahedin Organization of Iran v Department of State* 327 F 3d 1238, 1242 (DC Cir 2003).

49. PL 108–458, § 7019(a)(2), 18 Stat 3801; 8 USC § 1189(a)(4)(B).

50. *People's Mojahedin Organization of Iran v Department of State* 327 F 3d, 1244.

51. *National Council of Resistance of Iran v Department of State* 373 F 3d 152 (DC Cir 2004).

52. *People's Mojahedin Organization of Iran v United States* 613 F 3d 220 (DC Cir 2010).

53. Ibid., 230–31; but cf. Justice Henderson at 231.

54. *In re People's Mojahedin Organization of Iran* 680 F 3d 832 (DC Cir 2012).

55. United States, Department of State, 2012.

56. In the Kahane litigation, the court did advert to this issue, noting that while the 2004 designation had superseded the 2003 designation, the validity of the 2003 designation had not thereby been rendered moot: it would be of continued relevance in relation to anyone prosecuted for giving material support to any of the organizations (*Kahane Chai v Department of State* 466 F 3d 125, 133 (DC Cir 2006)).

57. Nine defendants were charged with a variety of activities related to the activi-

ties of MEK, but only seven were charged under section 2339B and were parties to the litigation surrounding MEK's designation.

58. *United States v Afshari* 426 F 3d 1150 (9th Cir, 2005).

59. *United States v Afshari* 446 F 3d 915 (9th Cir, 2006).

60. *Rahmani v United States* 2007 US LEXIS 43 (2007).

61. *United States v Afshari* 2009 US Dist LEXIS 31585, 8 (CD Cal 2009).

62. 50 USCS §§ 1701ff.

63. *United States v Al Arian* 308 F Supp 2d 1322, 1332 (D Fla 2004).

64. *Global Relief Foundation v O'Neill* 315 F 3d 748, 754 (7th Cir 2002); *Holy Land Foundation for Relief and Development v Ashcroft* 333 F 3d 156 (DC Cir 2003).

65. *Global Relief Foundation v O'Neill* 315 F 3d, 754; *Holy Land Foundation v Ashcroft* 219 F Supp 2d 57 (D DC 2002); Holy Land Foundation for Relief and Development v Ashcroft, 333 F 3d 156; *Islamic American Relief Agency v Gonzales* 477 F 3d 728 (DC Cir 2007) (where the court regarded the classified information as strengthening the government's case).

66. *Holy Land Foundation v Ashcroft* 219 F Supp 2d 57; Holy Land Foundation for Relief and Development v Ashcroft 333 F 3d 156; *Al Haramain Islamic Foundation v Department of the Treasury* 2009 US Dist LEXIS 103373, 15–27 (D Ore 2009).

67. *KindHearts for Charitable Humanitarian Development v Geithner* 710 F Supp. 2d 637 (ND Ohio 2010).

68. *Holy Land Foundation v Ashcroft* 219 F Supp 2d 57; *Holy Land Foundation for Relief and Development v Ashcroft* 333 F 3d 156; *Islamic American Relief Agency v Gonzales*, 734; *Al Haramain Islamic Foundation v United States Department of the Treasury* 585 F Supp 2d 1233 (D Ore 2008).

69. 2009 US Dist LEXIS 103373 (D Ore 2009).

70. *KindHearts for Charitable Humanitarian Development v Geithner* 647 F Supp 2d 857, 881 (ND Ohio 2009).

71. *KindHearts for Charitable Humanitarian Development v Geithner* 710 F Supp 2d 637.

72. American Civil Liberties Union 2012.

73. A history of the litigation is provided in *Holder v Humanitarian Law Project* 130 S Ct 2705, 2713–17 (2010).

74. *Holder v Humanitarian Law Project*, 2724.

75. Ibid., 2726.

76. Ibid., 2727–28.

77. Ibid., 2740–41 (2010).

78. Proscribed Organisations Appeal Commission (Procedure) Rules 2001 (UK), SI 2001/1286.

79. [2002] EWHC 644.

80. R *(Kurdistan Workers' Party and Others) v Secretary of State for the Home Department* [2002] EWHC 644, [76]–[77].

81. Relevant excerpts of the judgment are quoted in *Lord Alton v Secretary of State for the Home Department* (Proscribed Organisations Appeal Commission, unreported, 30 November 2007), [61].

82. The history of this litigation is set out in *Lord Alton v Secretary of State for the Home Department* (Proscribed Organisations Appeal Commission, unreported, 30 November 2007), [1]–[11].

83. Ibid., [62].

84. Ibid., [105]–[109].

85. Ibid., [110].
86. Ibid., [115].
87. Ibid., [355]–[358].
88. *Secretary of State for the Home Department v Lord Alton of Liverpool* [2008] EWCA Civ 443; [2008] 1 WLR 2341, [33]–[43].
89. *A and Others v HM Treasury* [2008] EWHC 869 (Admin); [2008] 3 All ER 361.
90. *A and Others v HM Treasury* [2008] EWCA Civ 1187; [2009] 3 WLR 25.
91. *Her Majesty's Treasury v Ahmed* [2010] UKSC 2; [2010] 2 AC 534, [56]–[61] (Lord Hope, with whom Lord Walker and Lady Hale agreed), [107]–[144] (Lord Phillips), [197]–[201] (Lord Brown), [225]–[231] (Lord Mance).
92. Ibid., [66]–[75] (Lord Hope, with whom Lord Walker and Lady Hale agreed), [89]–[106] (Lord Phillips), [203] (Lord Brown).
93. Ibid., [71] (Lord Hope, with whom Lord Walker and Lady Hale agreed), [203] (Lord Brown).
94. Ibid., [75]–[82] (Lord Hope, with whom Lord Walker and Lady Hale agreed), [184]–[185] (Lord Rodgers, with whom Lord Walker and Lady Hale agreed), [237]–[249] (Lord Mance).
95. Ibid., [183] (Lord Rogers, with whom Lord Walker and Lady Hale agreed).
96. Ibid., [203].
97. Terrorist Asset-Freezing (Temporary Provisions) Act 2010 (UK) c 2.
98. Ibid., ss 26, 28, 29.
99. Ibid., s 2 (1)(a).
100. Al Qaida and Taliban (Asset-Freezing) Regulations 2010, SI 2010/1197, giving effect to Council Regulation (EC) No 881/2002.
101. This was prior to the amendments under which entities are listed on no more than one list.
102. Cf. Dyzenaus 2005 (arguing that the procedure of the 1267 Committee is itself contrary to an overriding rule of international law: the requirement of legality).
103. Dosman 2004, 15–19.
104. *Abdelrazik v Canada (Minister of Foreign Affairs)* 2009 FC 580; [2010] 1 FCR 267, [51], [53].
105. Ibid.
106. British Columbia Civil Liberties Association 2010.
107. United Nations Security Council 2011.
108. Terrorism Suppression Amendment Act 2005 (NZ), s 6; Terrorism Suppression (Amendment) Act 2007 (NZ), s 20.

CHAPTER 7

1. *Rahman v R* [2008] EWCA Crim 1465; [2008] 4 All ER 661, [8] (Lord Phillips of Worth and Matravers CJ).
2. See Zabel and Benjamin 2008, 33–34, for a discussion of the relationship between the elements of material assistance offences and conspiracy and attempt offences.
3. Metcalfe 2007, 32–35; E. Parker 2007, 753 (citing arguments to this effect).
4. Roach 2001, 160.
5. Chesney 2007a, 447–75.
6. *R v Déry* 2006 SCC 53; [2006] 2 SCR 669, [34]–[35].

7. Ibid., [38].

8. Ashdown 2006, 780–81.

9. On the relationship between charitable provision and terrorist organisations, see, e.g., Flanigan 2006.

10. Roach and Trotter 2005, 994–95.

11. 18 USC § 2332b(g)(5). This requirement means that if a person contributes under the intent that the contribution be used for the group's nonterrorist activities, the enhancement is not attracted: see *United States v Chandia* 2010 US App LEXIS 19178 (4th Cir 2010) (citing *United States v Hammoud* 381 F 3d 316, 356 (4th Cir 2004), *United States v Benkhala* 530 F 3d 300, 313 (4th Cir 2008)).

12. Terrorism Act 2000 (UK), c 11, s 41, Sch 8; Crimes Act 1914 (Cth) (hereinafter CAA), ss 23DB-23DF.

13. CAA, ss 23CA, 23CB, 23DA.

14. Turner and Schulhofer 2005, 37–40.

15. 18 USC § 3142(e)(1).

16. 18 USC § 3142(e)(3)(C) (if the offence carries a maximum term of 10 years or more). The relevant amendment was made by PL 108–458, § 6952, 118 Stat 3775.

17. 18 USC § 3142(g)(1). The relevant amendment was made by PL 108–458, § 6952, 118 Stat 3775.

18. Criminal Code, RSC 1985, c C-46, s 515(6)(a)(ii), as amended by Anti-terrorism Act, SC 2001, c 41, s 19(4).

19. CAA, s 15AA. The relevant amendment was made by *Anti-terrorism Act 2004* (Cth), Sch item 1B.

20. See, e.g., *Rahman v* R [2008] EWCA 1465; [2008] 4 All ER 661.

21. United States Sentencing Guidelines § 3A1.4.

22. Counter-Terrorism Act 2008 c 28, ss 30–33, Sch 2; Criminal Code, RSC 1985, c C-46, s 718(a)(5).

23. CAA, s 19AG.

24. PL 104–132, § 303, 110 Stat 1250.

25. United States, House of Representatives, Judiciary Committee, 1995, 178–80 (dissent), 189 (dissenters).

26. PL 107–56, §§ 803, 805, 115 Stat 376, 377.

27. PL 108–458 § 6952, 118 Stat 3775.

28. United Kingdom, Parliament, Joint Committee on Human Rights, 2005.

29. Zabel and Benjamin 2008, 21–22.

30. Ibid.; Zabel and Benjamin 2009.

31. Chesney 2007c.

32. The Center on Law and Security (2010, 3) defines "terrorism charges" as offenses against §§ 2339A–2339D, Chapter 113B offences, and 18 USC §§ 1992, 1993 (terrorist attacks on mass transportation systems).

33. Chesney 2005, 18–20.

34. Chesney 2007c, 879, 885. The figure is 26, based on a comparison between the two lists of defendants given in Chesney's appendices A and B.

35. Zabel and Benjamin 2009, 9.

36. United Kingdom, Home Office, 2009, 10 (table 3(a)).

37. Ibid., 11 (table 3(b)).

38. Ibid., 5 (table A).

39. Kissane et al. 2008.

40. Catanzariti 2009, 13.

41. Hagan 2010, 3.

42. Munro 2010.

43. See *R v Mallah* [2005] NSWSC 317 (threat to kill official, but not for political purposes); Swanwick 2009 (bombs not for terrorist purposes); *R v Thomas* [2006] VSCA 165; (2006) 14 VR 475 (appeal on terrorism charge allowed).

44. *R v Ul-Haque* [2007] NSWSC 1251; (2007) 177 A Crim R 348.

45. *R v Khawaja* 2011 ONCA 862; 103 OR (3d) 321, special leave granted, *Khawaja v R* [2011] JSCC No 34103.

46. *R v Ahmad* 2009 CanLII 84788; 257 CCC (3d) 135.

47. *R v Thambaithurai* 2011 BCCA 137; 302 BCAC 288.

48. O'Toole 2011.

49. Cumming and Masters 2012.

50. Indeed, they sometimes consider them to be inadequate: see the trial judge's remarks, cited in *R v Sherif* [2008] EWCA Crim 2653, [45].

51. See, e.g., *R v Barot*, [2007] EWCA Crim 1119, [37] (a terrorism case where the principal offence was conspiracy to murder; but see at [61]: allowance also to be made for whether a conspiracy is likely to have led to an attempt and whether the attempt would have proved successful); *Lodhi v The Queen* (2007) A Crim R 470, [79] (Spiegelman CJ), [211] (Barr J), [229] (Price J); *R v Amara* 2010 ONSC 441; [2010] OJ No 181, [102]–[106].

52. See, e.g., *United States v Abu Ali* 528 F 3d 210 (4th Cir 2008); *Lodhi v R* [2006] NSWCCA 360; 2007 179 A Crim R 470, [221] (Price J, with whom Spiegelman CJ and Barr J agreed); *R v Amara*, [120], [121].

53. See, e.g., *R v Barot*, [54]; *Lodhi v R* [2006] NSWCCA 360; 2007 179 A Crim R 470; cf. *R v Roche* (2008) 188 FLR 336 (where there was evidence of remorse); *R v Sherif*, [45]; *R v Kent* [2009] VSC 375, [46].

54. Under Canadian law, those sentenced to "life" imprisonment may be released on parole as early as 10 years into their sentence.

55. *R v Amara* 2010 ONSC 441; [2010] OJ No 181.

56. *United States v Jayyousi* F 3d 1085, 1117 (11th Cir 2011) (citing *United States v Meskini* 319 F 3d 88, 92 (2d Cir 2003)).

57. Ibid., 1132–33.

58. Center on Law and Security 2010, 13.

59. Zabel and Benjamin 2009, 41–42.

60. Center on Law and Security 2010,14–15.

61. Zabel and Benjamin 2009, 9.

62. United Kingdom, Home Office, 2009, 18–19 (tables 8(a), 8(b). Sentencing data are provided only for 2007–8. The number of custodial sentences for terrorism offences exceeds the number of convictions in 2007–8 for which a terrorism offence was the most serious conviction charge. The number of custodial sentences for defendants not convicted under terrorism legislation falls far short of the number of defendants for whom a nonterrorist charge was the principal conviction charge.

63. Hagan 2010, 3.

64. *R v Amara* 2010 ONSC 441; [2010] OJ No 181 (9 years and life for sentences carrying maxima of 10 years and life, to be served concurrently).

65. *R v Amara*, ibid., [68]–[74].

66. *R v Thambaithurai* 2011 BCCA 137; 302 BCAC 288.

67. Zabel and Benjamin 2009, 7.

68. *Attorney General's Reference (No 4 of 2002)* [2004] UKHL 43; [2005] 1 AC 264.

69. *Zafar v R* [2008] EWCA Crim 184; *R v K* [2008] EWCA Crim 185; [2008] QB 827; R *v* M [2007] EWCA Crim 298; [2008] Crim LR 71 (interpreting sections 57 and 58 and the different operations of the two sections).

70. Roach 2008, 36.

71. Ibid., 36.

72. Sturcke 2009.

73. Kissane et al. 2008.

74. Catanzariti 2009, 13.

75. Ripley 2002.

76. CNN 2004.

77. In its narrative of the circumstances leading up to Abdi's being charged, the Fourth Circuit's judgment states that he had initially come to the notice of the authorities because Iyman Faris had told them that he had said he intended to "shoot up" a shopping center. Abdi denied this in subsequent interviews but was alleged to have admitted that he intended to bomb a shopping center (*United States v Abdi* 463 F 2d 547 (6th Cir 2006)). The judgment does not expressly say that he in fact confessed to this.

78. United States, Department of Justice, 2003.

79. See United States Department of Justice, Office of the Inspector General, 2006; and for additional details, see *Mayfield v United States* 504 F Supp 2d 1023, 1026–1029 (D Ore 2007) (the two sources yield slightly different versions of the story; that contained in the judgment is partly a narrative of claims by the plaintiffs).

80. Roach and Trotter 2005, 988–89; Turner and Schulhofer 2005, 70–71.

81. Roach and Trotter 2005, 975–81.

82. Smith 2005.

83. Clarke 2008, 1:45–206.

84. Cumming and Masters 2012.

85. Difo 2010, 8–10.

CHAPTER 8

1. Quoted in Chesney 2005, 31.

2. Obama 2010, 22.

3. Pilkington 2012, 6.

4. Boot and Kirkpatrick 2009.

5. Executive Order 13492 of 22 January 2009, 74 FR 4897; Amnesty International 2005; Fletcher and Stover 2009, 245.

6. See *Kiyemba v Obama* 605 F 3d 1046, 1048 (DC Cir 2010) (citing the legislation and ruling that it was not unconstitutional).

7. "US Could Allow Guantanamo Visits" 2011, 8; Pilkington 2012, 6; Harris 2013.

8. Goldsmith 2007, 107–9. For the legal advice, see Philbin and Yoo 2005, 29.

9. On the combatant status review tribunals, which found in favour of fewer than 8 percent of detainees, see Denbeaux and Hafetz 2009, 148–68; Forsythe 2011, 171–72. Others were released following recommendations by annual review boards. Wittes (2008, 72–102) is also critical of the procedures but argues that a considerable proportion of those detained had links with al-Qaeda or the Taliban.

10. Codified at 18 USC § 4001(a).

11. 542 US 507 (2004).

12. 115 Stat 224.

13. *Rasul v Bush* 542 US 466 (2004).

14. Detainee Treatment Act of 2005, PL 109–163, Title X, § 1405(e)(1), 119 Stat 3477, amending 28 USC § 2241.

15. *Hamdan v Rumsfeld* 548 US 557 (2006).

16. Military Commissions Act of 2006, PL 109–336, § 7, 120 Stat 2635, amending 28 USC § 2241.

17. *Boumediene v Bush* 553 US 723 (2008).

18. As to the implications of the decision, see, e.g., Fallon 2010, 378–96.

19. Wittes et al. 2010.

20. Cole 2010, 49; Worthington 2012b.

21. See *Al Maqaleh v Obama* 605 F 3d 84, 98 (DC Cir 2010) ("the writ [of habeas corpus] does not extend to the Bagram confinement in an active theatre of war in a territory under neither the *de facto* nor *de jure* sovereignty of the United States and within the territory of another *de jure* sovereign").

22. Grey 2007.

23. Ibid., 89 (CIA prisons), 267 (in 2006, the prisons were closed, and the remaining 14 prisoners were transferred to Guantánamo).

24. Grey (2007, 115) estimated that "hundreds" had been transferred.

25. Examples are Khaled El-Masri and Abu Omar, who was initially confined to Egypt following his release. See Grey 2007, 93–94,197.

26. Grey 2007, 237–39.

27. Bringing a person into the United States against the person's will and without resort to extradition procedures is permitted for the purpose of securing the person's presence at a trial before US courts for an offence against US law, but the extraordinary rendition program was devised because trial of suspected terrorists was often not feasible. Originally, rendition to third countries was approved on the basis that transferees would be given a fair trial in the third country. Those involved in the program knew otherwise. See Grey 2007, 125–42.

28. Grey 2007, 188–211; Shapiro 2012.

29. 66 FR 54909.

30. Amnesty International 2002; Tumlin 2004, 1186, 1197–1203.

31. Lobel 2002, 778–80; Cole 2009, 703–4.

32. *Turkmen v Ashcroft* 589 F 3d 542 (2d Cir 2009).

33. *Ashcroft v Iqbal* 129 S Ct 1937, 1951–52 (2009).

34. *Zadvydas v Davis* 533 US 678 (2001).

35. Ibid., 696 (per Breyer J, delivering the majority judgment).

36. PL 107–56 § 412, 115 Stat 351, codified at 8 USC § 1226a.

37. Cole 2009, 694; Wittes 2008, 136.

38. See, e.g., Chesney 2005, 34–37; Nesbitt 2007, 57–64.

39. Human Rights Watch 2005.

40. 403 US 368 (1999).

41. *Al-Kidd v Ashcroft* 580 F 3d 949 (9th Cir 2010), reh'g denied, 598 F 3d 1129 (9th Cir 2010); *Ashcroft v Al-Kidd* 131 S Ct 2074 (2011).

42. *Al-Kidd v Gonzales* 1:05-cv-093-EJL-MHW, docs 331, 332 (orders dismissing applications against senior officials, agencies, and Ashcroft), 336 (report re Agents Grencko and Mace), 337 (report re United States); 2012 US Dist LEXIS 141025 (Id D 2012).

43. Stent 1980.

44. English 2003, 139–42; T. Parker 2007; Blackbourn 2009, 137.

45. United Kingdom, Intelligence and Security Committee, 2005, [8] ("Handling of detainees"); *R (Maya Evans) v Secretary of State for Defence* [2010] EWHC 1445 (Admin), [19]–[48].

46. Memorandum of Understanding between the Government of the United Kingdom of Great Britain and Northern Ireland and the Government of the Islamic Republic of Afghanistan Concerning Transfer by the United Kingdom Armed Forces to Afghan Authorities of Persons Detained in Afghanistan, in United Kingdom, House of Commons, Foreign Affairs Committee, 2007, appendix 3, [3.1], [3.3]. Despite this agreement, three people had been transferred to US custody: see *R (Maya Evans) v Secretary of State for Defence*, [135].

47. On the nature of these arrangements and their implications for whether the internment power is governed by the ECHR, see *Al-Jedda v United Kingdom* [2011] ECHR 1092; (2011) 53 EHRR 23.

48. United Kingdom, House of Commons, Foreign Affairs Committee, 2007, [4]; Cobain and Norton-Taylor 2010.

49. Amnesty International 2005, 67–68; United Kingdom, House of Commons, Foreign Affairs Committee, 2007, 48, 50, 53, 54 (reporting views of the Foreign and Commonwealth Office).

50. Cobain and Norton-Taylor 2010.

51. United Kingdom, House of Commons, Foreign Affairs Committee, 2007, 28–29.

52. United Kingdom, House of Commons, Foreign Affairs Committee, 2005, [78]–[79]; 2006, [40].

53. Anti-terrorism, Crime and Security Act 2001 (UK), c 24, s 23; for background, see, e.g., Metcalfe 2007, 13–18.

54. As of December 2003, 16 foreign nationals had been detained; 2 had voluntarily left the United Kingdom, and 14 remained in detention: see United Kingdom, Privy Counsellor Review Committee, 2003, 51.

55. Ibid., 50.

56. Ibid., 52–56.

57. *A v Secretary of State for the Home Department* [2004] UKHL 56; [2005] 2 AC 68.

58. Prevention of Terrorism Act 2005 (UK), c 2.

59. Lord Carlile of Berriew 2011, 7.

60. Metcalfe 2007, 35.

61. *A v United Kingdom*, [2009] ECHR 301; (2009) EHRR 29, applied (albeit with limited enthusiasm) in *Secretary of State for the Home Department v AF* [2009] UKHL 28; [2010] AC 269.

62. Lord Carlile of Berriew 2011, 8.

63. May 2011, 36–42.

64. For an assessment of the legislation, see Roach 2006, 2198–2201.

65. United Kingdom, Parliament, Joint Committee on Human Rights, 2007, 9.

66. Quoted in *Amnesty International Canada v Canada (Attorney General)* 2008 FC 336; [2008] FCJ No 356, [55].

67. Ibid., [61]–[63], [66]–[67].

68. Ibid., [75]–[81].

69. Canada, Commission of Inquiry, 2005.

70. The periods were November 2001–January 2002 (Elmaati), May 2002–March 2004 (Almalki), and December 2003–January 2004 (Nureddin).

71. Iacobucci 2008, 349–57 (Elmaati), 438–46 (Nureddin).

72. *Amnesty International Canada v Canada (Attorney General)*, [85].

73. Immigration and Refugee Protection Act, SC 2001, c 27, ss 76–81.

74. *Charkaoui v Canada (Citizenship and Immigration)* 2007 SCC 9; [2007] 1 SCR 350.

75. Security certificates have been used on about 30 occasions: see *Harkat (Re)* 2010 FC 1242, [228].

76. Anti-terrorism Act, SC 2001, c 41, s 4, amending Criminal Code, RSC 1985, c C-46, by the addition of sections 83.29 (arrest to secure presence at an investigatory hearing) and 83.3 (detention where a peace officer reasonably believes a terrorist attack will be carried out and that arrest of a person is necessary to prevent it).

77. See Roach 2006, 2212–14 (use of the powers); Roach 2008, 25–28 (on the circumstances surrounding the refusal to extend the powers).

78. Roach 2008, 30–33; SC 2013, c 9, s 10.

79. For this reason, Hicks sought registration as a UK citizen. The home secretary refused registration. Hicks succeeded in an application for judicial review of the refusal: see *Hicks v Secretary of State for the Home Department* [2005] EWHC 2818 (Admin), appeal dismissed, *Secretary of State for the Home Department v Hicks* [2006] EWCA 400. The home secretary took six months to consider the application, granted citizenship, and then immediately cancelled it, using new powers: see Crabb 2006.

80. Coorey and Banham 2007.

81. For a critical analysis of the relevant proceedings, see Law Council of Australia 2007.

82. Criminal Code Act 1995 (Cth), Div 104, added by Anti-Terrorism Act (No 2) 2005, Sch 4, item 24.

83. Australian Security Intelligence Organisation Act 1979, ss 34F–34H, 34S, added by Australian Security Intelligence Organisation Legislation Amendment (Terrorism) Act 2003, Sch 1, item 24. For subsequent amendments, see Notes to the Act.

84. Criminal Code Act 1995 (Cth), Div 105, added by Anti-Terrorism Act (No 2) 2005, Sch 4, item 24.

85. *Al Kateb v Godwin* (2004) 219 CLR 562.

86. Munro 2011, 5.

87. Needham 2012, 5.

88. Australia, Parliament, Joint Select Committee, 2012, [6.125]–[6.152].

89. *Plaintiff M47 v Director General of Security* [2012] HCA 46; (2012) 292 ALR 243.

90. Immigration Act 1987 (NZ) Pt 4A, which was superseded by Immigration Act 2009 (NZ) Pt 9.

91. McCarthy 2002, 440, 449–50.

92. *Fox News*/Opinion Dynamics poll, September 2001, terrorism10.

93. *ABC News*/*Washington Post* poll, November 2001, terrorism8.

94. Howell 2004, 1203–05.

95. National Defense Authorization Act for Fiscal Year 2012, Pub L 112–81, §§ 1021, 1022, 125 Stat 1562. The former section stated that it did not purport to change existing law (§ 1021(d), (e)). The latter section, which targets al-Qaeda activists, may expose them to military detention for acts on US soil, but only if they are engaged in acts falling within the Authorization for Use of Military Force. A district court concluded that the scope of the act was much wider: see *Hedges v Obama* 2012 US Dist LEXIS 68683 (SD

NY 2012), clarified by *Hedges v Obama* 2012 US Dist LEXIS 78867 (SD NY 2012), which granted permanent injunctive relief, whose operation was almost immediately stayed by the court of appeals (*Hedges v Obama* 2012 US App LEXIS 19880 (2d Cir 2012)).

96. Section 19, which subsequently reversed the district court's decision, on the ground that the plaintiffs lacked standing: 740 F 3d 170 (2d Cir 2013).

97. Protection of Freedoms Act 2012 (UK), c 9, s 57.

98. ICM/BBC poll, 26 May 2004.

99. MORI poll, 7–9 April 2005, questions 24–26.

100. YouGov/*Spectator* survey, 14–15 August 2006.

101. Australian Security Intelligence Organisation Legislation Amendment Bill 2002 (Cth); Australian Security Intelligence Organisation Legislation Amendment (Terrorism) Act 2003 (Cth).

102. Anti-terrorism Act 2004 (Cth).

103. Anti-terrorism Act (No 2) 2005 (Cth).

104. *A v Secretary of State for the Home Department* [2004] UKHL 56; [2005] 2 AC 68.

105. *Charkaoui v Canada (Citizenship and Immigration)* 2007 SCC 9; [2007] 1 SCR 350, [129]–[132].

106. *Rahmatullah v Secretary of State for Foreign and Commonwealth Affairs* [2011] EWCA Civ 1540.

107. *Rahmatullah v Secretary of State for Foreign and Commonwealth Affairs (No 2)* [2012] EWCA Civ 182.

108. *Rasul v United States* 215 F Supp 2d 55 (D DC 2002); *Al Odah v United States* 321 F 3d 1134 (DC Cir 2003).

109. Chief Justice Roberts and Justices Thomas and Scalia dissented.

110. *Khalid v Bush* 355 F Supp 2d 311 (DC 2005); *In re Guantanamo Detainee Cases* 355 F Supp 2d 443 (DC Cir 2005).

111. 344 F Supp 2d 152 (D DC 2004); 415 F 3d 33 (DC Cir 2005).

112. 476 F 3d 981 (DC Cir 2007).

113. Worthington 2012a, 2012b.

114. For a summary of the history of some of the litigation given, see *Secretary of State for the Home Department v AF* [2010] EWHC 42 (Admin), [3]–[8].

115. *A v Secretary of State for the Home Department* [2002] EWCA (Civ) 1502; [2004] QB 335 (allowing appeal from Special Immigration Appeals Commission); [2004] UKHL 56, [2005] 2 AC 68 (of the nine Law Lords, only Lord Walker dissented on the validity issue).

116. *Charkaoui v Canada (Citizenship and Immigration)* 2007 SCC 9; [2007] 1 SCR 350.

117. Denbeaux and Hafetz 2009, 109ff.

118. United Kingdom, Parliament, Joint Committee on Human Rights, 2010, [42].

119. See, e.g., the case of *A/AF*, discussed in ibid., [89].

120. 2010 US App LEXIS 14263 (DC Cir 2010).

121. See chapter 9.

122. *Thomas v Mowbray* [2007] HCA 33; (2007) 233 CLR 307.

123. *Hicks v Ruddock* [2007] FCA 299; (2007) 156 FCR 574.

124. Human Rights Watch 2005, 45–58.

125. *Al-Adahi v Obama* 2010 US App LEXIS 14263 (DC Cir 2010); *United States v Chandia* 2010 US App LEXIS 19178, 11–12 (4th Cir 2010).

126. Jones 2009. See also Montopoli 2009.

127. Morales 2009. See also Jones 2009; Condon 2010.

128. Morales 2009.

129. ASSDA, Australian Survey of Social Attitudes (2007), v123, v545 by v539, weighted by v656.

130. United Kingdom, Parliament, Joint Committee on Human Rights, 2010c.

131. Cf. ibid., 46–48 (Dr. Evan Harris, MP, dissenting on several issues).

132. MORI poll, April 19, 2005.

133. YouGov poll, January 2011.

134. Detention at Guantánamo may be permitted in circumstances where information adverse to the detainee has been obtained by physical coercion. See *Salahi v Obama* 625 F 3d 745 (DC Cir 2010), noting that the circumstances in which admissions were made meant that while the detainee could not be prosecuted for providing material assistance, the court could nonetheless conclude that his detention might be justified.

135. Wittes 2008, 72–102.

CHAPTER 9

1. Cited in Taylor and Wittes 2009, 4, 6.

2. Grey 2007, 152.

3. Taguba 2004, [11].

4. Convention against Torture and Other Cruel, Inhuman or Degrading Treatment or Punishment 1465 UNTS 85, Arts 1, 2 (entered into force 26 June 1987) (hereinafter Torture Convention).

5. See, e.g., Parry 2010, 18–19, 28, 36–40.

6. Torture Convention, Art 1(1) ("any act by which severe pain or suffering, whether physical or mental, is intentionally inflicted on a person"), Art 16 (duty to prevent "other acts of cruel, inhuman or degrading treatment or punishment which do not amount to torture as defined in article 1").

7. Nowak 2006, 821–22.

8. Parry 2010, 55–75.

9. *Ahmed v R* [2011] EWCA Crim 184.

10. PL 103–236, § 506(a), 109 Stat 463, codified at 18 USC § 2340.

11. See, e.g., Fletcher and Stover 2009; Forsythe 2011; Sands 2009.

12. Mackey 2004.

13. See, e.g., Wittes 2008, 198–205.

14. Taguba 2004, [10].

15. Amnesty International 2005, 116–30.

16. Bybee 2005, 172; Yoo 2003.

17. These are discussed in United States, Department of Justice, Office of Professional Responsibility, 2009, 132–59, 241–51.

18. Goldsmith 2007, 150–51; Taylor and Wittes 2009, 9. For more details, see United States, Department of Justice, Office of Professional Responsibility, 2009, 30–37, 83–97.

19. Taylor and Wittes 2009, 11–14; Amnesty International 2005, 84–102, 103–6,124. As to the ill-treatment of those detained as "material witnesses," see Human Rights Watch 2005, 43–45.

20. Goldsmith 2007, 152–53.

21. PL 109–148, Div A Title X, § 1002, 119 Stat 2739.

22. Taylor and Wittes, 2009, 15.

23. PL 109–148, Div A, Title X, § 1004, 119 Stat 2740, codified at 42 USC § 2000dd-1.

24. *Hamdan v Rumsfeld* 548 US 557 (2006).

25. PL 109–336, §§ 5–8, 120 Stat 2639 (expanding the protections afforded by 42 USC § 2000dd-1).

26. HR 2082, Final Vote Results for Roll Call 117, 11 March 2008, http://clerk.house.gov/evs/2008/roll117.xml.

27. Executive Order 13491 of 22 January 2009, 74 FR 4893; Taylor and Wittes 2009, 2.

28. Davies et al. 2010.

29. Cobain et al. 2012.

30. *Ireland v UK* [1978] ECHR 1. The case was later to be cited in the US torture memoranda as authority for what constituted torture. As to its relevance to what constitutes torture, see United States, Department of Justice, Office of Professional Responsibility, 2009, 190–93.

31. Criminal Justice Act 1988 (UK), c 33, s 134.

32. Cited in R *(Mohamed) v Secretary of Foreign and Commonwealth Affairs* [2010] EWCA Civ 65; [2011] QB 218, [168].

33. United Kingdom, Intelligence and Security Committee, 2005, 13–18, 31.

34. Ibid., 31–32.

35. Ibid., 180–81.

36. *Al Rawi v Security Service* [2010] EWHC 1496 (QB).

37. United Kingdom 2010.

38. United Kingdom, Equality and Human Rights Commission, 2010. Its reservations about the suggestion that interrogation may proceed if risks are mitigated through caveats or assurances seems questionable if the effect of the caveats or assurances is that the interrogator believes that there is no longer a real risk of torture.

39. *(R) Mousa v Secretary of State for Defence* [2011] EWCA Civ 1334, [2]

40. Cobain and Norton-Taylor 2010.

41. The UK appears not to have been directly involved, but on two occasions, it has allowed the refuelling of planes that were en route to collect and transport detainees. The government denied awareness of the purpose of the flights. See, inter alia, Grey 2007, 228–30; Irfan Siddiq [Foreign Office] to Grace Cassy (assistant private secretary, 10 Downing Street), "Detainees," http://www.newstatesman.com/pdf/rendition/rendition.pdf (accessed 3 June 2011); Bright 2006.

42. Cobain 2012.

43. R *(Maya Evans) v Secretary of State for Defence* [2010] EWCA 1445 (Admin); Leigh 2010.

44. Davies et al. 2010.

45. Grey 2007; Cobain 2009 (list of questions provided by MI5 and Manchester police).

46. Grey 2007, 231.

47. Ibid. 226–27; Cobain 2009 (reporting both the current policy and instances of earlier cases of questioning by MI5 officials of people who had been tortured); Cobain and Norton-Taylor 2010.

48. United Kingdom, Intelligence and Security Committee, 2005, 9–10 (citing evidence given to the committee by the foreign secretary).

49. *A v Secretary of State for the Home Department (No 2)* [2005] UKHL 71; [2006] 2 AC 221, [115].

50. For summaries of the government's argument, see *A v Secretary of State for the Home Department (No 2)* [2005] UKHL 71; [2006] 2 AC 221, [46].

51. Criminal Code, RSC 1985, c C-46, s 269.
52. Canada, Commission of Inquiry, 2005.
53. Ibid., 360–95 (Elmaati), 405–35 (Almalki), 446–55 (Nureddin).
54. 2009 FC 580; [2010] 1 FCR 267, [91]–[93].
55. See *Canada (Prime Minister) v Khadr* 2010 SCC 3; [2010] SCJ No 3.
56. Canada. House of Commons. Special Committee on the Canadian Mission in Afghanistan 2009.
57. Canada, House of Commons, Standing Committee on Public Safety and National Security, 2009, appendix D.
58. BBC News 2012.
59. Criminal Code Act 1995 (Cth), Div 274. As to attempts, participation, and complicity, see sections 11.1, 11.2.
60. Banham 2006.
61. Australia, Defence Department, 2008.
62. No Australian died from enemy or friendly fire during Australia's period of involvement.
63. Australia, Senate, Foreign Affairs, Defence and Trade References Committee, 2005.
64. Habib 2008, 123–24, 127–28, 141, 150–51, 203, 225, 240–41.
65. *Habib v Commonwealth of Australia* [2010] FCAFC 12, [15]–[19] (Perram J, summarising the claims); (2010) 183 FCR 62.
66. Welch 2011, 7.
67. Australia, Inspector-General of Intelligence and Security, 2011.
68. Stephenson 2009.
69. Stephenson 2010.
70. Ibid.
71. "PM: Our Troops Don't Torture" 2010.
72. Taylor and Wittes report claims that coercive questioning has yielded valuable intelligence. They conclude that while these claims are generally far from conclusive, some claims (not relating to the War on Terror) are well documented, and other claims may not be without merit (Taylor and Wittes 2009, 10–12, 18–25; see also Wittes 2008, 190–98; United States, Department of Justice, Office of the Deputy Attorney General, 2010, 53). Indeed, media reports following the killing of Osama bin Laden claim that some of the information used in constructing the mosaic leading to the discovery of his whereabouts was derived from interrogation of prisoners at Guantánamo and elsewhere (Mazzetti et al. 2011, 18). For a more sceptical analysis, see United States, Department of Justice, Office of Professional Responsibility, 2009, 243–49. See also Sands 2009, 176–81. Chris Mackey (2004, xxii–xxiii), who is adamant that degradation is useless as a strategy, reports that one prisoner began cooperating after he realised that he was not going to be tortured. This last example suggests that the person being interrogated must at least have a fear that he might be tortured. This does not require that the belief have any grounds, and it might arise from enemy propaganda. But despite Mackey's confidence that torture would not work, one of the themes of his book is that he and those he worked with found it hard to extract information from prisoners without resorting to relatively coercive forms of questioning.
73. Phillips 2010, 96–109.
74. Mackey's 2004 account of his experiences as an interrogator in Afghanistan suggests the appeal of this reasoning.

75. Taft 2005, 129. The applicability question was distinct from the question of whether prisoners taken by the United States would enjoy prisoner-of-war status. There was general agreement that they would not. See Goldsmith 2007, 110–13; see also 154 (on military lawyers' opposition to the memoranda from the Office of Legal Counsel).

76. The CIA was determined that the State Department not learn of the program. See United States, Department of Justice, Office of Professional Responsibility, 2009, 38; see also 260 (where the report criticises the failure to circulate drafts of the torture memoranda to the State Department, given its interest in the interpretation of treaties).

77. Taylor and Wittes 2009, 12–13; Amnesty International 2005, 93; United States, Department of Justice, Office of Professional Responsibility, 2009, 30–33.

78. Morrow 2007.

79. On the centrality to the FBI of obtaining convictions, see Treverton 2009, 62–74.

80. See, e.g., Sands 2009.

81. See, e.g., Sands 2009; United States, Senate, Committee on Armed Services, 2008; Parry 2010, 171–203;, Forsythe 2011 (for the development of the legal responses).

82. United States, Department of Justice, Office of Professional Responsibility, 2009, 159–226.

83. Ibid., 252.

84. Ibid., 241–51.

85. United States, Department of Justice, Office of the Deputy Attorney General, 2010 (Margolis Memorandum).

86. *Mohammed v Obama* 704 F Supp 2d 1 (D DC 2009) (evidence adverse to petitioner); *Salahi v Obama* 625 F 3d 745 (DC Cir 2010).

87. E.g., *Al-Mithali v Bush* 2009 US Dist LEXIS 7033 (D DC 2009); *Lnu v Obama* 656 F Supp 2d 187 (D DC 2009); *Bin Attash v Obama* 628 F Supp 2d 24 (D DC 2009).

88. *Kiyemba v Obama* 561 F 3d 509 (DC Cir 2009), cert denied, 2010 US LEXIS 2462 (US, 22 March 2010), applying *Munaf v United States* 128 S Ct 2207, 2226 (2008) ("The judiciary is not suited to second-guess such determinations—determinations that would require federal courts to pass judgment on foreign justice systems and undermine the Government's ability to speak with one voice in this areas"). In *Kiyemba*, the government intended to return the detainees not to China (where they had come from) but to a country or countries willing to accept them.

89. *El-Masri v United States* 479 F 3d 296 (4th Cir 2007), cert denied, 552 US 947 (2007); *Mohamed v Jeppesen Dataplan* 614 F 3d 1070 (9th Cir, en banc, 2010), rev'g (6–5) 563 F 3d 992, 1007 (9th Cir 2009), cert denied, 131 S Ct 2442 (2011).

90. *Arar v Ashcroft* 585 F 3d 559 (2d Cir 2009), cert denied, 130 S Ct 3409 (2010).

91. *In re Iraq & Afghanistan Detainees Litigation* 479 F Supp 2d 85, 95 (D DC 2007).

92. *Ali v Rumsfeld* 649 F 3d 762, 773 (DC Cir 2011) (citing *In re Iraq & Afghanistan Detainees Litigation*, 105).

93. *Padilla v Yoo* 633 F Supp 2d 100 (ND Cal 2009).

94. *Lebron v Rumsfeld* 764 F Supp 2d 787, 799–800 (Charleston D SC 2011).

95. Ibid., 50–51.

96. *Lebron v Rumsfeld* 670 F 3d 540 (4th Cir 2012), cert denied, 132 S Ct 2751 (2012).

97. *Ashcroft v al-Kidd* 131 S Ct 2074, 2083 (2011).

98. *Padilla v Yoo* 678 F 3d 748 (9th Cir 2012).

99. Ibid., 766–68.

100. *Vance v Rumsfeld* 694 F Supp 2d 957 (ND Ill 2010); *Doe v Rumsfeld* 800 F Supp 2d 94 (D DC 2011)

101. *Vance v Rumsfeld* 653 F 3d 591 (7th Cir 2011), vacated by *Vance v Rumsfeld* 2011 US App LEXIS 22083 (7th Cir, 2011).

102. *Doe v Rumsfeld* 683 F 3d 390 (DC Cir 2012), reh'g, en banc, denied, 2012 US App LEXIS 15717 (DC Cir 2012).

103. *Vance v Rumsfeld* 701 F 3d 193 (7th Cir 2012).

104. Center for Constitutional Rights, *Turkmen v Ashcroft*, 2012, http://ccrjustice.org/ourcases/current-cases/turkmen-v.-ashcroft.

105. [2005] UKHL 71; [2006] 2 AC 221, [53] (Lord Bingham), [126] (Lord Hope).

106. *R v Ahmed* [2011] EWCA Crim 184, [30].

107. Ibid., [42]–[49].

108. *A v Secretary of State for the Home Department (No 2)* [2005] UKHL 71; [2006] 2 AC 221, per Lord Bingham [47] (prepared to accept); Lord Nicholls [69] (it might be ludicrous not to); Lord Hoffmann [93] (also noting [88] that evidence of the discovery of the ticking bomb would be admissible, notwithstanding that torture led to its discovery), Lord Rodger [132] (failure could involve breach of duty to protect); Lord Carswell [149] (a "very necessary ability"), Lord Brown [161]–[162], [171] ("bound to do so"; evidence of fruits admissible).

109. *R (Mohamed) v Secretary of Foreign and Commonwealth Affairs* [2010] EWCA Civ 65; [2011] QB 218, [168] (Neuberger LJ), and appendix, par (ix).

110. *R (Maya Evans) v Secretary of State for Defence* [2010] EWCA 1445 (Admin), [315]–[325].

111. [2011] EWCA Civ 1334.

112. *Al Rawi v Security Service* [2011] UKSC 34; [2012] AC 531.

113. Wintour 2010.

114. *Youssef v Home Office* [2004] EWHC 1884.

115. *Habib v Commonwealth of Australia* [2010] FCAFC 12; (2010) 183 FCR 62

116. See *Canada (Prime Minister) v Khadr* 2010 SCC 3; [2010] SCJ No 3.

117. *Abou-Elmaati v Canada (Attorney General)* 2011 ONSC 7720.

118. *Almalki v Canada (Attorney General)* 2012 ONSC 3023.

119. *Amnesty International Canada v Canada (Canadian Forces)* 2008 FCA 401; [2008] 4 FCR 546, application for special leave to appeal to Supreme Court dismissed, 2009 CanLII 25563.

120. Pew Research Center poll, 14–21 April 2009 (and earlier polls), http://www.pollingreport.com/terror2.htm.

121. Angus Reid Public Opinion poll, 19–21 February 2010 (torture against suspected terrorists by the US military and intelligence agencies always justified (13%), justified most of the time (21%), justified only sometimes (30%), never justified (30%)).

122. *Newsweek* poll, 10–11 November 2005, http://www.pollingreport.com/terror5.htm; Taylor and Wittes 2009, 4.

123. Ibid.

124. *USA Today*/Gallup poll, September 2006, http://www.pollingreport.com/terror3.htm.

125. *CBS News/New York Times* poll, 15–19 September 2006, http://www.pollingreport.com/terror3.htm. See also *ABC News/Washington Post* poll, 21–24 April 2009, http://www.pollingreport.com/terror2.htm.

126. CNN/Opinion Research Corporation poll, 2–4 November 2007, http://www.pollingreport.com/terror2.htm; *CBS News/New York Times* poll, 22–26 April 2009, http://www.pollingreport.com/terror2.htm; Angus Reid Public Opinion poll, 19–21 February 2010.

127. AP-GfK poll, 28 May–1 June 2009; CNN/Opinion Research Corporation poll, 23–26 April 2009, http://www.pollingreport.com/terror2.htm.

128. Angus Reid Public Opinion poll, 19–21 February 2010.

129. MORI poll, 7–9 April 2005, questions 24–26.

130. AP-Ipsos, September 2005, "Poll finds broad approval of terrorist torture" (61% of Americans as compared with "just over half" of British respondents), http://www.nbcnews.com/id/10345320/ns/world_news-americas/t/poll-finds-broad-approval-terrorist-torture/.

131. PIPA 2006.

132. United States, Department of Justice, Office of Professional Responsibility, 2009, 151–52.

133. Amnesty International 2005, 102n277.

134. Roll Call 117 of 2008.

135. *Newsweek* poll, 10–11 November 2005, terror5; Taylor and Wittes 2009, 4.

136. Angus Reid Public Opinion Poll, 19–21 February 2010.

137. Hetherington and Suhay 2012.

138. MORI poll, 7–9 April 2005.

139. ASSDA, Australian Survey of Social Attitudes (2007), v545 by v539, weighted by v656. For the logistic regression analysis, v545 was dichotomised, and low-frequency responses were excluded from the two categoric variables.

CONCLUSION

1. A case which might have resolved the question was decided against the plaintiffs on the grounds that the current circumstances of their detention did not make it unlawful: *Plaintiff M47 v Director General of Security* [2012] HCA 46; 292 ALR 243.

2. Daniels et al. 2001.

3. Howell 2004.

4. Wittes 2008.

5. *Al-Aulaqi v Obama* 727 F Supp 2d 1 (D DC 2010).

6. The only successful challenges related to the requirement that those served with NSLs keep this a secret. They must now be notified of their right to require the government to show cause why such an order should be made. Only one person has availed themselves of that right, and the matter was settled: Todd M Hinnen, Statement before the Subcommittee on Crime, Terrorism and Homeland Security, Committee on the Judiciary, United States House of Representatives, March 30, 2011, 8.

7. *A v Secretary of State for Home Affairs* [2005] AC 68, 102.

8. See chapter 4, note 13.

Bibliography

Publications

Aid, Matthew N. 2009. *The Secret Sentry: The Untold History of the National Security Agency*. New York: Bloomsbury.

Alford, John H., Carolyn L. Funk, and John R. Hibbing. 2005. "Are Political Attitudes Genetically Transmitted?" *American Political Science Review* 99:153–67.

Allen, M. 2007. "George W. Bush and the Nature of Executive Authority: The Role of Courts in a Time of Constitutional Change." *Brooklyn Law Review* 72: 871–938.

American Civil Liberties Union. 2012. "*KindHearts for Charitable Development, Inc. v. Geithner et al.*—Settlement." http://www.aclu.org/files/assets/kindhearts_v__geithner_-_settlement.pdf.

Amnesty International. 2002. *Amnesty International's Concerns Regarding Post September 11 Detentions in the USA*. http://www.amnesty.org/en/library/info/AMR51/044/2002.

Amnesty International. 2005. *Guantánamo and Beyond: The Continuing Pursuit of Unchecked Executive Power*. http://www.amnesty.org/en/library/info/AMR51/063/2005.

Ashdown, Gerald G. 2006. "The Blueing of America: The Bridge between the War on Drugs and the War on Terrorism." *University of Pittsburgh Law Review* 67:753–802.

ASIO (Australian Security Intelligence Organisation). 2003. *Report to Parliament, 2002–2003*. Available at http://www.asio.gov.au/Publications/Report-to-Parliament/Previous-Reports.html. Subsequent reports are also available at this site.

ASIO. 2004. *Report to Parliament, 2003–2004*.

ASIO. 2006. *Report to Parliament, 2005–2006*.

ASIO. 2007. *Report to Parliament, 2006–2007*.

ASIO, Director-General. 2006. "A Step Ahead: The Challenge for Counter-terrorism." Address delivered at the Security in Government Conference, 9 May. http://www.asio.gov.au/Publications/Speeches-and-Statements/2006/A-Step-Ahead-The-Challenge-for-Counter-Terrorism.html.

ASIO, Director-General. 2007. "National Security and Risk Management." Speech to Risk Management Institution of Australasia, 27 November.

Associated Press. 2005. "Bush: 'We Do Not Torture' Terror Suspects." http://www.nbcnews.com/id/9956644/ns/us_news-security/t/bush-we-do-not-torture-terror-suspects/.

Australia. Commonwealth Parliamentary Debates. http://www.aph.gov.au/Parliamentary_Business/Hansard/Hansreps_2011#2002.

Australia. 2006. *Terrorism Insurance Act Review 2006*. http://archive.treasury.gov.au/contentitem.asp?ContentID=1162.

Australia, Defence Department. 2008. *Inquiry Officer's Report into the Detention of Local*

Nationals on 29–30 April 2008 in Oruzgan Province, Afghanistan. www.defence.gov.au/publications/IOReportdetentionAfghanistan.pdf.

Australia, Inspector-General of Intelligence and Security. 2002–10. *Annual Reports, 2001–2002—2008–2009.* http://www.igis.gov.au/annual_report/index.cfm.

Australia, Inspector-General of Intelligence and Security. 2011. *Inquiry into the Actions of Australian Government Agencies in Relation to the Arrest and Detention Overseas of Mr Mamdouh Habib from 2001 to 2005.* http://www.igis.gov.au/inquiries/index.cfm#habib.

Australia, Parliament, Joint Select Committee on Australia's Immigration Network. 2012. *Final Report.* Accessed via http://www.aph.gov.au/Parliamentary_Business/Committees/Senate_Committees.

Australia, Senate, Foreign Affairs, Defence and Trade References Committee. 2005. *Duties of Australian Personnel in Iraq.* Accessed via http://www.aph.gov.au/Parliamentary_Business/Committees/Senate_Committees.

Australia, Senate, Legal and Constitutional Legislation Committee. 2002. *Inquiry into Security Legislation Amendment (Terrorism) Bill [No 2] [and Other Bills].* Report. Accessed via http://www.aph.gov.au/Parliamentary_Business/Committees/Senate_Committees.

Australia, Senate, Legal and Constitutional Legislation Committee. 2005. *Provisions of the Anti-terrorism Bill (No 2).* Accessed via http://www.aph.gov.au/Parliamentary_Business/Committees/Senate_Committees.

Australian Broadcasting Corporation. 2008. "3 Found Guilty over Liquid Bomb Plot." http://www.abc.net.au/news/2008–09–09/3-found-guilty-over-liquid-bomb-plot/503450.

Baker, Kevin. 2006. *Mutiny, Terrorism, Riots, and Murder: A History of Sedition in Australia and New Zealand.* Dural, New South Wales: Rosenberg.

Baker, Nancy V. 2006. *General Ashcroft: Attorney at War.* Lawrence: University of Kansas Press.

Banham, Cynthia. 2006. "Afghan POWs Denied Rights Because 'It's Not a War.'" *Sydney Morning Herald,* 16 July. http://www.smh.com.au/news/world/afghan-pows-denied-rights-because-its-not-a-war/2006/06/15/1149964675820.html.

Barros, Carlos Pestana, and Isabel Proença. 2005. "Mixed Logit Estimation of Radical Islamic Terrorism in Europe and North America." *Journal of Conflict Resolution* 49:298–314.

BBC News. 2012. "Canadian Security Services 'Can Use Torture Material.'" BBC News, 8 February 2012. http://www.bbc.co.uk/news/16943268?print=true.

Beall, Jennifer. 1998. "Are We Only Burning Witches? The Antiterrorism and Effective Death Penalty Act of 1996's Answer to Terrorism." *Indiana Law Journal* 71:693–710.

Bennett-Jones, Owen, 2012. "Terrorists? Us?" *London Review of Books,* 7 June, 10–12.

Bhabba, Faisal. 2003. "Tracking 'Terrorists' or Solidifying Stereotypes? Canada's Anti-terrorism Act in Light of the Charter's Equality Guarantee." *Windsor Review of Legal and Social Issues* 16:95–136.

Blackbourn, Jessie. 2009. "International Terrorism and Counterterrorist Legislation: The Case Study of Post-9/11 Northern Ireland." *Terrorism and Political Violence* 21:133–54.

Boot, Max, and Jeane J. Kirkpatrick. 2009. "U.S. and Allies Must Detain Afghan Prisoners." *Washington Post,* 29 December. http://www.cfr.org/publication/21084/us_and_allies_must_detain_afghan_prisoners.html.

Boyne, Shawn. 2004. "Law, Terrorism, and Social Movements: The Tensions between

Politics and Security in Germany's Anti-terrorism Legislation." *Cardozo Journal of International and Comparative Law* 12:41–82.

Bright, Martin. 2006. "Rendition: The Cover-up." *New Statesman*, 23 January. http://www.newstatesman.com/200601230005.

British Columbia Civil Liberties Association 2010. "Abdelrazik et al v Attorney General of Canada." http://bccla.org/our_work/abdelrazik-et-al-v-attorney-general-of-canada/.

Bush, George W. 2010. *Decision Points*. London: Virgin Books.

Bybee, Jay S. 2005. "Standards of Conduct for Interrogation under 18 USC §§ 2340–2340A: Memorandum for Alberto R Gonzales, Counsel to the President, August 1, 2002." In *The Torture Papers: The Road to Abu Ghraib*, edited by Karen J. Greenberg and Joshua L. Dratel, 172–217. New York: Cambridge University Press.

Canada. *House of Commons Hansard*. http://www.parl.gc.ca/housechamberbusiness/chambersittings.aspx?View=H&Parl=37&Ses=1&Language=E&Mode=1.

Canada. House of Commons Special Committee on the Canadian Mission in Afghanistan. 2009. *Evidence*, 18 November. Available at http://www.parl.gc.ca/committeebusiness/CommitteeHome.aspx?Cmte=AFGA&Language=E&Mode=1&Parl=40&Ses=2.

Canada, Commission of Inquiry into Certain Activities of the Royal Canadian Mounted Police. 1981. Vol. 1. *Freedom and Security under the Law*. Accessed via http://www.pco-bcp.gc.ca.

Canada, Commission of Inquiry into the Actions of Canadian Officials in Relation to Maher Arar. 2005. *Report of the Events Relating to Maher Arar: Analysis and Recommendations*. www.sirc-csars.gc.ca/pdfs/cm_arar_rec-eng.pdf.

Canada, House of Commons, Standing Committee on Justice and Human Rights. 2001. *Eighth Report*. http://www.parl.gc.ca/HousePublications/Publication.aspx?DocId=1032018&Language=E&Mode=1&Parl=37&Ses=1.

Canada, House of Commons, Standing Committee on Public Safety and National Security. 2009. *Third Report*. http://www.parl.gc.ca/HousePublications/Publication.aspx?DocId=4004074&Language=E&Mode=1&Parl=40&Ses=2.

Canada, House of Commons, Standing Committee on Public Safety and National Security and Subcommittee on the Review of the Anti-terrorism Act. 2007. *Rights, Limits, Security: A Comprehensive Review of the Anti-terrorism Act and Related Issues.*

Canada, House of Commons, Subcommittee on the Review of the Anti-terrorism Act. 2007. *Rights, Limits, Security: A Comprehensive Review of the Anti-terrorism Act and Related Issues*. http://www.parl.gc.ca/HousePublications/Publication.aspx?DocId=2798914&Language=E&Mode=1&Parl=39&Ses=1.

Canada, Senate, Special Committee on the Anti-terrorism Act. 2007. *Fundamental Justice in Extraordinary Times*. http://www.parl.gc.ca/sencommitteebusiness/CommitteeReports.aspx?parl=39&ses=1&Language=E&comm_id=597.

Canada, Senate, Special Committee on the Subject Matter of Bill C-36. 2001. *First Report*. http://www.parl.gc.ca/sencommitteebusiness/CommitteeReports.aspx?parl=41&ses=1&Language=E&comm_id=612.

Cassese, Antonio. 2006. "The Multifaceted Criminal Notion of Terrorism in International Law." *Journal of International Criminal Justice* 4:933–58.

Catanzariti, Katelyn. 2009. "NSW Terror Five Face Life Terms." *Age* (Melbourne), 17 October, 13.

Center on Law and Security. 2010. *Terrorist Trial Report Card: September 11, 2001–September 11, 2009*. http://www.lawandsecurity.org/Publications/Terrorism-Trial-Report-Card.

Chesney, Robert M. 2005. "The Sleeper Scenario: Terrorism-Support Laws and the Demands of Prevention." *Harvard Journal on Legislation* 42:1–89.

Chesney, Robert M. 2007a. "Beyond Conspiracy? Anticipatory Prosecution and the Challenge of Unaffiliated Terrorism." *Southern California Law Review* 80:425–99.

Chesney, Robert M. 2007b. "Enemy Combatants after *Hamdan v Rumsfeld*: State Secrets and the Limits of National Security Litigation." *George Washington Law Review* 75:1249–1315.

Chesney, Robert M. 2007c. "Federal Prosecution of Terrorism-Related Offenses: Conviction and Sentencing Data in Light of the 'Soft-Sentence' and 'Data-Reliability' Critiques." *Lewis and Clark Law Review* 11:851–901.

Chesney, Robert M. 2008. "Legislative Reform of the State Secrets Privilege." *Roger Williams University Law Review* 13:443–68.

Clarke, M. J. 2008. *Report of the Inquiry into the Case of Dr Haneef.*

CNN. 2004. "Somali charged in al Qaeda mall bombing plot." 15 June. http://edition.cnn.com/2004/LAW/06/14/terrorism.indictment/.

Cobain, Ian. 2009. "Tony Blair Knew of Secret Policy on Terror Interrogations." *Guardian*, 18 June. http://www.guardian.co.uk/politics.2009/jun/18/tony-blair-secret-torture-policy/print.

Cobain, Ian. 2012. "Rendition Ordeal Raises New Questions about Secret Trials." *Guardian Weekly*, 13 April, 14–15.

Cobain, Ian, and Richard Norton-Taylor. 2010. "Torture Warnings Pushed Aside for Britain to Join US in 'War on Terror.'" *Guardian*, 28 September. http://www.guardian.co.uk/world/2010/sep/28/torture-warnings-britain-us-ignored/print.

Cobain, Ian, et al. 2012. "Documents Detailing Scandals of Empire Were Hidden Away." *Guardian Weekly*, 27 April, 14–15.

Cole, David. 2009. "Out of the Shadows: Preventive Detention, Suspected Terrorists, and War." *California Law Review* 97:693–750.

Cole, David. 2010. "What to Do about Guantánamo?" *New York Review of Books* 14 October, 48–50.

Cole, David, and James Dempsey. 2006. *Terrorism and the Constitution: Sacrificing Civil Liberties in the Name of National Security* New York: Free Press.

Condon, Stephanie. 2010. "Poll: Most Americans Say Keep Gitmo Open." http://www.cbsnews.com/8301_503544_163-6084882503544.html.

Converse, Philip E. 1964. "The Nature of Belief Systems in Mass Publics." In *Ideology and Discontent*, edited by David E. Apter, 206–61. New York: Free Press.

Coorey, Phillip, and Cynthia Banham. 2007. "PM Tells the Party: 'I Could Free Hicks—but Won't.'" *Sydney Morning Herald*, 7 February.

Crabb, Annabel. 2006. "Law Strips Hicks of UK Citizenship." *Sydney Morning Herald*, 20 August. http://www.smh.com.au/news/world/law-strips-hicks-of-uk-citizenship-in-hours/2006/08/19/1155408075077.html.

CSIS (Canadian Security Intelligence Service). 2002. Public Report 2002. http//www.csis-scrs.gc.ca/pblctns/nnlrprt/2002/rprt2002-eng.asp. Accessed 27 January 2009.

CSIS (Canadian Security Intelligence Service). 2003. *Public Report 2003.* http://www.csis-scrs.gc.ca/pblctns/nnlrprt/2003/rprt2003-eng.asp.

CSIS. 2006. *Public Report 2006.* http//www.csis-scrs.gc.ca/pblctns/nnlrprt/2006/rprt2006-eng.asp. Accessed 27 January 2009.

CSIS. 2007. *Annual Public Report 2006–2007.* http://www.csis-scrs.gc.ca/pblctns/nnlrprt/index-eng.asp.

CSIS. 2009. *Public Report, 2008–2009.* http://www.csis-scrs.gc.ca/pblctns/nnlr-prt/2008/rprt2008-eng.asp.

Cumming, Geoff, and Catherine Masters. 2012. "A Nation Divided: Inside the Urewera Four Trial." *New Zealand Herald*, 24 March. http://www.nzherald.co.nz/nz/news/article.cfm?c_id=1&objectid=10794146.

Davies, Nick, et al. 2010. "Iraqi War Logs: Secret Files Show How US Ignored Torture." *Guardian*, 22 October. http://www.guardian.co.uk/world/2010/oct/22/iraq-war-logs-military-leaks?INTCMP=SRCH.

Davis, Darren W., and Brian D Silver. 2004. "Civil Liberties vs. Security: Public Opinion in the Context of the Terrorist Attacks on America." *American Journal of Political Science* 48:28–46.

Denbeaux, Mark P., and Jonathan Hafetz. 2009. *The Guantánamo Lawyers: Inside a Prison outside the Law*. New York: New York University Press.

Di Filippo, Marcello. 2008. "Terrorist Crimes and International Co-operation: Critical Remarks on the Definition and Inclusion of Terrorism in the Category of International Crimes." *European Journal of International Law* 19:533–70.

Difo, Germain. 2010. *Ordinary Measures, Extraordinary Results: An Assessment of Foiled Plots since 9/11*. Washington, DC: American Security Project.

Donohue, Laura K. 2006. "Anglo-American Privacy and Surveillance." *Journal of Criminal Law and Criminology* 96:1059–1208.

Donohue, Laura K. 2007. *Counter-terrorist Law and Emergency Powers in the United Kingdom, 1922–2000*. Dublin: Irish Academic Press.

Donohue, Laura K. 2008. *The Cost of Counterterrorism: Power, Politics, and Liberty*. New York: Cambridge University Press.

Dosman, E. Alexandra. 2004. "For the Record: Designating 'Listed Entities' for the Purposes of Terrorist Financing Offences at Canadian Law." *University of Toronto Faculty Law Review* 62:1–27.

Douglas, Roger. 2010. "Must Terrorists Act for a Cause?" *Commonwealth Law Bulletin* 36:295–312.

Dyzenaus, David. 2005. "The Rule of (Administrative) Law in International Law." *Law and Contemporary Problems* 68:127–66.

Electronic Privacy Information Center. 2007. *Foreign Intelligence Surveillance Orders, 1979–2007*. http://epic.org/privacy/wiretap/stats/fisa_stats.html.

Enders, Walter, and Todd Sandler. 2005. "After 9/11: Is It All Different Now?" *Journal of Conflict Resolution* 49:259–77.

English, Richard. 2003. *Armed Struggle: A History of the IRA*. London: Macmillan.

Eysenck, H. J. 1954. *The Psychology of Politics*. London: Routledge and Kegan Paul.

Fallon, Richard H., Jr. 2010. "The Supreme Court, Habeas Corpus, and the War on Terror: An Essay on Law and Political Science." *Columbia Law Review* 110:325–52.

Flanigan, Shawn Teresa. 2006. "Charity as Resistance: Connections between Charity, Contentious Politics, and Terror." *Studies in Conflict and Terrorism* 29:641–55.

Fletcher, Joseph F. 1989. "Mass and Elite Attitudes about Wiretapping in Canada: Implications for Democratic Theory and Politics." *Public Opinion Quarterly* 53:225–45.

Fletcher, Laurel E., and Eric Stover. 2009. *The Guantánamo Effect: Exposing the Consequences of U.S. Detention and Interrogation Practices*. Berkeley: University of California Press.

Forcese, Craig. n.d. "National Security Law, Chapter 10: Secrecy." http://craigforcese.squarespace.com/national-security-law-blog/category/chapter-10-secrecy.

Forcese, Craig, and Lorne Waldman. 2007. *Seeking Justice in an Unfair Process: Lessons from Canada, the United Kingdom, and New Zealand on the Use of "Special Advocates" in National Security Proceedings.* Ottawa: University of Ottawa Faculty of Law.

Forsythe, David P. 2011. *The Politics of Prisoner Abuse: The United States and Enemy Prisoners after 9/11.* Cambridge: Cambridge University Press.

Friscolanti, Michael, Jonathon Gatehouse, and Charlie Gillis. 2006. "Homegrown Terror: It's Not Over." *Maclean's*, 19 June. http://www.macleans.ca/article.jsp?content=20060619_128953_128953.

Gastil, John, et al. 2005. "The 'Wildavsky Heuristic': The Cultural Orientation of Mass Political Opinion." Public Law and Legal Theory Research Paper Series, Research Paper No 107, Yale Law School, New Haven, CT.

Gewald, Jan-Bart. 2007. "Coming through Slaughter: The Herero of Namibia, 1904–1940." In *The Practice of War: Production, Reproduction, and Communication of Armed Violence*, edited by Rao Aparna et al., 89–110. Oxford: Bergbahn Books.

Gibson, Sir Peter. 2010. *Report of the Intelligence Services Commissioner for 2009.* http://www.official-documents.gov.uk/document/hc1012/hc12/1240/1240.asp.

Global Terrorism Database. n.d. http://www.start.umd.edu.

Goldsmith, Jack. 2007. *The Terror Presidency: Law and Judgment inside the Bush Administration.* New York: W. W. Norton.

Grabosky, P. N. 1989. *Wayward Governance: Illegality and Its Control in the Public Sector.* Canberra: Australian Institute of Criminology.

Grey, Stephen. 2007. *Ghost Plane: The Untold Story of the CIA's Torture Programme.* Melbourne: Scribe.

Habib, Mamdouh. 2008. *My Story: The Tale of a Terrorist Who Wasn't.* With Julia Collingwood. Melbourne: Scribe.

Hagan, Kate. 2010. "Tamil Trio Accused of Terrorism Free on Bonds." *Age* (Melbourne), 1 April, 3.

Haggerty, Kevin D., and Amber Grazso. 2005. "The Public Politics of Opinion Research on Surveillance and Privacy." *Surveillance and Society* 3:173–80.

Haidt, Jonathan. 2012. *The Righteous Mind: Why Good People Are Divided by Politics and Religion.* London: Allen Lane.

Harris, Paul. 2013. "Detainee Release Will Get a Restart." *Guardian Weekly* 31 May, 4.

Hatemi, Peter K., et al. 2011. "A Genome-Wide Analysis of Liberal and Conservative Political Attitudes." *Journal of Politics* 73:271–85.

Hetherington, Marc J., and Elizabeth Suhay. 2012. "Authoritarianism, Threat, and Americans' Support for the War on Terror." *American Journal of Political Science* 55:546–60.

Henning, Anna C., and Edward C. Liu. 2009. *Amendments to the Foreign Intelligence Surveillance Act (FISA) Set to Expire February 28, 2010.* Washington, DC: Congressional Research Service.

Herman, Susan N. 2006. "The USA Patriot Act and the Submajoritarian Fourth Amendment." *Harvard Civil Rights–Civil Liberties Law Review* 41:67–132.

Hoffman, Grayson A. 2003. "Litigating Terrorism: The New FISA Regime, the Wall, and the Fourth Amendment." *American Criminal Law Review* 40:1655–82.

Howell, Beryl A. 2004. "Seven Weeks: The Making of the USA Patriot Act." *George Washington Law Review* 72:1145–1207.

Huddy, Leonie, et al. 2002. "The Polls—Trends: Reactions to the Terrorist Attacks of September 11, 2001." *Public Opinion Quarterly* 66:418–50.

Human Rights Watch and American Civil Liberties Union. 2005. *Witnesses to Abuse: Human Rights Abuses under the Material Witness Law since September 11*. http://www.hrw.org/reports/2005/06/26/witness-abuse-0.

Iacobucci, Frank. 2008. *Internal Inquiry into the Actions of Canadian Officials in Relation to Abdullah Almalki, Ahmad Abou-Elmaati, and Muayyed Nureddin*. Report. http://epe.lac-bac.gc.ca/100/200/301/pco-bcp/commissions-ef/iacobucci-e/final_report/index.html.

Jones, Jeffrey M. 2009. "Americans Oppose Closing Gitmo and Moving Prisoners to US." http://www.gallup.com/poll/119393/americans-oppose-closing-gitmo-moving-prisoners.

Kahneman, Daniel, Paul Slovic, and Amos Tversky, eds. 1982. *Judgment under Uncertainty: Heuristics and Biases*. New York: Cambridge University Press.

Keenan, Danny, ed. 2008. *Terror in Our Midst: Searching for Terror in Aotearoa New Zealand*. Wellington: Huia.

Kerr, Orin. 2003. "Internet Surveillance Law after the USA Patriot Act: The Big Brother That Isn't." *Northwestern University Law Review* 97:607–73.

Kissane, Karen, et al. 2008. "Benbrika and Five Followers Found Guilty on Terrorism Charges." *Age* (Melbourne), 16 September, 7.

Laberge, Cynthia. 2009. *To What Extent Should National Security Interests Override Privacy in a Post 9/11 World?* Wellington: Victoria University of Wellington Law Review.

Law Council of Australia. 2007. David Hicks v the United States: *Summary of the Report of the Independent Observer for the Law Council of Australia*. http://www.lawcouncil.asn.au/programs/criminal-law-human-rights/human-rights/hicks.cfm?fms_folder_uuid=8A2D2354-1E4F-17FA-D2CF-03C7F13E6BA7.

Leigh, David. 2010. "Iraqi War Logs: Prisoner Beaten to Death Days after British Handover to Police." *Guardian*, 28 October. http://www.guardian.co.uk/world/2010/oct/28/iraq-war-logs-abbas-alawiu/print.

Lobel, Jules. 2002. "The War on Terrorism and Civil Liberties." *University of Pittsburgh Law Review* 63:767–90.

"London Glasgow Terrorist Attacks: The Men in the Dock." 2008. *Independent* (London), 16 December.

Lord Carlile of Berriew. 2007. *The Definition of Terrorism*. Cm 7052. http:/www.official-documents.gov.uk/document/cm70/7052/7052.pdf.

Lord Carlile of Berriew. 2009. *Report on the Operation in 2008 of the Terrorism Act 2000 and of Part 1 of the Terrorism Act 2006*. http://www.statewatch.org/news/2009/jun/uk-carlile-report-2008.pdf.

Lord Carlile of Berriew. 2011. *Sixth Report of the Independent Reviewer Pursuant to Section 14(3) of the Prevention of Terrorism Act 2005*. https://www.gov.uk/government/uploads/ . . . /lord-carlile-sixth-report.pdf.

Lord Lloyd of Berwick. 1996. *Inquiry into Legislation against Terrorism*. 2 vols. Cm 3420. London: The Stationery Office.

Lum, Cynthia, et al. 2006. "Are Counter-terrorism Strategies Effective? The Results of the Campbell Systematic Review on Counter-terrorism Evaluation Research." *Journal of Experimental Criminology* 2:489–516.

Lynch, Andrew, et al. 2009. "The Proscription of Terrorist Organisations in Australia." *Federal Law Review* 37:1–40.

Mackey, Chris. 2004. *The Interrogator's War: Inside the Secret War against Al Qaeda*. With Greg Miller. London: John Murray.

Major, John C. 2010. *Air India Flight 182: A Canadian Tragedy*. Vol. 2. http://www.pco-bcp.gc.ca.

Manningham-Buller, Elizabeth. 2011. "2011 Reith Lecture Series: Securing Freedom." Parts 1 and 2. http://www.abc.net.au/rn/bigideas/series/2011/3328978.htm#transcript and http://www.abc.net.au/rn/bigideas/series/2011/3329559.htm#transcript.

Marks, Jonathan H. 2006. "What Counts in Counterterrorism?" *Columbia Human Rights Law Review* 37:559–626.

Martin, David A. 2009. *Refining Immigration Law's Role in Counterterrorism*. Washington, DC: Brookings Institution.

Martin, Thomas C. 2006. "The Comprehensive Terrorism Prevention Act of 1995." *Seton Hall Legislative Journal* 20:201–46.

Masters, David. 2008. "The Origin of Terrorist Threats: Religious, Separatist, or Something Else." *Terrorism and Political Violence* 20:396–414.

May, Theresa. 2011. *Review of Counter-terrorism and Security Powers: Review Findings and Recommendations*. Available at https://www.gov.uk/government/publications/review-of-counter-terrorism-and-security-powers.

Mazzetti, Mark, et al. 2011 "How Washington Got Its Man." *Saturday Age* (Melbourne), 7 May, 18.

McCarthy, Michael T. 2002. "USA Patriot Act." *Harvard Journal on Legislation* 39:435–53.

Metcalfe, Eric. 2007. *The Future of Counter-terrorism and Human Rights*. Accessed 24 July 2011.

Michaels, Jon D. 2008. "All the President's Men: Private-Public Intelligence Partnerships in the War on Terror." *California Law Review* 96:901–66.

Montopoli, Brian. 2009. "Poll Support for Closing Guantanamo Grows." http://www.cbsnews.com/8301_503544_162-509534-503544.html.

Morales, Lymari. 2009. "Americans Send No Clear Mandate on Guantanamo Bay." http://www.gallup.poll/113893/ameraicans-send-no-clear-mandate-on-guantanamo-bay.

Morrow, James D. 2007. "When Do States Follow the Laws of War?" *American Political Science Review* 101:559–72.

Mueller, John. 2006. *Overblown: How Politicians and the Terrorism Industry Inflate National Security Threats, and Why We Believe Them*. New York: Free Press.

Munro, Ian. 2010. "Three Guilty, Two Walk Free over Terror Attack Plan at Barracks." *Age* (Melbourne), 24 December, 1.

Munro, Peter 2011. "Court Backs ASIO Secrecy on Refugees." *Sunday Age* (Melbourne), 6 March, 5.

Needham, Kirsty. 2012. "Detained Teen Labelled 'Security Risk' to Get His Day in Court." *Age* (Melbourne) 14 January, 5.

Nesbitt, Katherine. 2007. "Preventative Detention of Terrorist Suspects in Australia and the United States: A Comparative Constitutional Analysis." *Boston University Public International Law Journal* 17:39–98.

New Zealand. Parliamentary Debates.

New Zealand, House of Representatives Justice and Electoral Committee. 2010. *Search and Surveillance Bill*. Available at http://www.parliament.nz/en-NZ/PB/SC/.

New Zealand Law Commission. 2007. *Search and Surveillance Powers*. http://www.nzlii.org/nz/other/nzlc/report/R97/R97.pdf.

"Northern Ireland Violence." 2009. Available at http://www.cain.ulst.ac.uk.

Nowak, Manfred. 2006. "What Practices Constitute Torture? US and UN Standards." *Human Rights Quarterly* 28:809–841.

NZSIS (New Zealand Security Intelligence Service). 2002. Reports for this and later years are available at http://www.nzsis.govt.nz/publications/annual-reports/. *Report to the House of Representatives for the Year Ended 30 June 2002.*

NZSIS. 2004. *Report to the House of Representatives for the Year Ended 30 June 2004.*

NZSIS. 2005. *Report to the House of Representatives for the Year Ended 30 June 2005.*

NZSIS. 2006. *Report to the House of Representatives for the Year Ended 30 June 2006.*

Obama, Barack 2010. *National Security Strategy.* http://www.whitehouse.gov/sites/default/files/rss_viewer/national_security_strategy.pdf.

OECD (Organisation for Economic Co-operation and Development). 2005. *Terrorism Risk Insurance in OECD Countries.*

O'Sullivan, Paul. 2006. Director-General's address to the Security in Government Conference—"A Step Ahead: The Challenge for Counter-Terrorism." http://www.asio.gov.au/Publications/Speeches-and-Statements/2006/A-Step-Ahead-The-Challenge-for-Counter-Terrorism.html.

O'Toole, Megan, 2011. "Terror Suspect Mohamed Hersi on Bail." *National Post*, April 29. http://news.nationalpost.com/2011/04/29/terror-suspect-mohamed-hersi-released-on-bail/.

Pape, Robert A. 2003. "The Strategic Logic of Suicide Terrorism." *American Political Science Review* 97:343–61.

Parker, Ellen. 2007. "Implementation of the UK Terrorism Act 2006—The Relationship between Counterterrorism Law, Free Speech, and the Muslim Community in the United Kingdom versus the United States." *Emory International Law Review* 21:711–57.

Parker, Tom. 2007. "Fighting an Antaean Enemy: How Democratic States Unintentionally Sustain the Terrorist Movements They Oppose." *Terrorism and Political Violence* 19:155–79.

Parry, John T. 2010. *Understanding Torture: Law, Violence, and Political Identity.* Ann Arbor: University of Michigan Press.

Philbin, Patrick F., and John C. Yoo. 2005. "Possible Habeas Jurisdiction over Aliens Held in Guantanamo Bay, Cuba." In *The Torture Papers: The Road to Abu Ghraib*, edited by Karen J. Greenberg and Joshua L. Dratel, 29–37. New York: Cambridge University Press.

Phillips, Joshua E. S. 2010. *None of Us Were Like This Before: American Soldiers and Torture.* London: Verso.

Pilkington, Ed. 2012. "Guantánamo: America's Lingering Failure." *Guardian Weekly*, 20 January, 6–7.

PIPA. 2006. *25 Nation Poll on Torture: Questionnaire and Methodology.* http://www.worldpublicopinion.org/pipa/pdf/feb06/ViewsCountries_Feb06_quaire.pdf.

"PM: Our Troops Don't Torture." 2010. *New Zealand Herald*, 17 August. http://www.nzherald.co.nz/nz/news/article.cfm?c_id=1&objectid=10666593.

Poole, Thomas. 2010. "Judicial Review at the Margins: Law, Power, and Prerogative." *University of Toronto Law Journal* 60:81–108.

Posner, Richard. 2008. "Privacy, Surveillance, and Law." *University of Chicago Law Review* 75:245–60.

Posner, Eric A and Adrian Vermeule. 2007. *Terrorism in the Balance: Security, Liberty, and the Courts*. New York: Oxford University Press.

Powe, Lucas A., Jr. 2009. *The Supreme Court and the American Elite, 1978–2008*. Cambridge, MA: Harvard University Press.

Pue, W. W. 2003. "The War on Terror: Constitutional Governance in a State of Permanent Warfare?" *Osgoode Hall Law Journal* 41:267–92.

Rahamim, Yoni. 2004. "Wiretapping and Electronic Surveillance in Canada: The Present State of the Law and Challenges to the Employment of Sophisticated and Intrusive Technology in Law Enforcement." *Windsor Review of Legal and Social Issues* 18:87–104.

Ramraj, V. V. 2009. "Terrorism, Risk Perception, and Judicial Review." In *Global Anti-terrorism Law and Policy*, edited by V. V. Ramraj, M. Hor, and Kent Roach, 107–26. Cambridge: Cambridge University Press.

Reinares, Fernando. 2004. "Who Are the Terrorists? Analyzing Changes in Sociological Profile among Members of ETA." *Studies in Conflict and Terrorism* 27:465–88.

Ripley, Amanda. 2002. "The Case of the Dirty Bomber." http://www.time.com/time/printout/0,8816,262917,00.html.

Roach, Kent. 2001. "The New Terrorism Offences and the Criminal Law." In *The Security of Freedom: Essays on Canada's Anti-terrorism Bill*, edited by Ronald J. Daniels, Patrick Macklem, and Kent Roach, 151–72. Toronto: University of Toronto Press.

Roach, Kent. 2006. "Must We Trade Rights for Security? The Choice between Smart, Harsh, or Proportionate Security Strategies in Canada and Britain." *Cardozo Law Review* 27:2151–2221.

Roach, Kent. 2008. "The Role and Capacities of Courts and Legislatures in Reviewing Canada's Anti-terrorism Law." *Windsor Review of Legal and Social Issues* 24:5–56.

Roach, Kent. 2009. "The Criminal Law and Terrorism." In *Global Anti-terrorism Law and Policy*, edited by V. V. Ramraj, M. Hor, and Kent Roach, 129–51. Cambridge: Cambridge University Press.

Roach, Kent, and Gary Trotter. 2005. "Miscarriages of Justice in the War against Terror." *Penn State Law Review* 109:967–1041.

Rosenthal, Peter. 2003. "Disclosure to the Defence after September 11: Sections 37 and 38 of the *Canada Evidence Act*." *Criminal Law Quarterly* 48:186–204.

Sands, Phillippe. 2009. *Torture Team: Uncovering War Crimes in the Land of the Free*. London: Penguin Books.

Saul, Ben. 2006. *Defining Terrorism in International Law*. Oxford: Oxford University Press.

Schmid, Alex. 2005. "Terrorism—the Definitional Problem." *Case Western Reserve Journal of International Law* 37:375–419.

Schwartz, Paul M. 2009. "Warrantless Wiretapping, FISA Reform, and the Lessons of Public Liberty: A Comment on Holmes's Jorde Lecture." *California Law Review* 97:407–32.

Seifert, Jeffrey W. 2007. *Data Mining and Homeland Security: An Overview*. Washington, DC: Congressional Research Service.

Shapiro, Ian. 2012. "Italy's High Court Upholds Convictions of 23 Americans in Abu Omar Rendition." *Washington Post*, 20 September. http://www.washingtonpost.com/local/italys-high-court-upholds-convictions-of-23-americans-in-abu-omar-rendition/2012/09/19/af06022c-0286–11e2–91e7–2962c74e7738_print.html.

Shapiro, Sidney A., and Rena I. Steinzor. 2006. "The People's Agent: Executive Branch

Secrecy and Accountability in an Age of Terrorism." *Law and Contemporary Problems* 69:99–129.

Smith, George. 2005. "UK Terror Trial Finds No Terror." *National Security Notes*, 11 April. http://www.globalsecurity.org/org/nsn/nsn-050411.htm.

Stent, Robert. 1980. *A Bespattered Page? The Internment of His Majesty's "Most Loyal Enemy Aliens."* London: André Deutsch.

Stephenson, Jon. 2009. "Kiwi Troops in 'War Crimes' Row." *Sunday Star Times*, 2 August. http://www.stuff.co.nz/national/2712026/Kiwi-troops-in-war-crimes-row.

Stephenson, Jon. 2010. "Prisoners Being Delivered to Brutal Afghan Secret Police." *Sunday Star Times*, 15 August.

Sturcke, James. 2009. "Convictions 'Prove Police Were Right to Pursue Retrial.'" *Guardian*, 7 September, http://www.guardian.co.uk/uk/2009/sep/07/terrorism-trial-carlile-cps.

Sunstein, Cass. 2007. "On the Divergent American Reactions to Terrorism and Climate Change." *Columbia Law Review* 107:503–57.

Swanwick, Tristan. 2009. "Alleged Stalker John Amundsen 'Used GPS on Ex-girlfriend.'" *Courier-Mail* (Brisbane), October 1. http://www.couriermail.com.au/news/alleged-stalker-john-amundsen-used-gps-on-ex-girlfriend/story-e6freon6–1225781304438.

Taft, William H., IV 2005. "Comments on Your Paper on the Geneva Conventions" and "Status of Legal Discussions." In *The Torture Papers: The Road to Abu Ghraib*, edited by Karen J. Greenberg and Joshua L. Dratel, 129–33. New York: Cambridge University Press.

Taguba, Antonio M. 2004. *Article 15-6 Investigation of the 800th Military Police Brigade.*

Taylor, Stuart, Jr., and Benjamin Wittes. 2009. *Looking Forward, Not Backward: Refining American Interrogation Law.* Brookings Institute Working Paper, Washington, DC.

Tomkins, A. 2010. "The Role of the Courts in the Political Constitution." *University of Toronto Law Journal* 60:1–22.

Torrance, Judy N. 1986. *Public Violence in Canada, 1867–1982.* Kingston: McGill-Queen's University Press.

Townley, Stephen. 2007. "The Use and Misuse of Secret Evidence in Immigration Cases: A Comparative Study of the United States, Canada, and the United Kingdom." *Yale Journal of International Law* 32:219–53.

Treverton, Gregory T. 2009. *Intelligence for an Age of Terror.* New York: Cambridge University Press.

Tumlin, Karen C. 2004. "Suspect First: How Terrorism Policy Is Reshaping Immigration Policy." *California Law Review* 92:1173–1239.

Turner, Serrin, and Stephen J. Schulhofer. 2005. *The Secrecy Problem in Terrorism Trials.* New York: Brennan Center for Justice.

United Kingdom. House of Commons Hansard. Available at http://www.parliament.uk/business/publications/hansard/.

United Kingdom. House of Lords Hansard. Available at http://www.parliament.uk/business/publications/hansard/.

United Kingdom. 2010. *Consolidated Guidance to Intelligence Officers and Service Personnel on the Detention and Interviewing of Detainees Overseas, and on the Passing and Receipt of Intelligence Relating to Detainees.* http://legislationline.org/download/action/download/id/3111/file/UK_%20Consolidated%20Guidance_on%20the%20Detention%20and%20Interviewing%20o.pdf.

United Kingdom. 2011. *Justice and Security Green Paper*. Cm 8194. https://www.gov.uk/government/consultations/justice-and-security-green-paper.

United Kingdom, Equality and Human Rights Commission. 2010. *Commission Advises Government That Torture Guidance May Breach the Law*. http://www.equality-humanrights.com/news/2010/september/commission-advises-government-that-torture-guidance-may-breach-the-law/.

United Kingdom, Home Office. 2009. *Home Office Statistical Bulletin: Statistics on Terrorism Arrests and Outcomes Great Britain*. http://webarchive.nationalarchives.gov.uk/search/?query=statistics+on+terrorism+arrests+and+outcomes+great+britain&where=text&x=14&y=10.

United Kingdom, Home Office. 2010. *Operation of Police Powers under the Terrorism Act 2000 and Subsequent Legislation: Arrests, Outcomes, and Stops & Searches, Great Britain 2009/10*. http://webarchive.nationalarchives.gov.uk/20110218135832/rds.homeoffice.gov.uk/rds/hosbpubs1.html.

United Kingdom, Home Office. 2012. "Current Threat Level." http://www.homeoffice.gov.uk/counter-terrorism/current-threat-level.

United Kingdom, House of Commons Foreign Affairs Committee. 2005. *Human Rights Annual Report*. http://www.publications.parliament.uk/pa/cm200405/cmselect/cmfaff/cmfaff.htm.

United Kingdom, House of Commons Foreign Affairs Committee. 2006. *Foreign Policy Aspects of the War against Terrorism*. http://www.publications.parliament.uk/pa/cm200506/cmselect/cmfaff/cmfaff.htm.

United Kingdom, House of Commons Foreign Affairs Committee. 2007. *Visit to Guantánamo Bay: Second Report of Session 2006–07*. HC 44. London: Stationery Office. http://www.publications.parliament.uk/pa/cm200607/cmselect/cmfaff/cmfaff.htm.

United Kingdom, Intelligence and Security Committee. 2005. *The Handling of Detainees by UK Intelligence Personnel in Afghanistan, Guantanamo Bay, and Iraq*. Cm 6469. http://isc.independent.gov.uk/committee-reports/special-reports.

United Kingdom, Intelligence and Security Committee. 2006. *Report into the London Terrorist Attacks on 7 July 2005*. Cm 6785. http://isc.independent.gov.uk/committee-reports/special-reports.

United Kingdom, Parliament, Joint Committee on Human Rights. 2005. *Counter-terrorism Policy and Human Rights: Terrorism Bill and Related Matters*. http://www.publications.parliament.uk/pa/jt200506/jtselect/jtrights/jtrights.htm.

United Kingdom, Parliament, Joint Committee on Human Rights. 2007. *Counter-terrorism Policy and Human Rights: 28 Days, Intercept, and Post-charge Questioning*. http://www.publications.parliament.uk/pa/jt200607/jtselect/jtrights/jtrights.htm.

United Kingdom, Parliament, Joint Committee on Human Rights. 2010. *Counter-terrorism Policy and Human Rights (Sixteenth Report): Annual Renewal of Control Orders Legislation*. http://www.publications.parliament.uk/pa/jt200910/jtselect/jtrights/jtrights.htm.

United Kingdom, Privy Counsellor Review Committee. 2003. *Anti-terrorism, Crime and Security Act 2001 Review: Report*. www.statewatch.org/news/2003/dec/atcsReport.pdf.

United Kingdom, Security Service. 2013a. "Attacks on UK Citizens and Interests Abroad." https://www.mi5.gov.uk/home/the-threats/terrorism/international-ter

rorism/international-terrorism-and-the-uk/attacks-on-uk-citizens-and-interests-abroad.html.

United Kingdom, Security Service. 2013b. "Threat Levels." https://www.mi5.gov.uk/home/the-threats/terrorism/threat-levels.html#history.

United Nations Security Council. 2011. "Security Council Al-Qaida Sanctions Committee Deletes Entry of Abu Sufian al-Salamabi Muhammed Ahmed Abd al-Razziq from Its List." http://www.un.org/News/Press/docs//2011/sc10467.doc.htm.

United States, Attorney General. 2009. Memorandum to the Heads of Executive Departments and Agencies, "Policies and Procedures Governing the Invocation of the State Secrets Privilege." http://www.justice.gov/opa/documents/state-secret-privileges.pdf.

United States, Department of Defense. 2001. *Military Commission Order No 1*, 21 March 21, 2002. http://www.defense.gov/news/mar2002/d20020321ord.pdf.

United States Department of Defense, Office of the Assistant Secretary of Defense (Public Affairs). 2002. DoD New Briefing–Secretary Rumsfeld and Gen. Myers, Feb 12, 2002, http://www.defense.gov/transcripts/transcript.aspx?transcriptid=2636.

United States, Department of Justice. 2003. "Iyman Faris Sentenced for Providing Material Assistance to Al Qaeda." http://www.usdoj.gov/opa/pr/2003/October/03_crm_589.htm.

United States, Department of Justice. 2004. "Somali Native Charged in a Bomb Plot, Ashcroft Says." http://usinfo.state.gov/xarchives/display.html?p=washfile-english&y=2004&m=June&x=20040614165038dmslahrelleko.7101862&t=livefeeds/wf-latest.html.

United States, Department of Justice. 2009. "Illinois Man Arrested in Plot to Bomb Courthouse and Murder Federal Employees." http://www.justice.gov/usao/ilc/press/2009/09September/24Finton.html.

United States, Department of Justice, Office of Professional Responsibility. 2009. *Report: Investigation into the Office of Legal Counsel's Memoranda Concerning Issues Relating to the Central Intelligence Agency's Use of "Enhanced Interrogation Techniques" on Suspected Terrorists.* http://www.judiciary.house.gov/hearings/pdf/OPRFinalReport090729.pdf.

United States, Department of Justice, Office of the Deputy Attorney General. 2010. Memorandum for the Attorney General. 5 January. http://www.judiciary.house.gov/hearings/pdf/DAGMargolisMemo100105.pdf.

United States, Department of Justice, Office of the Inspector General. 2006. *A Review of the FBI's Handling of the Brandon Mayfield Case.* http://www.justice.gov/oig/special/s0601/final.pdf.

United States, Department of Justice, Office of the Inspector General. 2010. *A Review of the Federal Bureau's Use of Exigent Letters and Other Informal Requests for Telephone Records.* http://www.justice.gov/oig/special/s1001r.pdf.

United States, Department of State. 2003. *Patterns of Global Terrorism, 2002.* http://www.state.gov/j/ct/rls/crt/2002.

United States, Department of State. 2004. *Patterns of Global Terrorism, 2003.* http://www.state.gov/j/ct/rls/crt/c14813.htm.

United States, Department of State. 2006. *Terrorism Deaths, Injuries, Kidnappings of Private U.S. Citizens, 2005.* http://www.state.gov/documents/organization/83383.pdf.

United States, Department of State. 2007. *National Counterterrorism Center: Annex of Statistical Information.* http://www.state.gov/j/ct/rls/crt/2006/82739.htm.

United States, Department of State. 2008. *National Counterterrorism Center: Annex of Statistical Information.* http://www.state.gov/j/ct/rls/crt/2007/103716.htm.

United States, Department of State. 2010. *Terrorism Deaths, Injuries, Kidnappings of Private U.S. Citizens, 2009.* http://www.state.gov/j/ct/rls/crt/2009/145700.htm.

United States, Department of State. 2011. *Terrorism Deaths, Injuries, Kidnappings of Private U.S. Citizens, 2010.* http://www.state.gov/j/ct/rls/crt/2010/170267.htm.

United States, Department of State. 2012. *Delisting of Mujahedin-e Khalq.* http://www.state.gov/r/pa/prs/ps/2012/09/198443.htm.

United States, Deputy Secretary of Defense. 2004. Memorandum for the Secretary of the Navy, "Order Establishing Combatant Review Tribunal." 7 July. http://www.defense.gov/news/jul2004/d20040707review.pdf.

United States. Federal Bureau of Investigation. 2002. *Terrorism 2000–2001.* http://www.fbi.gov/stats-services/publications/terror/terrorism-2000-2001#2001.

United States, Federal Bureau of Investigation. 2006. *Terrorism, 2002–2005.* http://www.fbi.gov/stats-services/publications/terrorism-2002-2005.

United States, General Accounting Office. 2004. *Terrorism Insurance: Implementation of the Terrorism Risk Insurance Act of 2002.* http://www.gao.gov/new.items/d04307.pdf.

United States, Homeland Security Advisory Council. 2009. *Homeland Security Advisory System: Task Force Report and Recommendations.* http:// www.dhs.gov/xlibrary/assets/hsac_final_report_09_15_09.pdf.

United States, House of Representatives, Judiciary Committee. 1995. *Comprehensive Antiterrorism Act of 1995.* Report 104–383. http://thomas.loc.gov/cgi-bin/cpquery/R?cp104:FLD010:@1(hr383).

United States, House of Representatives, Judiciary Committee. 2001. *Report of the Committee on the Judiciary, House of Representatives, to Accompany HR 2975 together with Additional Views.* Report 107–236, Part 1. http://thomas.loc.gov/cgi-bin/cpquery/R?cp107:FLD010:@1(hr236).

United States, National Counterterrorism Center. 2009. *2008 Report on Terrorism.* http://www.fbi.gov/stats-services/publications/terror_08.pdf.

United States, Offices of Inspector General of the Departments of Defense et al. 2009. *Unclassified Report on the President's Surveillance Program.* http://www.usdoj.gov/oig/special/s0907.pdf.

United States, President. Homeland Security Presidential Directive-3. http://georgewbush-whitehouse.archives.gov/news/releases/2002/03/20020312-5.html.

United States, Senate, Committee on Armed Services. 2008. *Inquiry into the Treatment of Detainees in US Custody: Report.* http://www.gwu.edu/~nsarchiv/torturingdemocracy/documents/20081211.pdf.

United States, Senate, Committee on the Judiciary. 2008. *State Secrets Protection Act: Report together with Minority Views to Accompany S 2533.* Report 110-442. http://thomas.loc.gov/cgi-bin/cpquery/?&sid=cp110IFPLj&r_n=sr442.110&dbname=cp110&&sel=TOC_0&.

"US Could Allow Guantanamo Visits." 2011. *Age* (Melbourne), 13 May, 8.

Varghese, George P. 2003. "The Role of Law Enforcement in Foreign Intelligence Surveillance." *University of Pennsylvania Law Review* 152:385–430.

Vermeule, Adrian. 2005. "Libertarian Panics." *Rutgers Law Journal* 36:871–88.

Viscusi, W. Kip, and Richard J. Zeckhauser. 2006. "Sacrificing Civil Liberties to Reduce Terrorism Risks." *Journal of Risk and Uncertainty* 26:99–120.

Walker, Clive. 2006. "Clamping Down on Terrorism in the United Kingdom." *Journal of International Criminal Justice* 4:1137–51.

Watkin, Kenneth. 2004. "Controlling the Use of Force: A Role for Human Rights Norms in Contemporary Armed Conflict." *American Journal of International Law* 94:1–34.

Watkin, Kenneth. 2005. "Canada/United States Military Inoperability and Humanitarian Law Issues: Land Mines, Terrorism, Military Objectives, and Targeted Killing." *Duke Journal of Comparative and International Law* 15:281–314.

Weaver, Robert C., and Robert M. Pallitto. 2005. "State Secrets and Executive Power." *Political Science Quarterly* 129:85–112.

Welch, Dylan. 2011. "Habib Settles Torture Case." *Age* (Melbourne), 8 January, 7.

Whitaker, Reg. 2003. "Keeping Up with the Neighbours? Canadian Responses to 9/11 in Historical and Comparative Context." *Osgoode Hall Law Journal* 41:241–65.

Wintour, Patrick. 2010. "Guantánamo Detainees 'to Get Millions.'" *Guardian Weekly*, 19 November, 16.

Wittes, Benjamin. 2008. *Law and the Long War: The Future of Justice in the Age of Terror*. Working Paper in the Project on Law and Security. New York: Penguin Press.

Wittes, Benjamin, et al. 2010. *The Emerging Law of Detention 2.0: The Guantánamo Habeas Cases as Lawmaking*. Washington, DC: Brookings Institution.

Worthington, Andy. 2012a. "As Judges Kill off Habeas Corpus for the Guantánamo Prisoners, Will the Supreme Court Act?" http://www.andyworthington.co.uk/2011/11/29/as-judges-kill-off-habeas-corpus-for-the-guantanamo-prisoners-will-the-supreme-court-act/.

Worthington, Andy. 2012b. "Guantánamo Habeas Results: The Definitive List." http://www.andyworthington.co.uk/guantanamo-habeas-results-the-definitive-list/.

Yoo, John C. 2003. Memorandum for William J Haynes II, General Counsel of the Department of Defense, "Military Interrogation of Alien Unlawful Combatants Held Outside the United States," 14 March. http://www.aclu.org/pdfs/safefree/yoo_army_torture_memo.pdf.

Zabel, Richard B., and James J. Benjamin, Jr. 2008. *In Pursuit of Justice: Prosecuting Terrorism in the Federal Courts*. New York: Human Rights First.

Zabel, Richard B. and James J. Benjamin, Jr. 2009. *In Pursuit of Justice: Prosecuting Terrorism Cases in the Federal Courts: 2009 Update and Recent Developments*. New York: Human Rights First.

Zuckerman, A. A. S. 1994. "Public Interest Immunity—a Matter of Prime Responsibility." *Modern Law Review* 57:703–25.

POLL DATA

To a considerable extent, the poll data used in this book are drawn from two major sources. One, www.pollingreport.com, is confined to US polls. Recent polls on terrorism-related issues are given at http://www.pollingreport.com/terror.htm, and details of earlier polls are accessible at http://www.pollingreport.com/terrorx.htm, where *x* is a number between 1 and 10, depending on the date of the poll. Notes cite PollingReport data by reference to "terror" or "terrorx," as appropriate. PollingReport gives details of the distribution of responses to particular terrorism-related questions and, occasionally, of the relationship between responses and party preference.

The other source is www.angus-reid.com. For US data, the Angus Reid site is less user-friendly than PollingReport. In general, each poll has its own address and must be downloaded separately. Each poll report is given its own number, with polls being numbered in more or less chronological order. The site includes details of non-US polls. It rarely gives details of the correlates of responses, but it occasionally does so and sometimes includes links to sites that provide considerable detail.

In addition, the home pages of polling organisations sometimes yield details of terrorism-related polls. Sites that have done so are www.compas.ca, www.ekos.com, www.gallup.com, www.ipsos-mori.com, www.yougov.com.

The Australian Social Science Data Archive (ASSDA) provides links to Australian poll data, and people registered with the ASSDA can download data sets. I have relied on data collected in the following polls: Timothy Phillips et al., The Australian Survey of Social Attitudes, 2007; Ian McAllister, ANU Poll 2009: Defence. Neither the ASSDA nor those who carried out the original analysis and collection of the data bear any responsibility for my further analysis or interpretation of it.

CASES

Recent (and some earlier) Australian, Canadian, New Zealand, United Kingdom, and European cases are cited by their medium-neutral reference and by the authorised report (if reported) or by reference to a parallel report (if there is one). Pinpoint references are to paragraph numbers.

Australia

A v Hayden [1984] HCA 67; (1984) 156 CLR 532.
Al Kateb v Godwin [2004] HCA 37; (2004) 219 CLR 562.
Australian Communist Party v The Commonwealth [1951] HCA 5; (1951) 83 CLR 1.
Habib v Commonwealth of Australia [2010] FCAFC 12; (2010) 183 FCR 62.
Hamed v R [2011] NZSC 101.
Hicks v Ruddock [2007] FCA 299; (2007) 156 FCR 574.
Hunt v R [2010] NZCA 528.
Leghaei v Director-General of Security [2005] FCA 1576.
Leghaei v Director-General of Security [2007] FCAFC 56.
Leghaei v Director-General of Security [2007] HCATrans 655.
Lodhi v R [2006] NSWCCA 360; (2007) 179 A Crim R 470. after Leghaei v DG [2007] HCATrans 655.
O'Sullivan v Parkin [2007] FCAFC 98.
Parkin v O'Sullivan [2006] FCA 1413; (2006) 162 FCR 444.
Parkin v O'Sullivan [2007] FCA 1647.
Parkin v O'Sullivan [2009] FCA 1096; (2009) 260 ALR 503.
Plaintiff M47 v Director General of Security [2012] HCA 46; (2012) 292 ALR 243.
R v Benbrika [2009] VSC 21; (2009) 222 FLR 433.
R v Benbrika (Ruling 1) [2007] VSC 141.
R v Kent [2009] VSC 375.
R v Khazaal [2006] NSWSC 1061.
R v Khazaal [2006] NSWSC 1335.
R v Lodhi [2006] NSWSC 571; (2006) 163 A Crim R 448.

R v Lodhi [2006] NSWSC 586.
R v Thomas [2006] VSC 18.
R v Thomas [2006] VSCA 165; (2006) 14 VR 475.
R v Touma [2008] NSWSC 1475.
R v Ul-Haque [2007] NSWSC 1251; (2007) 177 A Crim R 348.
Sagar v O'Sullivan [2011] FCA 192; (2011) 193 FCR 311.
Sankey v Whitlam [1978] HCA 43; (1978) 142 CLR 1.
Thomas v Mowbray [2007] HCA 33; (2007) 233 CLR 307.
Watson v AWB [2009] FCA 1047; (2009) 259 ALR 524.

Canada

Abdelrazik v Canada (Minister of Foreign Affairs) 2009 FC 580; [2010] 1 FCR 267.
Abou-Elmaati v Canada (Attorney-General) 2010 ONSC 2055; (2010) 101 OR (3d) 424.
Abou-Elmaati v Canada (Attorney General) 2011 ONCA 95.
Abou-Elmaati v Canada (Attorney-General) 2011 ONSC 7720.
Air Canada v Secretary of State for Trade [1983] 2 AC 394.
Almalki v Canada (Attorney General) 2012 ONSC 3023.
Almrei (Re) 2009 FC 240; [2010] 2 FCR 165.
Almrei (Re) 2009 FC 1263; [2009] FCJ No 1579.
Amnesty International Canada v Canada (Attorney General) 2008 FC 336; [2008] FCJ No 356.
Amnesty International Canada v Canada (Canadian Forces) 2008 FCA 401; [2008] 4 FCR 546.
Benatta v Canada (Attorney General) [2009] OJ No 5392; 2009 ON C LEXIS 4688.
Canada (Attorney General) v Almalki 2010 FC 1106.
Canada (Attorney General) v Commission of Inquiry into the Actions of Canadian Officials in Relation to Maher Arar 2007 FC 766; [2008] 3 FCR 248.
Canada (Attorney General) v Khawaja 2007 FC 463; [2008] 1 FCR 621.
Canada (Attorney General) v Khawaja 2007 FC 490; [2008] 1 FCR 547.
Canada (Attorney-General) v Khawaja 2007 FC 533; [2007] FCJ No 724.
Canada (Attorney-General) v Khawaja 2007 FCA 388; (2007) 289 DLR (4th) 260.
Canada (Attorney-General) v Ribic 2003 FCA 246; [2005] 1 FCR 33.
Canada (Prime Minister) v Khadr 2010 SCC 3; [2010] SCJ No 3.
Canadian Security Intelligence Service Act (Re) 2008 FC 300; [2010] 1 SCR 44.
Charkaoui (Re) 2009 FC 175; [2010] 4 FCR 448.
Charkaoui (Re) 2009 FC 342; [2010] 3 FCR 67.
Charkaoui v Canada (Citizenship and Immigration) 2007 SCC 9; [2007] 1 SCR 350.
Charkaoui v Canada (Citizenship and Immigration) 2008 SCC 38; [2008] 2 SCR 326.
Goguen v Gibson [1983] 2 FC 463; (1983) 7 DLR (4th) 144.
Harkat (Re) 2009 FC 1050; [2010] 4 FCR 149.
Harkat (Re) 2010 FC 1242; (2010) 224 CCR (3d) 93.
Henrie v Canada Security Intelligence Review Committee [1989] 2 FC 229; 1988 FC LEXIS 321.
Motehaver v Canada (Minister of Public Safety and Emergency Preparedness) 2009 FC 141; [2009] FCJ No 190.
R v Ahmad [2009] OJ No 6166; (2009) 257 CCC (3d) 135.
R v Ahmad 2011 SCC 6; [2011] 1 SCR 110.
R v Amara 2010 ONSC 441; [2010] OJ No 181.
R v Déry 2006 SCC 53; [2006] 2 SCR 669.
R v Khalid [2009] OJ No 3513; 2009 ON C LEXIS 3117.

R v Khawaja [2006] OJ No 4245; (2006) 214 CCC (3d) 399, special leave denied, *Khawaja v R* [2007] JSCC No 31776.
R v Khawaja [2008] OJ No 4244; 2008 ON C LEXIS 4226.
R v Khawaja 2011 ONCA 862; 103 OR (3d) 321, special leave granted, *Khawaja v R* [2011] JSCC No 34103.
R v Khawaja 2012 SCC 69.
Sriskandarajah v United States 2012 SCC 70.
R v Thambaithurai 2011 BCCA 137; (2011) 302 BCAC 288.
Suresh v Canada (Minister of Citizenship and Immigration) 2002 SCC 1; [2002] 1 SCR 3.
United States v Nadarajah [2009] OJ No 946; (2009) OR (3d) 514.
United States v Nadarajah 2010 ONCA 859; 109 OR (3d) 662, special leave granted, *Nadarajah v United States* [2011] JSCC No 34013.
United States v Sriskandarajah 2010 ONCA 857; 109 OR (3d) 680, special leave granted, *Sriskndarajah v United States* [2011] JSCC No 34009.

New Zealand

Attorney-General v Zaoui [2005] NZSC 38; [2006] 1 NZLR 289.
Hamed v R [2011] NZSC 101.
Hunt v R [2010] NZCA 528.
Attorney-General v Zaoui [2005] NZSC 38; [2006] 1 NZLR 289.

United Kingdom and the European Court of Human Rights

A v Secretary of State for the Home Department [2002] EWCA Civ 1502; [2004] QB 335.
A v Secretary of State for the Home Department [2004] UKHL 56; [2005] 2 AC 68.
A v Secretary of State for the Home Department (No 2) [2005] UKHL 71; [2006] 2 AC 221.
A and Others v HM Treasury [2008] EWCA Civ 1187; [2009] 3 WLR 25.
A and Others v HM Treasury [2008] EWHC 869 (Admin); [2008] 3 All ER 361.
Ahmed v R [2011] EWCA Crim 184; [2011] EWCA Crim 184.
Al-Jedda v United Kingdom [2011] ECHR 1092; (2011) 53 EHRR 23.
Al Rawi v Security Service [2009] EWHC 2959.
Al Rawi v Security Service [2010] EWCA Civ 482; [2010] 3 WLR 1069.
Al Rawi v Security Service [2010] EWHC 1496 (QB).
Al Rawi v Security Service [2011] UKSC 34; [2012] 1 AC 531.
Al-Sirri v Secretary of State for the Home Department [2009] EWCA Civ 222; [2009] INLR 586.
Attorney General's Reference (No 4 of 2002) [2003] EWCA Crim 762; [2005] 1 AC 264.
Attorney General's Reference (No 4 of 2002) [2004] UKHL 43; [2005] 1 AC 264.
Burmah Oil v Bank of England [1979] UKHL 4; [1980] AC 1090.
Carnduff v Rock [2001] EWCA Civ 680; [2001] 1 WLR 1786 (CA).
Conway v Rimmer [1968] UKHL 2; [1968] AC 910.
Edwards v United Kingdom [2003] ECHR 381.
Gillan v the United Kingdom (2010) ECHR 28; (2010) 50 EHRR 45.
Her Majesty's Treasury v Ahmed [2010] UKSC 2; [2010] 2 AC 534.
Hicks v Secretary of State for the Home Department [2005] EWCA 2818 (Admin).
Home Office v Tariq [2011] UKSC 35.
Ireland v UK [1978] ECHR 1; (1978) 2 EHRR 25.

Jasper v United Kingdom [2000] ECHR 90; (2000) 30 EHRR 441.
Kennedy v United Kingdom [2010] ECHR 682; (2011) 52 EHRR 4.
Liversidge v Anderson [1942] AC 206.
Lord Alton v Secretary of State for the Home Department (Proscribed Organisations Appeal Commission, unreported, 30 November 2007).
R v Ahmed [2011] EWCA Crim 184.
R v Barot [2007] EWCA Crim 1119.
R v Gul [2012] EWCA Crim 280.
R v H; R v C [2004] UKHL 3; [2004] 2 AC 134.
R v Ibrahim [2008] EWCA Crim 880.
R v K [2008] EWCA Crim 185; [2008] QB 827.
R v M [2007] EWCA Crim 298; [2008] Crim LJ 71.
R v M [2007] EWCA Crim 298; [2008] Crim LR 71.
R v Sherif [2008] EWCA Crim 2653.
R (A) v B [2009] UKSC 110.
R (Aamer) v Secretary of State for Foreign and Commonwealth Affairs [2009] EWHC 3316 (Admin).
R (Gillan) v Commissioner of Police of the Metropolis [2006] UKHL 12; [2006] 2 AC 307.
R (Gillan) v Metropolitan Police Commissioner [2003] EWHC 2545 (Admin).
R (Gillan) v Metropolitan Police Commissioner [2004] EWCA Civ 1067; [2005] QB 88.
R (Kurdistan Workers' Party and Others) v Secretary of State for the Home Department [2002] EWHC 644.
R (Maya Evans) v Secretary of State for Defence [2010] EWHC 1445 (Admin).
R (Mohamed) v Secretary of Foreign and Commonwealth Affairs [2010] EWCA Civ 65; [2011] QB 218.
(R) Mousa v Secretary of State for Defence [2011] EWCA Civ 1334.
Rahman v R [2008] EWCA Crim 1465; [2008] All ER 661.
Rahmatullah v Secretary of State for Foreign and Commonwealth Affairs [2011] EWCA Civ 1540.
Rahmatullah v Secretary of State for Foreign and Commonwealth Affairs (No 2) [2012] EWCA Civ 182.
Secretary of State for the Home Department v A [2010] EWHC 42.
Secretary of State for the Home Department v AF [2009] UKHL 28; [2010] AC 269.
Secretary of State for the Home Department v AF [2010] EWHC 42 (Admin).
Secretary of State for the Home Department v AHK [2009] EWCA Civ 287; [2009] 1 WLR 2049.
Secretary of State for the Home Department v Hicks [2006] EWCA 400.
Secretary of State for the Home Department v Lord Alton of Liverpool [2008] EWCA Civ 443; [2008] 1 WLR 2341.
Secretary of State for the Home Department v MB and AF [2007] UKHL 46; [2008] AC 40.
Youssef v Home Office [2004] EWHC 1884.
Zafar v R [2008] EWCA Crim 184.

United States

Al-Adahi v Obama 2010 US App LEXIS 14263 (DC Cir 2010).
Al-Aulaqi v Obama 727 F Supp 2d 1 (D DC 2010).
Al-Haramain Islamic Foundation v Bush 507 F 3d 1190 (9th Cir 2007).

Al Haramain Islamic Foundation v Department of the Treasury 2009 US Dist LEXIS 103373 (D Ore 2009).
Al-Haramain Islamic Foundation v Obama 2012 US App LEXIS 16379 (9th Cir 2012).
Al Haramain Islamic Foundation v United States Department of the Treasury 585 F Supp 2d 1233 (D Ore 2008).
Ali v Rumsfeld 649 F 3d 762 (DC Cir 2011).
Al-Kidd v Ashcroft 580 F 3d 949 (9th Cir 2010), rehearing denied, 598 F 3d 1129 (9th Cir 2010).
Al-Kidd v Gonzales 1:05-cv-093-EJL-MHW.
Al Maqaleh v Obama 605 F 3d 84 (DC Cir 2010).
Al-Mithali v Bush 2009 US Dist LEXIS 7033 (D DC 2009).
Al Odah v United States 321 F 3d 1134 (DC Cir 2003).
American Civil Liberties Union v National Security Agency 438 F Supp 2d 754 (ED Mich 2006).
American Civil Liberties Union v National Security Agency 493 F 3d 644 (6th Cir 2007).
American Civil Liberties Union v National Security Agency 128 S Ct 1334 (2008).
Amnesty International v Clapper 638 F 3d 118 (2d Cir 2011).
Amnesty International v Clapper 667 F 3d 163 (2d Cir 2011).
Amnesty International v McConnell 646 F Supp 2d 633 (SD NY 2009).
Arar v Ashcroft 585 F 3d 559 (2d Cir 2009).
Ashcroft v Al-Kidd 131 S Ct 2074 (2011).
Ashcroft v Iqbal 129 S Ct 1937 (2009).
Bin Attash v Obama 628 F Supp 2d 24 (D DC 2009).
Bismullah v Gates 2007 US App LEXIS (DC Cir 2007).
Bivens v Six Unknown Agents of Federal Bureau of Narcotics Agents 403 US 368 (1999).
Boumediene v Bush 476 F 3d 981 (DC Cir 2007).
Boumediene v Bush 553 US 723 (2008).
Cassidy v Chertoff 471 F 3d 67 (2d Cir 2006).
Clapper v Director of National Intelligence 133 S Ct 185 (2013).
Doe v Ashcroft 334 F Supp 2d 471 (SD NY 2004).
Doe v Gonzales 386 F Supp 2d 66 (D Conn 2005).
Doe v Gonzales 500 F Supp 2d 379 (SD NY 2007).
Doe v Rumsfeld 800 F Supp 2d 94 (D DC 2011).
Doe v Rumsfeld 683 F 3d 390 (DC Cir 2012), reh'g en banc, denied, 2012 US App LEXIS 15717 (DC Cir 2012).
Doe I v Gonzales 449 F 3d 415 (2d Cir 2006).
El-Masri v United States 479 F 3d 296 (4th Cir 2007).
El-Masri v United States 2007 US LEXIS 11351.
Ex parte Endo 323 US 283 (1944).
General Dynamics v United States 131 S Ct 1900 (2011).
Global Relief Foundation v O'Neill 315 F 3d 748 (7th Cir 2002), rehearing, en banc, denied, 2003 US App LEXIS 6708 (7th Cir 2003).
Global Relief Foundation v O'Neill 2003 US LEXIS 8207 (2003).
Hamdan v Rumsfeld 344 F Supp 2d 152 (D DC 2004).
Hamdan v Rumsfeld 415 F 3d 33 (DC Cir 2005).
Hamdan v Rumsfeld 548 US 557 (2006).
Hamdi v Rumsfeld 542 US 507 (2004).
Hedges v Obama 2012 US Dist LEXIS 68683 (SD NY 2012).
Hedges v Obama 2012 US Dist LEXIS 78867 (SD NY 2012).

Hedges v Obama 2012 US App LEXIS 19880 (2d Cir 2012).
Hepting v AT&T 439 F Supp 2d 974 (ND Cal 2006).
Holder v Humanitarian Law Project 130 S Ct 2705 (2010).
Holy Land Foundation v Ashcroft 219 F Supp 2d 57 (D DC 2002).
Holy Land Foundation for Relief and Development v Ashcroft 333 F 3d 156 (DC Cir 2003).
Holy Land Foundation for Relief and Development v Ashcroft 158 L Ed 2d 153 (2004).
In re Directives Pursuant to Section 105B of the Foreign Intelligence Surveillance Act 551 F 3d 1004 (FISCR 2008).
In re Grand Jury Proceedings in the Special April 2002 Grand Jury 347 F 3d 197 (7th Cir 2003).
In re Guantanamo Bay Detainee Litigation Case 1:08-mc-00442-TFH, document 409, filed 09.11.08; document 1496, filed 01.09.09.
In re Guantanamo Bay Detainee Litigation 634 F Supp 2d 17 (D DC 2009).
In re Guantanamo Detainee Cases 355 F Supp 2d 443 (DC Cir 2005).
In re Iraq & Afghanistan Detainees Litigation 479 F Supp 2d 85 (D DC 2007).
In re National Security Agency Telecommunications Records Litigation 564 F Supp 2d 1109 (ND Cal 2008).
In re National Security Agency Telecommunications Records Litigation 595 F Supp 2d 1077 (ND Cal 2009).
In re National Security Agency Telecommunications Records Litigation 630 F Supp 2d 1092 (ND Cal 2009).
In re National Security Agency Telecommunications Records Litigation 2009 US Dist LEXIS 62640 (ND Cal 2009).
In re National Security Agency Telecommunications Records Litigation 2009 US Dist LEXIS 64621 (ND Cal 2009).
In re National Security Agency Telecommunications Records Litigation 700 F Supp 2d 1182 (ND Cal 2010).
In re National Security Agency Telecommunications Records Litigation 669 F 3d 928 (9th Cir 2011).
In re National Security Agency Telecommunications Records Litigation 2012 US App LEXIS 16379 (9th Cir 2012).
In re People's Mojahedin Organization of Iran 680 F 3d 832 (DC Cir 2012).
In re Sealed Case No 02–001 310 F 3d 717 (FISCR 2002).
In the matter of Kevork 634 F Supp 1002 (CD Cal 1985).
Islamic American Relief Agency v Gonzales 477 F 3d 728 (DC Cir 2007).
Jewel v National Security Agency 2010 US Dist LEXIS 5110 (ND Cal).
John Doe v Holder 665 F Supp 2d 517 (SD NY 2009).
John Doe Inc v Mukasey 549 F 3d 861 (2d Cir 2008).
Johnson v Eisentrager 339 US 763 (1950).
Kahane Chai v Department of State 466 F 3d 125 (DC Cir 2006).
Khalid v Bush 355 F Supp 2d 311 (DC 2005).
KindHearts for Charitable Humanitarian Development v Geithner 647 F Supp 2d 857, 881 (ND Ohio 2009).
KindHearts for Charitable Humanitarian Development v Geithner 710 F Supp 2d 637 (ND Ohio 2010).
Kiyemba v Obama 561 F 3d 509 (DC Cir 2009), certiorari denied, 2010 US LEXIS 2462 (2010).
Kiyemba v Obama 605 F 3d 1046, 1048 (DC Cir 2010).
Korematsu v United States 323 US 214 (1944).

Lebron v Rumsfeld 2011 764 F Supp 2d 787 (Charleston D SC 2011).
Lebron v Rumsfeld 670 F 3d 540 (4th Cir 2012), cert denied, 132 S Ct 2751 (2012).
Lnu v Obama 656 F Supp 2d 187 (D DC 2009).
MacWade v Kelly 460 F 3d 260 (2d Cir 2006).
Mayfield v United States 504 F Supp 2d 1023 (D Ore 2007).
Mayfield v United States 599 F 3d 964 (9th Cir 2010).
McMurray v Verizon 2009 US Dist LEXIS 64621 (ND Cal 2009).
Mohamed v Jeppesen Dataplan 563 F 3d 992, 1007 (9th Cir 2009).
Mohamed v Jeppesen Dataplan 614 F 3d 1070 (9th Cir, en banc, 2010), certiorari denied, 131 S Ct 2442 (2011).
Mohammed v Obama 704 F Supp 2d 1 (D DC 2009).
Munaf v Geren 553 US 674 (2008).
National Council of Resistance of Iran v Department of State 251 F 3d 192 (DC Cir 2001).
National Council of Resistance of Iran v Department of State 373 F 3d 152 (DC Cir 2004).
Padilla v Yoo 633 F Supp 2d 100 (ND Cal 2009).
Padilla v Yoo 678 F 3d 748 (9th Cir 2012).
People's Mojahedin Organization of Iran v United States Department of State 182 F 3d 17 (DC Cir 1999).
People's Mojahedin Organization of Iran v United States Department of State 327 F 3d 1238 (DC Cir 2003).
People's Mojahedin Organization of Iran v United States 613 F 3d 220 (DC Cir 2010).
Rahmani v United States 2007 US LEXIS 43 (2007).
Rasul v Bush 542 US 466 (2004).
Rasul v United States 215 F Supp 2d 55 (D DC 2002).
Reynolds v United States 345 US 1 (1953).
Salahi v Obama 625 F 3d 745 (DC Cir 2010).
Turkmen v Ashcroft 589 F 3d 542 (2d Cir 2009).
United States v Abdi 463 F 2d 547 (6th Cir 2006).
United States v Abdulmuttalab 2:09-mj-30526, document 1 (complaint).
United States v Abu Ali 528 F 3d 210 (4th Cir 2008).
United States v Abu-Jihaad 531 F Supp 2d 299 (D Conn 2008)
United States v Abu-Jihaad 630 F 3d 102 (2d Cir 2011).
United States v Afshari 426 F 3d 1150 (9th Cir 2005).
United States v Afshari 446 F 3d 915 (9th Cir 2006).
United States v Afshari 2009 US Dist LEXIS 31585 (CD Cal 2009).
United States v Ahmed 2009 US Dist LEXIS 12007, 30 (ND Ga 2009).
United States v Al Arian 308 F Supp 2d 1322 (D Fla 2004).
United States v Benkhala 530 F 3d 300 (4th Cir 2008).
United States v Chandia 2010 US App LEXIS 19178 (4th Cir 2010).
United States v DeFreitas 1:07-cr-00543 (ED NY), document 1 (complaint). Available, after registration, with http://www.pacer.gov, at https://pcl.uscourts.gov/search.
United States v Dhafir 461 F 3d 211 (2d Cir 2006).
United States v Hammoud 381 F 3d 316 (4th Cir 2004).
United States v Holy Land Foundation 2007 US Dist LEXIS 50239, 21 (ND Tex 2007).
United States v Islamic American Relief Agency 2009 US Dist LEXIS 118505 (WD Mo 2009).
United States v Jayyousi F 3d 1085, 1117 (11th Cir 2011).
United States v Kashmiri 2010 US Dist LEXIS 119470 (ND Ill 2010).
United States v Lindh 212 F Supp 2d 541 (ED Va 2002).

United States v Meskini 319 F 3d 88, 92 (2d Cir 2003).
United States v Mubayyid 521 F Supp 2d 125 (D Mass 2007).
United States v Nixon 418 US 683 (1974).
United States v Reid 02-cr-10013 (D Mass 2003), Government's Sentencing Memorandum.
United States v Sattar 395 F Supp 2d 79 (SD NY 2005).
United States v Schnewer 2008 US Dist LEXIS 112001 (D NJ 2008).
United States v Shahzad 1:10-mj-00928, document 1 (complaint). Available, after registration, with http://www.pacer.gov, at https://pcl.uscourts.gov/search.
United States v Shareef 06-cr-00919 (ND Ill), affidavit of Jared Ruddy. Available, after registration, at http://www.pacer.gov, at https://pcl.uscourts.gov/search.
United States v Truong Dinh Hung 629 F 2d 908 (4th Cir 1980).
United States v United States District Court (Keith) 407 US 297 (1972).
United States v Warsame 547 F Supp 2d 982 (D Minn 2008).
Vance v Rumsfeld 2011 US App LEXIS 22083 (7th Cir 2011), reargued en banc and aff 701 F 3d 193 (7th Cir 2012).
Vance v Rumsfeld 2011 US App LEXIS 15717 (DC Cir 2012).
Vance v Rumsfeld 694 F Supp 2d 957 (ND Ill 2010).
Vance v Rumsfeld 653 F 3d 591 (7th Cir 2011).
Vance v Rumsfeld 701 F 3d 193 (7th Cir 2012).
Yates v United States 354 US 298 (1957).
Zadvydas v Davis 533 US 678 (2001).

Index